FUNDAMENTALS OF SOCIAL WORK PRACTICE

A Book of Readings

FUNDAMENTALS OF
SOCIAL WORK PRACTICE

A Book of Readings

Daniel S. Sanders
Oscar Kurren
Joel Fischer

University of Hawaii
School of Social Work

Wadsworth Publishing Company
Belmont, California
A Division of Wadsworth, Inc.

Social Work Editor: Curt Peoples
Production Editor: Diane Sipes
Art Director: Patricia Dunbar
Designer: Janet Wood
Copy Editor: Shirley Pitcher
Cover Designer: Janet Wood

Printed in the United States of America

2 3 4 5 6 7 8 9 10—86 85 84 83 82

Library of Congress Cataloging in Publication Data

Main entry under title:

Fundamentals of social work practice: a book of readings.

    1. Social service—Addresses, essays, lectures.
I. Sanders, Daniel S.   II. Kurren, Oscar.   III. Fischer, Joel.
HV37.F86   361.3   80-23458
ISBN 0-534-01009-1   AACR1

To our friend and colleague,
Herbert H. Aptekar.

You are missed.

PREFACE

The winds of change are blowing on social work. Over the years, social work has evolved into a dynamic and vital profession, which has at its core a configuration of values, ideology, knowledge, and skills that mark it as unique. The essence of the concept of social work presented in this book is that this unique configuration comprises the *fundamental* values, knowledge, and skills of social work. As noted in a report approved by the Board of Directors of our professional association, the National Association of Social Workers (NASW):

when referring to the elements that are taught to all beginning professionals, the profession should be pointing to social work fundamentals. *When discussing the knowledge and skill that all social workers have in common, we should be talking about the* fundamentals *of social work. When we seek to identify the base on which specializations in practice and education are built, the search should lead to* fundamentals. *In short, a professional . . . must know and be able to apply these* fundamentals. *This then becomes the heart of the general practice of social work.*

The purpose of this book is to help you to understand what these fundamentals are, both conceptually and for the purpose of actually integrating them into your practice. We develop the theme throughout the book that the social worker uses these fundamentals no matter what problems he or she is working with or what setting he or she is working in. We call this type of practice "general social work practice," and the individual who practices it a social work "generalist." This book is geared toward the preparation of an effective and competent generalist practitioner. It also provides a solid base for building more specialized knowledge and skills upon the formulation of fundamentals presented here.

ORGANIZATION

To help to accomplish these goals, we have organized the book into five parts.

Part I, Values and Ideology, focuses on the values and ideology central to the social work profession. It also examines emerging new developments and their implications for practice, models of social work practice, and the key goals of the profession.

Part II, The Context of Practice, focuses on the settings in which social work is practiced and the varying levels of intervention—that is, the micro-, mezzo-, and macrosystems. In addition, it examines the effect of organization and auspices on practice, the influence of social problem areas, and crosscultural and pluralistic perspectives in practice.

Part III, Knowledge for Practice, examines the knowledge base of general social work practice and identifies the core elements of the knowledge that has both evolved in practice and been developed for practice. This part also focuses on the generic processes of assessment and intervention in work with people in varying settings and at varying levels of intervention.

Part IV, Illustrations of Practice, provides a number of case examples and illustrations. These are illustrations of strategies in relation to varying goals of social work. A number of case studies are presented in order to afford an opportunity to engage in a differential analysis of the roles, tactics, and techniques of social work practice.

Part V, Issues, discusses several issues that appear crucial to the ongoing development of the profession. Among these are prospects and problems from the generalist perspective, preparation of social workers for practice for the future, and ensuring continuing effectiveness and accountability in practice.

This book is specifically addressed to undergraduate and graduate students in social work. We hope, however, that it will also be of value to practitioners, since the framework and the practical aspects of the book are intended to be timely as well as useful in updating social work knowledge. We hope it will lend clarity and provide new directions to social workers' efforts in the field.

Daniel S. Sanders
Oscar Kurren
Joel Fischer

CONTENTS

INTRODUCTION

Efforts are increasing within the social work profession in recent years to identify the common elements of its practice, to establish an orderly system of relationships among them, and to develop a broader, more integrated approach to practice. To understand the full significance of these efforts, it is necessary to take note of the different phases of the profession's development and the issues and dilemmas confronting the profession.

SOCIAL WORK IN THE CONTEXT OF SOCIAL WELFARE

We currently are part of—in the United States and around the world—a society in flux. Complex and varied social problems necessitate increasing flexibility and effectiveness on the part of social workers and a willingness to explore new approaches to practice. There are numerous demands being made on the profession to define the nature and scope of its practice and to clarify its relationship to other human service professions. Beginning students and practitioners, for example, will find it helpful if a clear distinction is made between terms such as *social work* and *social welfare,* despite the difficulty in defining such evolving terms. Social work and social welfare are historically related, changing concepts whose specific interpretation and meaning tend to vary to some extent from country to country. Because of the general professionalization of social work and the use of trained personnel in a complex and highly industrialized society such as the United States, a distinction is increasingly being made between social work and social welfare.

For some time, social welfare and social work were considered synonymous. While there might have been some justification for this usage earlier, it no longer appears to be valid and their separate identities need to be noted. Currently, social work is considered one of the human service professions within the social welfare *metainstitution* or complex of efforts institutionalized to provide social services (Siporin 1975, p. 9). *Social welfare* is a metainstitution that encompasses a wide range of helping professions and services, such as social work, health, education, housing, income security, and employment. Clearly *social welfare* is a broad term and denotes the full range of services and activities of government and voluntary agencies that are designed to prevent, control, or contribute to the solution of social problems (Kidneigh 1965, p. 3).

Social work is a more specific term that refers to the core functions and specialized helping services performed by social workers in their professional capacity as members of the profession. The functions and specialized tasks that are part of the social work practitioner's helping efforts are goal oriented and are geared toward problem solving and change. These helping efforts operate in the context of people interacting with their environment; that is, the transactions between people and their environments are at the core of social work concerns. In this sense social work can be viewed as a profession concerned with enhancing the social functioning of individuals in society, of improving social relationships, and of changing social institutions and policies with a view to contributing to the fullest possible development of all individuals. In essence, then, social work is a profession working in the context of the field of social welfare.

In an attempt to specify more clearly the characteristics of social work, the professional association, the National Association of Social Workers (NASW), has adopted the following definition:

Social work *is the professional activity of helping individuals, groups, or communities enhance or restore their capacity for social functioning and creating societal conditions favorable to that goal.* Social work practice *consists of the professional application of social work values, principles, and techniques to one or more of the following ends:*

helping people obtain tangible services;

counseling and psychotherapy with individuals, families, and groups;

helping communities or groups provide social and health services;

and participating in relevant legislative processes.

The practice of social work requires knowledge *of:*

human development and behavior;

social, economic, and cultural institutions;

and the interaction of all these factors. [National Association of Social Workers 1973, pp. 4–5]

Obvious interconnections exist between social work and social welfare even as we attempt to separate them for purposes of definition. Expertise in social work necessitates developing knowledge of and skill in methods of helping people. Expertise in social welfare necessitates developing knowledge and skills regarding organizational and institutional devices by which society deals with specific problems (Specht 1972, p. 14). Social work has claims to recognition as a profession different from other human service professions in that it has a broad knowledge base, a repertoire of interventive techniques, an integrative function, and a clear moral ideal embodied in its value position in which individuals and their relationship to their environment emerge as the central focus of concern (Romanyshyn 1971, p. 55).

FUNDAMENTAL ASPECTS OF PRACTICE

Social work practitioners, in their efforts to help people deal with problems at the individual and societal level, intervene directly in the life situations of people or seek to effect changes indirectly through planning, policy change, and related efforts. Numerous social work practice efforts have been in the area of working directly with people, whether in providing therapeutic services or in providing new information and resources to enable individuals to successfully deal with their problems.

Historically there has always been a tension in social work practice between efforts to help people by direct intervention and efforts to bring about institutional and policy changes in society that indirectly bear on people's lives and problems. Whatever the social problem to be dealt with and the level of intervention called for, there are certain fundamental attributes of practice—purpose, sanction, values, knowledge, and method—that are available to the social worker to draw on as appropriate in practice efforts. The following brief definitions are given of each of these attributes of practice to help especially the beginning student. Some of these attributes are not in and of themselves unique to social work practice; to a large extent they are attributes of all professional practice, for example, law, medicine, nursing, and architecture.

However, it is in their integration within one profession that their uniqueness emerges. The term *purpose* refers to an intended aim, end, goal, or desired result. The purpose of social work practice can be seen as effecting a deliberate change in the interaction of people and their environment, with a view to improving the capacity of individuals to cope with their life tasks in a way satisfying to themselves and to others, and in so doing, enhancing their capacity for a fuller realization of their values and aspirations (Compton and Galaway 1975, p. 145). *Sanction* refers to authoritative permission—formal or informal—that gives support to and legitimizes social work practice in society. Sanctions may be from such different sources as the agency, the profession, the client, and society as a whole. In the final analysis sanction for professional practice emanates from society itself. *Values* refer to ideal or normative conditions in behavior and human interaction and are intended to guide practitioners in their helping efforts. Values refer to what social workers think "ought" to be. Part I of the book, which focuses on values and ideology, points to the centrality of values in professional practice and discusses the value dilemmas faced by the social work practitioner. *Knowledge*, as understood in social work practice, refers to an organized body of information or the comprehension and understanding derived from the acquisition of an organized body of information. Part III of the book focuses on this fundamental aspect of social work practice. The last of the fundamental attributes of practice, *method*, refers to the systematic ways in which the social work practitioner mediates between individuals and their social environment (Compton and Galaway 1975, pp. 9–10). These methods constitute identifiable techniques and tasks that are to be utilized appropriately by practitioners in their helping efforts. (Later in the Introduction reference is made to the traditional methods of casework, group work, and community organization and how they are viewed today in the context of a more general approach to social work practice.)

All of these attributes can be integrated by viewing social work as the profession concerned with the fundamental zone of human existence where people and their environments are in exchange with each other. Social work has historically focused on this transaction zone, where the exchange between people and the environments that impinge on them results in changes in both. Social work intervention aims at the coping capabilities of people and the demands and resources of their environments so that the transaction between them is helpful to both. Social work's concern extends to both the dysfunctional or deficit conditions at the juncture between people and their environments and to the opportunities for producing growth and improving the environment. It is the duality of focus on people and their environments that distinguishes social work from other professions (National Association of Social Workers 1979).

As such, social workers practice in a wide variety of settings ranging from hospitals, clinics, and industrial settings to schools, public welfare departments, and family and child welfare agencies to counseling agencies, mental health clinics, and private practice. The societal mandate of social work is to be prepared to intervene at various levels: with individuals, families, and groups (clinical practice), with organizations and communities, and with broader levels of government, where the focus is on resource development and social policy changes. For example, in work with individuals—securing resources, mediating between the individual and organizations, acting as an advocate, and so on—social workers also consider and work with the effects of other systems on that individual.

Social work practitioners work independently or in collaboration with other helping professionals, depending on the problem area and the specific situation. The extent of collaboration is also likely to vary from situation to situation. In direct practice—in the area of child welfare, for example—the social work practitioner may work collaboratively with the school teacher, the psychologist, the psychiatrist, the home economist, and the marriage counselor in dealing with a child's problems at home and at school. Similarly in planning, policy change, and organizational efforts in an urban renewal project, the social work practitioner is likely to work collaboratively with the planner, the politician, the developer, and citizen groups to effect humane changes in urban renewal plans in a specific area.

The problem-solving effort in which the social worker is involved—whether the problem is at the individual or societal level—ideally consists of a partnership between the professional worker and the client or client system. Joint efforts are made to identify the problem, to understand the problem, and to map out a strategy for dealing with the problem. In the world of reality—which, after all, is the practitioner's world—such ideal conditions do not always exist and the nature of the helping effort and the extent of partnership between the practitioner and the client system tends to vary. In some contexts, such as child protective work or correctional service, the element of authority in the helping efforts of the practitioner is more evident; in such situations the social work practitioner has specific legal authority to intervene. This is not the case in other forms of intervention.

In all practice efforts, however, whether there is specific legal authority to intervene or not, a fundamental question emerges in social work practice as to who gives the sanction to the practitioners and their profession to intervene. The sanction for practice to some extent tends to come from the social agency, the social work profession, and client groups. But in the final analysis, sanction emanates from society itself. The social work profession and social work practice operate within the framework of societal support and sanction.

Herein lie some of the strengths and the limitations of the profession. Insofar as professional social work has the sanction of society and its major institutions, social work practice efforts tend to receive the necessary positive support. However, in the very process of helping people, the practitioner is also involved in issues of social reform and institutional change that at times may conflict with the views and the value premises of an appreciable number of people in society. Reform efforts and policy changes relating to minorities and other oppressed groups, for example, illustrate the tensions involved in the social work profession's facing up to its social reform and social critic roles. At its best, however, this tension provides the profession with the creative stimulus necessary to keep both the "reform" and the "service," the "prophetic" and the "priestly" aspects of the profession in balance (Chambers 1967, p. 264). The intent here, however, is not to minimize the difficulties and the ongoing debates within the profession that can at times be confusing to the beginning student and to the practitioner.

DEVELOPMENT OF THE PROFESSION AND CHANGES IN PRACTICE

Social work developed the attributes of a profession during the first half of the twentieth century. Even today there are some questions about the extent to which it has the full attributes of a profession when compared, for example, with medicine or law. During the early phase of the profession's development—the 1930s and 1940s—social work practice was fragmented into separate methods and there was no readily identifiable integrated body of knowledge and concepts to which they were related. The term *method,* as mentioned earlier, refers to a systematic way—involving techniques and tasks—in which the social work practitioner mediates between individuals and their social environment. The earliest methods associated with the profession of social work are casework, group work, and community organization. In simple terms *casework* refers to the process of intervening focused on helping individuals and families. *Group work* refers to the process of helping individuals through the medium of small groups. *Community organization* refers to a way of dealing with social problems through collective efforts; in this instance, the whole community is often perceived as the client or target group. The primary variable among these methods is *level of intervention*—that is, the number of persons with whom the social worker interacts: individuals and families, groups, and community representatives (Compton and Galaway 1975, p. 9).

This differentiation between methods on the basis of the size of the client system has been open to question; for one reason, it contributes to rigidly categorical thinking that advocates changing either the individual or the environment, when in point of fact the two are interrelated (Compton and Galaway 1975, p. 10). For another reason, it tends to lead social workers to respond to problems only on the basis of the techniques of their method, rather than in a more flexible way—that is, on the basis of the actual problem or situation.

Of the three methods—casework, group work, and community organization—casework, the clinical arm of social work, was in particular heavily emphasized in the early decades of this century. Preoccupation with a specific method, however, tended to stand in the way of the development of the profession. There was also a tendency for social work practitioners to accept the goals, functions, and standards of the agencies and programs as those of social work, without efforts to distinguish the profession itself and the requirements of its own practice (Bartlett 1965, p. 755). This acceptance, too, stood in the way of the development of the profession.

In the 1950s changes took place in the attempt to define social work practice and contributed to a shift in focus from the activity of the social agency to the activity of the professional practitioner. A significant development contributing to this trend of professional practice based on an identifiable knowledge base, values, interventive techniques, purposes, and sanction was the formation of the National Association of Social Workers (NASW) in 1955. The NASW paid attention to the definition and improvement of professional social work through its Commission on Social Work Practice. The commission, in the absence of any acceptable definition of social work, set about to develop its own working definition. In this context the commission developed the concept of a constellation of attributes—purpose, values, sanction, knowledge, method—that considered together seemed to distinguish the social worker's activity (Bartlett 1965, p. 756). Compared to earlier efforts in the profession's development, this formulation regarding practice—in citing common elements operative together with variations in application—was precise enough to justify claims to social work's being a profession.

During the 1960s the social work profession, after five decades of struggle and development, confronted a situation of phenomenal social change and questioning of its own role that posed new dilemmas and afforded unique opportunities. This statement is not meant to minimize the significance or the impact of social upheavals at earlier phases of the profession's development, especially the 1930s. The reform activities of Jane Addams, the movement for social security culminating in the Social Security Act of 1935 are just two examples of several early efforts of significance in response to social change. However, during the 1960s, in the context of the civil rights movement, the poverty programs, the demands of diverse ethnic and minority groups for greater justice and for social institutions and services more responsive to their needs, social work had to reexamine carefully the differing views within the profession, such as whether individualized treatment should take precedence over social reform and change efforts.

Advocates for the broader concerns and change efforts within the profession persisted in presenting the issues to educators and practitioners. A separation appeared to be growing between direct service that focused on resolution of problems largely in the treatment context—as defined by casework, group work, and certain aspects of community organization—and the more broadly based functions related to planning, policy, administration, and development that focused more on change efforts at the institutional and policy level (Meyer 1971, p. 964). This emphasis on institutional and structural changes in response to societal problems such as poverty and racism was nothing new. Social work from the very beginning has had roots in reform movements. What was perhaps new was the gradual acknowledgment by social workers of the professional legitimacy of the broader social concerns and intervention techniques along with the traditional direct service to clients (Meyer 1971, p. 964).

A new form of dichotomous thinking in practice had taken hold that had developed in the tendency to separate practice into two tracks: direct service on the one hand and planning, policy development, and institutional change efforts on the other. It should be noted that other forms of such categorical thinking in practice had been present in earlier phases of the profession's development; for example, in the somewhat rigid distinction between casework, group work, and community organization methods. It was increasingly evident that the profession had to address itself to both concerns: individual change and environmental change, in that the dichotomous, two-track thinking about practice simply did not meet the mission and realities of the profession. The social work profession increasingly expanded its definition of practice to accommodate institutional and policy change efforts as legitimate professional activities.

CURRENT STATUS AND CHARACTERISTICS OF THE PROFESSION

In the current phase of development, social work can claim to have the essential features of a profession. As noted previously the key elements of a profession were developed in the first half of the twentieth century. Social work's claim to professional status generally is no longer a major issue (Meyer 1971, p. 960). However, some reference made in this context to the essential features of a profession will be helpful. Greenwood (1957, pp. 45–55) referred to five attributes that are characteristic of a profession and that would constitute the model of a profession. The attributes are: (1) a systematic body of theory, (2) professional authority based upon professional education and knowledge, (3) sanctions of the community both formal and informal, (4) an acknowledged code of ethics, and (5) professional culture typified by a formal professional association.

While it is difficult to establish how closely social work has conformed to Greenwood's model or similar criteria referred to by others in the literature, it is evident that in examining each of the criteria described above social work has at least the minimal attributes of a profession.

The current issue is not so much whether social work is a profession as what kind of a profession it is becoming (Meyer 1971, p. 961). A key issue that needs to be resolved is whether the two views of professional practice and responsibility—that of providing direct service to clients and that of contributing to policy planning, development, and institutional and policy change—can be effectively contained in a single profession. While efforts have already been made to resolve this issue, it is important to point out that this is an ongoing issue. In a sense this issue and its dilemmas have been referred to in varying forms throughout the history of the profession, beginning perhaps with Mary Richmond, who in 1905 wrote of the "wholesale" and "retail" methods of social reform (Gilbert and Specht 1974, p. 965). Reference has been made in recent literature to social work as an "incomplete profession" and as a "subprofession." The profession is being challenged to develop the capacity to fulfill its commitment to direct services and its commitment to social welfare and in so doing to become a "complete profession" (Gilbert and Specht 1974, p. 674).

In responding to this challenge the profession needs to continue to address itself vigorously to basic problems of poverty, racism, discrimination, and oppression of varying minority groups, all problems that social workers witness in their practice at the individual and societal levels. During the 1960s social work, along with other professions, ironically rediscovered poverty and racism and rededicated itself to fighting these problems (Siporin 1975, p. 15). Poverty and racism are just two of many social problem areas (crime, drug abuse, and mental illness are some others) that call for collaborative efforts on the part of many professions and disciplines.

As a human service profession, social work has a special responsibility toward victims of poverty, racism, and other forms of oppression in society. The social work profession is guided by a code of ethics and individual members of the profession subscribe to a pattern of behavior. The Code of Ethics adopted by the Delegate Assembly of the National Association of Social Workers states:

Social work is based on humanitarian, democratic ideals. Professional social workers are dedicated to service for the welfare of mankind, to the disciplined use of a recognized body of knowledge about human beings and their interactions, and to the marshalling of community resources to promote the well-being of all without discrimination. Social work practice is a public trust that requires of its practitioners integrity, compassion, belief in the dignity and worth of human beings, respect for individual differences, a commitment to service, and a dedication to truth. . . . [Delegate Assembly, NASW 1971, p. 958]

The Code of Ethics clearly represents a collective stance against all forms of discrimination and injustice in society, and individual practitioners have the responsibility to condemn these practices and to work toward improving social conditions. However, it is a matter of concern that despite legislation, and efforts of governmental and private organizations, racism persists in our society. Due to the prevalence of institutional racism, many individuals are still subject in numerous ways to personal, social, and economic abuse; these inequities deny them opportunities to realize their fullest potential in American society (*NASW News* 1977, p. 35).

In a 1977 policy discussion on racism, the Delegate Assembly of the National Association of Social Workers identified racism as a specific professional concern. The assembly went on to say:

Social workers know more than anyone else the human costs of racism. In our profession we are in a position to see its particularly damaging effects in poverty, mortality rates, housing, employment, education, health care, and public welfare. . . . [NASW News 1977, p. 35]

This is not to minimize the efforts to combat racism and poverty undertaken in the past and some of the legislative breakthroughs that followed. Clearly much more needs to be done, however controversial the impact of such programs may be. Currently, institutionalized and systematic discrimination continues to exist in employment, education, housing, health, mental health, and public welfare, to mention only a few areas (*NASW News* 1977, p. 35).

Given the above developments, it is of particular interest to note the adoption of a policy statement on racism by the Delegate Assembly of the National Association of Social Workers. The policy statement on racism that addressed itself to several specific areas included the following key statements of intent:

> 1. *To work toward the building of an open society where racial differences are accepted and respected and within which individual and institutionalized racism can find no systemic supports and no residual practice maintenance.*
>
> 2. *To seek the institution of public, social, and economic policy through legislation, through regulation, and through judicial review which will protect rights, and ensure equity and social justice for the subordinated racial minorities....*
> [NASW News 1977]

While the cynical individual would perhaps dismiss such a statement of policy and efforts at implementation as mere rhetoric, it was a significant step by the national professional body of social workers to make a concerted effort to deal with the problem of racism. It is vital that individual social workers continue to foster the development of an open society in which differences of race, color, religion, age, sex, or national origin are acknowledged and appreciated.

Clearly, factors that contribute to social problems such as racism and poverty are complex and interrelated, and efforts to combat them require multidisciplinary approaches. Poverty, for example, is the lack of resources—not just the lack of money—and thus is determined by several interrelated factors such as the availability of an adequate occupation (income), the education of children, the nature and location of an individual's residence, the quality and accessibility of medical services, the types of justice received in the courts of law, the security afforded to an individual on retirement and opportunities for political, social, and cultural expression and participation (Pearl 1971, p. 921). The poor lack the resources necessary for optimizing their life opportunities and attainments; therefore, social workers generally are of the view that social resources and provisions should be redistributed more equally to the poor, especially through equal access to education, employment, housing, and income (Siporin 1975, p. 24).

The social work profession's concerns in the areas of poverty, racism, social justice, and redistribution of resources will continue to challenge the profession in the future. While these concerns related to the poor and disenfranchised in society are central to the profession, social work should not be equated solely with work with the poor. Social work as a helping profession has a commitment to serve all members of society including the non-poor, who may need help in handling interpersonal relations, in dealing with social and psychological concerns, and in optimizing their life opportunities and sense of fulfillment.

TOWARD A FRAMEWORK FOR PRACTICE

In the context of societal changes and changes within the profession, the need exists to identify and to explore further a suitable framework for practice. Such a framework, while allowing for new developments and innovations in practice, should ensure the possibility of integrating variations as they emerge in practice with a common base that has already been identified as fundamental to practice. Evidence of efforts to develop such a framework is reflected in current literature on social work practice; for example, the work of Pincus and Minahan (1973), Goldstein (1973), and Siporin (1975).

There is increasing realization of the need for a common base providing a framework for ongoing developments in practice and allowing for integration of diverse strands in practice (Bartlett 1970). The common base facilitates a unified approach and helps to integrate the fundamental elements in social work practice: purpose, knowledge, values, the repertoire of interventive techniques, and the varying contexts of practice. Hence, as noted in the Preface, social work practitioners are basically *generalist* practitioners, functioning as they do within a unified framework of a common base. Embodied in the generalist framework are basic concepts and principles that are applicable in a variety of specific settings and at all levels of intervention. Within this framework a comprehensive, holistic approach to practice is used. The holistic perspective is evident in the capacity of the generalist practitioner to function effectively at different interventive levels and to work with the client's total system as well as with the client per se (Klenk and Ryan 1974, p. 4). The holistic perspective is also evident in efforts to focus on the development of an integrated view of the individual in society by directing attention to improving services to individuals, families, and groups and to broader issues of social policy and social change in practice.

The suggested framework for practice draws from systems theory and assumes an open, dynamic, changing social system in which social problems are viewed as resulting from an interaction of complex interrelated factors (Compton and Galaway 1975, p. 61). Essentially, *systems theory* focuses not on individuals but on systems: the interaction between and the interrelatedness of units. It calls for a comprehensive long-term approach and an attack on structural factors contributing to social problems. Systems theory has been proposed by several authors as a likely conceptual framework for social work practice (Hearn 1969, Compton and Galaway 1975, Pincus and Minahan 1973). In the context of interrelatedness and interactions, systems theory provides a basis for developing approaches to problem solving. In Part III of the book there is further discussion of systems theory and its implications for social work. The generalist practitioner, functioning from the premise of a common base of knowledge and drawing selectively from a broad repertoire of skills, seeks to effect changes as necessary at different levels of intervention, varying from the individual to a broader society.

The main focus of this type of generalist practice is centered on change efforts whose broad goal is to enhance social functioning by attacking social problems that are a threat or a hindrance to the attainment of people's fullest potential. Earlier interpretations of social functioning focused mainly on the behavior of individuals in relation to their environment and would be construed as having a narrower meaning. *Social functioning* as used here is a more dynamic concept, focusing not so much on the behavior of a given individual (although this is included) as on the complex series of interactions between people and their environment (Bartlett 1970, p. 104).

Indeed, the key to understanding and changing social problems lies in this relationship between people and their exchange with their environment, specifically with regard to their access to and utilization of societal resources. In the practitioner's efforts to enhance these exchanges through intervention, several general objectives have been identified that serve as guidelines for the interventive efforts (Nann and Maas 1974, p. 59):

1. *Remedial or rehabilitative goals* where intervention aims at minimizing or eliminating already present adverse effects of social problems through material assistance and social services;

2. *Reform or redistribution of societal resources goals* where intervention focuses on alleviating factors that create social problems through attempts to bring about changes in policies and procedures of social resource agencies;

3. *Preventive goals* where interventive efforts focus on anticipating individual and social breakdown, foreseeing consequences of inadequate resources, and providing for necessary changes;

4. *Development goals* where intervention centers on broad-scale developmental efforts with a view to serving the entire population rather than specific target groups. Thus, developmental goals introduce more of a macroperspective, focusing on structural and institutional change in attacking the sources of problems.

Generalist social work practice begins with the assessment of problem situations that threaten to interfere with the social well-being of people. In this assessment process it is necessary to take into consideration the people who are affected by the problem and the societal resources—that is, the social institutions—that have contributed to the problem situation. Similarly, plans for intervention take note of the loci of intervention along a broad range of societal levels in order to determine the strategies and modes of intervention that will follow.

This approach to practice, which introduces a systems perspective in social intervention, involves in the broader sense three levels of intervention: macrosystem, mezzosystem, and microsystem. Because these are levels on a continuum, the distinctions between macro- (large), mezzo- (intermediate), and micro- (small) scale systems do not always lend themselves to precise definition. Macrosystem and mezzosystem problems do affect microsystems, and in this sense, a macrosystem or mezzosystem problem situation usually implies the fact that there are individuals and families needing help (Mullen and Dumpson 1972).

Macrosystem problems affect a large, geographically scattered population; the key determining factors go beyond individuals, groups, and neighborhoods. Problems such as poverty, sexism, racism, inadequate housing, or environmental pollution defy traditional, analytic problem-solving frameworks that focus on the individual personality, family, or locality (Mullen and Dumpson 1972, pp. 116–17). The ultimate goal of macrosystem practice is enhancement of the quality of life. The macrosystem practitioner's perspective is long-term and focuses on future conditions of social policy and societal directions. Social work practice at the mezzosystem level of intervention primarily involves work with middle-level institutions—their structures, processes, and supports—to enhance the social functioning of individuals, families, and groups (Mullen and Dumpson 1972, p. 129). Microsystem problems are those in which the key influences seem to be at the level of either the individual, family, or small group directly experiencing the problem (Mullen and Dumpson 1972, p. 158).

Successful outcome in practice is dependent on adequate problem definition, assessment, determination of the appropriate level of intervention, and the combination of roles and skills that are called for in relation to a specific target group. Practitioners may selectively engage in such diverse roles as clinicians, developers, consultants, organizers, and lobbyists in the course of their intervention efforts, depending on the nature of the problem, the level of intervention, the organizational auspices of the workers, the locus of intervention, and the specific kinds of exchange between people and the resource systems in the environment.

CURRENT ISSUES IN PRACTICE

Current issues in practice have not come upon us dramatically; they have been with us for some time. First, we are increasingly seeing the development of a continuum in practice that may increasingly be a pattern in the future. Practice is at different levels and is no longer identified exclusively with the work of the master's degree–trained personnel. There are two entry levels for social work practitioners—the bachelor's degree (BSW) and the master's degree (MSW)—although some social workers have had advanced training beyond the master's degree as well. This fact gives rise to issues of job classification, standards and levels of performance, and the relationship between BSW and MSW workers.

A second issue that practitioners are increasingly aware of in recent times is account-ability. More and more questions will be raised in the future as to whether we are meeting the stated goals and objectives of our programs, both short-term objectives and long-term objectives. There are issues of accountability of the worker to the clients, to the agency, to the board, to the funding agency, to the profession, and to the community that gives the practitioner the sanction to intervene to solve problems. The current crisis in social services is partly a crisis of credibility based on an inadequate system of accountability. Accountabil-ity implies a reasonable expectation that the purpose for which dollars were raised has been achieved with optimum efficiency and effectiveness.

Two other issues in social work are related to accountability: effective utilization of resources and evaluation of effectiveness of programs. Tougher questions than have pre-viously been asked will be asked in the future as to whether resources are being utilized in an optimal way. Does the present system of service delivery, organizational arrangement, and approach promise the best results? Are there alternate ways, using the same resources, that could produce better results? Is there need for more effective coordination among pri-vate agencies and between private and public agencies? Emphasis on evaluating the effec-tiveness of programs ensures the possibility of assessing whether the stated objectives are being met and whether the services provided are meeting the needs of people.

Another issue that will be emphasized increasingly in the future is the need to relate practice more to the life situations and family patterns of diverse ethnic and cultural minor-ity groups (Sanders 1973, p. 188). The social work practitioner is faced with such questions as: How do we avoid stereotyping ethnic and cultural groups with which we are not famil-iar? and How do we focus on the strengths and resources within these cultures as we at-tempt to help them? These and related questions have to be explored more thoroughly in practice.

Related to the foregoing issue is the increasing trend of involving the clients and consumers in the planning, organization, and delivery of services. This issue received con-siderable attention in the 1960s, as exemplified by the slogan of "maximum feasible par-ticipation" of the poor, consumers, and clients (Van Till and Van Till 1970). Despite the cynicism and the problems entailed, this is a trend that will continue with implications for practice. Increasingly in the future social work practitioners will be faced with the question of how far they are willing to go in involving clients and consumers in planning, organiza-tion, and delivery of services.

THE STRUCTURE OF THE BOOK

This book provides a framework for viewing practice analytically and in comprehensive terms. The framework developed for this book—that is, the common base—identifies the fundamental elements in social work practice: values and ideology; the varying contexts of practice; knowledge, the several roles, interventive strategies, and techniques used by prac-titioners; and the issues. This framework assumes that no matter what the problem area, certain basic concepts and principles—sufficiently general—are applicable in a variety of practice settings. The practice itself is the application of the general concepts and principles to specific situations at varying levels and in a variety of settings. In this sense the generalist practitioner's action is within the general social work frame of reference and is guided by the broadly defined knowledge, values, and techniques of the profession.

FRAMEWORK FOR SOCIAL WORK PRACTICE: A GUIDE TO THE BOOK

Part I. Values and Ideology

    A. Values and Philosophy
    B. Relation of Values to Goals
        1. Rem-Rehab
        2. Prevention
        3. Resource Development
        4. Social Change/Reform

Part II. The Context of Practice

    A. Levels of Intervention
        1. Macro
        2. Mezzo
        3. Micro
    B. Auspices and Organizations
    C. Fields

Part III. Knowledge for Practice

    A. Conceptual Framework: Generic Concepts and Principles
    B. Generic Processes of Assessment and Intervention
    C. Evaluation

Part IV. Illustrations of Practice

    A. Illustration of Strategies in Relation to Goals
    B. Illustrations of Differential Roles
        1. Clinician
        2. Organizer
        3. Planner
        4. Consultant
        5. Advocate
        6. Broker
        7. Developer
        8. Lobbyist
        9. Policy Analyst
      10. Reconciler
      11. Case Manager
    C. Differential Application of Strategies and Techniques

Part V. Issues

        1. Prospects for Generalists
        2. Effectiveness and Accountability
        3. The Future

The conceptualization of practice developed here goes beyond the tendency in the early years of the development of social work to focus heavily on method, whether a single method or combination of methods (casework, group work, and community organization); instead, practice is conceptualized at a broader level where no single method predominates. In fact, the major advantage of describing practice at the generalist level is the identification and integration of principles and practices that cut across all of the social work methods, thus facilitating the social worker's responding to the problem on the basis of client need, rather than on the basis of an artificial methodological designation. Consequently, a number of roles are involved in carrying out the interventive measures, such as clinician, organizer, planner, lobbyist, and so on. The practitioner assumes these roles depending on the nature of the problem encountered, the context in which the practitioner works, and the goals that have been established. Finally, the interventive measures—that is, the strategies and techniques (the "doing" aspects)—are goal oriented and must be viewed in relation to social work purposes, philosophy, and values. It is the authors' hope that the remainder of this book will help you both understand and integrate these fundamentals of social work into your own practice.

REFERENCES

Bartlett, Harriet M. "Social Work Practice."
    1965. In Harry L. Lurie, ed., *Encyclopedia of Social Work*. New York: National Association of Social Workers (NASW).

———.
    1970. *The Common Base of Social Work Practice*. New York: NASW.

Chambers, Clark A.
    1967. *Seedtime of Reform*. Ann Arbor: University of Michigan Press.

Compton, Beulah Roberts, and Burt Galaway.
    1975. *Social Work Processes*. Homewood, Ill.: Dorsey Press.

Delegate Assembly of the National Association of Social Workers.
    1971. "Profession of Social Work: Code of Ethics." In Robert Morris, ed., *Encyclopedia of Social Work*, vol. 11. New York: NASW, 1971.

Gilbert, Neil, and Harry Specht.
    1974. "The Incomplete Profession." *Social Work* 19, no. 6.

Goodman, James A.
    1973. *Dynamics of Racism in Social Work Practice*. Washington, D.C.: NASW.

Greenwood, Ernest.
    1957. "Attributes of a Profession." *Social Work* 2, no. 3:45–55.

Hearn, Gordon.
    1975. "General Systems Theory and Social Work." In Francis J. Turner, ed., *Social Work Treatment*. New York: Free Press.

Kahn, Alfred J., and Shela B. Kamerman.
    1976. *Social Services in the United States*. Philadelphia: Temple University Press.

Kidneigh, John C.
    1965. "History of American Social Work." In Harry L. Lurie, ed., *Encyclopedia of Social Work*. New York: NASW.

Klenk, Robert W., and Robert M. Ryan.
    1974. *The Practice of Social Work*. Belmont, Calif.: Wadsworth.

Meyer, Henry J.
    1971. "Profession of Social Work: Contemporary Characteristics." In Robert Morris, ed., *Encyclopedia of Social Work*, vol. 2. New York: NASW.

Mullen, Edward J., James R. Dumpson, & Associates.
    1972. *Evaluation of Social Intervention*. San Francisco: Jossey-Bass.

Nann, Richard C., and Henry S. Maas.
    1974. "Purpose and Framework for Curriculum Development in Social Work." *International Social Work* 17, no. 1:54–61.

National Association of Social Workers.
  1973.   *Standards for Social Service Manpower.* New York: NASW.
National Association of Social Workers.
  1977.   "Public Policy Issues." *NASW News* 22, no. 7:15, 16.
National Association of Social Workers.
  1979.   "Specialization in the Social Work Profession." *NASW News* 24, no. 4 (April):20, 31.
Pearl, Arthur.
  1971.   "Poverty: Strategies for Reduction." In Robert Morris, ed., *Encyclopedia of Social Work.* New York: NASW.
Pincus, Allen, and Anne Minahan.
  1973.   *Social Work Practice: Model and Method.* Itasca, Ill.: Peacock Publishers.
Romanyshyn, John M.
  1971.   *Social Welfare: Charity to Justice.* New York: Council on Social Work Education.
Sanders, Daniel S.
  1973.   *The Impact of Reform Movements on Social Policy Change: The Case of Social Insurance.* New York: Burdick Publishers.
Siporin, Max.
  1975.   "Introduction to Social Work Practice." New York: Macmillan.
Specht, Harry.
  1972.   "The Deprofessionalization of Social Work." *Social Work* 17, no. 2:3–15.
Van Till, J., and S. B. Van Till.
  1970.   "Citizen Participation in Social Policy: The End of the Cycle?" *Social Problems* 17, no. 3 (Winter):320–21.

PART I

Values and Ideology

Part I of this book, *Values and Ideology*, deals with a fundamental aspect of social work practice that is often glossed over. The social work profession has an explicit ideology and a set of values that provides a basis for professional practice. *Values* refer to ideal or preferred conditions and focus on what is desirable or good for humanity (Pincus and Minahan 1973, p. 38). They do not refer to the world as it is constituted or as we know it to be. Rather they point to what responses and relationships *ought* to be when individuals interact in society. Similarly, *ideology* refers to a system of beliefs and attitudes—that is, a group's "vision of desired reality" (Siporin 1975, p. 79). The social work profession derives its *ethical practice principles* from this fundamental core of values and ideology. The value orientations, the ideology, and the ethical principles of social work practice guide the professional worker in the helping process. The ethical practice principles are embodied in the professional code of ethics with the intent of providing more practical help in guiding the interventive efforts of the practitioner.

Values and ideology play a crucial role in shaping the purposes, concerns, and directions of the social work profession. In a sense every profession is marked by a set of beliefs and ideology. However, the nature of the value orientations and the extent of understanding and adherence to them vary from profession to profession. *Social work values* are those values that guide practitioners' interventions, responses, and behavior in their professional capacity (Levy 1977, p. 4). They provide a basis for rational choices in professional practice and are the values that social workers are committed to as members of a practice profession. One of the oldest and most widely held values in social work practice emphasizes the worth and dignity of every human being. Another basic value refers to the belief in the mutual responsibility of individuals for each other (Bartlett 1970, p. 65). A social work value that is increasingly important in both the national and international context is the belief in the right of individuals to be different from each other. The social work practitioner makes the assumption that each individual is unique and different, and helping efforts, plans for change, and intervention strategies are influenced by this and similar value assumptions. Thus, social work values influence and guide the practitioner's helping efforts.

While reference could be made to several more values, the primary values of social work that influence and shape practitioner intervention are stated succinctly by Pincus and Minahan as follows:

Table I-1. Summary of Major Principles of NASW Code of Ethics

I. THE SOCIAL WORKER'S CONDUCT AND COMPORTMENT AS A SOCIAL WORKER

A. *Propriety.* The social worker should maintain high standards of personal conduct in the capacity or identity as social worker.
B. *Competence and Professional Development.* The social worker should strive to become and remain proficient in professional practice and the performance of professional functions.
C. *Service.* The social worker should regard as primary the service obligation of the social work profession.
D. *Integrity.* The social worker should act in accordance with the highest standards of professional integrity.
E. *Scholarship and Research.* The social worker engaged in study and research should be guided by the conventions of scholarly inquiry.

II. THE SOCIAL WORKER'S ETHICAL RESPONSIBILITY TO CLIENTS

F. *Primacy of Clients' Interests.* The social worker's primary responsibility is to clients.
G. *Rights and Prerogatives of Clients.* The social worker should make every effort to foster maximum self-determination on the part of clients.
H. *Confidentiality and Privacy.* The social worker should respect the privacy of clients and hold in confidence all information obtained in the course of professional service.
I. *Fees.* When setting fees, the social worker should ensure that they are fair, reasonable, considerate, and commensurate with the service performed and with due regard for the clients' ability to pay.

III. THE SOCIAL WORKER'S ETHICAL RESPONSIBILITY TO COLLEAGUES

J. *Respect, Fairness, and Courtesy.* The social worker should treat colleagues with respect, courtesy, fairness, and good faith.
K. *Dealing with Colleagues' Clients.* The social worker has the responsibility to relate to the clients of colleagues with full professional consideration.

IV. THE SOCIAL WORKER'S ETHICAL RESPONSIBILITY TO EMPLOYERS AND EMPLOYING ORGANIZATIONS

L. *Commitments to Employing Organizations.* The social worker should adhere to commitments made to the employing organizations.

V. THE SOCIAL WORKER'S ETHICAL RESPONSIBILITY TO THE SOCIAL WORK PROFESSION

M. *Maintaining the Integrity of the Profession.* The social worker should uphold and advance the values, ethics, knowledge, and mission of the profession.
N. *Community Service.* The social worker should assist the profession in making social services available to the general public.
O. *Development of Knowledge.* The social worker should take responsibility for identifying, developing, and fully utilizing knowledge for professional practice.

VI. THE SOCIAL WORKER'S ETHICAL RESPONSIBILITY TO SOCIETY

P. *Promoting the General Welfare.* The social worker should promote the general welfare of society.

Source: *NASW News*, vol. 25, no. 1 (January 1980), p. 24. Reprinted with permission of the National Association of Social Workers.

a. Society has an obligation to ensure that people have access to the resources, services, and opportunities they need to meet various life tasks, alleviate distress, and realize their aspirations and values.

b. In providing societal resources, the dignity and individuality of people should be respected. [Pincus and Minahan 1973, p. 39]

The profession's code of ethics is derived from these primary values and the basic philosophy represented by them. The ethical principles of practice derived from the code of ethics are intended to provide more specific and practical guidelines to the professional worker. In a situation of rapid technological change, complexity of social problems, competing group interests, and value dilemmas, the demand for greater specificity and clarity in principles and guides to practice derived from social work values is increasing. It is not difficult to understand the demand for greater specificity and clarity in principles in the present context of rapid technological change, for many of the problems confronting workers and their clients or client system in the helping process are problems of values and "normative ethical conduct" (Siporin 1975, p. 68). While recognizing that a need for greater clarity and specificity exists, a vital question remains: How specific and prescriptive should a profession be? Although the profession's values and ethics can be seen as continuously evolving, a summary of the most recent Code of Ethics of NASW can be seen in Table I-1, while the entire Code of Ethics, approved in 1979 by NASW, is reprinted as Appendix A.

The shifts or changed emphases in values in relation to practice are a good example of the need to review constantly the fundamental elements of professional practice—knowledge, values, interventive techniques, and their interrelation—in the context of societal changes and new demands on the profession. Periods of rapid technological change intensify the need for human service professions such as social work to review, question, and reaffirm the basic values and the ideology of the profession (Wheeler 1977, p. 25). Periods of societal changes also require an ongoing review and examination of the values and goals of the profession. Societal changes, such as those that occurred in the 1960s and 1970s at an unprecedented pace, make new directions in social work practice necessary. Such review and assessment of the values and ideology of the profession should also take note of the pitfalls involved in the tendency to emphasize techniques to the detriment of basic value considerations in practice.

Ideology and values of the profession have to be rethought in terms of current realities and likely future developments. What new areas of emphases, modes of intervention, trends, and innovations will flow from a reexamination of the profession's present goals and values? The paradoxical situation must be noted that, while values and goals of the profession influence the future directions of practice in a society experiencing rapid change, it is also likely that shifts in emphases on specific values and goals of the profession may take place following the emergence of new problems and challenges.

Social work, for example, has emphasized two sets of values that are by and large complementary: the worth and dignity of the individual as related to the growth and well-being of the group, and the freedom and development of the individual in relation to the security of the individual and society (*An Intercultural Exploration* 1967). At varying stages in the development of a society, one or the other of these sets of values will probably receive more emphasis by the social work profession, leading to shifts in emphases and new directions in practice.

The social work profession, in its efforts to contribute to enhanced social functioning, improved quality of life and environment, development of institutions that are more responsive to the needs of people, and the quest for distributive justice, is inevitably concerned with the whole issue of the individual in society. The ideology of social work has an important contribution to make in the conceptual understanding of the place of the individual in society and in shaping the tangible interventive efforts that are necessary to ensure improved quality of life for all.

READING SELECTIONS IN PART I

The reading selections in Part I reflect the creative tension that exists in the profession from efforts to reexamine current ideology in the context of the rapid changes that have already taken place in a post-industrial society and the changes that are likely in the future (Bell 1973). Given the current changes and likely future developments, what ought to be the new emphases in values and goals, and what changes in practice seem necessary? In this reexamination of the ideology of social work in the context of a society in rapid change, the reading selections in Part I focus either directly or indirectly on many aspects that have direct implications for practice: the likely shifts in values and goals of the profession and the emergence of new goals and values, the possible changes in the profession's priorities and directions, the understanding of the changes likely to occur in the future, the new knowledge, contexts, and interventive efforts necessary for the practitioner of today and tomorrow, and an international code of ethics for professional social work practice.

"Social Work Values on the New Frontiers" by Pernell addresses itself to key questions of social values in an open, competitive, changing society faced with complex problems. A set of values largely based on the Puritan ethic that was so effective in making headway through "physical, biological, and economic barriers" in American society has created a host of problems in people's relationships to each other. The social worker stands at the "crossroads of competing values," and his or her influence in urging movement toward "the social good" by the rest of society seems significant. Pernell comments that, ideally, the social worker represents the social conscience of the community, prompting society toward action in keeping with its highest ideals. In applying social work values to specific situations—that is, at the operational level—the social work practitioner should be aware of his or her own values, including biases and prejudices, and the all-pervading influence that these are likely to have in practice. Related to this is the need for awareness on the part of the practitioner of the reality of diversity of values in society, based to some extent on variations in community, social class, and ethnic group.

"Cultural Differences and Social Work Philosophy" by Konopka highlights the role of philosophy in social work and stresses the need for social work practitioners to clarify the basic propositions of the profession in the context of cultural differences. Philosophy, she maintains, is the base of social work because it introduces the perspective of "ought" into practice and clarifies "what ought to be in relation to what is." Emphasizing the central place of goals and values of the profession, she challenges the practitioner to go beyond strategies and techniques in an effort to deal with the problems and life patterns of people in different cultures. Konopka sees the "clarification of philosophy" in the context of diverse cultures and subcultures as the basic premise of social work practice. She refers to two universal basic values: respect for the dignity of the individual and belief in the mutual responsibility of individuals. The differential applications of these basic values, she points out, are influenced by such factors as cultural, family, and ethnic variations; significant life experiences; precepts and demands of groups or systems to which people belong; and varying theories of human behavior that people subscribe to. Social work educators and practitioners would do well to pay heed to her admonition that focusing on techniques without an "underlying philosophy and thinking through of values" is fraught with serious difficulties, particularly in the context of social work practice in differing cultures.

"The Universal in Education for Social Work" by Rosenfeld is included in Part I for several special reasons. First, Rosenfeld, in discussing the universal components in social work education and practice, focuses a great deal on values and beliefs and identifies their central role in practice. The other two components of the universal content he refers to are skills and knowledge. Second, he makes the claim that the basic values, beliefs, skills, and knowledge in social work practice "are not culture bound" and may therefore be said to be universal. In this context the extent to which certain basic values, beliefs, and ideology in social work practice are universal needs critical study by educators and practitioners alike. Rosenfeld makes the point that while beliefs and values are universal, what is particular in social work is "the manner and the degree in which these values and beliefs" and, for that matter, skills and knowledge are used in a particular society. Third, Rosenfeld's claims regarding the universality of values—that is, that they are pertinent to all societies, regardless of a particular society's stage of development or its social philosophy—are certain to generate critical questioning and debate; this is to be especially welcomed in the area of social values and social thought, since values, however acceptable to the rational mind, may not be applicable to all situations in the real world. The need exists to examine specific societies or situations where the basic values or beliefs that are assumed to be universal are not fully acceptable or applicable. One question that emerges in this context is whether the values and beliefs that are assumed to be basic and universal in social work are to be thought of only in relation to a democratic society. How do these values and beliefs make sense in an authoritarian society? Insofar as social work practice assumes a democratic framework and related values as a given, the extent to which the core professional values in social work that are assumed to be universal could be operative in a society that does not embody basic freedoms and opportunities for the individual is questionable. In such societies the claims of social work values and ideology pose a challenge; and in such contexts the central purpose of social work—referred to as contributing to the humanization of society—takes on new significance.

"Between Values and Science: Education for the Profession During a Moral Crisis *or* Is Proof Truth," by Vigilante, introduces an important theme: the competing roles of values and science in the social work profession. The place assigned to values in the profession becomes crucial especially at a time of societal and moral crisis. Vigilante, while affirming the need for a scientific base in practice, questions the place assigned to values in professional education and practice. Professional values in social work are seen to be more than merely the philosophical base of practice, important as this aspect may be. He emphasizes the need for a recommitment and the assignment of a central place to values in social work theory and practice. In his view the difficulty in operationalizing values in our society has contributed to their being sheltered and, as he terms it, "being revered from a distance." This predicament has contributed to the search for an escape route through science. A strong plea is made for alternative research styles that stress values and for research efforts that would contribute to a more precise understanding of how values impact on practice. Vigilante suggests that, despite the relative lack of serious study or research on the place of values in the profession, they may provide the fundamental linkages in theory building for diverse forms of practice.

"International Code of Ethics for the Professional Social Worker" by Alexander is in the nature of a preamble that sets forth the humanitarian ideals, the democratic philosophy, the principles, and the standards of ethical conduct that provide the ideological basis and the broad guidelines for the practitioner. A code of ethics to which all practitioners subscribe is a vital element of professional practice and is evidence of the social work profession's maturity, discipline, and sense of accountability. The International Code of Ethics for the professional social worker, developed by the collaborative effort of several countries and adopted at the International Federation of Social Workers' Permanent Council Meeting in July 1976, is significant in that it provides tangible evidence that certain fundamental principles of social work practice may be "culture free." An international code of ethics based on practice experience in different countries and cultures introduces an international dimension to social work practice. This code is a necessary development today with increased travel, exchange of social work practitioners, and practitioner involvement in issues and concerns such as the refugee problem, intercountry adoption, and drug abuse that seem to defy narrow national approaches to their solution. Critics of the current code of ethics for professional social workers in the United States suggest that the code is designed more to protect the professional worker and the agencies that control the delivery of services than the clients (Absatz and Schwarz 1975). Questions have also been raised from time to time as to whether such statements of professional practice and conduct attempt to go beyond *maintenance concepts*—that is, efforts to maintain the status quo—and point to responsibility for action and change. In a context where there is skepticism—at least in some quarters—as to how far codes help to move the profession into social action and change efforts, the development of a new international code of ethics, with due thought and provision for action and change and due focus on resource development and social justice on the part of the practitioner, is to be welcomed.

REFERENCES

Absatz, Cecelia Love, and Al Schwarz.
    1975. "An Administrator and Practitioner Look At: The Impact of Professional Honesty in Work with Clients, Colleagues, Agency—Consequences for the Social Worker Who Practices Our Code of Ethics." Unpublished paper presented at the Twentieth Anniversary NASW Professional Symposium.

Bartlett, Harriet M.
    1970. *The Common Base of Social Work Practice.* New York: National Association of Social Workers.

Bell, Daniel.
    1973. *The Coming of Post-Industrial Society: A Venture in Forecasting.* New York: Basic Books.

Council on Social Work Education.
    1967. *An Intercultural Exploration: Universals and Differences in Social Work Values: Functions and Practice.* Report of the Intercultural Seminar held at the East-West Center, Hawaii, 1966. New York: Council on Social Work Education.

Levy, Charles S.
    1977. "Values in Social Work Education." In Boyd E. Oviatt, ed., *Values in Social Work Education: Cliché or Reality.* University of Utah.

Pincus, Allen, and Anne Minahan.
    1973. *Social Work: Practice Model and Method.* Itasca, Ill.: Peacock Publishers.
Siporin, Max.
    1975. *Introduction to Social Work Practice.* New York: Macmillan.
Wheeler, James P.
    1977. "Value Dilemmas in Social Work Practice." In Boyd E. Oviatt, ed., *Values in Social Work Education: Cliché or Reality.* University of Utah.

SOCIAL WORK VALUES ON THE NEW FRONTIERS

Ruby B. Pernell

O, Beautiful for Pilgrim's feet, whose stern impassioned stress
A thoroughfare for freedom beat across the wilderness . . .
America, America, God shed his grace on thee
And crown thy good with brotherhood from sea to shining sea

        [Katherine Lee Bates, America the Beautiful]

In these few lines are summed up some of the most compelling and persistent themes of American life: the stern, tight-lipped, driving discipline of Puritan ethos; the beckoning wilderness—the frontier existing but to be conquered; the struggle to keep open the paths of individual freedom; the expectation of a special meritorious relationship with God. The boastfulness, achievement, myth, and self-satisfaction are all there. It is descriptive of a vast do-it-yourself program except that it assigns to God the responsibility for the crowning gift of brotherhood.

From time to time in our history we have been confronted with the painful fact that not only freedom, but brotherhood, too, was our own, not God's responsibility. The outpourings of initiative and enterprise which have characterized American growth have been and still are much more easily directed toward the mastery and extension of our physical and biological world than to the world of human relationships; throughout our history one frontier after another has been breasted and the new territory beyond revealed, only to become a new target for conquest. Our physical frontiers are now somewhere in outer space. In biological sciences we are seeking the keys to creation and eternal life, as men once sought them through religion. In man's relationships with his fellow man, however, we remain, as it were, in barricaded settlements as timid newcomers on the edge of a vast, undeveloped, hostile land. Indeed, the wilderness is encroaching on what was thought to be cleared land. The creeping undergrowth and hanging fringes of moss are reclaiming their own. This is the true frontier of our times, resisting piecemeal attacks with inadequate tools, unbacked by sufficient will or courage to forge ahead. Despite the oratory of patriotic days, our good has not yet been crowned with brotherhood.

THE PURITAN ETHIC

The Puritan's code of conduct and action was peculiarly suited to the task he set himself, of conquering a strange, unknown, hostile land. As geographic and economic expansionist opportunities for a long time seemed unlimited, it is no wonder that his brand of ethics became the indelible mark on those who followed him to these shores and went beyond through the wilderness, working, fighting, destroying, and cheating their ways across the continent.

Source: From Katherine A. Kendall, ed., *Social Work Values in an Age of Discontent* (New York: Council on Social Work Education, 1970), pp. 46–61. Reprinted with permission of the Council on Social Work Education.

Tawney[1] said of the Puritan:

He drew from his idealization of personal responsibility a theory of individual rights, which, secularized and generalized, was to be among the most potent explosives that the world has known. He drew from it also a scale of ethical values, in which the traditional scheme of Christian virtues was almost exactly reversed, and which, since he was above all things practical, he carried as a dynamic into the routine of business and political life.*

The frontiers which stood before him in America presented the opportunity to continue the space exploration started by his voyage across the ocean and unfinished as yet. The frontier life demanded and repaid the individual initiative and unceasing toil and beckoned toward greater returns for those who would brave the hostile wilderness.

To quote Tawney again:

Limitless increase and expansion ... production ... systematic and methodical accumulation ... won the meed of praise that belongs to the good and faithful servant. The shrewd, calculating commercialism which tries all human relations by pecuniary standards, the acquisitiveness which cannot rest while there are competitors to be conquered or profits to be won, the love of social power and hunger for economic gain—these irrepressible appetites had evoked from time immemorial the warnings and denunciations of saints and sages. Plunged in the cleansing waters of later Puritanism, the qualities which less enlightened ages had denounced as social vices emerged as economic virtues. They emerged as moral virtues as well. For the world exists not to be enjoyed but to be conquered.[2]

And so men hacked their ways forward with social and moral sanction for their self-seeking behavior. The creed, severed from its religious base, is still with us as an everyday reality, still potent in the beliefs of those who succeed, still used as the screen through which to view the unsuccessful. But this set of values, proven so effective in clearing a way through physical, biological, and economic barriers, have in themselves created a host of problems in man's relationship with man.

---

* From R. A. Tawney, "Economic Virtues and Prescriptions for Poverty," in *Social Perspectives on Behavior*, Herman D. Stein and Richard A. Cloward, eds. (Glencoe, Ill.: Free Press, 1958). Reprinted by permission.

EXPLOITATION OF MINORITIES

It would seem that the concept of brotherhood has always been difficult for Americans. John Steinbeck, in his book *America and Americans*, comments in his pithy style:

The whole thing is crazy. Every single man in our emerging country was out for himself against all others— for his safety, his profit, his future. . . .[3]

The self-interest, the economic opportunities, and the social and moral sanction for exploitation of resources led inevitably not only to use and abuse of land and capital but of human beings as well. The destruction of the great forests were nothing as compared to the destruction of the Indians and their culture; the stripping of minerals from the earth nothing as compared to the stripping of culture and manhood from the black men brought as slaves; and on the newer frontiers of urban life and growing industrialization, the exploitation of men, women, and children as productive units was of much less concern than that of overworked farm animals. (In fact, the Society for the Prevention of Cruelty to Children was preceded by the Society for the Prevention of Cruelty to Animals.) To use Steinbeck's vivid language again:

From the first we have treated our minorities abominably. . . . All that was required to release this mechanism of oppression and sadism was that the newcomers be meek, poor, weak in numbers, and unprotected—although it helped if their skin, hair, eyes were different and they spoke some language other than English or worshipped in some church other than Protestant. The Pilgrim fathers took out after the Catholics, and both clobbered the Jews. The Irish had their turn running the gauntlet, and after them the Germans, the Poles, the Slovaks, the Italians, the Hindus, the Chinese, the Japanese, the Filipinos, the Mexicans. . . . The turn against each group continued until it became sound, solvent, self-defensive and economically anonymous—whereupon each group joined with the older boys and charged down on the newer ones.[4]

It only seems just that at this point in history the blacks, browns, and reds should be using the same mechanism against the white, Anglo-Saxon Protestants. If we are going to be full members in the same club, then everybody—even the first comers—ought to be initiated.

SOCIAL RESPONSIBILITY AND SELF-RIGHTEOUS VALUES

In a society conceiving of itself as "Christian," where there is both the opportunity for socioeconomic mobility and a sanctioned ruthlessness in human relations, somebody has to be the keeper of the Good. Someone has to care about safeguarding humanitarian values against predators. Someone has to be the other—rather than self-oriented. In our history these have been the humanitarians, the social workers, the social reformers. Fortunately, the same religious sources from which the Puritan ethic was derived also provided concepts for responsibility for the welfare of one's "brothers," while the pioneer communities of freedom-seeking men, newly formed in a new land, also provided a growth milieu for norms expressive of the interdependence motif of the collective moral and social values. Religious, philosophical, and political thought contributed to the development of a "social conscience," motivating not only acts of charity but of justice.

However, our major problem has been that the services and institutions growing out of the social responsibility–social conscience motivations have never quite been able to escape the entwinings of the more dominant values of our society. In the same way that the individualistic pursuit of the golden opportunities of expansionist America has been so destructive of human beings and human relations, so the pursuit of the common good has been constantly hampered by this righteously self-centered system of beliefs. While we give with the right hand to the poor, the unfortunate victims of the system, we manage in some fashion to deprive them with the left. The system of social work values—which in their basic generalizations embody the best of the humanistic beliefs of man's intrinsic worth, his potential, his right to make his own decisions, his rightful place within the community of men, and the responsibilities that the community of men have toward him—nevertheless is infiltrated at the operational level by those same sternly punitive, rejecting, prejudiced views of the Puritan. We are caught in our own myths, firmly believing in the land of golden opportunity and just as firmly not believing in the man who hasn't made the most of it. As individuals we will give to the United Fund or even vote for civil rights, but we rush home to barricade ourselves in the suburbs against a possible advent of even one poor or black person.

SOCIAL WORK AND THE SOCIAL GOOD

At this crossroads of competing values stands the social worker with a double historical task of urging movement toward the social good and rescuing those who have been lost or trampled on in the mass competitive rush toward personal affluence and social upgrading. The social worker ideally represents the social conscience of the community, prompting us toward action in keeping with our highest ideals; and the collectives of social workers should function in the same way in relation to their most earthbound members.

In the past the social worker was obvious, easily spotted in proverbial hat, gloves, and flat heels, going about "doing good," secure in her moral aims and in the knowledge of a community of similarly secure fellow workers. But now, in this season of our discontent, the social workers' faith in each other is shaken or lost. The normative behavior, goals, ethics, and values are being questioned by the young and the black and those who make common cause with them. The question is: Is social work (practice, values, organization, agencies, etc.) relevant to today's needs? There is no one correct answer; in fact, each questioner is likely to have his own answer ready before asking the question. We are too often like the student who undertook an inquiry on relevancy, stating, "In order to substantiate my point of view (which is 'no'), will you please fill out the attached questionnaire?"

There is no denying that today is not like yesterday. Every institution of American life does need to examine itself today for relevancy and gear itself to change in a rapidly changing world. The question of relevancy addresses itself to the selection of goals and the system of beliefs and explicit values of the institution, the integrity with which these inform every activity, and the utility of the institution in carrying out its social purposes.

American social work, both as an expression and instrument of American moral and social values, is inextricably tied up with what America is at any one period of time and thus tends to reflect the major concerns of the era. We have moved as the times demanded or permitted from a commitment to charity, to a commitment to justice, to a commitment to science. Though lessened in their power as choice determinants, the central motive of each of these periods has been carried forward as increments. Compassion, social justice, and disciplined knowledge are all part of our armamentarium, though we fall short in all three.

To quote John McDowell, writing in the Conference Bulletin:

The word "value" is used in the profession of social work to convey a concept ... to mean "that standard or principle which leads persons to select one option over another in making day-by-day choices." It is not what we say but what we do that reveals our value system. . . .

Values pose real choices because they always seem to come in pairs. The choice is seldom between good and evil, but between one good and another, or between an evil and lesser evil.[5]

Parsons defines values as:*

patterned conceptions of the qualities of meaning of the objects of human experience; by virtue of these qualities, the objects are considered desirable for the evaluating persons. Among such objects is the type of society considered to be good, not only in some abstract sense but also for "our kind of people." The value patterns that play a part in controlling action in a society are in the first instance the conceptions of the good type of society to which the members of the society are committed. Such a pattern exists at a very high level of generality, without any specifications of functions, or any level of internal differentiation or particularities of situation.[6]

The idea of what constitutes a "good" society can vary, particularly if it is cast in terms of "our kind of people," which can range in inclusiveness from family to all mankind. Indeed, this inclusiveness as well as exclusiveness is part of our problem, for in Steinbeck's words, "We speak about The American Way of Life as though it constitutes the ground rules for the governance of heaven" and want to impose it on everyone else.[7] At this level of generality we are talking of values such as democracy, individual freedom, justice for every man, and the common good. These, however, must filter down into an operational level at which they are internalized and institutionalized to give structure and direction to our daily choices of action. In this process a great many values, norms, and motives emanating from the substructures and individual conditioning enter the course, and the system sometimes gets out of line with its remoter values. Our most cherished myths lie at the remote ends of these misalignments where we still cling to the value and believe it is directing our choices, while in fact we have departed far from it.

It is important, however, that we continue to cherish the value even when departing from it, because it serves as the goal to turn toward at threatening moments in our history. With slavery, the exploitation of immigrant labor, with civil rights and poverty, the appeal for justice and human rights reaches into the moral realm—the collective conscience—for a response. Without these values the conscience would remain undisturbed.

Parsons describes the dominant American value pattern in its moral aspects as fundamentally individualistic, maximizing the desirability of individual autonomy and responsibility, and controlled normatively in two ways. First, it is premised on the idea of building the "good life" not only for the individual but for all of mankind—"a life that is considered desirable, not merely desired. This includes commitment to a good society." He goes on to say:

The society then has a dual meaning, from this moral point of view. On the other hand, it is perhaps the primary field in which valued achievement is possible for the individual. Insofar as it facilitates such achievements, the society is a good one. On the other hand, the building of a good society (that is, its progressive improvement) is the primary goal of valued action. . . . To the individual therefore, the most important goal to which he can orient himself is a contribution to the good society.[8]

This is, in effect, the value platform on which the social worker (used broadly here to designate the person who devotes himself to activities to improve the social conditions of individuals and the society as a whole) has stood: for himself he sees his major obligation to be his duty to his fellow man, to free him to function; i.e., to free him to make his own contribution to the building of a good society, and to work for those changes in the society which will permit greater individual initiative and autonomy.

THE QUESTION OF RELEVANCY OF SOCIAL WORK VALUES

Now [many] question the relevancy of our values in today's world. Yet, a reading of the stated goals

---

* Talcott Parsons, "Youth in the Context of American Society," *The Challenge of Youth*, Erik Erikson, ed. (New York: Anchor Books, 1965). Reprinted by permission.

of those who raise the question indicates the good society and individual autonomy to be the very self-same ends sought. This suggests some mis-connections between our values and our actions. Obviously social work itself must have a number of its own myths whose substantive realities have been corroded over time.

Parsons suggests that "the main pattern of [American] values has been and will probably continue to be stable, but . . . the structure of the society, including its subsystem values at lower levels, has . . . been involved in a rapid and far-reaching process of change."[9] The attempts to cope with the increasing complexity and differentiation in our society, the effects of science and technology, an increasing productivity and pursuit of affluence, rise of ethnic groups into the middle classes, the migratory waves of southern blacks from south to north and of northern whites from inner to outer urban America, have brought into prominence as determinants of choice those social values (as distinct from "moral" values) arising from desirability or expediency. "The common good" can be quite provincially perceived, and "our kind of people" can be taken as the only people who count. The guaranteed annual income may be all right for the farmer who agrees to let his fields lie fallow, because he is "our kind of people"; but a guaranteed annual income for a migrant or tenant family grossly exploited by that farmer is not to be countenanced. They are too common to be included in "the common good."

The social worker and social work institutions, as part of the mainstream of American life, have been caught up in these currents of change, too, so that while the main value pattern—the raison d'être—has remained stable, the lower-level values have changed greatly. In the process, some misalignments have occurred. There are two intermingling streams of development we may examine: one, the institutionalization of social work activities, and the other, the ascendance of the "scientific" or "professional" approach.

One of the more frequently referred-to historical writings is Porter Lee's 1929 Presidential Address to the National Conference on Social Work on the union of cause and function in social work in which he discussed the current concern that the capacity social work had shown for upholding and inspiring enthusiasm for a cause should not be lost as it became more of an established and well-organized function of community life.[10] [By the end of the 1960s] . . . once again [it had become] a concern, increasingly so

with the growing problems of society, the concomitant demands for services, and the further development of a "professional" who seemed more likely to respond to the demands for service than to those for social reform.

The early social workers were generally people who were clear about their mission to help those less fortunate than themselves, to root out social evils, and to rally others of their own class to support the cause. The chief motivation was altruism, and long, irregular hours with little monetary reward were to be expected.

With the social assistance programs of the thirties, social work began to be more of a "job," and then, with the growing development of university schools of social work, a profession. With these changes, other more personal motives entered in: earning a livelihood and occupational status, to mention two which have been of significant influence. Along with this, encouraging and encouraged by the trend, was the development of increasing numbers of organizations to carry on social welfare tasks. We were passing out of what Charlotte Towle referred to as phase one, "the stage in which social workers felt solely responsible passionately to persuade the community to support its good works," and into phase two (still with us), "in which social workers conceive of themselves as employees of the community, responsible to administer the community's good works and subject to its authority in so doing."[11]

Parsons points out that the moral value pattern of our society places heavy responsibility on the individual to help the society toward progressive improvement, but nevertheless subjects him to two crucial sets of limitations. One of these is the fact that individualism is bound within "a strongly emphasized framework of normative order," and that achievement must often be in the context of collective organization, thus limiting autonomy.[12]

For the social worker this means that he must rely on the organization with which he is affiliated to provide the moral conditions which make it possible for him to operate in line with the remoter values to which, hopefully, he subscribes. The misalignment of the organization, thrown off by the prevailing social values and demands at this earthbound level, therefore seriously hampers or completely blocks the potential contribution the individual worker may make to further the "good" society. . . . [However,] if the institution . . . can be perceived . . . as an expression of "the community's good works," the worker's identification with it and his acceptance of its authority may possibly give him a sense of fulfillment so far as his own value commitments are concerned. But this is not enough, for as Towle says:

> *Although a profession is an expression of the conscience of the community, its own conscience cannot be external. Out of the special knowledge and understanding of the human welfare implications of social conditions a profession is expected to contribute to the development of community conscience. Implicit in its function is the responsibility to foster social welfare causes. . . .*[13]

This, then, is a significant part of the problem before us: how to swing the earthbound social welfare institutions into better alignment with our basic values so that the worker within can find the way to make his own contribution to the good society, with the resultant good, not only to those served, but also to the community as it is moved to a higher level of commitment to the common good.

A concurrent stream of development which has contributed to the imperfect connections with our basic values has been the increasing emphasis on a knowledge-based technical skill in the performance of social work. Professionalization, with all its necessary and positive contributions, also has its hazards. The choice and execution of particular theoretical orientations and the elaborations of these into practice can and have led us into exclusiveness, denials of service to those who do not pass certain criteria of "readiness," focus on treatment of individuals, with neglect of attention to the social conditions which spawn the problems, and a general preoccupation with the techniques of making theory work. "Objectivity" and "professionalization" have become cold, negative terms to many present-day social workers and students because they conjure up feelings of, to use Towle's phrase, "the emptiness of the informed head divorced from the informed heart. . . ."[14] [For the reformer,] the "disciplined use of self and knowledge" . . . [thus loses] some of its appeal.

In Varley's illuminating study of social work values of students in two schools of social work [in 1968, a period of strong social change orientation,] she measured the impact of social work education on four social work values: equal rights, service, psychodynamic-mindedness, and universalism:

> *It was assumed that the service value (being primarily other- rather than self-oriented) was part of the foundation upon which social work had built its claim as a profession.*

> *Therefore, in rendering service, a social worker should limit the relationship to the technical task rather than to subjectivity and personal involvement (universalism), be impartial in giving service to all clients irrespective of personal sentiment (equal rights) and systematically apply a body of knowledge relevant to the client's problems (psychodynamic-mindedness).*[15]

Briefly, the study showed "a significant negative change at graduation time on service, psychodynamic-mindedness, and universalism. Only on equal rights was a trend on increasing commitment observed. . . . Graduating students appeared to reject the values of rendering service to clients based on the application of a systematic body of knowledge in a controlled, task-oriented relationship."

As Varley pointed out, "humanitarian values may appear to conflict with the universal technical task-orientation, or legal values applicable to the rights of social workers may conflict with dedication to service. On the other hand, the scientific values underlying psychodynamic-mindedness may conflict with humanitarian values, or the libertarian values within equal rights may appear to contraindicate a universalist approach."[16]

This brings us back to the question of relevancy [of a social work approach in a] . . . world in which . . . [there is a growing demand] for justice and equality—economic, political, and social; and . . . [many workers feel drawn to the newly articulated "radical social work" approaches.] The existing institutions and ways of life seem to stand as barriers between the individual's will to do good and the good he feels he could bring about. For a younger generation than those who hold the forts of the Establishment, this is the frontier—the hostile wilderness of demands and forms and requirements interlaced with attitudes which deny human need, dignity, or intelligence; and it is to be attacked with that same individual initiative, free enterprise, ruthlessness, and righteousness which took the pioneers across the American continent and up the economic ladders to conquest.

Probably nothing bothers the . . . [older generation of social workers] as much as the imputation that they never cared or tried to do anything about poverty or peace or prejudice—that their values have been weighed and found wanting. In their own freshness of youth they, too, were seized with the spirit of reform called forth by the times and [were] . . . stirred [again] by the call . . . [for action in the 1960s and 70s.] . . . [During that period a] study of attitudes on social action of members and those in leadership roles in the Chicago Chapter of the National Association of Social Workers in the writer's words "seemed to show greater liberalism than might be expected" on endorsement of an activist role for the chapter.[17] Sixty-six percent of the leaders in the sample were social work administrators or social work educators and 80 percent of the membership sample were caseworkers. In all the social action issues included in the study, the scores were generally on the liberal side for both groups, with the leaders scoring higher than the members. This . . . suggests that there are considerable numbers in the ranks and the lieutenancies who are not so irrelevant after all, and who are stirred by the beat of the same drums as the young, fresh troops.

We are each products of our own historical period, and most of us tend to follow or fall in with current developments, while a few emerge as leaders. However, very few people really rise above their times; that is, few have the vision and zeal and power to move forward at a strategic point in history and point the way to a new path. This is what Martin Luther King, Jr. did for America and the troubled conscience of America. For those searching for their own identity and integrity as whole or "real" persons—white or black—a direction appeared. Here in a social justice cause lay the opportunity to become one's best self. One path to affirmation of self is through an occupational role consistent with one's set of beliefs, which offers the opportunity for expression of those beliefs, through use of one's best skills. For many, then, stirred by indignation over injustice and inequality and the social values which perpetuate these, social work holds out the promise of fulfillment of one's mission. But, as Erikson points out, the evolvement of identity starts with trust and trust must be grounded in integrity.[18] If the . . . [reformers] among us are angry because they feel their trust betrayed, then the question is integrity not relevance, and we must address ourselves to this. Have we strayed in our daily practices so far from our moral value base that, like the Puritans, we are making virtues out of vices? Then let us reform.

SOCIAL WORK AS
CAUSE OR FUNCTION

If the question is whether we should be disciplined "professionals" and devote our energies to carrying on services rather than be "reformers"

drumming for a cause, . . . [is there any] necessity for a choice? Both are undoubtedly required. This is not to say that any specific professional service is to be perpetuated in whatever form or for whatever purpose it is presently given. We do not want to imply, as does the old report of a certain home for unmarried mothers, "how sad it will be if after a hundred years of service this Home has to close down for lack of girls needing help."[19] In a highly complex, heterogeneous, rapidly changing society in a scientific age, it is inconceivable that social and individual problems will disappear with the elimination of poverty or with a new power base for blacks. There are new problems emerging constantly and it takes training, skill, and experience to devise creative means for helping with their solution, and a good deal of just plain drudgery to carry on.

In Brustein's article "The Case for Professionalism," he comments that "the permanent dream of this nation, a dream still to be realized, has been a dream of equal opportunity—the right of each man to discover wherein he might excel."[20] Social work today attracts and should provide equal opportunity to two kinds of people whose excellence must complement each other and in each of whom a trace of the other should be discerned: the practitioner and the reformer. Neither plays his role alone; both require a broad public base of support and assistance. Porter Lee thought these two roles required different combinations of human qualities, and in a "flight into rhetoric" (his words), he drew this picture:

The emblazoned banner and the shibboleth for the cause, the program and the manual for the function; devoted sacrifice and the flaming spirit for the cause; fidelity, standards, and methods for the function; an embattled host for the cause, an efficient personnel for the function.[21]

Fortunately, the picture does not provide such stark contrasts today, although there are many who would have us think so. There are an infinite number of small causes fought daily over the program and the manual to win a little more dignity and respect and life for the people we serve. And this must go on while the big battles are being fought under emblazoned banners, with the help of a larger fellowship of those who care.

It is not to be wondered at that some persons with the temperament of the prophet rather than that of the executive deplore the preoccupation of social workers with orga-

nization, technique, standards, and efficiency which have followed the development of social work from cause to function. . . . [But] we cannot meet this challenge by going back to a day when social work was exclusively or predominantly a cause. We must meet it with the sober recognition that it is and must be both cause and function.[22]

I believe the cause must bind us all if we are to have our own validity, our own integrity, and each of us must find our own way to work for it. These are troubling times, and challenges come by the minute to raise questions within and among us about what we really believe—what we really value. We value life, we value man's humanity to man, we value respect for man, we value the true dignity that comes to the giver as well as the recipient of respect. We value the gifts that come with the abundant life, but only if these can be shared. We value the "good" society that permits these things to be. If these are not the values we hold and for which we earnestly work, then we shall perish.

In the words of Martin Luther King, Jr.:*

We must work passionately and indefatigably to bridge the gulf between our scientific progress and our moral progress. One of the great problems of mankind is that we suffer from a poverty of spirit which stands in glaring contrast to our scientific and technological abundance. The richer we have become materially, the poorer we have become morally and spiritually.

Every man lives in two realms, the internal and the external. The internal is that realm of spiritual ends expressed in art, literature, morals, and religion. The external is that complex of devices, techniques, mechanisms, and instrumentalities by means of which we live. Our problem today is that we have allowed the internal to become lost in the external. We have allowed the means by which we live to outdistance the ends for which we live. . . .

Our hope for creative living in this world house that we have inherited lies in our ability to re-establish the moral ends of our lives in personal character and social justice. Without this spiritual and moral reawakening we shall destroy ourselves in the misuse of our own instruments.[23]

Perhaps the true, unmastered frontier lies within our own hearts.

---

* Martin L. King, Jr., *Where Do We Go from Here: Chaos or Community?* (New York: Harper & Row, 1967). Reprinted by permission.

NOTES

[1] R.A. Tawney, "Economic Virtues and Prescriptions for Poverty," in *Social Perspectives on Behavior,* Stein and Cloward, eds. (Glencoe, Ill.: The Free Press, 1958), p. 267.

[2] Ibid, p. 276.

[3] John Steinbeck, *America and Americans* (New York: Viking Press, 1966), pp. 14–15.

[4] Ibid.

[5] John McDowell, "Guest Editorial," *The Conference Bulletin,* Columbus, Ohio, National Conference on Social Work, Vol. 72, No. 2 (Winter, 1969), p. 3.

[6] Talcott Parsons, "Youth in the Context of American Society," *The Challenge of Youth,* Erik Erikson, ed. (New York: Anchor Books, 1965).

[7] Steinbeck, op. cit., p. 32.

[8] Parsons, op. cit., p. 115.

[9] Ibid, p. 117.

[10] Porter Lee, "Social Work: Cause and Function," *Proceedings, National Conference on Social Work* (Chicago: National Conference on Social Work, 1929), pp. 3–20.

[11] Charlotte Towle, "The Role of Supervision in the Union of Cause and Function in Social Work," *Social Service Review,* Vol. 36, No. 4 (December, 1962), pp. 396–411.

[12] Parsons, op. cit., p. 116.

[13] Towle, op. cit.

[14] Towle, op. cit.

[15] Barbara K. Varley, "Social Work Values: Changes in Value Commitments of Students from Admission to MSW Graduation," *Journal of Education for Social Work,* Vol. 4, No. 2 (Fall, 1968), pp. 67–76.

[16] Ibid.

[17] Donald Brieland, "Attitudes on Social Action and NASW Member Participation: A Study of the Chicago Chapter," *NASW News,* Vol. 13, No. 1 (November, 1967), pp. 17–21, 23.

[18] Erik H. Erikson, *Childhood and Society* (New York: Norton, 1964).

[19] Quoted by Dorothy Emmet in "Ethics and the Social Worker," *British Journal of Psychiatric Social Work,* Vol. 6, No. 4 (1962).

[20] Robert Brustein, "The Case for Professionalism," *The New Republic,* Vol. 160, No. 17 (April 26, 1969), pp. 16–18.

[21] Lee, op. cit.

[22] Ibid.

[23] Martin L. King, Jr., *Where Do We Go from Here: Chaos or Community?* (New York: Harper & Row, 1967), pp. 171 and 173.

CULTURAL DIFFERENCES AND SOCIAL WORK PHILOSOPHY

Gisela Konopka

"I want to keep the extended family. That's the only way to safeguard the rights of old people." "They came from far away and suggested old-age homes. It's horrible," said a well-known social worker in a Far Eastern country.

"Forget about the beauties of the extended family. You always live under the whip—though sometimes gentle—of your mother-in-law. You are a slave of your husband's family," remarked a younger woman in this same country.

"Surely, I like self-determination," a lovely young social work faculty member says, "but when it comes to selecting my husband, I find it convenient that my father does it for me. Why make such an effort?" and she smiles with some embarrassment.

"We have no delinquent girls," insists a corrections official in a Middle Eastern country. I asked what is done when a girl becomes delinquent. He said, "It is handled in the family. If she is really bad, had sex outside of marriage or before marriage, she is killed by her father or her brother. It is illegal according to our laws, but it is honorable."

"You mean to tell me that suicide is considered a legal offense, and that a person can be arrested for attempting suicide? But they harm no one but themselves," was my own incredulous exclamation (then being new in this country) when a social worker told me of the arrest of a would-be suicide. Without question we could give thousands of examples of varying cultural responses. They occur in the areas of aesthetics—colors and forms beautiful to one group may seem lifeless and stilted to another; music pleasing to the ears of one nation sounds dreadful to another. But cultural differences are far more complex and difficult to understand when they occur in the area of ethics and human relations, the area in which social workers live, breathe, have to make decisions.

Philosophy, clarification of what ought to be in relation to what is, is therefore the base of social work. It is not a technical profession that can be practiced according to simple "know-how," like the straightening of bones or the application of chemical formulae. Clarification of philosophy in the face of a wide variety of cultures—and especially subcultures—is the premise of social work practice. It is the misconception that this profession has developed surefire techniques for dealing with human problems that has led to the present-day disillusionment with social work practice in this country and abroad. With a mechanistic way of perceiving "method" has gone a cultural blindness, which now is being followed by a radical relativism that stereotypes "culture" and suggests that there is no common base in working with people. There is a cacophony of voices proclaiming "this" is "white, Anglo-Saxon" (the value placed on hard work) or "that" is "Far Eastern" (the value put on spiritual development). Anyone familiar with these cultures knows of their diversity, knows how hard the Oriental person works, how much he is influenced by strong competition to succeed, how much he wants material goods which are often denied to him. An Indian educator who had just returned from a visit to the United States told me: "The students said they envied India's spiritual values and wanted to be like that. I said that we envied their material goods and wished we had them. It is the Gita."

For a brief period—right after the defeat of the Nazis, with their philosophy of supremacy of one race and their distortion of racial attributes, as well as their myth of pure races—it seemed as if the world was beginning to shed the superstitious belief in stereotyped national or racial characteristics and monolithic cultures. I fear that some of these attitudes have returned in disguised form, partly out of convenient political motives, and accepted through ignorance.

Let me make . . . [it as clear as I can:] I cannot and do not want to deny cultural differences. On the contrary, I find it tragic when we are not aware in our practice of being bound by culture, by the way we have been raised or fought the way we have been raised, by the impact of our environment. Social workers must know about cultural differences, and

Source: Gisela Konopka, "Cultural Differences and Social Work Philosophy." Reprinted with permission from *International Social Work* 14(1971):3–10.

not work on the basis of stereotypes, one-sided reports, hearsay. This is why I think that the international dimension in social work education is not only desirable but increasingly indispensable. In a country such as the United States, which includes people from a variety of cultures and subcultures, unawareness of the complexity of culture and of how to relate to this diversity makes work with individuals, groups, and communities and the establishment of social policy impossible. The comparative dimension also enhances a social worker's understanding of his own country's values and ideologies. Therefore, education about cultural differences and similarities should be part of the social work curriculum everywhere in the world, even in more monolithic countries. With the increasing interdependence of nations, social work's significance in national and even international policies becomes more prominent, so that stereotyped ideas—whether positive or negative—can influence policies. I was impressed by the words of an Arab official in the West Jordan area now occupied by Israel. He described the new system of rehabilitative services worked out together with Israeli officials. He stressed the concept of rehabilitation, of creating work for people, not keeping them "on the dole." His staff was trained to show respect for the clients, instead of treating them as inferiors. He spoke of the universality of our profession: "It seems that in social work at least we understand each other. We speak an international language." And in India a community worker who gives his nights to work with those shunned by others and who works as a researcher during the daytime commented: "Whatever you wrote in your [book], *Lindeman and Social Work Philosophy*, it fits right here. It is the I and Thou, it is the concern for everybody that binds us." But this is the moment when my pen or typewriter—I use them interchangeably when I try to put thoughts on paper—stops. I must continue with and repeat generalities we have heard so often about the respect for all people, the beauty of diversity, the never-changing injunction expressed through the ages in different forms, but with the same meaning: "Love thy neighbor"—"All men are brothers"—"The whole of humanity shall be a united people" (Ramakrishna, India's religious reformer)—"Wound no others, do no one injury by thought or deed, utter no word to pain thy fellow creatures" (the code of Manu, Hindu)—"Harm no living thing" (Buddhist)—"Never do to others what you would not like them to do to you" (Confucius)—"The moral law

within you" (Kant). Whether these religious leaders or philosophers adhered to a system of absolute values or stressed pragmatism, they always agreed with the fundamental demand for consideration of *all* people. The only counterforces to the precepts of the great religions or the great philosophers were those who—not only in practice but also in theory—restricted the ethical laws of human concern only to the group to which they belonged. Friedrich Nietsche was one philosopher who distinguished the "supermen" from the "common men." Fascism and Nazism have expressed in words and deeds their ideology of the superiority of one group over another, and so have the exponents of white racism. Unfortunately, more widespread than an expressed philosophical theory of superiority of one group over another is the day-to-day action of treating one group as inferior to another while expounding the lofty ideal that "all men are born equal."

This is not only apparent in the horror of racial superiority which continues in [. . . many] countries, but also in religious persecutions or confusions, in caste systems, and especially in national and economic exclusiveness in many countries. There are still Germans who consider the Southern and Eastern European workers in their country as inferior beings because they are Polish, Italian, or Turkish, though they will not say the same about a "Nordic" Swede. It is considered perfectly all right by many people in India that a person should be a street sweeper all his life if he belongs to the lowest caste, though official government policy opposes such practices. An alert student in Bombay raised the age-old question of how to get people of different religions and backgrounds to work together for the community group when they "always distrust each other, when the Parsi thinks he is better than the Hindu, etc."—There are no easy answers to such questions but a profession like social work, whose major responsibility is working with tensions, must try to find answers.

The underlying question is basically the same all over the world: How does one improve society so that it allows its people to live a "good life." But what is meant by the "good life?" Is it the same for everybody, or different in different cultures? I can only try to answer: It seems clear to me that all human beings want a level of physical comfort commensurate with their culture and the ecology of their environment. They all strive for at least physical survival for themselves and their children. But rarely do social tensions grow out of the need for these basic necessities.

If these basic needs are threatened or not available, there is frequently great apathy. In such desperate situations, people usually become very submissive to the powerful group controlling their very survival. Even in past history open rebellion or revolutions only started when the suppressed could see alternatives to their present state. The French Revolution did not break out under the harsh and oppressive regime of Louis XIV, but under the somewhat less punitive rule of his successor, which kept the injustices alive while exhibiting less strength.

The social tensions arising today all over the world are related to man's more spiritual needs, namely to be respected for himself, as an individual and as a member of the human race. This is basic and—as far as I can observe—universal. Alan Paton expressed this most beautifully:

To mean something in the world is the deepest hunger of the human soul, deeper than any bodily hunger and thirst, and when a man has lost it, he is no longer a man.

This wish to be "meaningful," this need to be someone, is expressed differently under different systems and cultures. But it is everywhere, as in the defiant and angry protest of many young people in the United States; the even deeper anger and frequent frustration of black people in several countries; the unhappy struggles of people of various nationalities against foreign exploitation; the rallying of the so-called lower classes or castes to gain the same opportunity as others; and the sullen wait of groups which do not belong to the ruling ideologies and are therefore prevented from speaking out in countries where only one opinion is considered permissible.

If tensions were always clearly recognizable as being between the haves and have-nots, or between the oppressed and oppressors, social workers would have easy decisions to make. Yet it is very important to recognize that the lines are not as sharply drawn, as clearly defined, as the popular media would indicate. We must recognize that what seems to one person persecution or deprivation might not mean the same to another person or group. For example, an American Indian who has felt all his life that he was discriminated against and treated as an inferior retaliates when he is the caretaker in a housing project by refusing to rent to black applicants. He feels that Indians, who were the "first Americans" and who have dealt with persecution with dignity and pride, are superior to those who have made what seems to him a

lot of noise. He feels that only Indians must have preferential treatment. The Polish immigrant, who has endured back-breaking work as a miner in the coalfields, and whose family has starved through strikes which finally produced better conditions, argues that he is discriminated against when any member of a minority group gets preferential treatment. We can argue that times have changed and preferential treatment is necessary today, but this does not change his feelings.

The international perspective helps us to see some of the causes for the confusion and the difficulty of distinguishing between what is just and unjust. For instance, nationalistic propaganda has for centuries told each nation that it alone was in the right. Such arguments were not always openly based on the assertion of supremacy, but were usually couched in terms of being "persecuted" or "threatened" and therefore having the right to fight some other nation. The Ottoman Empire justified that slaughter of Armenians by saying that they had tried to destroy the country; it was a "just" war. And the memory lingers. Today one of my Turkish friends complained bitterly that she is cold-shouldered by people of Armenian background, though she certainly had nothing to do with the massacre. Generalizations about people, falsification of actual situations, and phony invocation of ideals of justice and freedom have been, and are still, used all over the globe. They are some of the basic sources of tensions. They are partly due to the incapacity of the human being to see all sides of a situation, partly to a tendency to generalize from one experience with one member of a particular group to the whole group—as, "I know a Jew who overcharges for rent, therefore all Jews are exploiters"—and partly due to propaganda spread by powerful forces who want to disseminate dissent and false accusations. "The Negro is of inferior intelligence" was spread by powerful forces who needed cheap labor and segregation to keep people from finding out otherwise. "The Indian is lazy and by nature ignorant" was a conscious device to rationalize the breaking of treaties and depriving Indians of their lands. "The Jew is cunning, power-hungry, and sexually assaultive" was a consciously planned stereotype by the Naxis to eliminate any guilt in Germans when they destroyed Jews. "The poor are born into the low caste and must stay that way" allowed those who lived in luxury to solidify their wealth without guilt. The knowledge that generalizations about people are partly based on a certain laziness in human nature—

it is much easier to make simplifications than to investigate the complexities of life—and partly based on conscious distortion can help the social worker to deal better with tensions, without himself becoming dogmatic.

This insight should also tell our profession that it cannot deal alone with social tensions in the community. Neither can social work claim the power to solve all human relations problems, nor should it be expected by others to do so. At the International Conference in Manila, the young speaker from the Philippines accused social workers of having been too concerned with the problems of hygiene in rural areas, instead of the political aspirations of the people. I agree with him that work must be done on the political front but I doubt that social work can truly be accused of not having been involved at all in problems of public concern. The horrible conditions following a typhoon while we were in Manila, and in other parts of the Far East, showed that concern with hygiene is very important. Part of the hope for a good life is that families should not need to live under the constant fear that their children will die of dysentery or cholera. Social workers must be concerned with this part of life. They surely should not limit themselves to immediate problems of alleviation of specific crisis situations, but must be ready to help with individual problems, as well as to help change systems where they are harmful to people. The latter they cannot do alone. Recognition of political power structures should have a salutory effect on social workers as they learn to work together with others, professionals and community members, sometimes as leaders but often as co-workers. It will also guard them against the naive, simplistic, and therefore dangerous approach to problems of social tensions which assumes that goodwill alone can overcome unsatisfactory conditions, or that one has to become a dogmatic fanatic in order to achieve change.

What I have tried to convey is that the international perspective helps all of us, but especially students just entering the profession, to understand the vast complexity of human problems. A social worker must become imbued with the conviction that "instant solutions" would depend on "instant insight," and this is hardly possible. To fulfil the task of working with social tensions on a knowledgeable, not a superficial, base means constant probing, assessment, and a vast amount of knowledge in a great variety of areas reaching from systems analysis to understanding of individual behavior and motivation.

Philosophically, social work and social workers can never cease to work on clarification of the basic propositions of their profession. These propositions may not be exclusive to social work, but their particular combination and practical application spell out this profession's base.

What can we consider to be the propositions which encompass the universal basis of the social work profession? Let me suggest the following:

Proposition 1—Every social work decision involves a value judgment. Social work is not a value-free discipline.

Proposition 2—Social work is based on two absolute values:

a. The dignity of the individual,

b. The responsibility of the individual for others.

The different applications of these basic values are influenced by:

1. Cultural, family, and ethnic background;

2. Precepts and demands of given groups or systems to which people belong—nation, class, caste, subgroups like church, professional or social groups;

3. Significant personal experiences, like individual discrimination, illness, unusual success, death of important people;

4. Different perceptions or theories regarding human behavior.

It would be an excellent exercise in social work education to take these basic values and let students present and debate the way they would apply them, so that they become conscious of their own biases. For example, a Western social worker, recognizing the plight of elderly people in a Far Eastern country, began to work on the establishment of old-age homes. This created resentment and tension because, to people in this Eastern country, the dignity of an elderly person was violated by placing him in congregate living solely with people of his own age group. In this particular culture an elderly person is shown respect by being included in a family structure; everything else, whether sleeping in the street or living in a sheltered place, means violation of his or her human rights.

The value of the dignity of the individual is obviously derived from our general perception that human life is important. There have been stereotypes which assert that this value does not apply to some Eastern cultures. According to my knowledge this is not borne out by most of the philosophies of the Far East, nor by my encounter with the aspirations of people in the Far East for themselves or their children. Perhaps there are subgroups that deny this value, as there are in Western cultures. Social work, in any case, has accepted this value as supreme. Kierkegaard put this value most beautifully into the form of a demand:

To have a self, to be a self, is the greatest concession made to man, but at the same time, it is eternity's demand upon him.

His formulation includes the value of *self-actualization* which underlies, or should underlie, all programs of education and community development. This, too, has often been perceived as a Western value, with its emphasis on individuality, on "doing one's own thing." It was interesting to me to observe in my recent tour through the Far and Near East that this particular value is sweeping the world, is changing family structures, and is the beginning of unrest and tension. The practice of yoga was deep immersion into self, but what is added now is self-actualization in every aspect of life, beyond just the spiritual. No longer is there satisfaction with a system that submerged the individual. Women resent the "shadur" which separated them from the outside world and prevented them from developing their own personality. Young people cry out for participation in their own fate. They do not want to be dominated by authoritarian structures. Social work theory has stressed for a long time that we should not do *to* people, but *with* them. Yet general practice in many fields, especially public assistance and corrections, has not acted according to this precept. I remember when I first came to the United States, having come from a harsh fight against a dictatorship and any authoritarian approach, that I hesitated about becoming a social worker. My hesitation vanished when I saw the concepts of working *with* people and of accepting the group members' participation in their fate as basic principles in the practice of social group work. I have no doubt though, after thirty years in social work and loving it, that its precarious acceptance of social group work is directly related to a fear of realization of this principle. The somewhat easier acceptance of group therapy by social workers is influenced by the fact that the group therapist is more in control of pa-

tients than the group worker is in work with healthy people. The comparatively slow acceptance of group work approaches in community organization, in spite of its early development by Eduard C. Lindeman, is also influenced by the same fear of having people assert their strength in a group. Working with people, enhancing their participation in everything that concerns them, is a basic and universal application of one of the primary values that social workers must use in their practice.

The second value, namely responsibility for others, relates to the first, but makes it clear that self-actualization does not mean disregard for the significance and rights of other people. It is expressed in the demands of most of the great religions. Just as Kierkegaard put the value of individual dignity into existentialist terms and derived a demand from it, so did James Baldwin for the value of mutual responsibility. He says: "All lives are connected to other lives," and he derived from this the injunction: "The moment we cease to hold each other, the moment we break faith with each other, the sea engulfs us and the lights go out."[1]

Though the application of these two basic values is culture-bound, some principles of social work practice derived from them also seem to me universal. The teaching of pure techniques without underlying philosophy and thinking through of values is not only useless but harmful—especially if applied in the context of cultures different from the one system in which they were taught. Social work practice must include a constant scrutiny of not only the cultural values of people with whom the social worker works, but also his own. *Self-insight*, not primarily in terms of self-analysis of psychological motivation, but as a constant probing of one's culture-bound value system, is paramount in every aspect of social work practice and especially when one works with group tensions. Since it is very difficult to assess one's own culture—one of my friends in anthropology says: "Our own water does not have any taste"—one sharpens one's capacity to learn about this "taste" by learning about other value systems. It is, therefore, imperative to add historical and international perspectives to social work education.

Social tensions all over the world are heightened because one nation, one race, one religion, one ideology thinks its way of life is the only right one. Diversity among human beings—that is, considering each other valuable even though different—makes the world beautiful and an interesting one in which to live. Tensions are also heightened when groups, and sometimes individuals, see themselves as infallible. The recognition that judgments about human relations are influenced by a web of complex factors helps to erase or at least diminish this conceit of righteousness. An attitude of deep esteem for a variety of life styles and a certain appreciation of one's own fallibility are necessary for social workers when they enter the arena of group tensions. With such an attitude, with clarity about their own philosophy, with acceptance of the premise that their methods must be congruent with their ends, with a sharp mind that tries to analyze the situation beforehand, and with enough sense to enlist the help of others, social workers all over the globe can become more effective in dealing with the social tensions that tear this world apart.

I hope I have clarified some of the basic premises for our discussion. I do not think I have said anything brand-new. I feel sometimes very impatient when we constantly raise the same questions and start everything from the beginning. But perhaps this is the way it must be, because the context in which we live is always new. Rodin once wrote about his own art:

I have invented nothing; I only rediscover, and it seems to be new because the aim and the methods of my art have in a general way been lost sight of. People mistake for innovation which is only a return to the laws of the great statuary of antiquity.[2]

But his art was new because he infused it with his own personality, and the France of his day was different from the Greece of the antiquity.

Our basic philosophy is the distillation of the teachings of the great ethical writers of all times. Our particular times see the worldwide assertion of people as individuals, with the demand for participation in their fate and a hope for a good life in this world. This is universal and it is new.

NOTES

[1]Baldwin, James. *Nothing Personal*, New York, Atheneum Publishers, 1964.

[2]Sommerville Story, "August Rodin and His Work" in *Rodin*, London, Phaidon Press, 1949, p. 12.

THE UNIVERSAL IN EDUCATION FOR SOCIAL WORK

Jona M. Rosenfeld

Traveling in the different countries and continents and reading about the varieties of social work experience as they exist in different places of the world should have discouraged me from attempting to deal with the universal in social work education throughout the world. It may therefore be considered foolhardy to attempt to broach this subject, yet I wish to consider it for several reasons. First of all, I welcome the intellectual challenge which the struggle with this subject presents to me, and second, I hope that clarifying what is universal in social work education may counteract the tendency of social work educators in different lands to hide behind what they consider particular and unique to their own situation.

It is my conviction that we can identify and clarify what is universal and shared in social work without this being at the expense of what is particular and local for any country or part of the world. Furthermore, I believe that this is essential if we wish to stimulate the possible contributions of the social sciences and humanities to social work. Our profession is often accused of fostering an anti-intellectualism that results from the refusal of some of us to move beyond the parochial. I believe that relating to the universal will counteract this tendency. It will also counteract "the uncaring attitude" to people which, according to the Seebohm Report, is fostered by the absence of research and, in our context, is the conse-

---

Source: Jona M. Rosenfeld, "The Universal in Education for Social Work," trans. and ed. Maria Pintado de Rank and Ana Laura Cadilla de Delgado, paper presented at the XVIII International Congress of Schools of Social Work, San Juan, Puerto Rico, July 13–17, 1976.

quence of not mustering the contribution of science to the pursuit of social work.[1]

A third reason for taking up this challenge is connected to the theme of the International Association of Schools of Social Work's (IASSW) Fiftieth Anniversary Congress of Schools of Social Work: "The Knowledge Base of Social Work." I attribute great importance to this coming conference, not only because it is scheduled to take place in Israel, where I live, and because it is the fiftieth anniversary of an association I treasure, but also since I believe that its topic alone qualifies it as a jubilee conference. It seems to me that in order to move on to the knowledge base—which is the subject of that conference—it is essential to establish whether there are universal components of our profession.

THE UNIVERSALS IN SOCIAL WORK EDUCATION

As you may gather, all three reasons point to one of the main tenets which I shall claim is universal in social work education—that is, trust in and reliance on knowledge and the intellect; for without these our values and ethics are only a pavement of good intentions on the way to confusion.

I believe that in social work education, as in social work itself, the concept *universal* refers to the content of social work and the concept *particular* refers to the setting in which this universal content is expressed and transmitted. *Content* refers to values, knowledge, and skills at the disposal of the profession in the pursuit of its humanistic objectives and is thus the core of any curriculum in social work education. What is particular is the differential readiness and capacity of any society to employ this content and of any educational setting to impart it. What this statement implies is that the differences in social work are not endemic; that is, they do not result simply from the varieties of social problems or from the specific condition of any one country, just as the differences in the practice of medicine in different countries do not derive from the specific health problems of the particular country. They are rather a reflection of the differential readiness and willingness of any particular country or society to apply this content, be it of medicine or of social work. Similarly, insofar as social work education, entrusted with transmitting social work content, is different in our different countries, it is not due to the absence of a universal content but to the differences between the particular

settings which are engaged in education for social work.

The content of social work and, hence, that which is the core to be transmitted by those entrusted with education for social work are the beliefs and the values which guide and direct the activities and actions of the social worker and the skills and knowledge which are deployed, created, and developed in the pursuit of these values and beliefs.

What is particular in social work is the manner in and the degree to which these values and beliefs, these skills and this knowledge are used in a particular society. The same is the case for social work education. This implies that there are varieties of the "goodness of fit" between the universal content of social work and what is transmitted in the curriculum of any particular educational setting. One may add that in social work education this is, of course, also reflected in the manner in which this universal content is transmitted, developed, and reinforced.

The basic assumption of this thesis is that the basic values, beliefs, skills, and knowledge are not culture bound and may therefore be said to be universal. The tensions, both the constructive and the destructive ones that exist, are the consequence of the incongruence between these universals and the particular settings in which they are supposed to be taught. They reflect the readiness or the reluctance of a specific educational setting, as it is situated in its particular societal context, to imbibe these universals and to transmit them.

The transmission of these universals is determined by four modalities which describe the societal context of any particular educational setting. Each of them characterizes the particular tensions or conflicts which the interaction between these universals and any particular educational setting and its societal context might produce; that is, the crystallization of particular programs, with all their richness and diversity, reflects the conditions under which we live and work.

Yet within the diverse particularities of our professional lives, it might be said that we all subscribe to the notion that the purpose of social work—if you wish, its societal function—is to contribute to the humanization of society by fostering the well-being and development of individuals living in those societies. It is the effective pursuit of social work which ensures that humanization of society does not remain in ideological abstraction but [is] something realized in the lives of the most vulnerable people in our societies. This is so because in social work man is the measure of all things. He is the point of departure and the point of arrival in what is wrought and man's development and well-being constitutes the ultimate touchstone of the success of our work with people and on their behalf.

In concrete terms this is evident when one considers how this social responsibility of the profession is enacted everywhere via the two major categories of activities in which social workers are engaged: (1) delivery and development of personal social services to distinct individuals irrespective of their living on their own, in groups, or in communities; and (2) engagement in the propagation of social reform destined to benefit one or many individuals. Personal social services refer to direct services to people and comprise all publicly sponsored provisions, either on a universal or a selective basis. They might be considered as vehicles for translating such collective goals as equality or income security into the lives of people and into individual positive experiences so that each man feels entitled to what he is entitled to by law.[2] Social reform refers to changes in the macrosystem which range from the adaptation of existing systems to the needs of people to deliberate, though evolutionary, structural changes.

Societies which have embraced this humanistic social philosophy are bound to be more supportive of both personal social services and social reform. In these societies social work activities reflect and reinforce the prevalent social philosophy. In other societies, where humanization of society is at best a dormant social philosophy, the role of awakening it through personal social services and social reform is obviously more complex and more problematic, but also more challenging and more essential.

COMPONENTS OF THE PROFESSIONAL CORE

Still, regardless of the societal setting, it is the universal content of education for social work which we presume prepares people to perform these universally practiced activities of our profession. We shall now consider the three components of this universal content.

1. Values and Beliefs

The first component of the professional core of social work is values and beliefs. There are three interconnected foci of these beliefs and values, the first

of which is *man.* Social work assumes that man can develop fully if properly helped. It also assumes that man remains unfulfilled if this help is not forthcoming. Furthermore, in as far as man's development is hampered by familial and societal (and hence man-made) arrangements and provisions, it is up to man not to abdicate in the face of these lags in development, but to face them and to seek to remedy them deliberately with the tools of rationality. This trust in help is coupled with and supplemented by a belief in the nobility of help where people's capacity to define their problems and to alter them is fostered.

The second common belief or value concerns *society.* It is assumed that society has a moral obligation to provide the help needed for the development of man. This implies that the arrangements for and the provisions of societal help, be it via social security, social welfare, or social legislation, are a matter of right. Because there is this right to individual development, its translation into societal arrangements and provisions is not a matter of charity but rather an obligation which society must acknowledge.

The third focus of beliefs and values concerns *social work's* commitment to rationality itself. It is my contention that social work, in its pursuit of harnessing societal arrangements and provisions for the development of man and cognizant of the primacy of emotions as a determinant of one's thinking and actions, has a commitment to rationality. This belief in rationality is related to my contention that man's inhumanity to man exploits irrational motives. The consequences of this irrationality are more likely to be remedied with the forces of rationality even if "the voice of the intellect is silent but persistent." To hold to this belief is not easy and has to be maintained and nourished by developing tools of rationality.

One may wish to pause here not only to ponder whether these three are indeed universal beliefs and values of social work but also to ask whether there are additional ones that are equally important. I can only respond by saying that, while there may be others, these three headings constitute the most comprehensive and parsimonious way of summarizing what appears to me to be most essential. Whether they are universal might be gauged by finding out whether they are embraced by all who sit here. Another way of determining if indeed they are considered universal is to explore whether these three foci give rise to conflict and to controversy within the particular educational setting in which each of us works. If they do not, they are probably not specific to social work; that is, to what I have considered as constituting the societal function of this profession.

2. Skills

Let us now assume that we have exhausted the first component of social work—those beliefs and values which are the object of transmission in the education for social work. The second element is the skills or the crafts of social work, and the third is the knowledge needed in order to practice these crafts effectively. One way of determining what is to be included here is to explore which skills and what knowledge constitute the major vehicles through which the universal beliefs and values of social work are put into action. Another and complementary way of selecting skills and knowledge is to consider what is needed in order to develop and to deploy personal social services and to engage in effective social reform. I will attempt to spell this out, although within the bounds of this paper I shall not be able to do so as methodically as I might wish.

The crafts or the skills of social work are composed of two distinct parts. First, there is the repertoire of interventions to be deployed for either providing personal social services or for those social reform activities which social workers pursue. This repertoire is ideally composed of an entire range of interventions and the social worker is supposed to be able to master a modicum of all of them. He is also expected to decide which one to deploy in any particular situation in which he seeks to bring about change in the lives of people, either through personal social services or through social reform. It appears to me that there exists a finite repertoire of skills, even though they are in a constant state of flux and even though some of them are more useful to and hence more used by some than by others, possibly in line with the particular phase on the continuum of social development.

The second component of the craft of social work—and one which can be considered truly universal but which is universally underused—is that of "inventing interventions."[3] It is assumed that since the populations and needs to which social workers address themselves may vary and change much more than once in any social worker's lifetime, the repertoire of interventions acquired during the educational process can never be comprehensive enough to meet all changes. Thus the legendary knack of social workers to improvise and address themselves to ever-changing social problems cannot be left to chance. As this is something which every social worker has to master, it is also something to be taught. In fact, however, this is rarely the case. What is the case is that in our being wedded to teaching such holy trinities as casework, group work, and community organization we may unknowingly achieve two negative results. On the one hand we may be undercutting the natural development of this knack for improvisation by fostering adherence to what are at best conventional classifications of methods (casework, group work, community organization) and restricting our ability to create a rich variety of interventions. On the other hand we are not attempting to abstract this knack for improvisation or for inventing interventions and thus do not translate it into a craft to be taught, learned, and mastered.

3. Knowledge

Finally we come to what knowledge is universally essential for the pursuit of social work, both for the activation of beliefs and values and for the deployment and the invention of professional skills. At the risk of being somewhat simplistic, I shall confine myself to listing three spheres of knowledge, as well as a fourth one which is in some way, too, a sphere of knowledge, but actually is more in the nature of a conceptual framework or a technique developed in public health and adapted to social work.

The first sphere of knowledge concerns the behavior and development of man. The second is knowledge of the nature of society and of societies. A third is knowledge about the dimensions and development of societal arrangements for the delivery of social welfare provisions and of the organizations entrusted with providing them.

The last, and somewhat unconventional, sphere of knowledge—and hence one to be spelled out in somewhat greater detail—is the study of social welfare needs. This comprises: (1) the needs of a population, (2) provision of particular welfare services to meet these needs, and (3) discrepancies between the needs of a population and the welfare services that are provided. The use of this approach, which is an adaptation of a public health epidemiological model to social work, seems to be essential if one seeks to employ the crafts of social work in a rational manner; that is, based on systematic information on what are the changes in the priorities of groups of population which require the provision of social welfare services.

The availability of these tools for identifying unmet social needs counteracts any tendencies to serve populations on the basis of fads and fashions, inertia, impressions, or familiarity, rather than on the basis of verified information guiding decisions on priorities.

This summary of what is universal in social work covers that information which every educational program engaged in the training for this profession is expected to transmit, and this must be done in a manner in which values and beliefs are integrated, skills mastered, and knowledge absorbed. In addition, the institution has to launch a professional social worker who is able to reexamine his values and beliefs, develop his skills, and absorb new knowledge throughout his professional life. The achievements of these goals are vested in the particular educational setting and constitute what is particular in social work education.

4. The Educational Institution in a Societal Context

The problem which now presents itself concerns the conditions which determine the particular manner in which any educational institution goes about its job. In exploring this we assume that indeed the content is universal and that the choice about what to teach is limited to the differential emphasis given to any element within this, at least theoretically, common curriculum. This explains why I shall abstain from seeking cultural explanations for the tendency to concentrate more on one rather than another component of what I claim to be the non-culture-bound content of social work. The fact that some school may emphasize one subject more than another according to the society's phase of social development does not make a difference to my claim for a core curriculum. No one would claim that a medical school in the tropics that teaches more about malaria and one in a modern industrial state that teaches more about heart disease is an indication that the curricula in these schools are substantially different.

The state of our profession, to be sure, is not quite analogous to that of medicine. Social work as a profession is relatively new, and its coming-to-consciousness as a professional discipline is a recent and somewhat unruly phenomenon. If we recall the origins of the profession, we might easily lose ourselves in a maze of particularities—of blessed particularities—reflecting all the struggles of individuals and institutions to evolve a consistent and rational

basis of operation. Yet what seems clear is that we aspire to a clarity of purpose and a richness of resources similar to those that humane professions such as medicine have achieved, and that it would be useful if we had some way of classifying the diversities which characterize our actual work of educating the aspirants to our profession.

As previously mentioned the transmission of the universal content can be classified according to the modalities which describe the relation between the educational institution and the societal context in which it operates. These four modalities constitute combinations of whether the institution operates in a societal context which (1) does or does not embrace the universal values and beliefs of social work, and (2) does or does not dispose the resources to disseminate the universal content of the profession. To perceive these modalities is also to perceive the commonalties that lie behind them, in our consciousness as professionals, and to sensitize us to the nature of the struggle to implement universal aims within the very different conditions of our existence.

The first modality of relation between the school of social work and the social environment in which it must function is in fact the one characterized by the least tension. It describes the situation of the particular educational institution in a society that shares values and beliefs similar to those of social work and which has resources at its disposal to put the knowledge and skills into action. This is the case in many Western countries. In educational settings where this applies, our struggle to transmit the universal social work content is not excessive or is, at least, manageable. Similarly, in order to gain acceptance and support from faculty, public, or students, the rules of the game called "interpreting social work" should have much in common. They presumably include an appeal to humanistic ideals and base themselves as much on the presentation of such facts as on manpower needs. Within them we need not resort to covert strategies nor mask our aims and intentions and damn ourselves to splendid isolation at our work. We can appeal to our legislators, our colleagues, our students, from within the terms of values that may be presumed, formally at least, to be shared by all concerned.

A second modality lies at the other extreme. In this the particular society neither subscribes to many or most of the social work values nor does it muster the resources to activate social work knowledge and skills through social services. This has been the case in some of the economically deprived and poorly developed areas of the world.

One would assume that the prospects of the struggle for education for social work in this modality are dismal; however, the lonely road travelled by social workers who operate in these societies would be less lonely and more effective once the similarities of their struggle are recognized and shared. Even without enumerating the localities, societies, or continents in which these conditions prevail, it hardly needs to be stated that they are legion. What can be said in the nature of a generalization is that any advances made are probably due more to the work of one person with strong convictions than to any other factors. Splendid isolation may be painful, but it can bear rich fruits for those who have the strength to bear it—fruits the richer, I think, when there is consciousness of community with those outside the bounds of a particular society who also strive within the terms of a common, or universal, professional core such as I have outlined here.

A third modality refers to the vast parts of the world where the lack of economic and educational resources, rather than the opposition to social work values and beliefs, condemns social work to a low priority. Incidentally, this low priority is often the consequence of the belief—not always based on evidence—that economic and educational development has to precede, and is not dependent on, social development. The consequences of this policy are known to many of us. This unenviable and less-than-ideal "ideal type" of the "honest poor" raises sympathies in the outsider and solidarity among the insiders. If those of us working in situations in which the budgets of educational institutions are cut, yet where social problems are on the increase, were to compare notes, we would probably be struck by the similarity of the tactics we employed to uphold the course of education for social work, and we might possibly return home equipped with new ones. Again, consciousness of community would strengthen our hands.

The fourth modality is, in some ways, the most challenging one, as well as the one with the most potential for conflict. In this case, the development of social work education is not hampered by lack of resources, but the universal content of the profession can only be taught in terms of overt or covert challenges to prevalent beliefs and values in the society which are contradictory to those of social work. There are many examples of these kinds of value clashes or professional dilemmas, each of which is perhaps more prevalent in some one specific educational setting, but all of which are not unfamiliar to each of us. One example of these value dilemmas and of the controversies ensuing from them stems from the anti-revolutionary stance of social work which is based on a belief in evolution and growth. Another type of controversy is that which expresses itself in the dilemma of supporting economic, social, or political objectives and goals when they are clearly at the expense of societal obligations to meet the needs of individuals, groups, or communities. There are also national emergencies in which emotions stir up nationalistic feelings which tend to contradict and swamp social work's belief in upholding the voice of rationality. I have no doubt that it would be most revealing and instructive to spell out the strategies and tactics which are employed by us in facing these and other value dilemmas which are bound to bar the way for education for social work, but to do so would go beyond the scope of this paper. Yet, I dare say, perhaps we owe it to each other to collect such cases and to generalize from them in order to further our cause by being equipped with knowledge.

At this point one may ask what was the purpose of confining the many variations of styles and manners of social work education within the framework of these four modalities? My answer is that this shows, at least intuitively, that there are commonalities and common rules to the many varieties of our particular experiences.

From this, I would hope, also emerges the recognition that what may have seemed particular and parochial is indeed universal and common. If so, it has widened the scope of what we hold universally in common. Now it seems that we are beyond the particular and hence quite private views not shared by all of us. This is the reason for which such congresses as this one convene. After all we have learned, we believe and we teach that the application of what is universal and common to the lives of individual people constitutes an essential warranty for their development and well-being. If this is so, it should also apply to us as people engaged in the education for social work. If this is so, this paper will have contributed to our cognition and thinking more favorably on how much all of us have in common; and if indeed this is the case, we shall have strengthened each other in the always sufficiently lonely and endless road of social work toward humanization of society and, thus, toward the development and well-being of people everywhere.

NOTES

[1]Her Majesty's Stationery Office, *Report of the Committee on Local Authority and Allied Personal Social Services* (Chairman, Seebohm, HMSO, Comnd. 3703, 1968).

[2]Charlotte Towle, *Common Human Needs* (New York: National Association of Social Workers, 1945-, p. iv).

[3]Jona M. Rosenfeld, "Major Trends in Social Welfare and Practice in Developing Countries," in Nana A. Apt, ed., *Social Welfare and Practice in Developing Countries* (Ghana Association of Social Workers, 1972).

BETWEEN VALUES AND SCIENCE: EDUCATION FOR THE PROFESSION DURING A MORAL CRISIS *OR* IS PROOF TRUTH?

Joseph L. Vigilante

I believe that professional values in social work are more than merely the philosophical base of practice. In proper practice, values are part of the instrumentality for providing service, and they may be, as has been suggested recently, the fundamental linkages in theory building, both for direct practice and for social policy and planning.[1]

In spite of their endemic relationship to practice, values have caused some of our most persistent problems, not only in practice theory and decision making but in our relationships with other professions as well as with the community at large. We are sensitive about being identified as the conscience of the community. The role of a professional moralist is not one to which most individuals aspire, yet do-gooders *are* moralists.

To rephrase a quote from the *New York Times:* "Moral leadership is like great literature; everyone deplores the lack of it, but there is a tendency to prefer it from the safely dead."[2] Imagine what that thought could lead to for professional moralists these days. Regardless of the hazards that a strong preoccupation with values has and will bring upon us, I don't think we can escape them. Nor do I believe we should accept an escape route through logical positivism, no matter how academically "cool" (prestigious) that action may be.

VALUES AND PRACTICE

When we examine practice decisions we can see that professional values permeate decision making. Harold Lewis has emphasized the relationship between values and practice in this context:

The concern for consequences which justify practice, and the values that direct such concerns, are frequently overlooked in the history of science but can hardly be ignored in the development of a profession. When such values are evident in the product of professional effort, they constitute its morality. . . .

Professional authority is appropriately exercised in relation to the recipient since his authority is earned through furthering the moral maturity of the recipient in his service role. In sharp contrast, the exercise of professional authority to compel commitment and the involvement in service it would entail is more appropriately viewed as authoritarian and unprofessional. This difference is fundamental and poses the central issue that confronts the human service professions in our country today.[3]

Lewis's assertion that the use of professional authority to compel involvement in service is inappropriate clearly suggests the importance of values in decision making.

Source: Joseph L. Vigilante, "Between Values and Science: Education for the Profession During a Moral Crisis *or* Is Proof Truth?" *Journal of Education for Social Work* 10 (1974):107–15. Reprinted by permission.

Charles Levy, in a discussion of social work ethics, emphasized the importance of new understandings of ethics and values in the context of practice. In dealing with ethics as prescribed behaviors to carry out value commitments, he says:

> Social work ethics seem to be based, although not exclusively, on what the social worker does, the values to which he and his professional colleagues subscribe, the responsibility he shares for his profession's good name, etc. . . . However, a more practical and indicative basis for defining the social worker's ethical responsibility and guides for his ethical conduct might be obtained by focusing on the client and the system of mutual experiences and responses generated when he resorted to the social worker for help or service.[4]

Lewis and Levy are identifying the importance of involving the client in practice decision making, an often expressed professional value, but until recently not often specifically identified as an instrumentality for providing service.

A closer analysis of practice decision making, however, reveals the soft quality of our knowledge about values and demands that we and our students develop a more precise understanding of how values impact on practice. Our treatment of values as sacrosanct, religious-like beliefs has, perhaps, lowered their prestige. Sometimes I have the impression that our adoration of values may be part of the reason that many students don't take them seriously. Unfortunately, values are difficult to study in relation to practice behaviors.

Although we have identified social work practice as the amalgamation of values, knowledge, and skills, and we assume a preeminence of values, most of our sparse research efforts have been directed at the knowledge and skill components. By comparison the use of values in practice has been neglected as a target for research. Values have received only superficial attention from scholars, theory builders, and curriculum designers.

Eveline Burns called social policy the stepchild of the curriculum. Social policy's kinship with professional values probably has much to do with it. To continue Burns's metaphor, values may be viewed as the stepchild's security blanket. And like security blankets they are often overused or abused, and there is an emotional attachment to them that mitigates against their being examined, washed, or otherwise tampered with.[5]

SOCIAL MISSION

It is possible to define social work without a value emphasis, and we have done so when such forms of definition have been compatible with specialized, at times temporary, professional goals, or social agency goals. "Social" in social work can be interpreted in at least two distinguishing ways: one refers to a primary concern with the social interrelationships of people; the other, although not denying this functional description, suggests in addition the carrying forth of a societal goal, that is, a social mission. The social mission is a concept of mutual responsibility: each for the other in a social system. It is this latter definition that underscores the centrality of values in the profession.

The values of social work are those that fit under the broad rubric of humanitarianism. Central among these is the dignity and worth of the individual. Social work, therefore, is work with interrelationships among groups and individuals within the context of a societal goal. It is a good social responsibility. Humanitarianism is the philosophical justification. Its transmission into professional intervention creates the value-laden, "social" character of the social worker's function.

Nathan Cohen has called this effort to professionalize a value system "Humanitarianism in Search of a Method."[6] But Cohen's assertion of the relationship between values and practice illuminates a fundamental conflict that permeates our work as it does most contemporary human relationships. It forces an examination of the individual good vis-à-vis the community good, not in philosophical terms but in professional service terms. When we have to "do it" as well as "believe it," we have problems. The difficulty in operationalizing values in our society has led to their being shelved, to their being revered from a distance, but kept separate from the daily business of *succeeding*. We sometimes become embarrassed by them: a perfect condition for searching out an escape route through science.

SCIENCE AND THE INDIVIDUAL

By means of a fascinating course of intellectual development in Western society, the dignity and worth of the individual has become confused with individualism, which upon examination in action is revealed as quite a different concept. The popular reference to a contemporary breakdown in traditional values and morals might be more properly described as a distortion of the fundamental value of the rights and dignity of the individual. It is possible, therefore, to contrast "individualism" with "humanitarianism": the latter referring to the rights and dignity of the individual, the former to the distortion of these rights in an antisocial mode.

Richard N. Goodwin* relates our current value confusions to the rise of science in Western culture.[7] His observations, in my view, account for the rejection of value-dominated behavior both by political conservatives and radicals within the past several years. Would you believe that the immorality of Watergate can be traced to the same roots as the immoralities of extreme left-wing radicalism?

The excesses of our new individualistic orientations have led to a disdain for social structures, which are a manifestation of community values as instruments both for the continuance of stable social growth and the protection of individual dignity. There is an arrogance toward the law (the community's value) that permeates the expression of many political conservatives and radicals alike. For them the law is okay except when it protects the political enemy. Whether he is the president or the leader of a radical "revolutionary" movement, the individual decides.

Goodwin, referring to traditional exhortative value-laden descriptions of the relationship between the individual and society, says: "These phrases are not exhortations of self-sacrifice or Christian brotherhood but descriptions of a social condition wherein common values and shared inclinations are experienced by the individual as his own."[8] This is the crux of the *social* condition which I contrast with the *individualistic* condition.

Let me quote Goodwin more fully:

Our present condition was implicit in the earliest and most heroic statements of modern man's power, freedom, and unity. The centuries of Michelangelo and Columbus; Dante; Cervantes; and Leonardo, Galileo, and Shakespeare were labeled the Renaissance *to express a widespread belief that classical culture had been reborn. . . . we can see that it was not a Renaissance but a creation—the emergence of the modern world. . . . Its ideal was to be not in harmony with the "polis" or with the nature of things but, finally, man alone.*

---

*Richard Goodwin, "Reflections: The American Social Process," *The New Yorker,* 21 January, 28 January, 4 February 1974. Reprinted by permission.

The thought that helped to liberate man from the restraints of the medieval order also contained the possibilities of new enslavement . . . technology . . . provided the belief-compelling miracles of scientific reason. . . . by the nineteenth century many believed that the whole of existence could be compacted within the framework of scientific reason. . . . Its simplest litanies evoked the common response and belief requisite for a successful creed. It provided the feelings of domination and control necessary to individuals severing life-defining bonds. To calculate was to rule; to understand was to exploit; knowledge was power. [emphasis mine][9]

Science provided man with direction away from mysticism to the point where he eventually viewed *himself* in total control. Man, to a large extent, now controls nature, predicts what he will have to invent to satisfy his desire for comfort, protection, or just his curiosity, and then invents it. Science has permitted man to believe that he is indeed the master of his own destiny. Thus through the scientific process arises the new concept of the individual as the center of the universe: "man alone." The rise of individualism has challenged the social value of mutuality.

Although the early impact of industrialism created a mutual dependency among men, its later expansion and reliance on science has led to a growing denial of the phenomenon of mutual interdependence. The scientific method has become a hallmark of validity. Logical positivism, the objective scrutiny of available facts pointing toward factually revealed conclusions is science. Knowledge has become a value in itself, rather than knowledge for the social good.

We see manifestations of the individualistic orientation in a rejection of organizational structures developed for purposes of providing guidelines for human conduct; and a new value on free exercise of individual behavior with the implication that the individual defines his own ethics. Goodwin concludes that "there can be *no moral conduct* without community [note that he does not say 'without God.' His argument is not mystical, since values are mystical]; not only does the rise of individualism deny the value of community, it suffocates freedom, enforces an illogical effort to turn science into values—a second absurdity."[10]

Thus the ideology of individualism stemming from logical positivism looks on bonds as restraints, values as prejudices, customs as impositions, and the final absurdity emerges: it is only true if it can be proved and if it is proved it is true—*truth is proof.*

Turn the equation around and you have *proof is truth;* if it's proved it is true and it follows (like the social worker his intuition) that that which cannot be proved is not true.

The fallacy of the "proof is truth" axiom for the social sciences is clear when one becomes aware that proof in the logical positivist tradition is not possible for interpersonal phenomena, given the limitless variety of variables and the rudimentary nature of the research instruments.

The positivist approach in the social sciences is based on the assumption that these sciences are essentially no different from the natural sciences [except in their achievements]: that is to say that social phenomena are, for all analytic purposes, qualitatively the same as natural phenomena and can, therefore, be subjected to similar techniques of analysis.[11]

The values of Western society, established a priori, or as self-evident, or through "revelation" have been interpreted to imply a contrary state of man: a state of mutual dependency for the social good. Our value base is pre-Renaissance. This can be seen in the Old Testament, the writings of the canonists of the medieval church, and the Hebrew scholars of the Renaissance period.[12] It is a blending of values identified by Maimonides, Hillel, St. Thomas, and others. It is the golden rule, which implies community responsibility.

From both Christians and Jews came the natural rights interpretation of individual dignity. The meaning of the rights of the poor as expressed by Hillel and by the medieval canonists is clearly understood by twentieth century social workers. Muriel Pumphrey's work on social work values reveals the extent to which the humanitarian ethic has been absorbed into our professional value system.* As she describes a list of "ultimate professional social work values," she posits an integral relationship between individual and community:

1. Each human being should be regarded by all others as an object of infinite worth. He should be preserved in a state commensurate with his innate dignity and protected from suffering.

2. Human beings have large and as yet unknown capacities for developing both inner harmony and satisfaction and ability to make outward contributions to the development of others.

3. In order to realize his potentialities every human being must interact in giving and taking relationships with others, and has an equal right to opportunities to do so.

4. Human betterment is possible.... Change toward personal and social ideals affirmed by the profession, is something better.

5. Change in a positive direction, for individuals, groups, or organized societies, may be speeded by active and purposive assistance or encouragement from others. Change in a negative direction may be slowed or prevented by the intervention of others. In other words, "helping" is a process of demonstrated validity, and is a value to be respected in its own right.[13]

Pumphrey's research on values in social work led her to a "social" conclusion:

One of the major philosophic points of discussion going on currently in faculty curriculum planning is whether social work's primary commitment is to the individual or to the good of the whole society. It is this author's personal opinion that the two cannot be separated and must be seen constantly together as a field of interaction. Therefore, it seems possible that if many of social work's expressed values could be paired or grouped and taught as aspects of ultimate values, conflicts between the individual and others would be minimized and the student would gradually develop an intellectual habit of thinking of both. Social work's concepts of the interrelatedness and wholeness of man would be emphasized.[14]

According to Pumphrey, therefore, for a commitment to individuals to be reasonable in action terms, "pairing" with community is required. By this reasoning she underscores values as a social concept; indeed these values are a social testament, rather than a paean to individualism.

SCIENCE AND SOCIAL WORK

Having touched upon the value side of social work, let's examine its scientific side. The birth of professional social work at the turn of the century paralleled the appearance of the new social sciences. The new social sciences, Lester Ward's sociology, the new psychology, and the new political science were born before the sunset of the nineteenth century un-

---

*Muriel W. Pumphrey, *The Teaching of Values and Ethics in Social Work Education,* Vol. 13, A Project Report of the Curriculum Study (New York: Council on Social Work Education, 1959), pp. 43–45. Reprinted by permission.

der the elongated intellectual shadow of logical positivism. The social sciences throughout the twentieth century have adopted the scientific method as the prime instrument of their research. The psychology of Sigmund Freud, which has had the greatest impact upon social work theory, is an example of efforts to apply the scientific method to human systems. It is ironic that a major criticism of Freud is based upon applying the scientific test to his work, namely, that the "theory" has never been "proved."

As one might expect, due to its reliance on scholarship as its *raison d'être,* higher education has been perhaps most directly affected by the negative social results of the dominance of logical positivism. If administrative structure and bureaucratic systems are suspect these days, the university is a prime example; indeed it may be a microcosm of the ascendency of scientific thought toward social breakdown. Freedom with respect to scholarship—academic freedom—is the sine qua non of the free university. But this essential liberty depends on organizational and structural protection. Proper protection of academic freedom requires social control.

In the end, rules and procedures must be established and administered for academic freedom to thrive. The social system of the university requires social acceptance, an internal political arrangement. Scholarship cannot be apolitical in this sense and, thus, it cannot be valueless. It is dangerous and threatening to free systems when they cannot depend on social organization to guarantee their stability. Often academics tend to minimize the importance of organizational structures. It has been my experience that the most "scientific" disciplines reveal the most disdain for administrative structure.

Individualistic styles that denigrate social-institutional structures can be dystonic to the theory and practice of social work. Yet individualistic styles can be observed increasingly in service delivery patterns and in the extent to which social workers seem increasingly less willing to accept current structures for providing services. Perhaps it is more accurate to say that increasingly we social workers, appropriately discontented with present organizational means of distributing services, turn to antisocial-individualistic means for righting wrongs.

For example, our profession still requires supervision of the inexperienced worker. This has a fundamental and basic aim, namely, that of improving the skill of the worker to help assure the delivery of the best possible service to the client. The supervisory function has its administrative overtones. To rebel against the model of supervised practice because it represents old established bureaucratized methods of delivering services may deny the client his most fundamental protection.

What has been suggested in some of our most cherished professional documents regarding beginning professional competency is sometimes interpreted to deny, not only the need for skill development, but also the concept of community accountability and responsibility. The social agency, a community-based organization, the community's institution for delivering services, has certain advantages over individualistic systems of delivering service, such as private practice. It is at least more directly accountable to the community.

The autonomous social worker model and the detached social worker model represent advances in our thinking with respect to more efficient modes of delivering services, taking into account the variable and specialized needs of communities. They represent a "freeing up" of the social worker, but they can be distorted into an individualistic approach, free of accountability.[15] As we increasingly see social work faculties engaged in private practice, and as individual rather than group styles of curriculum development become more popular, and as we attempt to infuse more social sciences into the curriculum (all of these necessary for our professional growth), we move closer to the antisocial fallout of the scientific method. As we use social sciences more (as we must) we must be aware of the danger [that threatens] . . . a social orientation, [an orientation] necessary for the real preservation of human dignity.

NOTES

[1] Reuben Bitensky, "The Influence of Political Power in Determining the Theoretical Development of Social Work," *Journal of Social Policy,* Vol. 2, Part 2 (April 1973), pp. 119–30.

[2] Shirley Hazzard, review of *The Eye of the Storm* by Patrick White, *New York Times Book Review,* 6 January, 1974, p. 1. The precise quote is "Great literature is like moral leadership; everyone deplores the lack of it, but there is a tendency to prefer it from the safely dead."

[3] Harold Lewis, "Morality and the Politics of Practice," *Social Casework,* Vol. 53, No. 7 (July 1972), pp. 404–5.

[4]Charles Levy, "The Context of Social Work Ethics," *Social Work*, Vol. 17, No. 2 (March 1972), pp. 90–101.

[5]Eveline Burns, "Social Policy: The Stepchild of the Curriculum," *Education for Social Work, Proceedings of the Ninth Annual Program Meeting*, Council on Social Work Education, 1961, p. 23.

[6]Nathan Cohen, "Humanitarianism in Search of a Method," *Social Work in the American Tradition* (New York: Holt, Rinehart and Winston, 1958), p. 3.

[7]Richard Goodwin, "Reflections: The American Social Process," *The New Yorker*, 21 January, 28 January, and 4 February 1974.

[8]Ibid., 21 January 1974, p. 38.

[9]Ibid., pp. 40, 47–48.

[10]Ibid., 28 January 1974, p. 40.

[11]John Carrier and Ian Kendall, "Social Policy and Social Change," *Journal of Social Policy*, Vol. 2, Part 3 (July 1973), p. 210.

[12]Brian Tierney, *Medieval Poor Law: A Sketch of Canonical Theory and Its Application in England* (Berkeley: University of California Press, 1959), pp. 11–21, 22–27; and Moses Maimonides, *The Guide for the Perplexed* (London: Rutledge & Kegan Paul, 1951), pp. 232–33, 312–13, 328–29.

[13]Muriel W. Pumphrey, *The Teaching of Values and Ethics in Social Work Education*, Vol. 13, A Project Report of the Curriculum Study (New York: Council on Social Work Education, 1959), pp. 43–44.

[14]Ibid., pp. 44–45.

[15]Myron Blanchard and Joseph L. Vigilante, *Response to Change: The Educational Alliance & Its Future* (April 1970), pp. 17–20.

THE INTERNATIONAL CODE OF ETHICS FOR THE PROFESSIONAL SOCIAL WORKER

Chauncey A. Alexander

Are there fundamental principles of social work practice that are "culture free?" Has the social work profession reached a knowledge and experience level where it can agree on the values and principles of social work and prescribe the behavior of social workers through standards of ethical conduct?

The answer is a resounding YES, since an International Code of Ethics for the Professional Social Worker was adopted by the International Federation of Social Workers (IFSW), a representative body comprised of professional membership associations of fifty-six nations.[1] The adoption of such an international code represents a qualitative leap in the development and universality of the social work profession. The rationale and assumptions for the International Code were derived from the analysis of the codes from fourteen countries, an international working task force, and the debate and vote of the IFSW General Meeting, made up of three representatives from each national association.[2]

ORIGINS

The institutionalization of social welfare programs in most nations of the world has resulted in increased formalization of their labor force requirements. The drive for clarification of social work practice—its value base, knowledge, and methodology—has increased the standardization of practice and the professionalization of the workers. The rapid incorporation of practice theory and knowledge into formalized curricula in schools of social work, in in-service training and continuing education has consolidated a transmissible body of knowledge. Bodies of social workers, based upon educational and experiential qualifications for membership, have found it desirable to prescribe ethical standards for the professional behavior of their members.

In addition to these origins and outcomes of the social work profession, the exchange of a body of social work knowledge and practice throughout the

Source: This article was specially prepared for this volume by the author.

world has contributed to more universal understanding and application of the concepts of professional responsibility.

The biennial meetings and seminars of the IFSW, the International Conference on Social Welfare, and the International Association of Schools of Social Work, the meetings and policy creation of the United Nations and other international bodies, and the periodic international and regional meetings of national welfare ministers constitute conduits and networks of knowledge and practice exchange. These factors, combined with the increased travel and intermigration of social workers between countries, created the conditions for an international agreement on practice behavior.

THE RATIONALE OF DESIGN FOR A CODE OF ETHICS

If a social worker is to be guided by a code of ethics, the prescription must be specific enough to measure individual sets of behavior, such as the statements to clients and colleagues or the outcomes of nonaction. Many of the present national association codes set forth rather detailed conduct relative to what seems to be specific concerns within the country at the time. For example, the U.S. code specifies the social worker "will not discriminate because of race, color, religion, age, sex, or national ancestry and in my job capacity will work to prevent and eliminate such discrimination in rendering service, in work assignments, and in employment practices."[2] The Australian code stipulates the sources of remuneration: "In his professional work, the social worker is remunerated by the salary, fees, grants, or other payments allowable under the terms of his service and by no other source of gain connected with his work."[3]

These prescriptions were designated "Standards of Ethical Conduct" drawn from the definitions of *standard* as: "something used by general agreement to determine whether or not a thing is as it should be; type, model, or example established by usage; pattern; criterion" and that of *ethical* meaning: "conforming to the standards of conduct of a given profession."[4]

Since all of the possible practice situations cannot be anticipated, it is necessary to have some axioms that provide the basis for individual judgment in specific situations. Such axioms or guides were designated *principles* from the definition: "the ultimate

source, origin, or cause of something; a fundamental truth, law, doctrine, or motivating force upon which others are based." This differentiation between the motivating element (principles) and the criteria for measurement (standards) is most significant in providing a design for professional behavior. In addition to the above clarification, there is the special design problem created by the dialectics of a profession that at the same time encompasses, and yet must distinguish between, the dynamics of the individual and those of society. It is necessary to emphasize the dynamic relationship between these forces that create continuous tension. Such a dialectic occurs in many ways, yet must be incorporated in such a code. For example, it is necessary to describe opposite or different modes of conduct within the same standard; that is, status quo versus developmental responsibilities, the conduct of rehabilitation and maintenance activities as well as responsibility for change, the prevention versus solution considerations, the professional versus the agency identity, and the distinguishing between form and substance in all areas of practice.

Another critical element in the code design was consideration of the purpose of the professional behavior at any particular time. The basis and form of the behavior of professionals stems from the nature of the responsibility and relationship they hold to others, the factors conditioning the purpose. Therefore, it was desirable to divide the "Standards of Ethical Conduct" into those standards that had general application and those directly related to clients, agencies and organizations, colleagues, and to the social work profession as a collective body.

THE GUIDING PHILOSOPHY

The origins of social work and its place in the historical context of the industrial revolution have been well described. The idiosyncratic development of social work in each nation and international comparisons are much less complete. Nevertheless, general agreement and documentation exists as to the humanitarian, religious, and democractic movements that have initiated personal, group, and community services to deal with the dysfunctions of personal-societal interactions.

It is important to distinguish between the *ideals*—existing as ideas, models, or archetypes; consisting of ideas—and the *philosophies*—the general principles or laws of a field of knowledge, activity, and so forth. It is also necessary, in an international context, to indicate that *democratic* does not refer to a specific political party or structure, but to a broad philosophy of social organization that has application to capitalist, socialist, and other governmental forms to the degree that it is their guiding doctrine.

The historical basis and the ultimate purposes of social work are then summarized in the foreword of the International Code as follows:

Social work originates variously from humanitarian, religious, and democratic ideals and philosophies and has universal application to meet human needs arising from personal-societal interactions and to develop human potential. Professional social workers are dedicated to service for the welfare and self-fulfillment of human beings; to the development and disciplined use of scientific knowledge regarding human and societal behavior; to the development of resources to meet individual, group, national, and international needs and aspirations; and to the achievement of social justice.

THE BASIC PRINCIPLES

All codes of ethics of national professional associations have their stated or implied principles incorporated in the following five principles of the international code:

1. Every human being has a unique value, irrespective of origin, ethnicity, sex, age, beliefs, social and economic status, or contribution to society;

2. Each individual has the right of self-fulfillment to the degree that it does not encroach upon the same right of others;

3. Each society, regardless of its form, should function to provide the maximum benefits for all of its members;

4. The professional social worker has the responsibility to devote objective and disciplined knowledge and skill to aid individuals, groups, communities, and societies in their development and resolution of personal-societal conflicts and their consequences;

5. The professional social worker has a primary obligation to the objective of service, which must take precedence over self-interest or views.

The first principle, concerning the unique value of each human being, appears to be the most consis-tently stated in national codes. There are many ways in which the opposite actions or disregard of human values are demonstrated. Most of them have economic and attitudinal biases particularly directed toward origin, status, or belief of an individual. However, sex, age, and contributions to society have been commonplace enough discriminations to warrant reference in the international code.

The right of self-determination, that atomic ingredient of the social work process, has been stated in many ways in different codes. For example, the Norwegian association's ethical guidelines cites "respect for the client's right to decide over his own actions," and "accepts the client's self-worth regardless of his personal and moral beliefs." In order to extend a more developmental aspect to the concept of self-determination, it was formulated as the right of self-fulfillment. In order to clarify past confusions in the literature and in practice regarding the question of the limits on self-determination, it was necessary to qualify that right by recognition of the limit of the "impingement on the same rights of others."

The third principle, referring to societal responsibility, is usually stated as responsibility for "the greatest good for the greatest number." However, in order to introduce equity into the concept and to recognize the difference in resources from one nation to another, it was considered that society should provide the "maximum benefits for all of its members."

In order to deal with the conflicts between knowledge and skill, client differences, prevention and solution, and personal and societal demands whose interplay and integration test the professional's ability, the principle of dependence on the worker's professional discipline is stated. The role and responsibility of the professional worker is further explicated in the declaration concerning the ascendency of service over self-interest. This commitment to a calling and to a service orientation constitutes two of the six characteristics of a professional as described by Moore.[5]

THE GENERAL STANDARDS OF ETHICAL CONDUCT

Since the basis and form of the behavior of professionals stem from the nature of the responsibility and relationship they hold to others, clarity and precision of the standard's prescriptions were obtained by dividing the standards into five classifications: those for general conduct and those relative to clients, to organizations, to colleagues, and to the profession. Although not observed in most codes, it seemed important to distinguish between those ethical practices with colleagues as peers and the broader responsibilities to the profession of social work or the organized collective of social workers, their professional association.

The translation of the principles into specific standards often made it necessary to state the action requirements in two ways in order to include the mandate of initiative; for example, "seek and understand," "uphold and advance," "recognize and respect," and others.

The general standards of the International Code are:

1. Seek and understand the worth of each individual and the elements that condition behavior and the service required;

2. Uphold and advance the values, knowledge, and methodology of the profession, refraining from any behavior that damages the functioning of the profession;

3. Clarify all public statements or actions, whether on an individual basis or as a representative of a professional association, agency, or organization;

4. Recognize professional and personal limitations, encourage the utilization of all relevant knowledge and skills, and apply scientific methods of inquiry;

5. Contribute professional expertise to the development of sound policies and programs to better the quality of life in each society;

6. Identify and interpret the social needs, the basis, and nature of individual, group, community, national, and international social problems, and the work of the social work profession.

Two general standards warrant special comments. The fourth standard, referring to practice limitations, opts for methods or means justifiable by scientific method. Those who are trapped in the art versus science dialogue may quarrel with this criterion. Nevertheless, it was considered that even though individual skill could determine the degree of effectiveness of different practitioners, no profession could claim efficacy for its methods without resorting to verifiable means.

The fifth general standard takes an affirmative position on the necessity for all professional social workers to be concerned with social change. Rather than the usual broad declaration applicable to any citizen, this standard is stated within the boundaries of realistic and special contribution, that of "professional expertise."

Ethical Standards Relative to Clients

The standards relative to clients are described in a more detailed fashion, not only to ensure understanding, but because they are at the core of the ethical responsibility.

The standards relative to clients of the International Code are:

1. Maintain the client's right to a relationship of mutual trust, to privacy and confidentiality, and to responsible use of information. The collection and sharing of information or data shall only be related to the professional service function to be performed with the client informed as to its necessity and use. No information shall be released without prior knowledge and informed consent of the client, except where the client cannot be responsible or others may be seriously jeopardized;

2. Recognize and respect the individual goals, responsibilities, and differences of clients. Within the scope of the agency and the client's social milieu, the professional service shall assist clients to take responsibility for personal actions and to help all clients with equal willingness. Where the professional service cannot be provided under such conditions, the client shall be so informed in such a way as to leave the client free to act;

3. Help the client—individual, group, community, or society—to achieve self-fulfillment and maximum potential within the limits of the equal rights of others. The service shall be based upon helping the client to understand and use the professional relationship in furtherance of the client's legitimate desires and interests.

An important qualifier was built into the relationship standard; that is, that of information being related, in collection or distribution, to the professional service function. Experience with adjudication of violations of ethical practice has shown confusion over what information is really necessary to obtain from clients to perform the professional service. Clarity as to the purpose and function of the relationship prevents unprofessional behavior.

It was necessary in the second standard that applies the self-determination principle to the client to specify the professional's responsibility relative to clients with whom there may be personal or ideological conflict. This necessitated indicating responsibility to inform the client in a helpful manner that leaves the client free to act.

The third standard states the application of the self-fulfillment principle to helping the client within the limits of the equal rights of others. The focus of this standard emphasizes the professional relationship and its use and understanding for the client. Another important limit for the professional is built into this standard; that is, that of the "legitimate" desires and interests of the client. This establishes another important cutoff point in the client-professional relationship, clearly placing a judgmental responsibility with the practitioner.

Ethical Standards Relative to Agencies and Organizations

The standards relative to agencies and organizations required dealing with two reality problems: (1) the difference between the quality of service of agencies and the service standards of the profession and (2) the precedence of accountability to the client and the profession over that of the agency. The standards are as follows:

1. Work or cooperate with those agencies and organizations whose policies, procedures, and operations are directed toward adequate service delivery and encouragement of professional practice consistent with the code of ethics;

2. Responsibly execute the stated aims and functions of the agency or organization, contributing to the development of sound policies, procedures, and practice in order to obtain the best possible standards of service;

3. Sustain ultimate responsibility to the client, initiating desirable alterations of policy, procedures, and practice through appropriate agency and organizational channels. If necessary remedies are not achieved after channels have been exhausted, initiate appropriate appeals to higher authorities or the wider community of interest;

4. Ensure professional accountability to client and community for efficiency and effectiveness through periodic review of client, agency, and organizational problems and self-performance.

The appropriate professional approach is defined within the combination of the four standards, including (1) work and cooperation with organizations with adequate service delivery; (2) contributing to development of sound policies, procedures, and practices; (3) initiating desirable alterations; and (4) the ensurance of agency accounting.

In the first of these standards, the phrase "are directed toward" is of special significance. Some purists among practitioners would argue that a professional should not work for an agency that did not meet the profession's standards. The present wording was decided upon to encourage practitioners to assist substandard agencies to work toward adequate standards.

Two important action requirements are built into the third and fourth standards: (1) the exhaustion of organizational channels as a method of change, and (2) the action obligation of appeals to higher authorities and to the wider community. Both of these are seen as a necessity and means for professional accountability. The forms or procedures of appeals were not defined because of the variance in situations and techniques in each country.

Ethical Standards Relative to Colleagues

The standards relative to colleagues represent an important advance in an area of professional accountability and performance that has usually been disregarded or taken for granted. The positive affirmations, formalizing responsibility for professional cooperation, accepting differences, and sharing knowledge should be the basis for initiating new levels of understanding and action.

1. Respect the training and performance of colleagues and other professionals, extending all necessary cooperation that will enhance effective services;

2. Respect differences of opinion and practice of colleagues and other professionals, expressing criticism through appropriate channels in a responsible manner;

3. Promote and share opportunities for knowledge, experience, and ideas with all professional colleagues, other professionals, and volunteers for the purpose of mutual improvement and validation;

4. Bring any violations of client interest or professional ethics and standards to the attention of the appropriate bodies and defend colleagues against unjust actions.

Several components of these standards define clear responsibilities in areas of practice that were formerly obscure or debatable. The responsibility to express criticism, and through appropriate channels, is now a standard for professional maturity and behavior. A second clarification is the requirement for sharing of expertise beyond other colleagues to include other professionals and particularly volunteers. This moves the social work profession away from a guild psychology to community responsibility.

Probably most important of all of the components is the defined requirement to take action on violations of client interest and professional ethics and standards. It is no longer acceptable to sit back when violations occur. One's inaction is a cause for being subject to professional sanctions.

Ethical Standards
Relative to the Profession

An affirmative action concept, as used relative to colleagues, is carried through to the standards relative to the profession, with practitioner responsibility fixed for individual action. The following four standards are defined:

1. Maintain the values, knowledge, and methodology of the profession and contribute to their clarification and improvement;

2. Uphold the professional standards of practice and work for their advancement;

3. Defend the profession against unjust criticism and work to increase confidence in the necessity for professional practice;

4. Encourage new approaches and methodologies needed to meet new and existing needs.

Although the exact measurements of a higher obligation are not set forth (because of national differences), the necessity to evaluate personal performance in the light of peer judgments and consensus is established in these standards.

SUMMARY

The International Code of Ethics for Professional Social Workers is a qualitative step for the social work profession at an international level. This code is now being utilized and tested by national professional associations throughout the world. It makes clear decisions in areas of professional behavior that have not been fully specified in the past.

The next important step is to develop guidelines for the implementation of the code, so as to speed up its application and to avoid criticisms of it that may occur from its misuse. It is also important to assemble case examples of both upholding and violation of the code in order to embellish the necessary guidelines. Many examples that now exist in various countries can form the basis for the collection, with the IFSW providing the continuous reference center for future information and data.

NOTES

[1]International Code of Ethics; adopted at the IFSW General Meeting, San Juan, Puerto Rico, July 10, 1976.

[2]USA, *Code of Ethics*, 1 page (printed: National Association of Social Workers, 1967).

[3]Australia, *Aims, Organisation, Activities*, 6 pages, (multilithed: Australian Association of Social Workers, 1974).

[4]All definitions are from *Webster's New World Dictionary*.

[5]Moore, Wilbert E., *The Professions: Roles and Rules*, Russell Sage Foundation, New York, 1970. Pages 5–19.

PART II

The Context of Practice

Analysis of the context of social work practice entails consideration of broad societal forces—sociocultural, historical, political, and economic—along with the institutionalized system of social welfare. The first section of this introduction addresses the broad forces, followed by a more detailed discussion of the changes occurring in the system of social welfare. The broader sociocultural, political, economic, historical context and the immediate context of the field of social welfare form an interrelated constellation of factors that shapes the ideology, structure, and processes of social work practice.

In a very real sense the profession of social work as we know it today is a product of Western industrialization and bureaucratization. Historically, societal forms of helping individuals and families in need are traceable to a Judeo-Christian heritage. Giving succor to the distressed is a Judeo-Christian religious concept that carries through to the present. As Christianity gained in influence and acceptance throughout the medieval world, its leaders assumed responsibility for distributing alms to the poor and utilizing monasteries to shelter the orphaned, the ill, and the handicapped.

The present professional model of social work is embedded in a highly bureaucratic system of social welfare programs, and although in part the model draws on the Judeo-Christian background, it is also a product of increasing industrialization and urbanization in the twentieth century. We are discovering that prevailing social problems, including structural unemployment of millions (unemployment created or sustained by our system), the growing number of neglected elderly, the blight and slum of our inner cities, the high incidence of crime, the extensive poverty amidst unparalleled affluence, and even the chronic illnesses such as heart disease and cancer have their origins in a polluted, unsafe, and debilitating environment. Industrialization often creates the clientele for social changes. Forced mobility of a great percentage of the country's work force seeking employment in a rapidly changing and dynamic economy strains the limited resources of the modern nuclear family and thus creates the need for a wide range of human services. Technology regularly discards millions of workers, forcing early reliance on public income maintenance programs and services for survival.

On the other hand, resources made available through industrialization have made possible the development of large-scale social welfare programs. Social security, public welfare, national, state, and local health programs, public education, public-sponsored housing, employment services and training, and the broad range of social services to the various populations at risk—the young, the elderly, the one-parent families, youthful and adult offenders, the handicapped—have been institutionalized by public policy and public spon-sorship in all Western industrialized nations and throughout the world where a sufficient level of industrialization has been achieved.

Industrialization has transformed America into an urban nation. More than 50 per-cent of the U.S. population resides in urban areas, defined as communities with populations in excess of 25,000 (see Hauser 1977). Differentiation, diversification, and complexity—the characteristics of an urbanized, industrialized society—mandate the need for social workers with knowledge and skills, particularly as connectors of services and facilities, individuals and families. A fragmented, complex environment requires social workers with skills in planning, designing, organizing, and delivering a broad range of human services. Linking the patient in the acute-care hospital to community-based programs in long-term care and organizing a personal support system that includes the case services and public social util-ities (described later in Part II in reading selection 9 by Kahn) are the new roles expected of the social worker in the present environment for practice.

By way of summary, the consequences of industrialization and urbanization include:

1.   A growing dependence of the individual on society for meeting basic needs, a conse-quence of division of labor and specialization in modern society;

2.   A changed role for and impact on the family. The extended intergenerational family is disappearing; the modern family relies to an ever-increasing extent on society for meeting its needs. A consequence is the greater vulnerability of the family in meeting major crises and dependence on community programs for the care of children and for aging parents;

3.   A sharp increase in women entering the work force. This phenomenon has created opportunities and tensions in realigning traditional approaches to work status and role as-signments and has stimulated the need for child care services and greater reliance on com-munity support programs for basic services;

4.   A shift to a post-industrial society. A consequence of this shift has been the develop-ment of a new and vast service industry to meet the needs of a more consumer-oriented society, as well as the needs of a society that contains a growing percentage of members that are beyond age sixty-five.

SOCIAL WELFARE SYSTEM: IMMEDIATE CONTEXT FOR SOCIAL WORK PRACTICE

Dramatic changes that have occurred in the broader societal context have transformed the institution of social welfare into a vastly different system. Changes have taken place in the basic value and belief system undergirding social welfare programs and services, organiza-tion and delivery of human services, and the roles played by the prime actor in the system, the professional social worker.

Changes in Definition of Basic Terminology Reflecting a Change in Ideology

Increasing use of the term *human services* in place of *social services* reflects a fundamental change in program orientation. *Human services* reflects a discontent with current practice and a recognition of the common elements underlying the concerted helping actions of a diverse group of caregivers and consumers working together with a mutual support system. Human services represent a variety of programs and services that communities require for their own social health and for the expression of the essential humanity of interpersonal and social relations and services (see Morris 1974).

From a broad perspective human services could include all of the basic social welfare programs: health, education, employment, housing, income maintenance, and justice and lay compliance with the law. Human services in practice are the programs that span the boundaries between the basic social programs (Kurren 1977).

Human services facilitate individuals' and families' coping with the social roles and requirements necessary for meaningful participation in society by providing services that the primary family or extended family might have provided but are not now providing. Alternative primary care—in reality substitute family arrangements—include foster care, group home care, protective services, counseling, day care, and nutrition programs for the elderly. Human services also have the function of facilitating access to and utilization of the broad basic social programs: health, employment, education, housing, information and referral, and crisis intervention. Human services can augment basic social programs through community-based arrangements that include neighborhood health centers, alternative schools for the school dropout, and halfway houses for the recently discharged patient from state institutions.

Changes in Value and Belief System

Social work is one of the primary professions involved in providing these human services. However, a counter trend is emerging, signaling new directions and recasting priorities for social work. Replacing a traditional preoccupation with social pathology are a number of belief trends that place a higher value on securing a more adequate fit between human needs and conditions, public policies, and programs. These include:

> Human services as a right rather than a privilege extended to select populations. The fundamental value principle of equity has moved from the rhetoric stage to policy implementation in the basic areas of living: health care, housing, income maintenance, education, and employment;

> Protection of the individual's right to participate in the conditions of treatment provided by the care-giving systems. These include the person's right to decide on the provision or cessation of heroic medical care procedures in the interest of prolonging or terminating life;

> The citizen's right to participate in policy, planning, and development in the organization and delivery of essential social services;

> The individual's right to community-based care rather than institutionalization for indefinite extended periods in isolated, archaic facilities;

> A move away from the labeling and categorizing of people with certain needs and problems to a more humanistic, nonstigmatizing, common needs–common problems orientation to the delivery of social services;

> Protection of the rights of people for confidentiality, for due process, and for equal opportunity;

> Protection of the individual from the hazards of human experimentation, frequently conducted without securing consent or authentic involvement of the individuals or groups concerned.

The focus for social work practice within the context of the above-mentioned belief trends is on common needs of people who are experiencing problems in their efforts to achieve a desired level of social functioning. When viewed from a social developmental perspective, poverty, unemployment, physical and mental illness, and disability are manifestations of social underdevelopment; that is, the problematic conditions noted above stem from inadequacies in the fit between human needs and the quality of organization and development of society itself (Hollister 1975). The primary nuclear family has steadily lost its capability for socializing, preparing, and sustaining its members and is now forced to rely on secondary institutions created by society. It should come as no surprise to discover that as prosperity and affluence increase in modern society, social services and social work occupy a more central position. Social services are part of the modern world. They continue to exist and even expand as productivity increases and as average standards of living are raised. Indeed they are seen as part of the improved standards (Kahn 1976).

Changes in the Organizational and Administrative Context for Social Work Practice

Bureaucracy has become synonymous with professionalization, to some extent accompanied by public discontent with both developments. The American social welfare scene has been described as a series of pyramid-shaped structures, each with peaks of power located far from the community scene of social service delivery. Decisions made in Washington are transmitted down through layers of officialdom. Neighborhood autonomy and control, community decision making, local management of resources—all the hallmarks of an earlier period in American social welfare—have been supplanted by centralized superstructures that have until recently often made service delivery at the neighborhood level more of a myth than a reality. Unquestionably a high has been reached in public discontent, distrust, and frustration with the unresponsiveness and ineffectiveness of large-scale bureaucracy. Alternative approaches that are based on new themes—decentralization, decategorization, and devolution (delegation of authority)—are replacing traditional policies and programs. As a result of the new insights into the nature of organization and administration required for locality-oriented and locality-directed programs, program planners have developed a keener appreciation for unintended consequences of well-meaning interventions. Families and individuals seeking social welfare assistance and protection frequently find themselves worse off. Clients often are shunted off to institutions, nursing homes, mental hospitals; social welfare program protection often means protecting society from delinquent youth, the disabled, the chronically ill, the elderly, and the poor (Pierce 1970) by removing them to state institutions far from their community.

Neighborhood-based, community-centered systems for the delivery of social services are slowly replacing the "pyramids" of centralized power. The categorical centralized system that evolved piecemeal over time as society recognized a problem and devised a program in response to it is being replaced by a more locality-oriented, comprehensive framework of services. Human service centers and human resource systems that provide a broad range of necessary services are replacing the traditional welfare departments, health agencies, and rehabilitation programs. New legislation, including amendments to the Social Security Act, has made these changes possible.

These changes challenge social work motivation and capacity for change. Sarri's (1975) observation is therefore especially relevant: "Unless the profession can demonstrate conclusively that it can assist effectively in the resolution of critical social problems in the design and delivery of services, and in evaluation of the outcomes of the programs, social workers will be relegated to handmaiden and subordinate roles."

READING SELECTIONS IN PART II

A prime objective of Part II of the book is to sensitize the social work practitioner to some of the basic issues as well as some of the changes in the context of social work practice, not the least of which, as noted above, has been the profound change in the organization and administration of social services.

The introductory remarks to Part II noted changes occurring in the definition of human needs, social problems, and the organizational and administrative concepts and practices that now shape the directions and priorities in social work. A discussion of the changing context for social work would not be complete without referring to the impact of a new awareness of ethnic and cultural factors influencing social work practice. As concern for the rights of people and their social functioning becomes increasingly highlighted as the most important organizing framework for practice, heightened awareness and appreciation of ethnic and cultural factors will emerge.

The reading selections in this part of the book were chosen to illustrate the following points: presentation of a framework for reviewing the roles and objectives of social work in the context of social problems; the place of social work amidst the vast array of human services; the cross-national and cross-cultural context of practice; some new directions in public social services; and some bureaucratic influences on social work practitioners.

"A Framework for Practice in Social Welfare: Objectives and Roles" by Teare and McPheeter provides a comprehensive framework for examining the context of social work practice. Major areas of human need—health, education, employment, family functioning, financial needs, and integration into the neighborhood and community—are designated as *domains of living*. Individual and family functioning within each of the domains of living is viewed as a continuum from well-being (low risk) to disability (the condition in which problems have already surfaced). Major environmental obstacles to functioning are identified, including institutional racism, natural catastrophes, rigid or archaic laws, rules and regulations, and environmental and personal deficiencies. The social worker must become familiar with this continuum of functioning as visualized by the authors and begin to see the natural history of social problems from well-being to stress to crisis to disability as complex interrelated phenomena. Other major contributions of the reading selection are the presentation of a system of objectives and functions for the field of social welfare and a format for clustering the work activities of the social worker in relation to the target of intervention, objective worker attributes, skills, abilities, work activity, and the work setting.

"The Place of Social Work in the Human Services" by Robert Morris provides considerable insight into the changes that are occurring in the context of social work practice. Morris has the facility for viewing in macro fashion the major events and influences shaping the growth and development of social welfare programs and for forecasting their implications for social work practice. Morris believes that social work can become much more central to the field of human services by recognizing and accommodating to the changes that are occurring in the conceptualization, organization, and delivery of human services. Social work often acts as a force resisting change when it fails to consider the context of social organization and social structure of post-industrial society, of which social work is an integral part.

It is significant that Morris joins with others in the social work literature in using the more general term *human services*. Human services, in contrast to the term social services, provides a more comprehensive, noncategorizing approach to human needs. Societal mandate within a human services orientation is a more comprehensive and inclusive approach to problem resolution.

Health and mental health are identified by Morris as major growth areas for the foreseeable future in their utilization of a wide range of human services personnel. Changes occurring in the health and mental health areas, and undoubtedly in all of the other major areas or domains of living, reflect a universal theme or concern for humanitarianism and a desire to meet the common needs of people. Social work will have to accommodate to change by shifting its present orientation from a largely rehabilitative or social treatment-and-cure orientation to one of helping people maintain a desirable level of social functioning or well-being.

When—particularly in the 1960s—the charge of institutional racism was leveled at social institutions including the social welfare system, profound changes were set in motion, one of which was a thorough assessment of the value premises and belief systems undergirding social work practice. "Social Work Practice in Cross-National and Cross-Cultural Perspective" by Pernell presents the mandate for a cross-cultural perspective to social work practice. Basic themes of social work, such as the "dignity of man" and "self-actualization," are examined within the context of the *person-in-situation*. What may have been labeled as resistance behavior or considered maladaptive behavior may in fact be, as Pernell notes, adaptive behavior quite appropriate for the presenting circumstances.

Pernell identifies a key principle, in essence, that social work is basically concerned with assisting people to cope productively with their environment. It is therefore most important that social workers know how the person perceives his or her environment and what behaviors and responses he or she considers appropriate to this perception.

The person-in-situation—which in reality is a primary context of social work practice—serves as a framework for cross-cultural learning. Developing an appreciation of cultural expressions can be enhanced in a number of ways, particularly through the use of curriculum materials that draw heavily on lifestyles and systems of various ethnic and racial population groups. The cross-cultural perspective—a key aspect of the context of social work practice—can effectively influence the social worker's understanding and use of intervention approaches.

Kahn's "New Directions in Social Services" defines an important context of social work practice with clarity, precision, and authority. Kahn has been in the forefront for many years in forecasting with accuracy the changes occurring in the basic social welfare system. His main theme is that "an urbanized industrial society cannot forego social services." The question is not "whether," but "what kind," "for whom," "of what quality," and "who pays?"

Kahn perceives general or personal social services as a communal effort to enhance individual and group development and well-being and to aid, rehabilitate, or treat those in difficulty or need. General social services are further identified in terms of specific services described as interpersonal, therapeutic services, and public social utilities (the concrete array of services such as day care, transportation, and nutritional services).

Kahn's model for a modern public social welfare system provides for the following services: an access service system consisting of a network of neighborhood information and referral centers located in shopping centers throughout the community; and specialized programs consisting of case services and public social utilities for various populations at risk (foster homes, group therapy, day care, counseling for the elderly, and so forth). Sponsorship of the specialized programs would either be public, voluntary, or a consortium of both auspices.

Key program principles for Kahn's presentation include: (1) a universal framework for social services, which means that services are made available to the entire population on the basis of need and not income; (2) therapeutic relational services and public social utilities organized on the basis of geographic and administrative boundaries; and (3) the development of a network of specialized programs.

For the student of social work examining for the first time the current community scene of social service or human service programs, the scene might look like a crazy-quilt network of services. Along with the bewildering array of programs and services, it is becoming increasingly difficult to make the distinction between those programs that are publicly sponsored and those that are privately sponsored. For example, some of those that are in the public sector include local and state health departments, public welfare agencies, and state vocational rehabilitation agencies. The private or voluntary sector, where social work as we know it today had its beginning, is represented by agencies such as child and family services, settlement houses, and day care programs. There had been a time when a principal difference between the public and voluntary sectors was the source of their funding. Public agencies received their support directly from public taxation, and voluntary agencies relied on voluntary giving from the public through campaigns such as the United Way. The great change that has blurred the boundaries between public and voluntary programs is the increasing use of purchase of service arrangements. Public agencies can now purchase needed services from voluntary agencies. This has resulted in a growing partnership between public and voluntary agencies in communities throughout the United States.

Indeed it is difficult to understand the development of social work without understanding the crucial role that agencies have played over the years. In large part, social workers have depended on formal organizations such as agencies for a large part of their sanction and legitimacy as professionals. Agencies can provide or allow: a marshaling of a wide variety of resources, a clear location for delivery of services, an opportunity for ongoing educational and professional growth for social workers through peer contacts and consultations, and numerous advantages in providing the critical human services. Similarly, as noted above, agencies can be: public or voluntary, primary (run by and for social workers, such as a family service agency) or host (with primary services provided by another professional, as in a hospital or a school). Agencies can also vary among themselves in numerous dimensions, including size, types of services, internal structure and organization, and so on.

While agencies can provide numerous benefits, the social worker entering agency practice for the first time may encounter certain difficulties. "The Professional Social Worker in a Bureaucracy" by Wasserman observes that it is time for social workers to stop hiding their knowledge of bureaucracy and to move forward with new ideas and models for achieving organizational change. The organization or the bureaucracy (which literally means formal organization involving government by bureaus) occupies a central position in social work and is a primary context for social work practice. Formal organizations or bureaucracies are a product of industrialization and urbanization of society and have made possible the complex system of social welfare programs and services that now serve millions of Americans. The distinctive characteristics of bureaucracy are: (1) a high degree of specialization; (2) a definite structure or hierarchy of authority within the organization, with the clear defining of roles and responsibilities; and (3) a code of conduct for workers within the organization that defines the nature of relationships between workers and workers to clients. Undoubtedly the greatest contribution of bureaucracy is efficiency in the performance of complex services for mass consumption.

A way of life and a major concern of social work, therefore, has been and continues to be with organizations. How to make organizations more humanistic and more responsive to the needs of clients and how to provide an environment compatible with professional social work practice are the issues addressed in this reading selection. Wasserman identifies the dysfunctional elements of worker relationships with organizations; for example, the phenomenon of *situation ethics*, the process whereby the worker shades facts and operates in borderline fashion in terms of ethical considerations in an effort to secure needed services for the client concerned.

Four major areas of organizational dynamics are examined in the article:

1. Bureaucratic structure as supporting and/or constraining professional workers' activity;

2. Nature of transactions and interactions in role performances of social workers;

3. Maneuvering by organizations to either serve or deflect services to clients;

4. Overall effects of organization on the professional worker.

If the premise is accepted that organizations will almost inevitably exhibit varying degrees of "social lag"—that is, the purposes for which they were created become irrelevant to the needs of the client group they now serve—then the need to understand the dynamics and strategies of organizational change must also be seen as essential (see, for example, Patti and Resnick 1972).

REFERENCES

Hauser, Philip M.
1977 "Meeting Human Needs—An Integral Component of Public Policy." Reprinted with permission from *Public Welfare* 30, no. 1 (Winter):8–15.

Hollister, C. David.
1975 "Social Work Skills for Social Development." Paper presented at the National Association of Social Workers, Twentieth Anniversary Professional Symposium, Hollywood-by-Sea, Florida, October 24.

Kahn, Alfred J.
1976 "New Directions in Social Services." *Public Welfare* 34, no. 2 (Spring):26–32.

Kurren, Oscar.
1977 "The Design of Human Service Programs—Toward a Model for Excellence." Paper presented at the National Association of Social Workers, Fifth Biennial Professional Symposium, San Diego, November 20.

Morris, Robert.
1974 "The Place of Social Work in the Human Services." *Social Work* 19, no. 5 (September):519–31.

Patti, Rino J., and Herman Resnick.
1972 "Changing the Agency from Within." *Social Work* 17, no. 4 (July):48–57.

Pierce, F. J.
1970 "A Functional Perspective of Social Welfare." *Current Views and Issues in Social Welfare.*

Sarri, Rosemary C.
1975 "Essential Skills for Administration and Policy Roles in Social Work." Paper presented at National Association of Social Workers, Twentieth Anniversary Professional Symposium Plenary Session on "The Essence of Social Work Skills," Hollywood-by-Sea, Florida, October 23, p. 2.

A FRAMEWORK FOR PRACTICE IN SOCIAL WELFARE: OBJECTIVES AND ROLES

Robert J. Teare, Harold L. McPheeters

THE FIELD OF SOCIAL WELFARE

The Problem

The focus of this paper springs from a basic problem facing persons charged with responsibility for planning, operating, and evaluating delivery systems for various types of services in the United States.* Couched in its simplest terms, the problem is this: Given the current and projected availability of

*Funding for the activities of the Social Welfare Manpower Project which produced this report was through a Section 1115 grant from the Social and Rehabilitation Service of the Department of Health, Education, and Welfare.

Source: Abridged and edited from Robert J. Teare and Harold L. McPheeters, "A Framework for Practice in Social Welfare: Objectives and Roles," in *Manpower Utilization in Social Welfare* (Atlanta: Southern Regional Education Board, 1970). Reprinted with permission of the Southern Regional Education Board. Figure appearing in this article is not included here; for further information consult the original version.

manpower and under present patterns of utilization, health care and social service systems simply cannot adequately meet the needs of the general public. Because this shortage of trained manpower is a general condition, all of the helping professions are faced with the problems it creates.

This situation has reached critical proportions in the area of activity charged with the responsibility of providing social welfare services to the public.* Like their counterparts in other professions, social welfare planners are faced with the dilemma of trying to provide a wider range of services to an increasing population while having to draw upon a cadre of trained workers which diminishes proportionately each year. Because the problem is of great concern to many individuals, it has been thoroughly documented and discussed (Barder and Briggs 1966; Department of Health, Education, and Welfare 1965; Monahan 1967; Schwartz 1966; Szaloczi 1967; Wittman 1965). Thus to most knowledgeable professionals, the above statements do not come as a revelation.

We have long been aware that half of all the social welfare work positions in the agencies are filled with persons who hold only bachelor's degrees. As we look at other parts of the social welfare field such as public welfare, child welfare, probation and parole, corrections, and vocational rehabilitation, we see that more than 75 percent of the positions are filled with persons with bachelor's degrees. Most agencies have used these people either in lieu of fully trained persons (i.e., MSWs) without rewriting the job descriptions, or as case "aides" working under the direct supervision of fully qualified workers.

Approaches to the solution of the problem can and do differ widely in terms of scope and focus. Some have attempted to reduce or redesign the spectrum of services open to the public; others have concentrated on ways to increase the number of individuals who enter the education and training channels or to accelerate the educational process; and a third major approach has focused on the tasks carried out by the social welfare worker. Although there are several variations in this third approach, all have been basically concerned with the reformulation and reallocation of existing tasks and the creation and development of new tasks and functions to be included as part of the purview of social welfare activities.

The authors decided to focus their efforts in the third major area: the reformulation of existing tasks and the development of new tasks to be carried out by baccalaureate workers. Our goal was to find more rational guidelines for the utilization of workers with BSWs and B.A. degrees in subject matter areas related to social welfare problems. If more rational guidelines could be developed, they might be used by social welfare agencies in reformulating work activities for B.A. workers and in developing new activities for these people.

Needs, Problems, and Scope of Social Welfare

The authors, in consultation with several professionals in the social welfare field, identified between nine hundred and one thousand illustrations of examples of specific needs and problems that people present to agencies as social welfare problems.** From this material we endeavored to develop a preliminary taxonomy to describe the field of social welfare and the range of client, family, and community needs that fall within its purview.

In analyzing the illustrations we first grouped these needs and problems into several basic areas of living. These were:

1. Health,
2. Education,
3. Employment,
4. Integrity of the family,
5. Money and financial resources,
6. Integrity of the neighborhood and community.

It seemed to us that we were talking about certain basic content categories in each of these areas of living. As a result, we further subdivided the areas into finer groupings. Under "Health" we classified needs as being associated with:

---

*The term *social welfare services* is used in this document in the broadest possible sense. Perhaps the closest definition is that which has been articulated by the Department of Health, Education, and Welfare (1965); that is, "... the organized system of functions and services, under public and private auspices, that promote community conditions essential to the harmonious interaction of services directed toward alleviating and contributing to the solution of social problems, with particular emphasis on strengthening the family...."

**See Teare & McPheeters (1970) for a complete description of this project and a list of the participants.

1. Prevention of illness,

2. Detection of illness,

3. Maintenance of health,

4. Treatment of illness,

5. Care,

6. Restoration to proper functioning (rehabilitation).

In like manner, subcategories were abstracted out of the problem content in each of the other major areas (education, employment, fiscal resources, etc.). More complete descriptions of these content areas are presented in Appendix 6-A.

If we could guarantee that all persons would have their needs met through the usual institutions developed by our society, there would be no need for the corrective aspects of the field of social welfare to exist. Obviously this is not the case; there is a host of forces that often blocks individuals, families, or groups from meeting their needs. In describing these problems, it seemed the obstacles could be classified into four major areas:

1. *Deficiencies within individuals*—that is, lack of education or training, inappropriate values, personal instability, poor physical health;

2. *Environmental deficiencies* (lack of resources or lack of access to them)—that is, shortage of housing, no medical facilities in area, no jobs in the central city;

3. *Rigid or inequitable laws, regulations, policies, and practices*—that is, employers will not hire blacks; inequitable requirements for services; fraudulent contracts;

4. *Results of catastrophes*—that is, death in the family, sudden severe brain damage, natural tragedies.

Based on this material, we have developed a system of social services. . . .

The problems to which social welfare service systems respond are conceptualized in three basic dimensions:

1. Domains of living,

2. Status of functioning,

3. Obstacles to functioning.

Some explanation of these terms is in order at this time.

Domains of Living. This dimension is simply an expansion of the basic content areas described in the taxonomy in Appendix 6-A. The categories are intended to be neither exhaustive nor precise. . . . They have been chosen merely to reflect the simple fact that social welfare workers are called upon to deal with problems that exist in a variety of domains of living and quite often they will have to deal simultaneously with problems in more than one area (the multiproblem client).

Status of Functioning. Quite often we have heard social welfare practitioners talking about unexpected catastrophes—fires, theft, death of a breadwinner, disabling accidents—that precipitated problems or crises for individuals or groups. Just as often they spoke with a sense of frustration of not being able to intervene early in the development of a problem in order to prevent disability. These apparently different orientations have a common conceptual thread: individuals can move, precipitously or gradually, along a continuum of funtioning ranging from a high level of well-being to permanent disability. Furthermore, in more cases than we realize or admit, this progression is systematic and predictable.* Given the appropriate data this progression would lend itself to description in much the same way that the *natural history* concept is used in public health and medicine.

. . . Five stages of functioning [exist]. . . . As with the domains, the labels are merely convenient anchor points on a continuum of functioning. They are taken from the work by Levine and Lipscomb (1966). *Well-being* depicts a status of high level "wellness." At this stage all appropriate social indicators would point to a situation of low risk, low vulnerability status. The second stage, *stress*, is a condition wherein, although no problems have arisen yet, indicators (as part of the natural history) have begun to point to an increase in risk and vulnerability. The *problems* stage depicts the condition that although problems have begun to occur, they are manageable within the resources of the individual or system. At *crisis*, problems have exceeded the capacity of the individuals' ability to cope. Vulnerability may lead to pathology or damage.

---

*The writings of Harrington (1962, 1970), in describing the "magnetic field" of poverty, eloquently capture the dynamics of this concept. A similar notion, couched in terms of social work practice, has been advocated by Levine and Lipscomb (1966) in their "levels of intervention."

(Many participants indicated that this is the typical status of clients or groups when they finally come under the purview of social service systems.) The final stage is that of *disability*. At this stage damage has occurred. Problems, more often than not, are now of a chronic or continuous nature.

This notion of a continuum of functioning and a natural history of social problems is probably the most important aspect of the conceptual framework. Without it the idea of early intervention, or preventive intervention, would be difficult to conceive. As we will demonstrate later in the document, it will have important implications for the specification of the objectives of social welfare activity.

Obstacles to Functioning. This last dimension simply reflects the three major classes of obstacles or barriers that were described by practitioners. Each one of these basic problem types has already played a major role in shaping the type of interventive methods that have been developed in social welfare (i.e., casework, group work, and community organization). When coupled with the other two dimensions, they will be equally important in shaping the functions and objectives described in this document.

In summary, as we see it now, *a social welfare problem is an alteration in the status of functioning (movement toward dysfunction) of individuals, groups, or institutions, in one or more domains of living, brought about or made worse by any one of several obstacles to optimum functioning.* Futhermore, these problems rarely occur in isolation or in just one domain. For example, deficiencies in education generally result in occupational vulnerability. This vulnerability, when it reaches crisis (unemployment), will lead to crises in financial resources and housing. Eventually the integrity of family life is threatened and this has implications for the physical and mental well-being of the family and ultimately the community.

Finally, although many crises are brought about by unexpected catastrophes, there is also a potential for interrupting this chain of events (or natural history) if the proper pattern of utilization of workers is developed.

Objectives and Functions of Social Welfare

Focusing on the taxonomy from the previous section, we would like to speculate on the major points of intervention for the field of social welfare. A summary of those social welfare objectives are listed and described below. We have tried to define these objectives broadly enough so that they will encompass all relevant areas and, at the same time, make them specific enough so that they will suggest the strategies and tasks that would be needed to accomplish them. We have derived nine major objectives to social welfare activity. They are defined as follows:

1. *Detection*—The primary objective is to identify the individuals or groups who are experiencing difficulty (at crisis) or who are in danger of becoming vulnerable (at risk). A further objective is to detect and identify conditions in the environment that are contributing to the problems or are raising the level of risk;

2. *Linkage or connection*—The primary objective is to steer people toward the existing services which can be of benefit to them. Its primary focus is on enabling people (clients/groups) to utilize the system and to negotiate its pathways. A further objective is to link elements of the service system with one another. The essential quality of this objective is the physical hookup of the client/group with the source of help and the physical connection of elements of the service system with one another;

3. *Advocacy*—The primary objective is to fight for the rights and dignity of people in need of help. The key assumption is that there will be instances where practices, regulations, and general conditions will prevent individuals from receiving services, from using resources, or from obtaining help. This includes the notion of fighting for services on behalf of a single client and the notion of fighting for changes in laws, regulations, etc., on behalf of a whole class of persons or segment of the society. Therefore, advocacy aims at removing the obstacles or barriers that prevent people from exercising their rights or receiving the benefits and using the resources they need;

4. *Mobilization*—The primary objective is to assemble and energize existing groups, resources, organizations, and structures, or to create new groups, organizations, or resources, and bring them to bear to deal with problems that exist or to prevent problems from developing. Its principal focus is on available or existing institutions, organizations, and resources within the community;

5. *Instruction–Education*—We are using these in the sense of objectives rather than methods. The primary objectives are to convey and impart information and knowledge and to develop various kinds of skills;

6. *Behavior change and modification*—This is a broad one. Its primary objective is to bring about change in the behavior patterns, habits, and perceptions of individuals or groups. The key assumption is that problems may be alleviated or crises may be prevented by modifying, adding, or extinguishing discrete bits of behavior, by increasing insights, or by changing the values and perceptions of clients, client groups, and organizations;

7. *Information processing*—This is an often ignored objective within social welfare. Its primary focus is the collection, classification, and analysis of data generated within the social welfare environment. Its contents would include data about the client, the community, and the institution;

8. *Administration*—Again, we are using the term as an objective rather than a method. The principal focus here is the management of a facility, an organization, a program, or a service unit;

9. *Continuing care*—The primary objective is to provide for persons who need ongoing support or care on an extended and continuing basis. The key assumption is that there will be individuals who will require constant surveillance or monitoring or who will need continuing support and services (for example, financial assistance, twenty-four-hour care), perhaps in an institutional setting or on an outpatient basis.

For us the nine concepts are the "centers of gravity" of social welfare. They are the primary sets of objectives that came into being by virtue of the problems and needs discussed by the participants. It is significant to note that the principal focus in their definition is on objectives, not methods or tools. They are, to paraphrase Kadushin (1965), "goal-oriented" and not "process-oriented" concepts.

Clustering Work Activity

As we considered the many possible ways in which the work in the social welfare field might be organized into jobs, it became apparent that there is only a limited number of options. Work can be grouped according to:

1. *The target*—Here we are referring to the object which is acted upon by the worker. This object will have attributes or properties that can have a direct influence on what is done and who does it. When we speak of such characteristics as types of client needs and problems, lack of resources or skills, size of groups, community problems or deficits, client vulnerabilities, and people at risk, we are using *target-oriented* concepts and we are focusing on the properties of the individuals, groups, social structures, and policies on which we operate. Finestone's (unpublished) "case unit of differentiation" and Richan's (1961) "client vulnerability" concept fall into this category;

2. *The objectives*—As we have seen earlier, the objectives of the work—the goals it is seeking to accomplish—will also be an important factor in determining the way in which tasks are grouped together. Since we have already described these objectives, we will not repeat them here;

3. *The worker*—We refer to the individual who carries out the social welfare activity. The worker brings to the work activity a variety of attributes and characteristics which will have a real bearing on the ways in which the work gets done. When we talk about professions, education levels, years of experience, professional standards, skills, and abilities, we are using *worker-oriented* concepts and are talking about aspects of the people who carry out the work activity of social welfare;

4. *The work activity*—Here we are referring to the work itself—the things that workers do in social welfare. The dimensions and attributes which underlie the activities, determine the relationships between them, and influence their clustering will have profound effect on the configurations we design and the assignments we give to workers. When we talk about such concepts as tasks, task clusters, work functions, and methods, and when we use terms like "difficulty," "complexity," "work sequence," "repetitiveness," and "discretion," we are giving recognition to the fact that there are *work-oriented* variables that must be taken into account. Again, the literature contains examples of these variables being used as organizing concepts. Richan's (1961) "degree

of task complexity," Finestone's (unpublished) "task unit of differentiation," and Fine's (1955) "levels of worker functions" are examples of work-oriented variables;

5. *The work setting*—Here we are talking about attributes and characteristics of the work environments in which social welfare activities are carried out. We are referring to factors related to the logistics of the agencies, the organizations, and the institutions within which people are employed. Thus, when we speak of types of supervision, programs, kinds of service units, agency charters, and personnel systems, we are giving recognition to the fact that these *setting-oriented* variables have had an impact on the organization of work activity.

It appears that the natural propensity of social welfare agencies and systems is to choose one of the latter three of these options as the major organizing focus for jobs. Yet these are the rationales that may be least sensitive to the needs of the clients they are supposed to serve in meeting the basic objectives of their programs. Rather they are the rationales most sensitive to the "system" and to the status of the professions. While there is no doubt that there will always be a need to establish some jobs on the basis of these three rationales (i.e., workers, work activity, and settings), we strongly recommend that they be given low priority in grouping the work of an agency into jobs.

As we consider the primary need of clients or families for a single person whom they can trust to help them through the maze of agencies and specialists and to be their personal agent for all of their needs, we believe that *the primary focus for jobs in social welfare must be on the target person or group.* With any other focus the poor, the weak, the sick, the disabled, and the distressed simply will not find fulfillment of their basic human need for personal concern for the totality of their problem.

This is the basic notion of the *generalist*: the person who plays whatever roles and does whatever activities are necessary for his client at the time the client needs them. His primary assignment or concern is the client, not specific tasks or techniques.

Because the notion of objective is one of the possible rationales that we identified as closely related to the program goals, we recommend that *objectives be*

the second priority of focus for organizing the work of social welfare into jobs. That is, if the job cannot be focused entirely on clients or families for all of their needs, we should at least keep it focused on filling some combination of objectives or goals that the agency feels are appropriate to its mission. We feel strongly that individual jobs should not be made up from single objectives. This tends too strongly in the direction of specialization and again fragments services to clients. The ideal combination would be the blending of several objectives to provide the most comprehensive service to clients and the most satisfying jobs. In this sense, it closely resembles the notion of the "episode of service" developed by Barker and Briggs (1965).

Levels of Work

Our social welfare jobs can be characterized as consisting of tasks that will vary simultaneously in terms of objectives and levels. For us, *level of work* is a multidimensional concept. Tasks differ in terms of level as a function of three important intrinsic characteristics:

1. Complexity of the problem being dealt with by worker,

2. Difficulty of the task (in terms of technical skills and knowledge),

3. Risk (in terms of vulnerability of the client) if the work is poorly performed.

In the social welfare field, the great majority of jobs that workers [will] have will be those that deal primarily with "people" or "data" dimensions. In the people-oriented (or clinical) jobs, a relatively heuristic system for describing levels has been proposed by Levine and Lipscomb (1966). Their "levels of intervention" come closest to characterizing what we mean when we use the term work levels associated with the objectives that relate primarily to these people-oriented functions. Other jobs will center around data-oriented goals and objectives. In these instances, Fine's (1955) "levels of worker functions" (associated with "data") lend themselves very nicely to the task of characterizing work of differing levels of complexity. Still other jobs will involve objectives that require work with both data and people. To describe work levels in these instances, an integrative notion combining the Levine-Lipscomb, and Fine concepts will have to be used.

Given these notions we would propose that a fruitful characterization of social welfare activity would be a depiction in terms of objectives and levels. . . . Any given job, existing or proposed, can thus be depicted as consisting of a cluster of tasks. This cluster of tasks may be narrow or broad in terms of both objectives and levels (complexity-difficulty-risk) at which the worker is operating. This variability is what the job descriptions or job specifications must capture. If the cluster is narrow (in terms of objectives), the job becomes that of a specialist; if there is great spread, we are describing the work functions of a generalist.

We have intentionally avoided a detailed listing or illustrations of specific work activities at each level. The inclusion of this kind of detailed material would have resulted in the staff preparing preliminary job descriptions rather than guidelines around which such descriptions should be written. It is the task of each agency to carry out this activity in accordance with its own policies and mandates. We would, in summary, make the following general recommendations:

1. Jobs should be oriented around the needs of the client or the target group;

2. Whenever possible jobs should be centered on objectives rather than methods;

3. Job boundaries, for any type of worker, should be made as broad as possible (in terms of objectives and levels), thus providing for a variety of experience and personal growth;

4. Skill requirements rather than educational requirements should be emphasized.

APPLICATIONS: PRACTICE ROLES

As we move from a theoretical framework describing the work of the field of social welfare to the practical applications of the framework for agencies, we must be more concerned with the workers and how they will function and relate to each other and to their clients and less concerned with the work itself. It is analogous to describing the functions of a musician rather than the concepts of music theory.

The Generalist

In the course of our discussions with social welfare experts, we have repeatedly heard that the client

in distress or need is already at the mercy of too many specialists and agencies. Especially in complex urban areas, the client and his family are shunted from specialist to specialist and agency to agency, each with its different policies, procedures, and eligibility limits. The client—usually a person in distress and with limited abilities—finds himself confused by the maze, intimidated by the specialists' jargon and manner, and rebuffed by the system's rules and regulations. What poor people and people in distress need is not more specialists, or even worse, a proliferation of subspecialists, but a single person whom they can trust and through whom they can relate to all of the specialists and agencies.

The client needs a person like himself who talks his language, understands his culture, and can be his agent to help him meet his needs. Social scientists have long told us that the poor, the immigrant, the aged, and the ill have dealt with official society on a highly personal basis. They consulted the neighborhood grocer, the precinct captain, a neighbor or friend with some special talent in dealing with officialdom. Today this person-to-person need is as great as ever, but our social structure has become more complex and impersonal so that people feel more frustrated and isolated than before.

Thus the recommendation that the *highest priority for focusing the activities of social welfare workers be the target person or group* will provide a personal agent to meet this basic human need. In social welfare we have models of this concept in probation and parole workers. Whenever possible this kind of generalist, client-oriented focus should be built into worker jobs and assignments.

Roles

We recognize that in many agencies or institutions it may not be possible to assign workers to single clients to meet all of their needs. This may be because of distance or because of limits to a scope of the agency's responsibility. In this case the recommendation is made that the *second level of priority of focus be objectives.*

Thus we begin to speak of *roles,* by which we mean a cluster of alternative activities that are performed toward a common objective. The roles we have identified are generally the worker-related terms that correspond to the objectives presented earlier. Thus:

Objective	Role
Linkage	Broker
Advocacy	Advocate
Instruction	Teacher

Obviously the following roles might further be expanded into a greater number of roles, or they might be condensed into fewer:

1. *Outreach Worker*—implies an active reaching out into the community to detect people with problems and help them to find help and to follow up to assure that they continue toward as full as possible a fulfillment of their needs;

2. *Broker*—involves helping a person or family get to the needed services. It includes assessing the situation, knowing the alternative resources, preparing and counseling the person, contacting the appropriate service, and assuring that the client gets to it and is served;

3. *Advocate*—has two major aspects:

   a. Pleading and fighting for services for a single client whom the service system would otherwise reject (regulations, policies, practices, etc.);

   b. Pleading or fighting for changes in laws, rules, regulations, policies, practices, etc., for *all* clients who would otherwise be rejected;

4. *Evaluator*—involves gathering information, assessing client or community problems, weighing alternatives and priorities, and making decisions for action;

5. *Teacher*—includes a range of teaching from simple teaching (i.e., how to dress, how to plan a meal) to teaching courses in budget or home management, to teaching in staff development programs; that is, teaching [staff developers] aims to increase peoples' knowledge and skills;

6. *Behavior Changer*—includes a range of activities directed to changing peoples' behavior rather precisely. Among them are simple coaching, counseling, behavior modification, and psychotherapy;

7. *Mobilizer*—involves working to develop new facilities, resources, and programs or to make them available to persons who are not being served;

8. *Consultant*—involves working with other persons or agencies to help them increase their skills and to help them in solving their clients' social welfare problems;

9. *Community Planner*—involves participating and assisting in planning of neighborhood groups, agencies, community agencies, or governments in the development of community programs to assure that the human service needs of the community are represented and met to the greatest extent feasible;

10. *Care Giver*—involves giving supportive services to people who are not able to fully resolve their problems and meet their own needs, such as supportive counseling, fiscal support, protective services, day care, twenty-four-hour care;

11. *Data Manager*—includes all kinds of data gathering, tabulating, analysis, and synthesis for making decisions and taking action. It ranges from simple case data gathering, through preparing statistical reports of program activities, to evaluation and sophisticated research;

12. *Administrator*—includes all of the activities directed toward planning and carrying out a program such as planning, personnel, budgeting and fiscal operation, supervising, directing, and controlling.

It must be made clear that these roles are only the components of jobs. Jobs for individual workers will be some blend of these roles. Very seldom should a job be made up of a single role. This is tending too much in the direction of specialization.

The rationale for grouping roles into single jobs will depend to some degree on client needs and to some degree on agency goals. Thus an agency concerned with services to individual clients would group functional roles (broker, advocate, teacher, behavior changer) having to do with individuals, while an agency that serves neighborhoods or communities would more likely group the roles having to do with communities (mobilizer, community planner, administrator, data manager) into single jobs. . . .

CONCLUSIONS

The addition of new kinds of workers to any organization is always difficult and complicated. It makes ripples that affect many parts of the system—existing workers, personnel, financing, tables of organization, etc. In the field of social welfare we must also consider the effects on the professions, on the professional schools, and on the organizations themselves. We must consider the total manpower system, not just single organizations.

We must also be aware that introducing the notion of the generalist worker at the entry levels rather than as an assistant to a specialist will be especially upsetting, particularly to institutions such as mental hospitals that have been organized according to professional specialties.

In addition there will be special problems in introducing new workers into the field of social welfare, since the basic goals and objectives of the field, which have never been well defined, seem to be in substantial transition. We seem to be moving from notions of public assistance to the guaranteed annual income; from notions of punishment to rehabilitation in corrections; from notions of crisis intervention to social system intervention; from treatment to prevention; etc. Until these basic goals of social welfare are better defined, we can expect many persons in our agencies to want to stay with traditional personnel patterns. At the same time, the agencies that can redefine their goals most clearly may find that the changeover period offers a special opportunity to redefine worker roles to introduce new types of workers.

APPENDIX 6-A

Taxonomy of Problem Areas

Health

Functions	Obstacles
Prevention	Lack of access (inaccessibility)
	Location
Detection	Transportation
Mental illness	
Infectious diseases	Lack of Availability
Degenerative illnesses	Quantity
Chronic illness	Facilities
Acute illness	Personnel
	Quality
Maintenance of good health	Range-diversity-variety
Treatment	Lack of ability to pay or purchase
Rehabilitation	
(restorative functions)	Lack of knowledge and information
	About illness
Care	About resources
	Lack of Motivation
	Opposition to values and beliefs
	Stigma
	Cultural bias
	Religious scruples
	Restrictive laws and regulations
	Restrictive policies and practices
	Environmental deficiencies
	Garbage, sewage
	Rats, pests, vermin

Taxonomy of Problem Areas (continued)

Education

Functions	Obstacles
Basic literacy (reading, writing)	Lack of access (inaccessibility)
	Location
Preparation for higher education (content)	Transportation
	Personal (situational) obstacles, i.e., child must stay home and babysit
Family and social living skills	
	Lack of availability
"Hidden" curriculum (behavioral maturity, adaptive skills)	Quantity
	Facilities
	Programs-curricula
Extended, continuing education	Personnel
Avocational	Quality
Leisure time	Irrelevant curricula
Hobbies	Personnel
Retirement	Improper training
	Insensitivity
	Lack of adaptive skills
	Work habits
	Conformity-discipline
	Grooming, cosmetics
	Lack of physical necessities
	Diet, nutrition
	Sleep
	Clothing
	Incongruent or competing values
	Destruction of motivation
	Costs
	Restrictive laws and regulations
	Restrictive policies and practices

Taxonomy of Problem Areas (continued)

Employment

Functions	Obstacles
Securing employment	Lack of access (inaccessibility)
Retaining employment	Location
Conditions and characteristics of work	Transportation
Working environment (light, heat, smell, dirt, risk)	Personal obstacle, i.e., need for child care during working hours
Job characteristics	Lack of availability
Security	Quantity
Status	Diversity
Meaningfulness	Lack of information (about job opportunities)
Compensation	Negative characteristics inherent in jobs
Full employment	Lack of basic educational skills
Advancement	Lack of specific job skills
	Lack of adaptive skills
	Grooming
	Discipline-conformity
	Personal habits (punctuality)
	Lack of health and stamina
	Personal problems
	Transitory
	Chronic
	Restrictive policies and practices
	Race, creed, color
	Disability
	High risks

Taxonomy of Problem Areas (continued)

Integrity of the Family

Functions	Obstacles
Husband-wife relationships	Composition of family
Parent-child (child-parent) relationships	Ratio of parents-children age span (elderly-young) sex
Sibling relationships	Number of members
Total intrafamily relationships	Role conflicts
Extended family relationships (aunts, uncles, grandparents, etc.)	Authority sources Breadwinners
Autonomy and individuality of family members	Psychological and cultural "drift"
	Cultural barriers
	Achievement changes
	Education shifts
	Disability or incapacity of member(s)
	Parent(s)
	Breadwinner
	Child (children)
	Elderly member
	Prolonged separation (of unit); prolonged absence (of member[s])
	Employment
	Incarceration
	Desertion
	Military service
	Termination of family unit
	Orphans
	Children grown
	Widows, widowers
	Lack of adequate resources and necessities
	Money
	Food
	Shelter
	Clothing

Taxonomy of Problem Areas (continued)

Integrity of the Family

Functions	Obstacles
	Disruptive behavior on part of family member 　Acting-out 　Alcoholism 　Emotional instability

Money

Functions	Obstacles
Provision or securing of income Retaining or maintaining income Management of finances	Lack of access (inaccessibility) 　Inability to get credit 　Inability to get loans, financing Lack of employment Lack of availability 　Poor money market 　Lack of funds in general welfare and financial assistance programs Lack of information 　Credit 　Investments, savings 　Budgeting 　Shrewd purchasing (bulk purchasing, comparative shopping) 　Sources of money Loss of buying power 　Fixed income (pensions, Social Security) 　Inflation 　Tax, fee inequities Vulnerability to fraudulent schemes 　Home improvement 　Used cars Lack of motivation vis-à-vis saving, investments Incongruent values, beliefs Laws, regulations Policies, practices 　Garnishment

Taxonomy of Problem Areas (continued)

Integrity of the Community-Neighborhood

Functions	Obstacles
Mobility (accessability, transportation)	Lack of access
	Transportation
Protection and safety	Location
(physical, i.e., fire, police, legal, public health, psychological, social)	Barriers or obstacles
	Inability to negotiate
Shelter (public–low-cost, institutions, detention)	Linkage of institutions, government, etc.
Growth and development	Lack of availability
(individual and community)	Quantity
Cultural	Facilities
Educational	Manpower
Psychological	Quality
Economic	Administration deficiencies
Enjoyment	Planning
Recreation (organized or individual)	Coordination
	Enforcement
	Delivery
Esthetic experience	Evaluation of impact
Parks	Diversity
Architecture	Cost
Permanence and stability	Inability to raise funds
	Inability to use available funds
Maintenance	
Public works	

REFERENCES

Barker, R. L., and T. L. Briggs.
1966 *Trends in the Utilization of Social Work Personnel: An Evaluation Research of the Literature.* Research Report Number 2. New York: National Association of Social Workers.

———.
1968 *Differential Use of Social Work Manpower.* New York: National Association of Social Workers.

Cudaback, Dorothea.
1967 Preliminary Report of Welfare Service Aide Project. School of Social Welfare, University of California.

Department of Health, Education, and Welfare.
1965 *Closing the Gap in Social Work Manpower.* Washington, D.C.

Elston, Patricia.
1967 *New Careers in Welfare for Professionals and Nonprofessionals.* New York: New Careers Development Center, New York University.

Fine, S. A.
1967 *Guidelines for the Design of New Careers.* Staff Paper of the Upjohn Institute for Employment Research. Washington, D.C.

———.
1955 "A Structure of Worker Functions." *Personnel and Guidance Journal*, October.

Finestone, S.

Unpublished "Differential Utilization of Casework Staff in Public Welfare: Major Dimensions." Background memorandum.

Harrington, M.

1962 *The Other America*. Baltimore, Md.: Penguin Books.

———.

1970 "The Other America Revisited." *The Establishment and All That*. Santa Barbara, Calif.: Center for the Study of Democratic Institutions.

Kadushin, Alfred.

1965 "Introduction of New Orientations in Child Welfare Research." *The Known and Unknown in Child Welfare Research: An Appraisal*, Miriam Norris and Barbara Wallace, eds. New York: Child Welfare League of America and National Association of Social Workers.

Kattan, Joseph.

1970 "New Breed of Workers in Human Services Occupations." Unpublished research paper (mimeo). Ann Arbor: School of Social Work, University of Michigan.

Levine, D. L., and E. B. Lipscomb.

1966 "Toward an Epidemiological Framework for Social Work Practice: An Application to the Field of Aging." *Gerontologist* 6, no. 3 (Part II).

Monahan, F. T.

1967 "Manpower for Treatment and Prevention in an Era of Abundance." Paper presented at the National Association of Social Workers Southern Regional Institute, Birmingham, Alabama, June.

Reiff, R., and F. Riessman.

1964 *The Indigenous Nonprofessional: A Strategy of Change in Community Action and Community Mental Health Programs*. Research Report Number 3. New York: National Institute of Labor Education, November.

Richan, W. C.

1961 "A Theoretical Scheme for Determining Roles of Professional and Nonprofessional Personnel." *Social Work* 4, no. 4 (October): 22–28.

Schwartz, E. E.

1966 "A Strategy of Research on Manpower Problems." *Manpower in Social Welfare*. New York: National Association of Social Workers.

Szaloczi, Jean K.

1967 "Some Conceptual Issues in Social Welfare Manpower Statistics." *Welfare in Review* (March).

Taylor, F. W.

1911 *Shop Management*. New York: Harper & Brothers.

Teare, R. J.

1968 *Working Paper: Symposium on Career Development for Baccalaureate Level Workers in Social Welfare*. Atlanta, Ga.: Southern Regional Education Board, August.

———.

(In preparation.) "The Developmental Approach to Program Planning and Career Design in the Human Services Occupations."

Wiley, Wretha.

1967 *An Illustration of the Functional Approach to Designing Jobs and Careers*. New York: New Careers Development Center, New York University.

Wittman, M.

1965 "The Implications of Social Welfare Manpower Needs in 1975 for Professional Education and Social Planning." *Social Service Review* 39 (December): 459–67.

THE PLACE OF SOCIAL WORK IN THE HUMAN SERVICES

Robert Morris

Many of the forces that will shape the role of social work in the human services in ten years cannot be clearly defined, nor can their effect be predicted with certainty. Some assumptions are made about more general phenomena, however: (1) there will be no major wars, (2) the economy will continue to move by fits and starts, . . . (3) the population will continue to grow at the rate of approximately .8–1.0 percent per year, even though the long-term trend is for slower growth, (4) there will be no major redistribution of income or wealth in the population, and (5) the base of income for the lowest 10 percent of the population will rise slightly, but the gap between that group and higher income groups will remain the same or will increase. Further, minority groups will continue their slow penetration of professional, technical, and higher-income activities without producing a dramatic redistribution or universal equalization of income or position.

The people's uncertainty about the value of scientific changes and skepticism about the reliability and trustworthiness of government will make it difficult to develop any grand national plan or significantly reduce their level of anxiety. Moreover, national values and attitudes will remain about what they are today: a high premium will still be placed on the private acquisition of material goods and people will continue to try to satisfy their private desires with little regard to the adverse effect this may have on the common well-being. Generous, idealistic movements will persist, but society will not be radically altered.

DEFINITIONS

And what will be the place of social work in the human services in ten years? This question contains ambiguity because social workers have not agreed on the exact meaning of the terms "social work" or "human services." Thus before continuing his discussion, the author proposes the following definitions, which should be kept in mind when reading this article.

Social work refers to all the interpersonal and social tasks and the roles performed by persons holding either a bachelor's or master's degree in social work. Not all persons who happen to be employed in social welfare activities are social workers.

The term *human services* covers several subsystems of the social welfare system that employ social workers in either a dominant or peripheral position. These subsystems include health and medical care, law and justice, education, income security, and the reinforcement of personal growth and family cohesiveness (family services, character-building, and the like).

The *place* of social work refers to the relative statuses of social workers in these human service subsystems—that is, how important they are to the subsystems.

The author recognizes that these definitions leave the boundaries of the subject overlarge. In many states the human services, thus interpreted, include as much as 50 percent of state government employees and account for between 50 and 65 percent of state governmental expenditures. The human services have room for the most varied activities: protecting society against destructive members; punishing deviance according to current mores; safeguarding and sheltering the helpless and vulnerable, be they children, the disabled, or the aged; correcting economic inequities through income maintenance programs; and reinforcing social and personal strength or integrity through a variety of family or community services. And social workers must find their place in relation to the variety of other professional, quasi-professional, and nonprofessional persons also involved in similar activities—physicians, nurses, teachers, psychologists, college graduates in the humanities, and paraprofessional personnel without college degrees.

This article will consider three perspectives from which to anticipate the shape of social work in the 1980s. And it does so within the larger context of national change, which is also ambiguous. The three perspectives are: (1) an estimate of the forces for change and the forces against change, (2) the roles to be filled in the various human service subsystems, and (3) the functions of the professional practices to be performed in the systems.

FORCES FOR CHANGE

The two most significant forces in the direction of change seem to be demographic trends and the erosion of public confidence in the national government.

Demography. Although no significant alteration in population growth is expected in so short a time, the effect of population shifts in the past twenty years will begin to impose an inexorable force for change. Since World War II the proportion of persons in the work force aged 25–45 has decreased from 30.1 percent to 23.7 percent and of those aged 45–65 has increased from 18.8 to 20.5 percent. During the same period persons aged 65 and older have grown from 6.8 percent to 9.9 percent, while those over age 75 have increased at the rate of nearly 50 percent.[1]

In addition, the number of severely disabled persons continues to grow, although the percentage increase has not been dramatic. In this group are children born of genetic anomalies as well as those with a variety of birth defects, including mental retardation and the whole range of difficulties that comprise the term "developmental disabilities." Medical and technical means permit the survival of an infinitely diverse group of persons, young and old alike, with disabilities severe enough to require not only therapeutic intervention but continuing personal care from others. For example, the survival rate of young adults with spinal cord injury has grown from 10 percent to 84 percent since 1946.[2] The startling increase in survival beyond age 75, when the demand for both medical and personal-care services is four times the average demand of the population, has and will continue to enlarge the group of disabled confronting society.

Medical technologies, such as renal dialysis, suddenly make possible the long-term survival of thousands of persons each year with kidney diseases. At the same time, the tide of revulsion against warehousing large numbers of law violators, addicts, and

mentally ill persons in vast institutions will continue to swell. Taken together these factors will force attention to the alternatives of institutional versus community care and the balance to be struck between short-term therapeutic intervention and the long-term requirements of maintenance.

Public Confidence. A second major force for change is the public's shifting and eroding confidence in the national government as an instrument with which to shape specific remedies for distressing human situations. Although the national government still is recognized as the primary financial resource, a marked decline in confidence is evident about the national government's ability to organize programs that will satisfy both the recipient of service and the voting citizen.

Although some citizens and even political figures hope that the problems can just be ignored, most are trying to find some approach that will join the collection of taxes at the national level with decision making at the local level about how the tax moneys are to be spent. Sometimes the hope is expressed that the capacity of local governments to deal with the citizens' social needs will be revived; more often it is a nostalgic wish that voluntary associations will be restored with enough strength to assume social responsibilities, even if this must be done with extensive tax support.

These two forces (demography and the erosion of public confidence) create a tension that will continue into the 1980s—a groping for ways to shape life, given the prevailing conditions in society. In such an environment, experimentation and the generation of new ideas will be encouraged, although widespread support for any clear course is unlikely to emerge.

FORCES AGAINST CHANGE

Against the forces for change can be posited several forces in the direction of stability and maintenance of the status quo.

Institutionalized Opinions. The professions and the government have institutionalized their opinions, which are therefore frozen and not subject to rapid change. Civil service at all levels embodies a set of practices that argue against a rapid shift in the nature of personnel employed or in their tenure.

In general the adult labor force has been educated and therefore conditioned by old ways of thinking. It adopts new ideas slowly, if not reluctantly. This conservative tendency is reinforced by the fact that key policy- and decisionmakers are likely to be older than the average worker. In addition, civil service regulations, union contracts, and agency personnel practices often link the rewards of promotion and the security of tenure to years of service, which further strengthens the proclivity toward maintaining the status quo.

Social Work Education. Professional training and the standards of professional associations also change slowly. For example, graduate education for social work has had a distinctive character for at least twenty years, and this character has shaped the thinking and activities of virtually all persons now employed. And these social workers are primarily responsible for shaping whatever programs will exist in ten years. If the imprinting of professional education does exist, the influence of the past ten years will govern the shape of practice during the next ten years. The major shift—recognition of the bachelor's degree in social work (BSW)—cannot yet be tested, but it is reasonable to assume that much of the BSW education will draw heavily on the curriculum of the master's degree (MSW) and will rely heavily on persons who received an MSW in the past.

The bias in favor of the MSW will certainly be moderated by persistent efforts to create an educational base that will produce more qualified generic personnel. At the same time the opportunities for experimentation in state and local governments will grow because of pressure to produce better results in services. In addition, there will be stronger and more widespread objections to increases in taxes and governmental spending. These two factors should increase the influence of major specialized service agencies in shaping the staffs they will employ for both specialized and specific positions. The outcome of this war between the efforts of educators to generalize and the tendency of employers to specialize is not easy to predict, but it is likely that there will be an increase in short-term post-BSW training by schools and employers alike, while the MSW programs will experiment with the development of advanced forms of specialized skills. . . .

. . . [I]t is doubtful that the number of direct service personnel will again increase so fast. Rather, cash benefits through social security will grow at a more rapid rate than expenditures for services. In 1970, cash benefits, housing, and education represented at least 80 percent of all governmental social welfare expenditures, and it is unlikely that social services will ever dominate the rest of welfare expenditures.[3] If these forces are operative, as the author believes them to be, then the period of the 1980s is likely to see a redistribution of roles and functions rather than a dramatic alteration in the shape of social work.

Most analyses of professional efforts have been based on the educational qualifications for social work practice rather than on the place of social workers in the major welfare systems. However, the author believes that social work should be examined in the context of the social organization or social structure of which it is a part. If one takes this approach, it is possible to borrow a framework from census studies. Census studies identify employment categories (e.g., professional, technical, and kindred workers), and it should be possible to examine the place of social work according to the proportion of social workers found in these categories in the various human service subsystems.

Social workers are distributed throughout four types of human service subsystems: (1) those that are controlled by social work and in which 75 percent or more of all professional and technical personnel are social workers (voluntary family service agencies and children's programs); (2) those in which social work is recognized as an important ancillary function, but social workers represent only a small proportion of the professional and technical personnel (medical care, mental health services, and income security programs); (3) those in which social workers are found in small numbers and their function is not universally accepted and may be considered peripheral or experimental (school social work and corrections); and (4) private practice.

FAMILY AND CHILD WELFARE

Social work will control only a small sector of the human service system—the subsystem made up of family and child welfare agencies. Although there are no adequate figures on the proportion of the total system devoted to this area of practice, it is clearly minor. In the 1980s, social workers will continue to perform their functions much as they do today. The professional hierarchy will be weighted in favor of employing MSWs, and a limited number of BSWs will be hired as social work aides. The functions performed by these agencies will be as diverse as in the past, but such agencies will continue to be much like those in the 1970s. Self-selected caseloads, small-scale penetration of target populations (accounted for by limited support for such agencies), and reliance on one-to-one relationships or family or small-group therapy will be buttressed by practice that is primarily psychotherapeutic.

However, in the 1980s there will be more experiments to supplement counseling with a variety of more tangible services, often funded under contract with third parties or public purchasers. For example, foster care and the development of small group residences for children displaying serious adjustment problems will more and more be supported by contracts from public agencies. The expansion of homemaker services for the chronically lonely elderly may likewise be paid for through public third-party payments. Day care for children will continue to grow, but it is still moot whether its leadership will be from the profession of education or social work. As of now it seems that social work will concentrate on day care for children with special behavioral problems, while education will lead in general child development programs.

The family and child welfare agencies and their staffs will continue to experiment with trying to reach trouble spots in urban areas—the urban ghettos, the centers of high delinquency rates and high dependency. However, these experiments, given the characteristics just noted, are not expected to lay the foundation for a massive approach so that penetration of the at-risk population will continue to be insignificant.

MENTAL HEALTH

The greatest changes that social work can anticipate in the next ten years will be in the second human service subsystem—agencies in which social work is recognized as an important ancillary function. The mental health subsystem is the one in which social workers are now most firmly embedded. For example, in 1968, 14,427 social work positions were identified in various psychiatric facilities. And 11,000 of over 50,000 members of the National Association of Social Workers were employed in psychiatric settings in 1969.[4] Approximately one-quarter of all full-time professional personnel in community mental health centers were social workers in that year. More social workers will be accepted as administrators of such psychiatric facilities as the shortage of physicians and psychiatrists becomes more pronounced and the demand for administrators grows.

The use of large state hospitals will continue to decline, and treatment will increase in psychiatric wards of acute general hospitals, in community mental health centers, or through community-care treatment that combines chemotherapy and psychotherapy. Greater attention will be given to community living and community care for the mentally ill, with or without treatment, and this will also increase demands on social workers to arrange for facilities for community care, such as halfway houses. Individualized treatment and mobilization of a variety of community resources to buoy up disturbed, mentally ill, or distracted individuals will become increasingly important adjuncts to chemotherapy and psychotherapy. Thus instead of concentrating on rehabilitation, social treatment, and "cure," social workers will be involved more and more in activities designed to help the mentally ill maintain themselves for long periods with their illness or limitations only partially reduced.

Social work will rediscover the close association between the individual psyche and the social environment. It will realize that social vulnerability is as significant as psychic vulnerability and that long-term modification of the living environment is essential. In fact environmental modification will become a key rationale. It is the blend of psychological insight and readiness to take social responsibility for the living arrangements of others that is expected to make social workers more important in maintaining the mental health system.

HEALTH CARE

Health care represents the second major arena for the development of social work. The congressional debate on national health insurance has stimulated a massive reappraisal of the organization of health services. Whatever the outcome of the debate, it is clear that the investment in health services will not decline. Moreover, numerous experiments, both large and small, will be undertaken to reorganize the system for delivering health care and the personnel to provide the care, as well as to bring about slowly an equitable redistribution of health services to the poor, whose social needs complicate their health needs.

The attempt to minimize or control the phase of acute care in hospitals will continue, and this will place an increasing demand on health-based services to move patients from one to another of the various kinds of health facilities (e.g., hospitals, nursing homes, extended care facilities, hospitals for chronic illness, protected environments, and home care) so that the interface between medical services and social welfare services will become more significant. Medical institutions will become dependent on those persons responsible for making appropriate arrangements for transferring to community facilities those patients with acute conditions during periods of convalescence and those with long-continuing disabilities.

The unresolved question facing the health subsystem is this: How much responsibility should health agencies assume in caring for as well as treating persons with long-term conditions? A simple listing of such conditions indicates the scope of this problem: children born with severe genetic or birth defects; degenerative neurological conditions of cerebral palsy, multiple sclerosis, Parkinson's disease, and the like; severe traumatic injury resulting in spinal cord severance or loss of limbs; and the wasting diseases—including cancer—as well as the accumulating burden of long-term conditions of older adults, including hypertension, heart disease, and the crippling form of arthritis.

The position of social workers in the health subsystem will be similar to their position in the mental health subsystem. That is, they will be required to handle the enlarged set of relationships between the intricate network of health services and social services in the community that the long-term conditions require. In addition, they will be called on to manage and coordinate complexes of such services on behalf of individual patients. Although social workers will continue to help physically ill and emotionally disturbed persons face the realities of their health conditions and to use the health care system adequately, they will be expected to assume the much wider responsibilities involved in managing the liaison between health care and social services in the community.

The proposed new requirements of the Joint Commission on Accreditation of Hospitals signal this future role.[5] If they are adopted all hospitals, to be accredited, will be required either to have a social work department of their own or to arrange for appropriate social work services from other sources. Another indication of what is to come is the fact that group health practices and health maintenance organizations are beginning to employ social workers in addition to the usual clinical complement of physicians, nurses, and the like. Numerous proprietary institutions, such as nursing homes, are also starting to hire social workers and to respond to mounting pressures to improve the quality of care by individualizing the treatment of patients.

ROLE IN THE COMMUNITY

Although medical social workers have up to now worked primarily in hospitals, it is likely that with experimentation, they will expand their role in the community to encompass more than doing referrals and acting as liaisons to community agencies. Whether hospital and health facilities will assume responsibility for developing supportive out-of-hospital social work services (such as providing home helps or home health aides) depends on whether health insurance companies will reimburse them for such services. While reimbursement for home health aides is already well established, the current narrow definitions of home health aides may be broadened to include duties not limited to completing treatment of an acute episode of illness. Social work can assume responsibility for these functions if they become part of the health care continuum.

Social workers have the pertinent experience to manage such out-of-hospital and hospital-community services, although public health nurses and nurse's aides also perform these functions in many places. Social workers have no monopoly on this aspect of medical care today, but the demand for such services can be expected to increase in the next decade. And if the profession recognizes this opportunity it can become *the profession* responsible for this dimension of medical care. If social work is recognized as being responsible for such community roles, social workers at both the bachelor's degree and master's degree levels will be in great demand. A recognizable hierarchy based on promotion from one level to the next will develop, encompassing management, social assessment, and provision of both tangible (home help) and intangible (casework) services.

It is likely that in this area social workers will be recognized as the professionals who perform a range of specialized activities for which they will have requisite professional authority to exercise judgment. Today physicians overburdened by their clinical tasks rely on the opinions of social workers but make the final judgment themselves. In the future the social worker's decision about the social conditions appropriate for a patient's discharge from an institution will be comparable to the physician's clinical judgment about the patient's physical condition. The social worker of the future will decide, for instance, whether the available residential, family, and community environment is suitable for a specific patient and will try to provide such an environment if it does not exist.

In addition, social workers might assume authority in determining whether patients are entitled to various social benefits—a function now performed by physicians. For example, they might decide when a patient with a complicated illness is to be judged disabled according to the definition in the Social Security Act or in a specific program for the permanently and totally disabled. In the field of mental health, it is possible that the clinical diagnosis of whether the patient is ready for medical discharge from a mental hospital may be accompanied by the social worker's decision about whether the patient is capable of adapting to society or the community environment is ready to receive him. Such an enlargement of authority as well as responsibility has already occurred in the United Kingdom, where physicians are required to consult social workers in all cases of involuntary commitment to a mental hospital on the grounds that a social worker's judgment about the suitability of an alternative environment is vital.

These expectations for social workers in the health field are buttressed by the extent to which social work has become professionalized in this field. Fifty-five percent of the medical social workers and 12 percent of the psychiatric social workers have had two years of professional education, the definition of a professional until recently.[6] This base of professionals provides an excellent springboard from which the field can be further extended; additional manpower for expanded functions can be provided by professionally trained personnel at both the bachelor's degree and master's degree levels.

INCOME SECURITY PROGRAMS

Income security programs are the bedrock on which the human service system rests, but social work's role in this subsystem, especially in public assistance and social security, has been marginal in the past and probably will be even more so in the future. Although professional social workers constitute a fraction of all public assistance employees, they are frequently supervisors or administrators. Nonetheless, it is difficult to assert with any confidence that

throughout the country the social work profession is in a position to administer the vast public assistance program. Now that the separation of income and social services under the Social Security Act is becoming a reality, social workers in public welfare are likely to become even further removed from the provision of income.

How does one reconcile these facts with the general public's identification of social work with public assistance? The answer, of course, may be found in the use of the term "social worker" to apply to *all* public assistance employees. However, in a 1972 survey of NASW members, only 8.2 percent with a professional education indicated that they were employed in public assistance agencies.[7]

There has been a long-term, steady trend toward the development of a standardized flat-grant system for handling income security, recognized first through the Old Age, Survivors, Disability, and Health Insurance Program, and more recently in the federalization of the adult categories in public assistance. This has been paralleled by attempts to develop Allied Services legislation to deal with social work services for recipients of assistance that are independent of income.[8]

This trend toward a separation of the management of financial security and the provision of services to recipients of assistance is expected to continue. The separation will be confused by the fact that the public tax fund will support only those social services directed primarily to recipients of assistance, although changing regulations of the Department of Health and Human Services permit limited public funds for persons recently on relief or likely to become eligible for relief. Despite the current limitation, this author predicts that by the middle 1980s there will be a network of comprehensive tax-supported social service agencies throughout the United States, as part of state and local governments, that will offer some services directly to clients and not be responsible for income security programs. These agencies will represent a small splintering off of public welfare social services from the antecedent public assistance program, but will have the potential for greater development in the future.

A small group of social workers with advanced degrees will be responsible for administering a large staff with diverse qualifications (BAs and paraprofessionals). It is expected that persons with bachelor's degrees will constitute the majority of personnel, and persons with advanced training will be involved mainly in administration, research, and the development of policy.

The direct-service agencies will be responsible initially for handling cases of persons who are and some who are likely to become eligible for public financial aid. They will eventually carry out many activities previously handled only by voluntary family and children's agencies for nonrecipients of relief. They can be expected to perform the following functions: placing dependent and neglected children in foster homes; attempting to manage predelinquent youths; and providing day-care services for poor families and working mothers, home helps and homemakers, and counseling services for a variety of other public programs, such as those dealing with alcoholics, addicts, the aged, and the severely disabled.

By the 1980s these agencies will still be concerned primarily with rehabilitation, counseling, and the provision of those concrete services such as day care and homemaker services that enable persons with physical or mental handicaps or social disabilities (unmarried mothers with small children) to seek employment and economic independence to the extent of their abilities. When economic independence is not possible, functional independence for the severely handicapped in lieu of institutional placement will emerge as a secondary goal. Functional independence is the ability of a handicapped person to manage the requirements of daily living despite his handicap. Many persons with severe physical handicaps can maintain functional independence with supplemental personal care assistance, while remaining in charge of their life decisions. Recent revisions in the legislation on rehabilitation . . . have provided for just such a development.

It is doubtful that services in this network of agencies will be based solely on the conventional skills of casework or individual counseling. Rather, sensitivity to human beings and assessment of individual needs will be buttressed by responsibility for managing and administering a variety of concrete services (e.g., those previously mentioned) which will constitute the public responsibility for strengthening family life and personal adjustment. The concept of managing or administering social services is used to distinguish this function from the more prevalent idea that professional social workers refer clients to others who provide concrete services. In this case "management" implies that the professional social worker is to be responsible for delivering concrete services, directing a variety of staff workers, deciding who shall be served and when, choosing which services take priority over others, making a budget, and being accountable to the supporting community.

One may ask: Why choose social workers for such a function? The answer is simple: No other profession, except perhaps community nursing, has shown the slightest interest in looking after troubled people day after day by becoming responsible for their basic living conditions. Others may move in a crisis, e.g., law and medicine, but few are prepared to live for long with the unpleasant aspects of living.

A strong basis for such a network already exists in local communities. Departments of public wefare already offer child care services through which neglected children are frequently placed in foster homes by public agency staffs. In addition several departments of public welfare maintain or purchase from private sources a variety of home-health-aide and homemaker services for the disabled. It is likely that there will be different forms of organization throughout the country, but whether programs of child care, day care, foster home, child guardianship, and home help are developed through separate public agencies or become the consolidated function of one comprehensive public social service agency need not obscure the growth of this sector.

THE BRITISH EXPERIENCE

Such a program would represent the beginning in this country of the remarkable chain of events that took place twenty-five years ago in the United Kingdom, when income payments were separated from social services. In the current United Kingdom pattern, which was mandated by Parliament, each local jurisdiction is required to have a local public personal social services department staffed both by qualified social workers and by a large complement of persons providing a variety of concrete services. The department's responsibility is not limited to assistance recipients but is extended to all vulnerable persons in the defined geographic area. In a typical area, perhaps 100,000 to 250,000 persons are served by area teams of social workers who reach out to the community, are up-to-date about the people in their area, and construct means whereby persons in need are brought to the staff's attention. The staff then assesses these persons' needs and orders and manages a complex variety of concrete services available in each jurisdiction. Varying from community to community, these concrete services include some or all of the following: home health services provided for varying periods of time and at various levels of skill; day centers that train persons released from mental hospitals and the severely disabled either in employment or in socialization and that provide retarded children and adults with educational, occupational, and social programs and the elderly with rehabilitation and social activities; foster care and small institutional programs for dependent children; small training institutions for delinquent youths; and day care centers for children.

In the United Kingdom the local department is strong because it is responsible for assessing the needs of individuals, case counseling, and managing a complex of concrete services. It is no longer wholly dependent on services provided or controlled by other independent agencies, but instead controls its own network of tangible services, which does much to enhance the morale and self-confidence of the staff. In many jurisdictions, the department is also able to purchase some supplementary services from willing, cooperating voluntary agencies to fill out the public services. Payment for such services is controlled by judgments made by the staff of the public personal social services department.

It is remarkable how decentralized the United Kingdom program is. Local departments are not required to distribute cash payments. Instead staffs are assessed primarily on their ability to reach out and be receptive to people with a variety of needs. They are responsible for a population in a geographic area, *not* for a caseload screened and sifted by regulations that are barriers to eligibility. Responsibility decentralized to small area teams has encouraged an atmosphere of helpfulness rather than rejection, since meeting the needs of the population is the criterion of success. Decentralization is extended to include case authority, which means that area teams are free to determine how to use their personnel and budgetary resources according to the unique needs of their immediate population as long as they stay within the broad policy guidelines. This situation is in sharp contrast to that in the United States, where the national government and state governments superimpose their detailed standards on local jurisdictions.

It has also been possible in the United Kingdom to use only a small cadre of professional social workers (perhaps 10 to 15 percent in any department). The remaining personnel comprise persons with varied backgrounds who are chosen because of their interest in helping people and their personal qualifications rather than their educational credentials. Although it is expected that in time a common educational base will be established for this diverse group, at present it has been possible to launch a varied program without awaiting the development of standardized training for personnel. As a result young people with only a high school diploma or some college education, college graduates with concentrations in the social sciences but no social work training, mature adults dissatisfied with routine tasks who want to help other human beings, and middle-aged housewives seeking to supplement their income through part-time work are blended together around the core of a trained cadre of social workers.

Although the experience in the United Kingdom cannot be simulated exactly in the United States, it does seem reasonable to expect that there will be a practical evolution in this country by which local public social services will be separated from the provision of income, that it will start in the 1980s and that it might well evolve along the same lines over a longer time span as it has in England.

WORK IN OTHER SYSTEMS

Social workers will continue to be employed in a variety of other human welfare systems such as corrections, probation, and the public schools. Although they will perform important functions, they are not expected to assume significant positions in these systems for a variety of reasons. Schools are heavily influenced by the training that teachers receive, and the philosophy and methodology of the corrections system differ from those of social work too much; these factors will discourage widespread employment of social workers in positions of primary responsibility.

What about the private practice of social work? In 1967, 8 to 10 percent of practicing social workers were engaged in private practice at least on a part-time basis.[9] However, private practice is expected to expand and to become more attractive to those persons with exceptional skills and interests in psychotherapy and social counseling. Most private practice has been some form of therapy, and the almost inexhaustible American demand for such counseling indicates that social workers will have an increased opportunity to practice, along with psychologists, psychiatrists, rehabilitation counselors, and the like.

Private practice is likely to fit into the mainstream of the development of social work in much the same way as the private practice of medicine has fitted into the growth of the institutionalized practice of medicine and such phenomena as third-party payments and hospital systems.

The most important functions of social work in the human services have already been discussed. There are two other parallel functions that will be significant in the 1980s—research and social action, and planning.

RESEARCH

Advanced social work training at the doctoral level will slowly produce a sufficient cadre of systematic investigators to make possible the application of modern scientific approaches to human resources. Until recently basic research into the functioning of the social service systems and the human services has been left to researchers from the fields of sociology, economics, and public administration. Social work researchers have been concerned mainly with practice with individuals or groups. By the mid-1980s, doctoral-level and master's-level training in social planning and research should have proceeded far enough for trained investigators to make useful contributions to the assessment of the fundamental operations of the major human service systems; their focus will be on improving the responsiveness of these systems to human needs as well as trying to validate social work case methods.

Research into the effectiveness and suitability of social work methods will become more critical. It will lead to the development of more effective forms of practice by all social workers. Such research should finally bridge the gap that has separated work with individuals from an assessment of the ability of service systems to meet the needs of large populations of vulnerable persons. This research capability will be carried forward by small numbers of persons employed in key positions in major human service systems. It will not become exclusive to social work, but rather will be shared by researchers drawn from other fields. The major contribution of the social work researcher will be to create a balance between individual needs and a rigorous, critical evaluation of institutional approaches to meeting those needs, whether through the practice of individuals or through the structuring of service delivery systems.

SOCIAL ACTION AND PLANNING

The traditional social action and social planning functions of social work are not expected to change materially in the next ten years. The demand for coordination and linkage among a variety of services will continue, and the function of managing resources in various systems, such as income maintenance, medical care, and mental health, will continue to be supplemented by formalized mechanisms devoted to various types of coordination and planning. Examples of such mechanisms may already be found in comprehensive health planning agencies, agencies for the aged, community mental health centers, and in the attempts to improve general-purpose governmental planning at state, local-regional, and metropolitan levels.

United Way of America will continue to operate, but this association probably will concentrate more and more on the links between voluntary agencies and will represent the interests of voluntary agencies in various contractual relationships with governmental bodies seeking to purchase services mandated by law. At the same time a variety of governmental coordinating mechanisms will expand to join together public organizations. These will draw on the traditional social work skills of coordination and community organization, notably in state and area planning agencies for mental health, comprehensive health planning, work with the aging, and the like.

Other forms of social action will provide scattered opportunities for employment. Organizations representing minority groups and some community action organizations will continue to provide career opportunities that will probably be dominated by bachelor's degree social workers and a few committed social workers with master's and doctoral degrees. However, employment opportunities will be as limited as they are now. Workers in this area of social action will continue to act as public consciences, to bear witness against injustice and inequality, and to prod society to move faster toward improving conditions.

It is doubtful whether most social workers will have an opportunity to be paid to engage in what has been conventionally defined as social action. However, it is possible and even expected that most professional membership associations will find their most acceptable function to be the expression of the social conscience of its members. However, the conversion of the membership associations of social workers primarily into social action bodies remains fraught with uncertainty. In the past social workers at the master's and doctoral levels first acquired a sufficient professional security and then sought additional outlets for their concern with social injustice. They asked their membership associations to engage in the expression of such concern in various ways. However, bachelor's degree social workers, who have not as yet been overwhelmingly attracted to professional or association membership, may require primary attention to their economic and status positions in a changing employment and professional scene. It is not clear whether any one national organization can adequately represent the status needs of this much larger base of the profession and simultaneously give attention to social action and legislative change. It can be expected that the next ten years will see a competition among professional organizations comparable to that which took place in the late 1930s and early 1940s among such associations as the American Association of Social Workers, the American Association of Medical Social Workers, and the American Association of Psychiatric Social Workers on the one hand and the various unions representing the economic interests of employees in public and private agencies on the other hand.

CONCLUSION

In the 1980s social work will continue to find its greatest strength in using the interests, concerns, and skills of its members, at both the bachelor's and master's degree levels, to come to grips with the problems of living encountered by the disadvantaged. The uncertainties of life will broaden the definition of "disadvantaged populations," and the interpersonal skills of social workers will be much expanded. Regardless of economic class, the problems of addiction, injury, mental and physical illness, retirement, family disorganization, and other hazards of daily living will continue to exist and perhaps even increase. These conditions will stimulate the demand for social work skills.

The strength of the profession will continue to be its readiness to go into the homes of the persons it serves and to look clearly at the problems it confronts. However, in the future the profession will be stronger in its readiness to combine assessment and counseling with management of other more tangible services. It is expected that control of new resources

will gravitate to social work, and the effective management of such resources will become the hallmark of the profession, humanized as it will be by insight into human needs to moderate the impersonality of large-scale programs.

None of this can be accomplished with the current focus of professional social work education. However, it is expected that schools of social work will respond to the predicted developments by enriching their basic curricula. BSW programs will supplement their courses in the concepts of human development with training in techniques of providing a variety of tangible services, such as home health, homemaker, home help, day care, and institutional or residential care. On the MSW and Ph.D. levels there will be increased attention to the management side of administering such services and to complexities of team leadership, especially when such leadership includes administrative responsibilities. Advanced training in interpersonal treatment skills will be offered by some schools of social work, but will also be sought by social workers in other educational institutions as well. New patterns of study and work—and challenging opportunities—may come out of the interweaving of the various levels of practice. It is clear that the newly defined manpower needs of the field will play a crucial role in shaping future professional education.

NOTES

[1]*Statistical Abstract of the United States, 1972* (Washington, D.C.: U.S. Department of Commerce, Bureau of the Census, 1972), Table 37: "Population by Age, 1940–1970."

[2]Data refer to veterans surviving for one year in 1946 and in 1958. *See Mortality Report on Spinal Cord Injury* (Washington, D.C.: Veterans Administration, November 13, 1958).

[3]Annual Statistical Supplement, *Social Security Bulletin*, 1971, Table 3.

[4]*See* Martin Nacman, "Mental Health Services, Social Workers in." *Encyclopedia of Social Work* (New York: National Association of Social Workers, 1971), p. 823.

[5]*Accreditation Manual for Hospitals* (Chicago: Joint Commission on Accreditation of Hospitals, December 1976), pp. 139–42.

[6]*See* Arnold Gurin, "Education for the Profession of Social Work," in Everett C. Hughes, ed., *Education for Changing Practice*, to be published by McGraw Hill.

[7]"NASW Manpower Data Bank Survey" (Washington, D.C.: National Association of Social Workers, 1972).

[8]The adult categories include income for the aged, permanently and totally disabled, and the blind. "Allied Services" is the term coined in legislation to cover federal grants to the states for those social services previously administered in state public assistance programs—an uneven mixture of services such as casework, homemaker, employment, day care, child care, protective, and family services.

[9]See Margaret A. Golton, "Private Practice in Social Work," Encyclopedia of Social Work (New York: National Association of Social Workers, 1971), p. 952.

SOCIAL WORK PRACTICE IN CROSS-NATIONAL AND CROSS-CULTURAL PERSPECTIVE

Ruby B. Pernell

A radical shift has occurred . . . in our concepts of what constitutes professional social work, the relative weighting of its various activities, and the universality of a particular model. Among many other influences, two concurrent and related social and political movements have jarred the old images and created new perceptions in much the same way as kaleidoscopic patterns change.

The black movement within the United States, setting in motion similar movements of other ethnic and racial minorities, and the self-conscious nationalism among developing nations abroad have both had the effect of making groups assertive about who they are, what has made them that way, and what they want from others.

This affirmation of personal and national identity as distinctive from that of others and the bars to opportunity for self-actualization and nation actualization have raised the question of the relevance of social work's values, goals, roles, and methods to the needed social challenges and tasks. Indigenization has become a key concept in many places as a response to the question of relevance; and the attempts to indigenize have sharpened our awareness of cultural and national differences, forcing us to begin to give attention to further questions of the adequacy, breadth, and bias of our knowledge base about the individuals and groups with whom we work and the suitability of our goals and methods.

At the same time, influenced by these and other external and internal stirrings, the social work profession has been examining its models of practice and reconceptualizing them in ways that have greater promise for applicability and utility in a wider world of concerns and differing contexts. This strand of development makes it easier to bring together practice concepts and indigenous requirements.

In this article we will look at some of the special considerations, understandings, and skills called for in working with diverse ethnic, cultural, and national groups either within the United States or in other parts of the world.

PERSON-IN-SITUATION: THE SOCIOPOLITICAL-SOCIOECONOMIC CONTEXT

In the United States there are two major cultural groupings of current interest and concern: the white ethnics of European stock and the disadvantaged minorities of African, Asian, and North and Latin American backgrounds. A third group—which dominates both—has no particular concern about its cultural identity except as Americans; it holds and exercises power—political and economic—occupies superior social status, and controls the access routes to opportunity. In many ways this pattern mirrors the international scene of three worlds: the Western one of dominance and power, the so-called second world of the Eastern European block, and the Third World of nations struggling for development against odds of limited economic and political resources. And within

Source: This article was specially prepared for this volume by the author.

most of these nations are cultural groups who enjoy or endure similar inequalities. These relationships of nations and groups to each other, of those who control resources and opportunity and those who need them, are dominant contextual elements influencing values, goals, perceptions of self and others, and activities of each group. The urge for social and economic development and justice and the right to control one's own destiny have become major themes among the third world people at home and abroad.

The thrust toward development essentially means moving rapidly from a folk culture to a modern, technological one. The stress of coping with rapid change, impersonal demands on the person, and increased demands on the system creates an uncomfortable disequilibrium. There are reorientations of values and new behaviors and the old and new exist side by side, in conflict with each other. The value of modernization is often in conflict with the value placed on conserving some of the older aspects of the culture.

It is this broad, seeking, changing situation within which the members of these groups exist and which exists in the consciousness of the individuals that must be within the range of awareness of the social worker in his individual and group encounters.

The social worker whose practice takes him across cultural or national boundaries must examine his assumptions, definitions, theories, and practice models with specific reference to the group to which he intends to apply them. We tend to be culture bound by our own milieu, which includes the parts of the social work profession with which we identify. Because the basic values and goals of social work are concerned with the dignity of persons and their potential and opportunity for self-actualization, most will agree that we are dealing with universal themes. However, the ways in which man's situation is defined by and for him, his immediate and intermediate goals, his tasks and motivations, and his ways of coping may vary greatly. So also the most useful modes of helping may need to vary.

THE ASSUMPTIONS

Can we assume, for example, in working with individuals that self-directing autonomy is the most desirable state toward which growth should be encouraged? Perhaps, but not without knowledge of the social expectations and constraints of which the person is a part and the value he puts on conformity to

these; and not without clarification of what we mean by autonomy and how it should manifest itself.

Among population groups, the nuclear family, the joint family, the extended kinship group, the tribe or clan, neighborhood, village, racial, ethnic, or religious group will have various holds on their members. While some of these groups expect individual decision making and exert control through indicating approval or disapproval, others expect or require that individuals take consultation and guidance from their elders or other respected persons before making a decision. In some instances—such as the arranged marriage—the value is attached to the parents having fulfilled their responsibility to the child and to the couple fulfilling their responsibility to their families. Marriage is literally a family affair and the rights of the individuals are reduced to a minimum. The emphasis on self-directing autonomy has been sustained by a cultural and philosophical tradition that nurtures the individualistic family type in which individual goals have precedence over goals of specific collateral or lineal groups. This is in sharp contrast to a society in which "duty" in fulfillment of obligations to other family members, as prescribed by one's own role, is considered a primary virtue enshrined in the cultural and religious traditions.

Spiegel,[1] who has made some interesting cross-cultural observations of client-therapist relationships, has used Kluckholm's[2] classification of value orientations to describe some of the problematic areas. Spiegel identifies the model middle-class American family orientation as *individualistic*: "Every attempt is made to foster the autonomy of the individual family member and to allow children to make their own decisions." By contrast, the orientation of the model Irish-American family in his sample gives the *lineal* principle the first rank; that is, training its children for dependent behavior that is reinforced through the mutual care and aid offered by the extended family, religious, and community networks. For the Italian-American, the *collateral* relationships take first place, with lineal second, the reverse of the Irish-American group.

Comparing the value orientations of the middle-class therapist with the Irish-American client, Spiegel describes the therapist's first order of emphasis to be mastery-over-nature, while the client's is subjugation-to-nature. The therapist's dominant time orientation is on the future, with present second in importance, and past in low position; the present is most important to the client, the past second, and the future third. The American middle-class therapist puts emphasis on *doing,* while the Irish-American client puts it on *being.*

Spiegel discusses the conflicts these differences cause in the therapy situation where client and therapist misread each other's motives and actions and neither's expectations are met. As he says: "There is much question about the extent to which the therapist can actually be freed of his original values. The experiences my colleagues and I have had working with patients whose cultural backgrounds differed greatly from our own is that the value discrepancy sets up a very complicated strain within the therapist."[3] It also sets up a very complicated strain within the client.

If social work practice is centered on assisting people to cope productively with their environments, then it is necessary to know how they perceive their environment and what behaviors and responses they consider appropriate to these perceptions. Problems may be similar across cultures, but solutions that seem right in one environment will not necessarily fit another.

Bartlett points out: "If social functioning is to be enhanced, then criteria for *effective* functioning become necessary. Under these circumstances, the concept covers not only what is but what *ought to be,* namely, norms and values as well as knowledge and this has proved difficult to handle. Thus social workers have become involved in the risk of imposing, often unconsciously and unintentionally, their own social work values, middle-class values, or requirements for conformity to societal expectations."[4]

PERSON-IN-SITUATION: PEOPLE'S COPING EFFORTS AND DEMANDS OF THE SOCIAL ENVIRONMENT

The cross-cultural and cross-national perspective in practice must be one that views the person or group within the context of their environment and in interaction with it. In the search for universalities in social work practice, the person is sometimes viewed in terms of generalized strivings for self-actualization. His or her "goal-directed" activity is interpreted as appropriate or inappropriate, and the social worker's role is to help him or her cope more adequately with the particular developmental and incidental tasks at hand. This presupposes the person's or group's ability to do something about their situation or in spite of it. However, in a great many instances,

the client or group is trying to cope with an iceberg-like problem, external to himself, freezing him, with the visible piece representing only a fraction of the reality with which he is dealing. As many have pointed out, one characteristic of being a "disadvantaged" group or member of such a group is the sense of powerlessness in transactions with others. The limited resources or access to these transactions constitute a further block to effective action. The sense of powerlessness applies not only to the situation of some ethnic and racial groups within the United States, but to the majority of the population in countries where opportunities for access to resources are controlled by political or bureaucratic establishments. Social work practice aimed at helping the individual or group sort out the problem and select from alternatives the means for coping with it is not enough. The necessity is for the social worker to have a much broader concept of problems, valid targets, and worker roles. The advocacy or broker roles, the provision of technical help, the attempts to influence policy of bureaucratic organizations, the seeking-out of potential resources, or the teaching of effective forms of action become necessities. This may be the case for problems ranging from an individual's health care to a community development self-help project. At the individual direct-service level, Schwartz and Schwartz have indicated a distinction between "treatment" and "help" that applies here.[5] They see "help" as a shift from concepts of "norms" and "cure," implying instead a large variety of influence efforts based on a different conception of who is to be helped with what and a different view of the conditions and processes that affect the progress of the client to whom the help is being given.

In defining a problem, then, both its context and locus are important. The dimensions and meanings of a given problem may be situational contextual factors affected by, or functions of, certain internal norms and expectations of the cultural or national group or of the societal arrangements of the group vis-à-vis others. The historical and present social and economic realities constitute a field wherein a number of problems are generated and the bureaucratic, economic, and political structures may act as both cause and barrier to effective coping.

KNOWLEDGE ASSESSMENT

The utilization of the casework method has carried along with it—until very recent modifications—

a psychoanalytic theory about behavior that served as the major basis for diagnosis of client problems. While useful, it has undoubtedly been limited in scope and value as related to the variety of problems in social functioning that claim the attention of the social worker. Stretched to explain behavior in diverse cultural settings, it has sometimes been an outstanding misfit, as Mukundarao notes in his comment on social work education in India, "where students were learning about the traumatic implications of overstrict toilet training in a country with an extraordinarily casual attitude to defecation."[6]

Role theory, socialization theory, opportunity theory, general systems theory, and neo-Freudian formulations, such as Erikson's[7] Stages of Man, that have expanded the view of persons interacting with social demands have also expanded the potential for better assessing the behavior of persons and groups in diverse cultures interacting within their own context and in transactions with the wider environment or impinging culture.

Torrey[8] says whenever therapists from one culture diagnose and prescribe treatment for patients from another culture, there is an inherent probability of professional misjudgment. The same can be true of community development specialists, social policy consultants, and other professionals operating outside their own cultural milieu. This is probably partly due to the intrusion of one's own values, partly to the limitations of the theory being utilized, but perhaps largely due to lacunae in our knowledge of the other culture and its forms of expression Someone has pointed out that our models may also unwittingly limit us. The medical model, for instance, dictates certain kinds of information gathering, but misses ethnographic data. Thus we easily misread cues, misinterpret data we do have, or proceed in ignorance of the character of the resources available to the client within his own setting and how he makes use of these. Sometimes it is the worker's prejudice that leads to stereotyped readings of information and behavior.

Minority groups in the United States have called attention to the proneness of workers to consider certain behaviors of a particular cultural group as "abnormal" or "inappropriate" when, in fact, they are adaptive behaviors, appropriate for the circumstances, anxiety-reducing, and directed toward problem solving. Similarly, what is interpreted as "resistance" may be the client's misunderstanding of worker's objectives or techniques or inability to connect with the "inappropriate" behavior of the *worker*. Sometimes clients do not understand the relevance to their problems of certain questions asked in the interview. Sometimes the client is waiting for *advice*, particularly where the worker represents authority or superior status. In community development the marginal existence of men may make the risk of changing an old practice too great, so they resist innovative techniques.

Spiegel,[9] in the study mentioned earlier, provides an example of abortive communication in a case situation involving an Irish-American father of a disturbed child. The father's value structure is primarily *present time, being,* and *lineal,* all of which are in oppositon to the model of psychotherapy utilized by the therapist, who is *future time, being,* and *collaterally* oriented. The client keeps asking the therapist what he should be doing and is unable to act without this direction. He feels he is wasting his time because nothing is happening. Repeated attempts of the therapist to involve him in the interview in "proper" fashion fail. Spiegel asks, "Exposed to these responses, how will the therapist conduct himself? For a while he will identify the patient's response as 'resistance' and keep on trying to use his usual techniques. After a . . . time he will feel intensely frustrated . . . [but] his therapeutic values will order him to stick to the technique . . . [he] will feel guilty if he wants to stop treatment before the patient is ready to quit. . . . But if he continues under the guidance of these values, he will reach a stalemate, not being able to make progress or to terminate treatment."

Chu[10] provides an example from a Chinese village of the worker's failure to correctly interpret the client's behavior, which, from the worker's point of view, was irrational, but quite rational when viewed within the context of his own social situation. Utilizing the mutual-aid mechanism in his village, the father borrowed money from his neighbors to pay for his child's hospitalization. Miss Chu writes:

In my hospital one parent demanded removal of his child who had been hospitalized for his TB-meningitis and was required to stay in the hospital for a long time. Despite the doctor's threat to report to the police, the man went ahead and removed his child without the doctor's permission. He explained that he had to do this because he had no more money to pay the hospital bill. In all this process, the social worker assured him that the hospital would pay any extra expenses since he was known to be destitute. Both the doctor and the social worker thought that this man must have been crazy to remove the child before he was completely healed, even in the face of promised financial assistance.

A home visit that followed revealed that this man was continually being pressured by his neighbors to remove the child from the hospital. The neighbors who had lent him money reasoned with him that if he could let his child stay in the hospital for a longer period, then he must have extra money to pay for the extra hospital expenses. If he had the extra money, then he should have used it to repay the loan from his neighbors. They could not believe that the hospital would not eventually come to them for any extra expenses which they were afraid they could not raise. The neighbors, according to their observations, were convinced that since the child could eat, walk, talk, and had no fever at all, he could then be taken home.

It is obvious that this man was operating under extra social pressure from his community. He had to conform so as to be on good terms with his neighbors with whom he had shared, and would continue to share, mutual-aid interest, confidence, and trust. Perhaps, in this situation, it is understandable that he could even sacrifice his own child's welfare by removing him from the hospital.

The example illustrates the importance of cultural institutions and social networks and how they sustain and control the lives of clients. The family is one of the institutions on which there is a great deal of cross-cultural data revealing its variations in size, structure, and functions. For the social worker, knowledge of the roles and role expectations, the claims on its members, the resources it provides may be the keys to understanding much of a client's behavior that otherwise is either misinterpreted, unutilized, or just mysterious.

In direct practice the client's perception of reality may be a source of surprise and suspicion for the worker from a different cultural tradition. For example, the Mexican-American who reports on "hearing voices" may be assessed as hallucinating; whereas, when one understands the nuances of the language and the cultural connotations, the expression loses its pathological meaning and may be similarly understood as when an Anglo-American says he "heard the call" to join an evangelical religion.[11]

Another example of problem communication across language barriers is in the conveying of concepts. *Salud mental*, the Spanish word equivalent of mental health, does not exist as a *concept* for the Spanish-speaking person. Since he makes no separation between the psychological and total well-being of the

individual, all his terms to describe his condition imply a physical as well as a psychological component.[12]

Another kind of cultural expression that requires understanding is that of a subcultural group in disadvantaged status with a dominant and repressive culture or caste. Members of such a group develop personality and social traits that make it possible to cope with what may be the injustice, inconsistency, and impotence in their transactions with the dominant group. This has been true for colonialized people such as the Indian vis-à-vis the British and those in similar circumstances brought into daily contacts in which response and feeling may be at continued variance. Novelist E. M. Forster, in *A Passage to India*,[13] beautifully catches this double stream of consciousness in the relationships between the Indians and the British ruling class. Chestang discusses this with reference to black-white relationships in the United States:

Coping under the circumstances imposed by the society has required the development of ego-syntonic modes that are often at variance with personality trends considered normal by the majority group. The black is socialized into black and white society, developing skills to function effectively in both. The experience of being black in American society has resulted in the development of two parallel and opposing thought structures—each based on values, norms, and beliefs and supported by attitudes, feelings, and behaviors—that imply feelings of depreciation on the one hand and a push for transcendance on the other. Effective social functioning and environmental reality require that black individuals incorporate both these trends into their personalities—the one to assure competence in dealing with reality, the other as an impetus for transcending reality.[14]

For the white worker whose practice takes him across racial lines, this formulation can be very helpful in the attempt to understand some behavior and attitudinal responses that are otherwise confusing. They are responses to a reality partly created or represented by the worker, as white, of which the worker is a part but does not experience in the same way. This is to say, while white worker and black clients are participants in the same event, the reality experienced by each may well differ; thus, in situations in which communication is especially frustrating, it may not be that the client is out of touch with reality, but that the worker is out of touch with the client's reality.

Although most of the content here has been particularly relative to direct practice with individuals, families, or groups, there is also special knowledge required of the community practitioners for accurate assessment. The basis for social stratification at the community level, the realities of economic and political relationships, the norms governing social relationships, the kinship system as these affect participation and decision making, the traditional forms of organization and collective activity, all vary from one society to another, retarding or facilitating the achievement of national or group development goals.

Most important is recognition that with cultures in transition—as is true everywhere today—generalizations are only that; and the actual values, norms, beliefs, behaviors, aspirations, realities of individuals, families, or groups in a dynamic society will be scattered throughout the range of possible combinations.

THE CONCEPTS
AND MODELS OF PRACTICE

To think in terms of adjustment rather than maladjustment, health instead of pathology; to find conditions of normal living . . . to win with each person his own best balance.[15]

Much of the export of the American models of social work practice and their subsequent primacy in social work education abroad occurred at a time when we were trying to refine the medical model in casework; group work was still committed to both individual development and social goals; and community organization meant process, not program. In some developing countries, methods were gradually combined into "generic" courses more suitable to the social worker's tasks in those countries, centered as they were around problems; and community organization was broadening into community development in response to the social development objectives and programs through which significant national goals were to be reached. However, in social work with microsystems, the practice models remained much the same. The growth-and-development/social-goals model of group work with its educational and leisure activity and its decision-making, program-building, and group-action tasks was especially adaptable to social development needs and programs. The medical model of casework and the supportive Freudian theory base probably persisted because they have their utility in certain situations. There are always sick and troubled people in a society, and within the urban setting it is possible to develop specialized services where the helping activity can be carried on. Also, the culture of professional social work displaces to some degree facets of one's indigenous culture, causing some loss of awareness of the inappropriateness or lesser utility of certain approved or status-accorded activities.

While practice has undoubtedly been modified, especially in this self-conscious period of seeking for indigenous bases for the professional activity, there has been little work on reconceptualizing practice models. There is certainly much more utilization of cultural concepts, but not always awareness of relevant social research done in one's own country. And there is increased seeking for indigenous materials for teaching social work. The South East Asian Seminar for Social Work Educators convened in Bombay, India, in 1971, saw its major concerns as indigenous curriculum development and regional self-reliance. Emphasis on cultural identity and uniqueness was strong and was especially expressed in the workshop on the use of creative indigenous literature as teaching material.[16] Since that date some excellent materials have been developed. However, it was obvious then that a very great deal still needed to be done in the realm of new conceptions of practice.

The use of concepts such as *person-in-situation* and *social functioning* and identification of the *central focus of social work as being on people coping with the demands of the social environment* seem to hold great promise for a way of analyzing and conceptualizing practice in diverse cultures where, in fact, the circumstances of daily living and the thrust of development programs have made such a bifocal vision a necessity. The Asian educators referred to earlier reaffirmed that individual needs and social change were twin tasks of social work and of equal importance. Practice theory needs to give form to the linkage between them, filling out and making self-conscious and transmissible the practice models and techniques already being utilized by workers in many different cultural and national settings. Techniques of directiveness, advice-giving, demonstrating, and teaching may be wholly appropriate to the setting and problem, as well as activities with other parts of the system in behalf of those served; but the professional social work–acculturated individual may feel guilty at using these in direct service—if they aren't completely rejected—as long as the medical model and the dictates of engaging and helping the client via a particular set of techniques remain his major frame of reference.

New frames of references are being offered. The ecological perspective for the individualizing social work services has been incorporated in the *Life Model* as conceptualized by Germain and Gitterman.[17] It is focused on the transacting forces in the man-environment ecosystem, with concern for a humane environment as well as for the strengthening of the adaptive capacity of individuals to cope with the processes of change. It incorporates a philosophy of man's interdependence with his environment that is close to traditional Eastern concepts of man's oneness with nature and provides a framework for the unified or integrated approaches already being utilized in many places.

The identity and liberation movements of disadvantaged populations within the United States and elsewhere in the world have sparked some other models that are focused on the structural or systemic elements as determining factors in the ability of individuals, communities, or societies to solve the problems facing them. Both general-systems theory and political analysis provide theoretical and ideological underpinnings for these models that have the goal of transforming society. *Conscientization*, developed in the 1960s out of the particular social, economic, and political circumstances of Latin America, is concerned with the "awakening of consciousness" to the reality of one's place in nature and society, the ability to analyze the causes and consequences of this order of things, and action aimed at transformation.[18] In many parts of the world, social workers are utilizing this approach as they tackle the massive structural problems that limit the life-chances of the people they work with.

By the 1970s *radical social work* had entered our terminology, "emphasizing change rather than adjustment and . . . raising people's consciousness of the systemic sources of many of the tensions and problems which we experience."[19] The approach merges with that of conscientization and in both instances are political orientations, though not in every case articulated as the expression of a particular ideology. Basically they are concerned with issues of equity and justice, and no social worker who moves within the cross-cultural, cross-national arenas can afford to be unaware of the pressures for change nor the consequences of change for social work practice.

NOTES

[1]John P. Spiegel, "Some Cultural Aspects of Transference and Countertransference," in Jules Mas-serman, ed., *Individual and Familial Dynamics* (New York: Grune & Stratton, 1959), pp. 160–82.

[2]Florence Kluckholm, "Variations in the Basic Values of Family Systems," *Social Casework* 39, nos. 3 and 4 (February–March 1958): 63–72.

[3]Spiegel, "Some Cultural Aspects of Transference," p. 174.

[4]Harriet Bartlett, *The Common Base of Social Work Practice* (New York: National Association of Social Workers, 1970), p. 110.

[5]M. D. Schwartz and Charlotte G. Schwartz, *Social Approaches to Mental Patient Care* (New York: Columbia University Press, 1964), p. 85.

[6]K. Mukundarao, "Social Work in India: Indigenous Cultural Bases and Processes of Modernization," *International Social Work* 12, no. 3 (1969): 29–39.

[7]Erik K. Erikson, *Childhood and Society.* (New York: Norton, 1963).

[8]E. Fuller Torrey, "The Case for the Indigenous Therapist," *Archives of General Psychiatry* 20, no. 3 (1969): 365–73.

[9]Spiegel, "Some Cultural Aspects of Transference," p. 174.

[10]Sylvia Sui Feng Chu, "Utilizing Traditional Elements in the Society in Casework Practice," unpublished paper, 1974.

[11]Amado M. Padillo and Rene A. Ruiz. *Latino Mental Health* (Rockville, Md.: National Institute of Mental Health, 1973), pp. 31–32.

[12]Ibid., p. 14.

[13]E. M. Forster, *A Passage to India* (New York: Harcourt Brace, 1949).

[14]Leon W. Chestang, *Character Development in a Hostile Environment,* Occasional Paper, No. 3, University of Chicago, School of Social Service Administration, November 1972.

[15]Bertha C. Reynolds, "The Social Casework of an Uncharted Journey," *Social Work* 9, no. 4, (October 1964): 13–17.

[16]A. S. Desai and A. C. Almanzor, eds., *Curriculum Development and Teachings,* Proceedings of the South East Asian Seminar for Social Work Educators, Bombay (New York: Athenaeum Press, 1972).

[17]Carel B. Germain and Alex Gitterman, *The Life Model of Social Work Practice* (New York: Columbia University Press, 1980).

[18]R. P. Resnick, "Conscientization: An Indigenous Approach to International Social Work," *International Social Work* 19, no. 1 (1976): 21–29.

[19]Jeffrey Galper. *Social Work Practice—A Radical Perspective* (Englewood Cliffs, N.J.: Prentice-Hall, 1980).

NEW DIRECTIONS IN SOCIAL SERVICES

Alfred J. Kahn

NEW CONCEPTS IN SOCIAL SERVICES

We have been too long satisfied with anachronism, ambiguity, half measures, and mediocrity in social service policy and practice. Despite short-run policy failure, the society has recognized, come to value, and institutionalized (1) education, (2) income security, and (3) health systems. It has begun to consider (4) employment-manpower and (5) housing as essential public institutions. But these five systems (the "social" or "human" services) clearly do not provide all the supports essential to human welfare in an urban industrial world. My thesis thus is that the time has arrived to recognize as the *sixth* human service system what the British now call the "personal social services." This identifiable domain of crucial supports is growing in importance and would benefit by conceptualization, organization, and evaluation.

Definition

We have long known how much more there is after the five established and largely universal systems have been covered. Among the elements are child welfare; family services; community-based programs for the aged; community centers and settlements; homemakers; day care; congregate meals and meals-on-wheels; self-help and mutual aid activities among handicapped groups; institutional care and residential treatment for delinquents and children in need of supervision; advice services for adolescents; and protected residential arrangements for young workers. These programs—which prove on analysis to be more than a list of unrelated items—should and must be conceptualized as the sixth system, the sixth social service.

"Should" because the personal social services have developed out of response to need and to consumer demand. "Must" because only if defined, organized, and supported with what it takes to shape a working system—and I emphasize system—will the personal social services be able to eliminate so much of what is now unsatisfactory in the social welfare service sector in the United States and help this sector develop its full potential. In short, while we need to define personal or general social services, we need even more to proceed to do them well.

Cross-National Study. My colleagues and I have prepared a report of an eight-country study in which we examined the status of these activities. We "sampled" the large domain with a series of different topics and perspectives: child care (day care and preschool programs); programs to identify and respond to child abuse and neglect; residential and institutional services for delinquent and neglected children and the community-based alternatives; family planning; community programs for the aged; and the local delivery system for these and related services.

The work was carried out in collaboration with research teams in Canada, England, France, West Germany, Poland, Yugoslavia, and Israel. A parallel United States study covered all the indicated topics, and included a review of how each of these services looks "on the ground" in a medium-sized American city and how they interrelate for administrative and service delivery. Special attention was devoted to the delivery system as defined and constrained by law, regulation, structure, and professional practice.

Out of the study and from our earlier work, we have concluded that "something" is occurring. It is accurate to speak internationally of the emergence of a sixth social service, the "personal or general social service," and there is convergence upon common tasks for the delivery system. Both here and abroad we observe a group of related activities, functions, and service models; but though they are sometimes coordinated or even integrated in policy and deliv-

Source: Alfred J. Kahn, "New Directions in Social Services," *Public Welfare* 34(1976):26–32, Reprinted with permission of the American Public Welfare Association. © 1976 American Public Welfare Association.

ery, in the rigorous sense of the term there is a lack of system in most places for formally and effectively identifying elements which belong among the personal social services and organizing them as such.

Conceptual Base. The conceptual base for defining the system may be specified: *The personal social services are services available by nonmarketplace criteria.* Need, demographic category, or status are determining, not ability or inability to pay, even though there may be fees, partial fees, or no fees. Society organizes some services because the market will not function to assure them. Drug abuse, alcoholism, marital problems, parent-child difficulty, child abuse, emotional disturbance, and physical handicaps do not spare even people with enough money, good housing, advanced education, or jobs. Old age, adolescent separation from families, developmental and socialization needs of children are normal, nonproblem conditions which cross income and class lines. Personal social services cannot substitute for sufficient money, adequate housing, or a good education; but such resources cannot substitute for the services in question either. The personal social services are needed as part of the total societal response to modern living.

Function. The personal social services as we have observed them are addressed to one or more of the following tasks:

Contributing to socialization and development—that is, offering daily living and growth supports for ordinary, average people (not just problem groups), a role shared with other nonmarket services but involving unique programs;

Disseminating information about and facilitating access to services and entitlements anywhere in the social sector (all six social service fields);

Assuring for the frail aged, the handicapped, the retarded, and the incapacitated, a basic level of social care and aid necessary to support functioning in the community or in substitute living arrangements.

Providing help, counseling, and guidance which will assist individuals and families facing problems, crises, or pathology to reestablish functional capacity and overcome their difficulties;

Supporting mutual aid, self-help, and activities aimed at prevention, overcoming problems in community living, and service planning;

Integrating the variety of appropriate programs or services as they impact upon individuals and families to assure coordination for maximum effect.

Existing Programs

Many of the personal social services are or should be public social utilities. The utilities are programs available at consumer initiative for which entitlement is a matter of citizenship, age, or related status. They are largely programs which buttress daily living and contribute to socialization and development, functioning under present social circumstances as family, primary group, or village once did. Examples are preschool programs, senior citizen centers, community centers, residential schools, and family planning services.

Other personal social services are by definition case services—programs for abused and neglected children, institutions for delinquents, nursing homes for the disabled. The case services, by contrast, require a diagnostic or assessment process and certification that there is need or eligibility. The process may be a court adjudication, a medical review, a social study, a psychiatric assessment, or a psychological test.

A personal social service network clearly requires both case services and public social utilities. A single program model (day care, for example) may be a utility (for all eligible children whose parents choose to use the service) or a case service (for children in disorganized homes who need supportive help).

Utilities, by their nature, are universal and not limited to those who pass a means test. Case services may be either selective (for the poor alone) or universal; universal services may impose differentiated fees determined by income so long as the right to service is not reserved for those below a specified income level. Case services involve illness, problems, maladjustment, difficulty; social utilities may serve average people facing ordinary circumstances.

The personal social services, because they include both utilities and case services, are significant for average people; they are for those with occasional or constant personal problems as well as for those whose disadvantage or disorganization is pervasive. Selectivity—organizing services for the poor alone—would unnecessarily and unwisely close out needed services to many users. Services which are universally available and good enough for any citizen are the cross-national trend. The organizational task under universalism is to assure access and to allocate priorities if rationing is needed so as to guarantee that the poor are not closed out by more aggressive, advantaged, or sophisticated people.

Organization.   Any effort to organize personal social services into an effective and efficient system faces difficult boundary problems. One begins with a partially developed series of case services and utilities fragmented by eligibility rules and administrative structures, some of them currently selective and some universal. These services merge and overlap with the health, education, corrections, housing, or manpower efforts. The boundaries may be quite vague, but they are nonetheless important to practitioners in each system. Even where the mood favors collaboration, it may be difficult to formulate collaborative arrangements and division of roles which grow out of solid knowledge as to what works best. To illustrate we may note the need to define medical and social work roles in programs for abused and battered children or services to the frail elderly.

We found, internationally, convergence toward common elements in the delivery system for personal social services, even though some trends are not yet resolved. In general there is a tendency toward a freestanding system, with some personal social services outposted as adjuncts to other systems. That is, personal social services are being organized as a network, with some staff based in other agencies and institutions such as schools, hospitals, and Social Security offices. A possible and far less frequent alternative which creates enormous problems of program coordination and case integration attaches personal social services to other systems without creating a freestanding delivery system as a "home base."

The American Milieu.   The American picture favors a core freestanding personal social service system which, in turn, could outpost staff to other institutions, much as health departments currently outpost doctors to schools to serve school health programs. The elements out of which a system could develop are the structures for public welfare services and child welfare in most counties; antipoverty and housing service programs; those components of community mental health which really are personal social services; and a variety of categorically based social services in such fields as health, education, and rehabilitation.

Universalism in the personal social services supports the mandated separation of means-tested income maintenance programs from service programs—a separation developed both to objectify and protect the right to money (since acceptance of service must not be conceived of as a valid test of finan-cial need) and to avoid program stigma, an inevitable consequence if services are reserved or required for relief recipients alone. The remaining problem is that of the high-risk, vulnerable client who comes only for financial assistance and does not request what may be badly needed help. The separation of income maintenance and service programs, therefore, requires special provision for identifying such cases and channeling them for appropriate aid.

Public-Voluntary Coordination.   The public-voluntary separation is everywhere a constraint upon a creation of system. Voluntary programs tend to be restricted to certain categories of individuals (aged, children, etc.) or directed toward specific problems (delinquency, mental health, etc.). This orientation has a long and understandable history, but it is an obstacle to program coordination and to case integration at the operational level and is a major block to accountability as well.

It would, however, be possible to create a personal social service system which integrates the public and voluntary effectively and joins them in a true network. Our cross-national studies show this to be the case in a number of countries. However, creation of such a private-public coverage system, with enforcement of standards and assurance of case accountability, apparently requires both legal mandate and public-sector commitment. These are found in some United States jurisdictions but are not general, nor are they called for in recent social service legislation in the United States.

The public-voluntary relationship in the United States is most frequently viewed as a "partnership." Because this term is so vague, such formulation really dodges the basic issue. An integrated and accountable system cannot be achieved without a clearer and more assertive public role and formal public-voluntary compacts, publicly sanctioned. Differences among the states as far back as a decade ago document the fact that the public role is the crucial variable in determining whether an integrated delivery system can be achieved. If public authority will guarantee standards, system, and accountability, the voluntary sector resources can be extremely well deployed; well deployed, that is, not merely as expert separate services, but as components of a responsible network of coverage governed by public priorities.

Value.   Affirmation of the significance and validity of a personal social service system does not require exaggerated claims or a lack of balance. Our studies show that a social policy which does not base itself on availability of suitable employment and adequate income maintenance, health, housing, and educational programs will be continually frustrating and incapable of progress. The personal social services are a needed component of social policy, not a substitute for it. They are a complement of cash, in-kind, housing, and health provisions—not a cheaper alternative or a diversion. They require only modest funding (perhaps 1 percent of the gross national product), as contrasted with income maintenance, education, or health programs; however, this modest cost does not signify unimportance.

These related and necessary services have emerged throughout the industrialized world in recent decades and are everywhere identifiable and significant. The time has come to move beyond the haphazard, fragmented, and temporary arrangements of the past toward administrative autonomy and relative stability. One cannot speak of child care or programs for the aged as transitory needs. Women are in the labor force. Families want their children to have group experiences. Medical research has extended life expectancy, and our citizens want opportunities and options in their later years. These are not temporary conditions, but rather signify permanent trends and changes in human experience which require large-scale institutional response. The personal social services are there to meet the challenge if we can learn how to use them to their maximum potential.

DESIGNING SOCIAL
SERVICES FOR THE FUTURE

In a fundamental sense the pace and scope of the development will reflect basic social and economic forces in the next several years: the state of the economy, the balance of political power, the evolution of major interest groups and professions, and emerging ideologies. Although these larger societal trends will play a major role in shaping the future, those involved directly in social service planning, administration, and practice will also have an impact on the direction taken. It is, therefore, important to focus on the substantive issues which define the targets and delivery systems so that our choices may be made conscious and visible.

Title XX

Public social utilities follow general principles of public administration. We have found that a free-standing personal social service delivery system may organize its case services around the following processes: information, referral, and other access activities; case assessment and evaluation; delivery of direct benefits and social care services; counseling; program and service coordination and case integration; accountability; and reporting, evaluation, and feedback. Such organization is not easy to implement; it requires the settling of boundary issues, reassignment of tasks, agreements on case flow and procedures, definitions of agency rights and sanctions, assignment of personnel and resources, and public interpretations of roles and relationships—all after the universalism/selectivity balance has been determined!

Potentials and Limitations. I believe that Title XX, the new social services title in the Social Security Act, has been underestimated in its potential for strengthening several of the service fields. It is possibly even more significant in relation to the future delivery system for the personal social services.

Title XX makes states eligible for high-level matching federal funds earmarked for flexibly defined social services. The states, which are responsible for planning and implementation of the services, are required to meet certain federal guidelines: specified goals to be addressed (a service for each of five goals); expenditure reserved for recipients of public assistance and related programs (half of all the budgeted money in the state); and specified programs to serve recipients of the adult assistance categories (aged, disabled, blind). Two services are mandated: family planning and foster care. Some services are to be universal, "without regard to income": that is, information and referral services and protective services.

Several elements in this legislation are especially interesting in their potential. The eligibility provisions are implemented by regulations which would permit a universal system to be constructed. One delivery system could serve nonpaying, partially paying, and full-paying service recipients. A comprehensive universal system for people of all income groups is a prerequisite for effective organization of social services. Further, there is a mandate for popular response to and participation in planning and enough flexibility to permit states to define and develop services which reflect their own demographic and cultural uniqueness and needs. Each state can develop its own blend of services appropriate to its constituency. What is more, the permeable boundaries would allow unique state experimentation with multi-disciplinary mixes and choice in placement of various service components within different systems.

Impediments to Action.   Despite these possibilities, states have not gone vary far with their programs as yet for a number of reasons. First, the new legislation arrived with an expenditure ceiling, and several of the states were near or beyond their entitlements, while others could not manage more matching funds. In general, this is a difficult time financially for state and local government.

Second, politicians, consumers, and staff need to get used to the new ideas, and there has been little time. For example, there is a tradition of selectivity in public welfare, namely services for the poor alone ("current, former, potential relief recipients"). We need to learn how to think about social services for all.

Then, categorical interests have been preoccupied with getting what they define as their fair share of funding in this zero-sum game. It is a pie of limited size. In the midst of that kind of struggle, particularly with a cost inflation that has created real problems for public and private agencies, it was inevitable that the various interest groups would struggle to receive funding and recognition without regard to the larger picture.

Also the intent and consistency of the Congress and the administration is very uncertain. The track record has not been encouraging. It is difficult to know whether we are on the brink of a real break with tradition and opportunity to develop new ideas, or whether this is just a passing stage. Is the new approach sound, basic, no matter who sits in the White House or who is secretary of Health and Human Services? Will Congress . . . categorize programs, modifying their very essence? . . .

Finally, the legislation fails to mandate an administrative structure which could serve as a basis for coordinating social service delivery, which is presently scattered among the various categorical programs and several other systems (education, health, etc.). The regulations implementing Title XX contain a mandate to coordinate. Mandate there is, but there is no real interference with much other legislation in child welfare, child care, the field of the aging, in-kind benefits, the handicapped or retarded or delin-

quent—and so on—upon which the real evolution of system will rest.

The United States has provided social services on a categorical basis which fragments and duplicates efforts in many instances. Categorical approaches, whatever their appeal, do not by their nature make adequate provision for service coherence or service integration. They cannot assure balanced social provision to meet need. Those who would serve families in a preventive or therapeutic sense cannot assure them the cash assistance, housing, health service, special education, and personal social services they require to fit their specific circumstances because that is not how social institutions are organized.

Furthermore, there has been a tendency in this country to periodically focus on individuals in spotlighted categories. The spotlighting follows upsetting incidents, dramatic case stories, or new research findings; but it may be short-lived. The legislation and funding follow the public arousal or new fad. All too often it is not knowledge of effective intervention, but concern, sentiment, or organizational dynamics which take over. Each special program meets real needs, but it is not in balance with other programs or institutions.

Nor does the coordination mandate assure significant leverage vis à vis related systems or networks which, for maximum impact should also be integrated with social services and grow in tandem with them: special revenue-sharing programs in manpower, urban development, health, and education. Title XX calls for coordination, but so does other legislation; Title XX authorizes personal social services, and so do other laws. The Congress has not created a hierarchy, nor does such hierarchy exist within the administrative structure. In effect, each system sees itself in the lead role and rejects others who would take the lead. Each develops its own components and does not address balance from the consumer's perspective.

Thus, if the personal social services are to discharge their potential, they must emerge as a system vis à vis categorical and related area social service programs which have specific mandates and over which Title XX administrators as yet have limited prerogatives. At present, then, the entire initiative embodied in Title XX—the policy, the planning, and the resolution—are partial. There is no lead agency with mandate and resources to create an integrated personal social service system and to develop the necessary pattern of relationships with agencies and systems at its boundaries. Title XX is promising, but hardly a guarantee.

Possibilities

I believe administration at the state and federal levels must be strengthened if we are to achieve our goals. For a decade or more we in the United States have coped with problems of federal fragmentation and indecision by raising the slogan of decentralization. Where federal programs were fragmented, unrelated, even inconsistent, we sometimes gave program initiative in the social sector to cities or counties, often even bypassing state irresolution, saying, "We don't seem to be able to work it out in Washington, why don't you try?" And when local government could not overcome barriers, it transferred initiative to the neighborhood. It adopted multiservice centers and community control as integrating devices and often implied, "We don't know how, but certainly you service providers must." These devices are escapes. They seldom achieve desired objectives. They do not even assure the qualitatively improved or even expanded services justified by the larger investment. They certainly do not alone end fragmentation, offer balance, and achieve service integration, case integration, and accountability in service delivery.

Federal categorical programs carry regulations, procedures, reporting requirements, standards, and staffing patterns which often supersede the announced solutions through local initiative. No multiservice center can satisfy the needs of a group of independent administrative systems at higher levels. It is not possible to create an integrated operation without coping with elements of professional culture and modal delivery patterns associated with specialized bureaucratic systems. It is not possible to devise an integrated local system while reporting to four or five or seven different administrative structures at the state level.

Thus, while not closing off devices allowing local and county initiative, we had better do even more at the middle tier—the state—and the intermediate tier—the city—as well as at the top tier—the federal government and its several parts. For there cannot be an integrated personal social service system unless there is attention to the conditions for its realization.

Federal Initiatives.   Progress in creating a personal social service system will depend in part on further

sorting out at the federal level. Perhaps this requires that local jurisdictions be freed from some legislative and regulatory mandates and reporting. There may also be need for amalgamation among the several forms of social sector special revenue sharing through new legislation. Whether through administrative action or legislation and budgetary practice, the initiatives will need to be reflected in federal guidelines and regulations which are not merely mutually consistent among themselves, but are also mutually supportive.

The Department of Health, Education, and Welfare [currently the Department of Health and Human Services] . . . reflects the current fragmentation and confusion of goals in the social services. Responsibility for social services is divided between the Social and Rehabilitation Service (SRS), which administers some programs picked up from the old welfare system and also some new programs, and the Office of Human Development (OHD), which handles problem and age-status groups. The evolution of a personal social services delivery system would be enhanced if services to the aged, children, families, and special problem groups were consolidated under one administration. Such a move would provide the necessary framework for creation of a universal, comprehensive system with the necessary mandate to deal with boundary and coordination problems.

State Role.   Some states have probably moved further than the federal government in providing necessary conditions for an integrated personal social service system. There are several types of human resource and public welfare agencies at the state level which are experimenting with integrated management or integrated delivery systems under their own auspices, through direct operation, or by encouragement and support of local activities. Federal backing and reorganization would enhance the prospect. Exchange of experience and cooperation would help substantially. Development of planning capacity would be useful if the interest were in results, not in compliance with required ritual.

Some states, I noted, have probably gone further toward creating conditions auspicious for a personal social services system than has Washington. But others apparently have given up the game. Title XX may be read in two ways. A Title XX agency at the state level may become a mere fiscal agent used to funnel funds through to other human service programs:

mental health, education, corrections, and so forth. Or the state Title XX agency may operate and support at the local level the core service programs, the basic public foundations for a personal social service system. The personal social services cannot develop as system without the public front-line delivery presence that will structure access, accountability, and case integration. State decisions will thus be determining. So far there is no clear trend visible, but the issue is critical. State agencies which merely channel funds and do not have a personal social service delivery structure under their own auspices are signaling their real decision: no freestanding personal social service system.

Delivery at the Local Level. Obviously, in a country which could not manage without pluralism, there is required a range of experimentation and testing, and the ultimate adoption of diverse solutions. Those who would do this work at the local level need guidance, models, training supports, and encouragement. The planned variations within and between localities are the way to shape the system. Our cross-national study of delivery systems found that the personal social services are converging toward a model offering general social work practice at the front line (team or outposted individual), supported by specialized services or resources (public or private) in the same or related units, and assigned responsibility for social care programs, access services, direct counseling, and case integration.

For the United States the newest element in the local system is what might be called "social care." Social care is a term describing a cluster of practical helping measures, including: (a) personal care and hygiene for old and handicapped people; (b) home-health services, including light practical nursing and assistance in taking medication; (c) homemaker or home help services, such as medical preparation, light cleaning, personal laundry; (d) chore, shopping, and escort services; (e) friendly visiting and telephone reassurance services.

Social care programs clearly require both medical and social work elements. They could be located either in medical or personal social services systems or operate out of a neutral base and serve both. But the personal social service unit must offer access to and work in close relation with social care services, whatever the operating base. The aged, handicapped, retarded, emotionally disturbed, or victims of personal and family emergencies have great need for

such services. The personal social service delivery system as a whole could be organized to offer social care, substitute care, intensive counseling, in-kind benefits, information, and referral.

CONCLUSION

The commitment to system coherence and coverage as noted will require some resolution of public-voluntary roles; the leadership must be assumed by the state or federal levels since the burden of resolution will be too great for any locality. Clearly responsibility for policy, coverage, and funding is public. The base-line access and case integration system, too, probably require public operation. But if preferred, the remainder of the system could be constructed out of a mix. The public system could integrate voluntary resources, as specialized programs or as front-line "contract" services, if there were a mandate and will for strong public auditing and enforcement of standards.

In brief: To translate the beginnings of a personal social service system into a reality will require:

> Federal legislative, administrative, and budgetary mandates to cope with categorization and fragmentation of programs;
>
> Reorganization and new support structures at the federal level;
>
> State-level design and reorganization of programs to meet state needs;
>
> Local experimentation to shape alternative models for personal social service systems;
>
> Coordination of a delivery system combining access provision, general practice, provision for case integration, and accountability arrangements;
>
> Development of a core of essential social care services;
>
> Public operation of front-line services and public accountability for purchased services.

You will note that I have concluded my program and policy analysis with both projection and advocacy. I see the stirrings of the sixth social service and recognize its potential. I observe widespread need, but am aware of obstacles. The development is worldwide and there is knowledge and experience, so there is a basis for hope. Yet the legislative, organizational, professional, and cultural obstacles are substantial, so there is uncertainty.

The personal social services have come too far to disappear. They are too vital and sought by too many elements in our society to be wiped out. But they could grow slowly, serve the well-to-do one way and the poor in another, and remain fragmented and less effective than they might be. That would be too bad. The personal social services as a comprehensive, universal system could gain in effectiveness and thus in their value to the society. They could be integrating elements, forces for social cohesion and even for some resource redistribtuion. The need is all around, and effective response is within grasp. We are quite close. What are essential now are wisdom, commitment, and serious work.

THE PROFESSIONAL SOCIAL WORKER IN A BUREAUCRACY

Harry Wasserman

The professional social worker in a public welfare bureaucracy serves two masters—his professional self, embodying intellectual and moral criteria, and his employing organization, with its demands and constraints. In a previous article the author discussed the general question of the comparative influence of social work education and structural constraints on social work practice.[1] In this article he discusses specifically the neophyte professional social worker's life in a bureaucracy. Some of the areas that will be explored are the following: How does the bureaucratic structure support or constrain the worker's professional activities? What is the nature of the transactions and interactions he makes in order to perform his role as efficiently and effectively as possible? How does he maneuver within the bureaucracy to gain what he needs for his clients? In what ways does the bureaucratic structure manipulate him?

POSITION OF RELATIVE POWERLESSNESS

The formal organization of the agency involved in this study places the professional social worker at one of the lower levels of authority and power. Administratively he is responsible to the following ascending hierarchy: a supervisor who is his immediate superior, a deputy director who fills the role of a chief of supervisors, a district director, and higher administrators who are physically and operationally removed from the worker's daily activities because they are located in the agency's central office. Operationally, however, it is the supervisor to whom the worker turns for expertise, guidance, and organizational support.

An analysis of supervisor–worker transactions reveals some apsects of the way the bureaucratic structure works. Each supervisor is administratively responsible for five workers and generally meets with each one on a regular basis (e.g., once a week or once every two weeks). The supervisor is also available as an emergency consultant at unscheduled times. During supervisory conferences, the worker explains what he has been doing, discusses problems in case management, negotiates for the fulfillment of clients' material needs, and seeks advice and guidance concerning the problems of specific clients. This practice is fairly typical of supervisor–worker transactions. It is quite striking, however, that the supervisor rarely meets with his five workers as a group except when new regulations, rules, and procedures must be explained. During the two-year span of the study there were no group meetings with a supervisor for the purpose of discussing case problems rather than administrative procedures. This fact raises the following questions: Why are so few group meetings of supervisors and workers initiated by the supervisor? Conversely, why is it that professional social workers never insist on having group meetings to discuss and grapple with the common recurrent problems and issues they face?

There are several factors that when acting together militate against group meetings. The administration can more effectively maintain control over

Source: Copyright 1971, National Association of Social Workers, Inc. Reprinted with permission, from *Social Work*, Vol. 16, No. 1 (January 1971), pp. 89–95.

the workers if workers must deal with their supervisor as individual entrepreneurs or contractors. For instance, a particularly resourceful and ingenious young worker who is capable of providing special items for his clients might inadvertently disclose in formal sessions the many ways to "work the system."*

By negotiating with the worker at the formal level of supervision as if he were a private entrepreneur, the administration avoids the introduction of resourcefulness and ingenuity into the formal system. On the other hand, by accomplishing things for his clients, the worker receives gratification that sustains him in his work. Paradoxically, however, it is clear that the individual worker's successes serve to gloss over or cover up the harsh inadequacies of the system. In struggling for successful outcomes within his own caseload, the worker tends to forget that the penurious institutional resources are abrasive and harmful to significant numbers of families and children whose social workers are less endowed with the qualities of resourcefulness and ingenuity.

The questionable legal maneuvers to protect clients from what, in the worker's opinion, are excessively harsh rules and regulations are justified by the worker as "situation ethics."[2] For example, the worker obtains an increase in a foster family's monthly grant because the foster child has a behavior disorder (the child actually does not, but the worker feels that because the foster parents are doing a good job they deserve a few extra dollars per month); an adolescent foster child earns enough money to necessitate recomputing his grant, but the worker "forgets" about it; or an AFDC mother has a friend who contributes financially, but the worker "forgets" about it. Although the worker may try to convince himself of the validity of his position, he does not quite succeed. He feels guilty, tense, and uneasy when he has acted in a questionable, unethical manner.

---

*In "working the system," some workers develop informal alliances with supervisors, cashiers, and clerks, who then serve as expediters. If the workers are relatively moderate in their demands, they can be quite successful in obtaining material goods for their clients, as well as jobs, housing, and medical care. Evidently these alliances are known to those who must process special requests, and the worker may discuss some of his moves with others, but the extralegal moves are kept secret.

WORKERS' PERCEPTION OF SUPERVISION

Most of the workers in the study had more than one line supervisor during their period of employment with the agency; only three of the twelve judged their supervisors to be competent and therefore helpful. The majority of these young workers perceived the supervisory position to be primarily a bureaucratic control device; thus the way the supervisors functioned had little or nothing to do with social work values, knowledge, and skills.

The supervisor performs the function of organizational mediator; he makes judgments and decisions about workers' claims and demands on behalf of their clients on the basis of the agency's scarce resources. In other words, he negotiates on behalf of the organization with the worker who represents the clients.

The supervisor rarely sees the worker's clients except in emergencies. His role is to talk about clients, not to them. Thus he only knows the client through the worker and must make reasoned judgments and decisions based on a complex of variables that includes the client's actual situation, the worker's perception and definition of that situation, and the agency's capacity to provide an item or series of items. If the supervisor is responsible for five workers with a total of 175–200 cases or more, one questions whether he can make reasoned and balanced judgments about any problematic human situations, particularly when he must base his judgments on what the workers say about clients.

The majority of the new workers viewed their supervisors as insecure and frightened people who were unsure of their authority and power, conforming, lacking courage, unwilling to take a stand on critical issues involving either workers or clients, and more sensitized and attuned to organizational demands and needs than to those of the clients. They also believed that the system wanted passive, uninspired people in supervisory positions, that the need for supervisors with master's degrees was just another manifestation of our "credential society";[3] that credentials and comformity were more important for system maintenance than knowledge, competence, and skill; and that image and facade were valued more highly than reality and substance.

The agency's utilization, whenever possible, of graduate social work supervisory personnel and the lack of resistance of supervisory personnel to the impediments of the system probably accounted in part for the noticeable increase in cynicism among the new workers during the two-year period of study. This growing cynicism, plus the frustrations of working with difficult clients (many of whom were chronically in disastrous situations), and the cumulative reactions of physical and emotional fatigue inevitably produced situations of great stress. The workers protected themselves in such situations, but the cost was the reinforcement of their natural defense mechanisms to the point of rigidity and brittleness.* Functionally this meant that they worked with many of their clients in a routine, uninspired way.

There are two solutions to such a dilemma. The worker can remain in the agency and eventually be promoted to a supervisory position, which will remove him from the clients, or he can leave the agency for another job (the solution chosen by six of the workers in the study).** If he remains and becomes a supervisor, he will adapt to the system. He may rationalize that he will do things differently and try to change the system, but he realizes that because bureaucracies do not change easily, structural change is a tremendously difficult, long-term undertaking. As Dahrendorf explains:

> Bureaucratic organizations typically display continuous gradations of competence and authority and are hierarchical. Within dichotomous organizations class conflict is possible; within hierarchical organizations it is not. This difference has an important consequence for the definition of bureaucratic roles. Insofar as bureaucratic roles are defined in the context of a career hierarchy, they do not generate a [class] conflict of interest with other bureaucratic roles.[4]

This means that all employees of a bureaucracy, regardless of their hierarchical status, are essentially "... on the same side of the fence that divides the positions of dominance from those of subjection."[5] In the long run, it is extremely difficult for a professional social worker in a bureaucracy to be an impassioned advocate for his clients, because in so doing he must come into conflict with agency administrators as well as professional colleagues. If he cannot mobilize the support of both colleagues and welfare rights or other organizations that represent clients, he will be forced to leave the agency. If the new professional remains in the agency and eventually moves to the position of supervisor, he is constrained to "play the game," which includes accepting the meager systemic inputs and the dysfunctional aspects of the bureaucratic structure.*

WORKERS' VIEW
OF THE ADMINISTRATION

Almost invariably the new professionals in this study looked on the higher administrators of the agency as "them." The administrators were not quite "the enemy," but they were viewed as being unconcerned about the worker's involvements with his clients except when financial accountability was an issue. The most important indication of the administrators' lack of concern for clients, according to the observations of the workers, was the nature of the communication system, which was generally a one-way flow from top to bottom.

One of the assumptions of the "rational" system of organization is that knowledge, competence, authority, and important decision making are at the top of the organizational pyramid, and ignorance, passivity, and capacity for routine performance are on the bottom. As Blau and Scott point out, when the need for a highly coordinated organization is imperative, communication is of low organizational value.[6] This generalization also applies to the agency in which the flow of information from top to bottom is considered the normal pathway and direction of communication. It is true that workers can write memorandums to higher administrators through their supervisor, but these are rarely acted on. Therefore, the workers virtually have no way to voice their work needs, observations, good ideas, or creative innovations.

The social work education of these neophyte professionals apparently gave them no experience in

---

*As reported in Wasserman, op. cit., three of the twelve new professionals in the study suffered from psychiatric difficulties that they believed were triggered by their work situations.
**At the termination of the study, eight of the twelve new professionals had left the agency. Six of the resignations were voluntary and two were involuntary (one worker was drafted into the armed forces; the other moved to another city as a consequence of her husband's employment situation).

---

*In a bureaucracy a skeleton of "permanent cadre"—supervisors and administrators, professional and nonprofessional—maintain the system. Many of them have become thoroughly acclimated to the system. Little research has been done on either the self-concepts or the sociological functions of these long-term employees.

working together as members of a professional collectivity, e.g., in identifying their clients' needs or gaps in programs, social resources, and social utilities. As a professional group with a sense of collective responsibility, social workers do not pressure the system on behalf of clients—they accept the system. For example, the workers studied were prone to make such statements as the following: "You can't fight city hall," "The county supervisors (commissioners) are the real bosses," "What's the use of trying to change things when it's impossible to do so," and so forth. Such statements connote more than poor morale; they are part of a system of beliefs. Such defeatism and cynicism (as cognitive and emotional "sets") are psychological reflections of what Kenniston calls the "institutionalization of hypocrisy."

Of course, no society ever fully lives up to its own professed ideals. In every society there is a gap between creedal values and actual practices, and in every society the recognition of this gap constitutes a powerful motor for social change. But in most societies, especially when change is slow and institutions are powerful and unchanging, there occurs what can be termed institutionalization of hypocrisy.[7]

The social welfare bureaucracy only expresses the profound hypocrisy of a larger society. The agency is neither the conspiracy of a small group nor the perpetual fiefdom of cruel men who have deliberately decided to harm or destroy families and children. The agency's cruelty reflects society's pejorative attitudes about broken, poor families who must rely on the public for special kinds of aid.

Dahrendorf explains the purposes and functions of bureaucracies and their power position in a society as follows:

... although ... [bureaucracies] always belong to the ruling class, because bureaucratic roles are roles of dominance, bureaucracies as such never are the ruling class. Their latent interests aim at the maintenance of what exists; but what it is that exists is not decided by bureaucracies, but given to them....[8]

Dahrendorf's conceptualization of the purposes and functions of bureaucracies is dramatically illustrated by the fact that financial accountability is the supreme value and all other values are subordinate to it. For example, the social worker with a master's degree is not permitted to make a judgment or decision about a client's need for an extra grocery order; he must obtain authorization from two higher supervisor-administrators. If translated into whether the professional social worker is capable of making judgments and decisions about a client whose immediate future is hunger, the overriding organizational value of financial accountability means, in an objective sense, indignity and humiliation for the worker. Subjectively, some of the new workers felt this indignity and humiliation; others did not.

CLIENTS AS OBJECTS

Bureaucratic inefficiency is usually equated with an excessive amount of menial activities, e.g., red tape, paper work, and the like. The new professionals in the study complained about the amount of paper work, but when emotionally unable to see clients even the most committed workers found respite in paper work and other office routines. Most professional social workers protest that such routine activities as maintaining files, keeping records, and collating statistics are beneath their professional competence; yet it is such menial work that allows them to objectify their clients, i.e., to regard them as objects rather than people. To preserve his mental health, a worker must not be too sensitive about the clients' plights or become too involved with their "outcomes." Thus, although bureaucratic procedures that cause dehumanization of clients are severely criticized, they are probably a psychic necessity for some workers.

What then is questionable and inevitably harmful in the process of client "objectification"? It is that the bureaucracy tends to dehumanize recipients by viewing them as cases and numbers or as objects related to financial accountability. If it is inevitable that workers will dehumanize their clients because psychologically they need to perceive them as abstractions, what does finally intervene on behalf of the client? It is simply the "sometimes" humanity of the worker. The word *sometimes* is critical, because it is psychologically impossible for a worker constantly to be a feeling, responsible human who is prepared at all times to cope with human disorder and disaster. However, the fact that the worker sometimes treats the client as a worthwhile human being keeps the system partially viable and, more important, the client feels that someone does care for him.

However, the cumulative effects of insufficient resources, bureaucratic structure, and personal fallibility finally can force the workers toward:

working on a different set of problems from those the . . . [organization] has set for them. . . . There is a sharp distinction that must be made between behavior that copes with the requirements of a problem and behavior that is designed to defend against entry into the problem. It is the distinction one might make between playing tennis on the one hand and fighting like fury to stay off the tennis court altogether on the other.[9]

The worker can defend himself by becoming overinvolved in paper work, a specific case, informal meetings with colleagues, aimless driving, and so on. In other words, he can spend a large amount of time avoiding meaningful encounters with clients.

The bureaucratic system stimulates and reinforces defending rather than coping behavior by keeping the worker off balance. The constant changes in caseloads, rules, regulations, and procedures imposed from above produce a state of insecurity and instability in the worker. Thus the new professional's underinvolvement in initiating or participating in the creation of policies and procedures was undoubtedly another important cause of excessive defending behavior and low morale.

INFORMAL ORGANIZATIONS

According to Gouldner, informal organizations are "spontaneously emergent and normatively sanctioned structures in the organization.[10] Although one of the latent functions of the informal organization is to permit people to act as people rather than as occupants of specific positions or as incumbents of a structured role, organizational theorists generally assume that the informal organization in a bureaucracy tends to support the goals of the formal organization.

The informal organization—which must be understood specifically in this context as small groups of two or more people who are peers—primarily serves two functions: (1) it is the focal point for expressing complaints about the agency and (2) it is the most important social system for providing emotional support for workers and a sense of mutuality among them.[11] Workers let off steam in their informal meetings with colleagues while working at their desks, when they meet with other workers accidentally in the halls, and during planned and unplanned coffee breaks. Their complaints cover a wide range of difficulties involving clients, other workers, supervisors, bureaucratic obstacles, and so on.

More important than the content of the complaints, however, are the latent functions of these informal gripe sessions: They provide emotional support for the worker in the sense that he can talk to a peer who understands, and they are a mechanism for draining off and deflecting the worker's need for a more formally organized, systematic approach to his problem as a worker in a bureaucracy. Thus, although some of the verbal attacks against the agency are subversive in the sense that they frequently carry a high anti-authority component, the complaining done in the informal group is essentially functional to the maintenance of the formal system's equilibrium. As Coser has shown, much social conflict can be encapsulated within a social structure; in fact social conflict often supports it.[12]

In district offices where there were other professional workers, the new professionals were members of small informal groups. In those offices in which there were few, if any, professional social workers, the new professional was almost totally isolated. The workers who gave and received emotional support from informal relationships unquestionably had higher morale than those who were deprived of this experience. When the new worker was the only professional, or one of few professionals, he tended to reject the camaraderie of the nonprofessionals because he saw himself as different from them. This was probably a defensive reaction against the nonprofessionals, who saw him as a threat because he was engaged in the same work but received greater financial rewards and a higher status.

CONCLUSION

The large public welfare agency—with its bureaucratic structure—is the embodiment of a profound moral ambivalence toward the people it serves. On the one hand its manifest purpose is to help needy persons; on the other hand its latent function is to "punish" those who are unable to maintain independent successful lives by failing to provide conditions by which they can help themselves or be helped. Its main aim is financial accountability—not accountability to the people it serves.

The social worker in such a bureaucracy is

caught up in this brutal intersection of contradictory values. If he actually tries to help his clients and "buck" the organization, he often suffers from emotional and physical fatigue and becomes cynical and defeatist about the nature of social work. If he adapts to the bureaucracy, he at best experiences massive frustration; at worst he becomes a "mindless functionary."[13]

It is time for the social work profession, bureaucrats, and schools of social work to stop hiding their knowledge of bureaucracies. What we now need is new ideas, concepts, and models—in short, a new vision to reconstruct our working lives and new ways to relate to each other and to those we serve.

NOTES

[1]The study on which this article and the author's previous article were based involved observing twelve new professional social workers over a two-year period. For an overall discussion of the study and some general theoretical considerations, *see* Harry Wasserman, "Early Careers of Professional Social Workers in a Public Child Welfare Agency," *Social Work*, Vol. 15, No. 3 (July 1970); pp. 93–101.

[2]Joseph Fletcher, *Situation Ethics* (Philadelphia: Westminister Press, 1966).

[3]*See* Edgar Z. Friedenberg, "Status and Role in Education," *Humanist*, Vol. 28, No. 5 (September–October 1968): 13.

[4]Ralf Dahrendorf, *Class and Class Conflict in Industrial Society* (Stanford, Calif.: Stanford University Press, 1959), p. 296.

[5]Ibid.

[6]Peter M. Blau and W. Richard Scott, *Formal Organizations: A Comparative Approach* (San Francisco: Chandler Publishing, 1962), p. 242.

[7]Kenneth Kenniston, "Youth, Change, and Violence," *American Scholar*, Vol. 37, No. 2 (Spring 1968): p. 239.

[8]Dahrendorf, op. cit., p. 300.

[9]Jerome S. Bruner, *Toward a Theory of Instruction* (Cambridge, Mass.: Harvard University Press, 1966), pp. 3–4.

[10]Alvin W. Gouldner, "Organizational Analysis," in Robert K. Merton et al., eds., *Sociology Today* (New York: Basic Books, 1959), p. 406.

[11]*See* Earl Bogdanoff and Arnold Glass, *The Sociology of the Public Assistance Caseworker in an Urban Area.* Unpublished master's thesis, University of Chicago, 1954.

[12]Lewis A. Coser, *The Functions of Social Conflict* (London: Routledge & Kegan Paul, 1956).

[13]Hannah Arendt, *Eichmann in Jerusalem: A Report on the Banality of Evil* (New York: Viking Press, 1964), p. 289.

PART III

Knowledge for Practice

The material presented in the first two parts serves as an important foundation for that which is at the heart of every profession: the knowledge used by its practitioners. Unless a profession can demonstrate possession of a common body of knowledge for use by its practitioners, it can scarcely lay claim to professional status (Greenwood 1957; Bartlett 1970). The task of Part III of the book, then, is to present some of the fundamental elements of the knowledge used in social work practice.

WHAT IS KNOWLEDGE FOR SOCIAL WORK?

In his review of issues regarding knowledge for social work, Kadushin (1959) defined the knowledge base of social work as a topic "which encompasses the facts and theories, skills and attitudes necessary for effective, efficient practice" (p. 39). In other words, the knowledge base of social work is a complex amalgam of ideas, principles, facts, theories and parts of theories, and assumptions. For Gordon (1965), knowledge is that which has been established by high standards of objectivity and rationality. This is a view seconded by Bartlett (1970), who states that knowledge refers to verifiable experiences that appear in the form of rigorous statements that are made as objective as possible. Both of these authors define knowledge in contrast to values—that is, that which is preferred, or desired, or "should be." Hence, one distinction between knowledge and values is that the former may be confirmed objectively while the latter may not.

For purposes of this book, *knowledge* is defined as an organized body of information or the comprehension and understanding derived from the acquisition of an organized body of information. This definition in particular takes into account one of the key elements that Greenwood (1957) has suggested can distinguish a profession from a nonprofession or occupation: a systematic body of theory. The chief difference between this and the Greenwood position is that this definition of knowledge includes but goes beyond the use of theory, if theory is defined only as any more or less formalized conceptualization of the relationship of variables (Marx 1963). Hence, Greenwood's key "attribute" of a profession might more properly be redefined or extended to include a whole range of concepts, principles, and models that might not be theory related, but still might—as knowledge—furnish direction for social workers in practice. (One of the best reviews of the variety of terms relevant to this discussion is available in Siporin, 1975, pp. 350–68).

Knowledge to What End?

The latter part of the above discussion defined a crucial characteristic of knowledge for social work practice: it should be used to guide and direct practice. Hence, to narrow this elusive concept somewhat further, knowledge for social work can be seen as composed of two, often overlapping, categories. The first is *developmental knowledge,* knowledge that is used as an aid in understanding the development of a particular problem, person, situation, or even specific behavior. Such knowledge is intended to answer the question "why did a particular state of affairs come about?" The second category is *intervention knowledge,* which is used to prescribe principles and procedures for inducing change in problematic situations and/or behaviors. Intervention knowledge is designed to answer the question "what can be done to modify this particular state of affairs and will it be effective?"

Both of these types of knowledge, to be most effective for social work practice, should be used together. By definition, a professional practice rests on a body of knowledge, the purpose of which is to supply the practitioner with the capacity to influence or change events. Indeed, *practice knowledge* can be described as being composed of two parts, those parts corresponding to the two categories described above. The first part involves a systematic presentation of assessment principles with the goal of understanding the client/system, problem, or situation about which we are concerned and using the results as a guide to selection of methods of intervention. This is where developmental knowledge is used—to furnish direction for the processes of social work *assessment.* The second part involves a systematic explication of principles of induced change and procedures for implementing those principles, with the goal of inducing change in the phenomena of concern. This, of course, involves *intervention* knowledge.

Now, hypothetically, assessment and intervention principles are utilized together, with one leading to the other. A body of knowledge for professional practice comprised only of developmental/assessment principles would leave the social worker with clear understanding of the problem, but an inability to change it. Similarly, a body of knowledge comprised only of interventive principles and procedures might leave the social worker knowing how to implement change, but with an inability to know where, when, and with whom. This is to say, then, that the fundamentals of knowledge for social work practice are knowledge to undergird assessment practices and knowledge to provide interventive strategies and procedures.

Knowledge from Where?

There are two primary sources of knowledge for social work practice: (1) knowledge derived from other fields and (2) knowledge derived from within the social work profession. A large part of the knowledge used in social work is based on material adapted from other fields—that is, from sociology, psychology, medicine, and from most of the social and behavioral sciences. Over the many years of the history of social work, knowledge has been selected from these sources based on its apparent relevance for social work, tested in practice, and sometimes extended or reformulated in social work terms (Bartlett 1970).

Of course there are several problems inherent in derivation of knowledge from other fields (Kadushin 1959):

1.   Because of a time lag in such derivation, we may tend to adapt outdated knowledge; hence, it behooves social workers to be constantly on the alert—through use of the litera-

ture—for advances in other fields and, especially, to evaluate those advances to determine their usefulness;

2.   We may well endow the borrowed knowledge with a greater degree of certainty than the donor discipline itself; hence, social workers must evaluate the relevance and utility of borrowed knowledge with regard to the specific social work problems for which it is to be used;

3.   It is possible to be misled by oversimplified versions of the borrowed knowledge; hence, it is important to avoid the temptation of seeking quick, simple answers to some of the complex problems with which social workers deal;

4.   There is a danger of confusion of professional identities resulting from borrowed knowledge;

5.   There is a potential danger that borrowed knowledge will become "an undigested lump" in social work practice: somehow there, but never thoroughly understood nor wisely used.

While these are indeed real problems, it is possible that sensitivity to and awareness of them will minimize their effects. But even though borrowed knowledge does present social work—or any profession—with certain difficulties, an even greater danger to the profession would be ignoring knowledge developed by others, because knowledge developed in other fields might be immensely productive to social workers in terms of being translatable into demonstrable benefits for our clients. Thus, the key principle is that social workers must continue to look wherever they can—both within and without their own field—for knowledge and methods of practice that may increase their chances of providing more effective services to clients. The distinctive configuration of values, philosophy, and goals described in Parts I and II of this book, plus the unique concentration of social work on enhancing client social functioning, are all safeguards to ensure that the knowledge will be used in accordance with basic social work principles. The allegiance of social workers must be to finding and utilizing the best knowledge available, whether developed by social workers or other professionals.

Because social workers—as do physicians, engineers, and all other professions—utilize knowledge developed by others, does this mean that social work should be content to let all its knowledge be imported from "outside?" As was stated earlier, the second important source of knowledge for social work practice is knowledge derived from social work experience. Most of the reading selections in this part of the book comprise knowledge developed by and for social workers, which has been and can be a major source of knowledge for practice. Much of this knowledge comes from the experience of professional social workers' working with people and helping them meet a wide range of life problems; this is the *practice wisdom* of the profession (Bartlett 1970). This is knowledge that may not have been rigorously tested in experimental research, but might be extracted from case studies in the literature, taught in courses in schools of social work, and passed on through supervision, consultation, and conferences.

Practice wisdom is not the only form of knowledge that social workers themselves can produce. Indeed, not only must social workers be aware of the methods professionals in other fields are using and the research they are conducting, but social workers can and have developed their own methods and conducted their own research into approaches that work best (Hollis 1973; Roberts and Nee 1970; Turner 1974). Thus, what is ultimately sought is a blend of knowledge from within and without the profession to be integrated with the common values and philosophy of social work and focused on one overriding concern: the benefit of our clients.

How Should Knowledge Be Selected?

It should be clear that, above all else, the knowledge base of social work practice is an eclectic one, in the sense of social workers' owing no particular allegiance to any one particular theoretical orientation. Further, it is eclectic in the sense of "not following any one system as of philosophy, medicine, etc., but selecting and using whatever is best in all systems" (*American College Dictionary* 1957, p. 381). This definition calls for the knowledge selected and used by social workers to be carefully evaluated and systematically integrated in such a way that different aspects of the whole support and buttress each other and provide a broader range of options for the social worker in his practice. Indeed, there are many principles that social workers might consider as useful criteria for selecting and integrating different approaches for practice. These principles or criteria suggest an integration at the professional rather than theoretical level, since each offers philosophical, conceptual, and/or empirical evidence for use or nonuse of a given approach by social workers. (The principles that follow consist of an abridgement of several dozen criteria that might be applied in selection of an approach; see Fischer [1978] for a more extensive discussion of these points.)

As presented in Part I, the first set of principles is related to the basic philosophy of social work, particularly the key value of our respect for the *dignity and worth of every individual.* Hence, at the broadest level, the first set of principles involves the extent to which utilization of an approach would be congruent with the values of a profession. In actual practice, a given approach can be evaluated as ethically suitable if its utilization does not demean—rather, if it enhances or maintains—the dignity and individuality of the people involved, both the worker and the client.

A second dimension for use in selecting and integrating knowledge involves the area of knowledge to be examined. Given the explosion of knowledge in recent years in the social and behavioral sciences, a social worker must have some guidelines to help in wending one's way through the constantly expanding maze of ideas. As noted by Bartlett (1970), social work must identify an area of central concern that is: (1) common to the profession as a whole, (2) meaningful in relation to the profession's values and goals, (3) practical in terms of available and attainable knowledge and techniques, and (4) sufficiently distinctive so that it does not simply duplicate what other professions are doing. For social work, this area of central concern is *social functioning.* Social functioning refers to the behavior of individuals as they attempt to cope with life tasks and environmental demands, to the active and exchanging relationships of individuals with their environment, and to the feedback and consequences to both individuals and environment flowing from that relationship (see Bartlett 1970, Chapter 6; and Butler 1970). Based on this affirmation of the importance of knowledge for practice that leads to the enhancement of client social functioning, the criterion for knowledge selection is that the knowledge be relevant to understanding and affecting social functioning and pertinent to understanding and affecting the social, interpersonal, and psychological characteristics of human beings.

A third dimension to be considered in knowledge selection is the extent to which an approach deals with interventive practice. Thus, if it is developmental knowledge under consideration, that knowledge would provide understanding that would have direct implications for selection of *intervention methods.* If the knowledge were interventive knowledge, it would be composed of a systematic explanation of how change comes about, plus prescription of specific procedures or techniques so that the social worker can actually implement, or apply in practice, the approach.

Another criterion to be considered is the extent to which aspects of the approach have been validated in *empirical research.* Thus if, for developmental knowledge, an approach has predictive value or, for intervention knowledge, there is clear evidence of effectiveness in practice with clients, these approaches must be considered as prime candidates for use by social workers. This is not to say that approaches without evidence are to be ignored; the approach may be new and the evidence not yet developed. Rather the principle is that the greater the degree of empirical validation contained within an approach, the more likely is the approach one that must be seriously considered by social workers.

A final criterion for selection and integration of knowledge for practice is the *heuristic value* of an approach: Is it useful in serving as a tool for guiding empirical investigation, for ordering relevant knowledge, and for facilitating understanding of complex phenomena?

TWO EXAMPLES OF KNOWLEDGE FOR PRACTICE

Given the discussion in the Introduction of the two types of knowledge for practice—developmental and intervention—two perspectives that are being increasingly utilized by social workers are briefly discussed below as illustrations. The first is *systems theory*, an example of developmental knowledge for practice; the second is *behavior modification*, an example of intervention knowledge for practice.

Systems Theory

Actually systems theory is technically not a theory, but more of a model that provides the tools for analysis and a way of thinking about and organizing data (Janchill 1969). Systems theory has been proposed by several authors as a likely conceptual framework for social work: Hearn (1969); Compton and Galaway (1975); and Pincus and Minahan (1973). Essentially, *systems theory* focuses not on individuals but on *systems*: the interactions between and interrelatedness of units. Hence, it allows a holistic orientation to complex organizations in which individuals and their social and physical environments are viewed as interacting wholes; specifically:

> *General systems theory is a series of related definitions, assumptions, and postulates about all levels of systems from atomic particles through ... galaxies. General behavior systems theory is a subcategory of such theory dealing with living systems, extending roughly from viruses to societies. Perhaps the most significant fact about living systems is that they are open systems, with important inputs and outputs. Laws which apply to them differ from those applying to relatively closed systems. [Miller 1955]*

A system is a set of objects together with relationships between the objects and between their attributes (Hearn 1974). Systems can be open or closed; have boundaries; contain various stresses, strains, and conflicts; have a tendency to achieve a balance among their various parts; are constantly in the process of change and movement; and provide mechanisms for feedback—that is, inputs and outputs across boundaries. (All of these terms and the basic characteristics of systems are defined in Chin [1961]; Hearn [1969, 1974]; and Janchill [1969]).

What is important about systems theory is the use to which social workers can put this body of knowledge. Many of the potential values of systems theory as a conceptual framework for social work have been summarized by Compton and Galaway (1975, pp. 66, 67):

1. Systems theory allows social workers to bring order into a massive amount of information from all the different disciplines from which social work must draw;

2. The concepts of systems theory are equally applicable to the range of clients seen by social workers, from the individual to society;

3.   Systems theory provides a framework for gaining an appreciation of the entire range of elements that bears on social problems;

4.   Systems theory focuses attention on the *interaction* between people and their environment, allowing the concept of social functioning to be more adequately studied and understood;

5.   Systems theory tends to negate interactive disturbances of people as "sick" or "pathological" and moves the social worker into the present life of the system;

6.   Systems theory, focused on transactions between systems, provides a framework for viewing the important social work function of providing and maintaining such interchange opportunities;

7.   Systems theory focuses social work's attention on populations and systems headed toward isolation and on the strains impelling such isolation;

8.   The concepts of change and tensions in open systems focuses social workers' attention on how and why such changes can be generated and often are resisted;

9.   The systems theory conception of change in one part of the system often greatly affecting changes in other parts or even the whole, focuses attention on the impact of social work intervention at one point—which must be carefully selected—affecting other aspects of the system. This broadens the concepts of the point at which social workers can enter a system, making such entry more efficient and more effective.

Behavior Modification.

The emerging technology of behavior modification is an excellent example of a body of intervention knowledge. Behavior modification is a technology of helping that has implications particularly for social work intervention with individuals, families, and groups, and some work is proceeding using behavioral principles with larger collectivities. Essentially, *behavior modification* can be defined as the planned, systematic application of experimentally established principles of learning to the modification of maladaptive behavior. There are basically three general fields or areas of behavior modification: the *operant, respondent,* and *modeling* or *social learning* (see Fischer and Gochros [1975] for in-depth discussion of these terms). From these three areas and their basic principles, researchers and practitioners have devised a range of specific procedures for decreasing undesired behaviors and increasing desired behaviors. The socioenvironmental emphasis of behavior modification, which focuses on the total person and change goals involved in social functioning, is particularly congruent with the type of intervention knowledge central to the development of a common base for social work (Bartlett 1970).

There are numerous advantages for social work in the use of behavior modification (Fischer and Gochros 1975, pp. xi, xii): (1) It respects the integrity of the client by focusing on observed behavior and limiting itself to diminishing maladaptive functioning and increasing adaptive functioning; (2) there is accumulating research evidence of the effectiveness of behavior modification procedures with a variety of problem situations. Furthermore, the fact that each case in which behavior modification is used allows for—indeed demands—specifying the problematic behaviors and systematically recording the changes in these behaviors, leads to testing the effectiveness of the procedure with each situation; (3) there is a clear, logical connection between the assessment of the case and the resulting intervention plan for modifying the behavior by changing these conditions; (4) the basic principles of behavior modification are clear and easily communicated and may be taught to nonprofessional personnel and individuals within the natural environment of the client, thereby giving such personnel an effective, easily comprehensible method of assisting in the process of altering dysfunctional behavior; (5) the behavior modification approach has generated numerous specific procedures that the social worker can differentially apply, depending on the nature of the problem, situation, and client; (6) the behavior modification approach is efficient; many cases and situations can be handled more quickly and with less professional time, either directly or by utilizing people in the client's natural environment, than is possible with other approaches; (7) the behavior modification approach encourages "self-change" by the clients themselves by teaching them how to arrange the conditions that affect their behavior outside the interview situation; (8) behavior modification is oriented toward prevention; as noted above, parents, teachers, and others within the natural environment of the client may be taught change procedures in order to more directly affect the behavior in the client or individual; (9) there is a wide range of applicability of behavior modification, both in terms of problems and clients. The procedures of behavior modification have been effectively applied with individuals from upper- and lower-income groups, including clients without skills at verbal communication. Behavior modification has been effectively used with clients typically seen in family service agencies, outpatient clinics, and with a range of people and problems that traditionally have been considered "hopeless," such as "retarded" or "autistic" residents in psychiatric hospitals, delinquents, and so on; (10) behavior modification provides principles and procedures for socioenvironmental change that are to be applied directly to people, or—if their natural ecology must be altered—to the systems of which they are a part. Further, these basic principles are the same at all levels of intervention—individual, family, group, social system; (11) behavior modification is compatible with major ideas of other current conceptual frameworks utilized in social work practice that attempt to understand and modify human behavior in terms of its environmental context, such as role theory, system theory, and group dynamics. Thus, these approaches—and a range of others with empirical evidence of success—can supplement behavior modification and its base in learning theory to give a more comprehensive view of both interpersonal behavior and, more importantly for social work, intervention into human problems.

READING SELECTIONS IN PART III

Much of the knowledge presented in Part III of the book has been developed in relatively recent times. Of the seven papers, four were written or revised specifically for this book and the other three were published in the 1970s. The point is not only that these are relatively new developments, but that they portend a fertile and exciting future for continuing innovations and knowledge-building in social work. Indeed, the first book to be published that attempted to conceptualize a generic or common base for the profession was published only in 1970 (Bartlett 1970).

Most of the material in the reading selections that follow was developed by and for social workers—that is, the focus here is less on knowledge that has been derived from other fields than it is on knowledge that social workers themselves have conceptualized and begun to test out in order to enhance social work practice. Of course, precisely because the knowledge used in social work has such a broad base, a great deal of selectivity was exercised in choosing articles for this part. The purpose here is to present a conceptual framework for social work practice that develops the fundamentals in terms of presenting specific models to guide practice and providing some core knowledge that can actually be used in practice. The knowledge presented in Part III is not intended to be viewed in isolation from parts I and II. Thus, when such knowledge is implemented in practice, it should be done in a manner congruent with the values and special emphases of the profession.

The reading selections presented in Part III were chosen on the basis of their relevance to the development of a common base for practice, their interrelationships with each other, and their implications for actual practice. Specifically, they illustrate the following: the issues involved in considering the development of generalist practice and some of the ensuing consequences for the profession; a rationale and conceptual framework for generalist practice; a model that focuses on integrating interventive efforts with both individuals and environments at the conceptual level; the use of role and system concepts to develop a framework for assessing points for intervention; a framework that presents a step-by-step guide for practice with individuals and their environments, integrating both assessment and interventive considerations; and an overview of some of the research required for enhancing the effectiveness of social work practice. In summary, these reading selections focus on: (1) fundamentals of the practice of social work both at general and specific levels and in relation to models that guide practice, (2) specific knowledge that can be used in practice, and (3) research for evaluating and monitoring practice.

"General Practice and Specialization in Professional Social Work" by Aptekar refers to a seeming tension in professional practice between general practice and specialization. Paradoxically, even as we come to a realization of the need for a more generic emphasis in practice, there is a newer appreciation of the need for specialization, even within a generic framework. Aptekar contributes significantly to further conceptualization in the area of social work practice by developing diverse models of general social work practice. Included in his models of the generalist social work practitioner are: generalist in terms of outlook and orientation; generalist in terms of methods and skills; generalist in the sense of an ability to work effectively across at least two methods; generalist in terms of the agency's framework, where the practitioner is exposed to a broad range of problems that necessitates versatility in the use of a broad range of skills selectively applied; generalist within a specific field of practice; and generalist within a specialized method.

"Rationale for a Generalist Approach to Social Work Practice" by Brown also helps set the tone for the remainder of the selections. Brown goes beyond establishing a rationale for a generalist practice and develops a conceptual framework for such practice based on a "solution-seeking stance" for the social worker within a social problems context whereby all methods of social work can be used singly, serially, or in combination. Brown also provides a framework for generalist assessment and intervention, gives several examples of generalist practice, and discusses the implications for social work practice of proceeding from a generalist base.

"Social Work Practice: A Life Model" by Gitterman and Germain presents a model of practice that attempts to integrate two historic social work positions: (1) emphasis on knowledge and skill to effect change in persons, and (2) emphasis on knowledge and skill to effect change in environments. The authors call this a *life model*: an ecological/reciprocal perspective that also helps to integrate the traditional methodological specializations of casework, group work, and community organization. The goal here is to provide people and their environments simultaneous professional attention through an ecological theoretical perspective and a reciprocal conception of social work function. Traditionally defined needs and issues are reconceptualized from "personality states" and "environmental states" to problems in living as a guide for developing professional interventions.

"The Integration of Individual and Environmental Change Efforts: A Conceptual Framework" by Garvin and Glasser moves to a more specific level. Garvin and Glasser actually integrate not only individual and environmental change efforts, but a substantial body of knowledge about both assessment and intervention, such as the material presented in previous reading selections. Their article concretely describes processes for assessment and intervention in a particularly helpful way: by operationalizing a model that is based on the varying functions of social welfare organizations. Their *organizational-environmental model* therefore allows for the identification of similarities and differences across a variety of practice situations. The focus in this reading selection is on social work practice with individuals, families, and groups; but the model itself—proceeding as it does in a planned, systematic way through assessment of and intervention with both individual and environment—facilitates the social worker's providing broader services based on client need rather than providing limited services based only on a narrow range of worker techniques.

"Locating and Using Points for Intervention" by Atherton, Mitchell, and Schein uses role and system concepts to develop a scheme for classifying some of the common problems with which social workers are faced in practice. Their classification uses three major categories: (1) problems related to performance of legitimate and acceptable roles, (2) problematical roles, and (3) problems in the structure in social systems. Next the authors discuss the various interventive roles for social workers to assume in relation to those problems. The table at the end of this reading selection relates the problem—that is, point for intervention—to the worker role and to the appropriate activity performed, given the client (or system) problem and the worker's role. Although the authors offer this as a tentative scheme, it nevertheless represents one of the best attempts to provide a basic and crucial element of professional social work practice: a framework for relating assessment to intervention. As such, this framework can facilitate both efficient and effective practice.

The essence of professionalism is a commitment to developing effective practice methods. Unfortunately, social workers too often accept as a given that their practice is effective and do not bother to assess objectively the effectiveness of their own interventions. Kirk's "Evaluating the Effectiveness of Social Work Intervention" provides an overview of basic elements of evaluative research. He discusses the various types of evaluation research, why practice needs to be evaluated, and four issues central to the actual evaluation of social work intervention: (1) definition of the problem to be changed, (2) determination of goals to be sought, (3) specification of the interventions used, and (4) the design of research. This reading selection provides the social worker not only with basic knowledge about evaluative research in general, but with several strategies that each social worker can consider using in evaluating the effectiveness of his or her own practice. This type of research, called *time-series* or *single-system design*, consists of formal case studies in which clear objectives are identified and measurements of the behaviors that the client desires to change are taken prior to, during, and after intervention. This design allows the worker to monitor progress with all of his or her cases and to make changes in the intervention program if the data so indicate. There has been increasing attention to this type of research in recent years in the social work literature (see, for example, Howe [1974] and Bloom and Block [1977]; see also Hersen and Barlow [1976], Jayaratne and Levy [1979], and Bloom and Fischer [1981]), and it is hoped that this trend will also mark an increase in the effectiveness of the services that social workers provide for their clients.

REFERENCES

Bartlett, Harriet.
   1970 *The Common Base of Social Work Practice.* New York: National Association of Social Workers.
Bloom, M., and S. R. Block.
   1977 "Evaluating One's Own Effectiveness and Efficiency." *Social Work* 22, no. 2: 130–36.
Bloom, M., and J. Fischer.
   1981 *Evaluating Practice: Guidelines for the Accountable Professional.* Englewood Cliffs, N.J.: Prentice-Hall.
Butler, R. M.
   1970 *Social Functioning Framework.* New York: Council on Social Work Education.

Chin, Robert.
1961 "The Utility of Systems Models and Developmental Models for Practitioners." In Warren G. Bennis, Kenneth D. Benne, and Robert Chin, eds., *Planning of Change.* New York: Holt, Rinehart and Winston.

Compton, Beulah Roberts and Galaway, eds.
1975 *Social Work Processes.* Homewood, Ill.: Dorsey Press.

Fischer, Joel.
1978 *Effective Casework Practice: An Eclectic Approach.* New York: McGraw-Hill.

Fischer, Joel and Harvey L. Gochros.
1975 *Planned Behavior Change: Behavior Modification in Social Work.* New York: Free Press.

Grodon, William E.
1965 "Knowledge and Value: Their Distinction and Relationship in Clarifying Social Work Practice." *Social Work* 10, no. 3: 32–35.

Greenwood, Ernest.
1957 "Attributes of a Profession." *Social Work* 2, no. 3: 45–55.

Hearn, Gordon.
1969 *The General Systems Approach: Contributions toward an Holistic Conception of Social Work.* New York: Council on Social Work Education.

———.
1975 "General Systems Theory and Social Work." In Francis J. Turner, ed., *Social Work Treatment.* New York: Free Press, pp. 343–71.

Hersen, M. and D. H. Barlow.
1976 *Single Case Experimental Designs.* Elmsford, N.Y.: Pergamon Press.

Hollis, Florence.
1973 *Casework: A Psycho-Social Therapy,* 2nd ed. New York: Random House.

Howe, M. W.
1974 "Casework Self-Evaluation: A Single-Subject Approach." *Social Service Review* 48 (March): 1–23.

Janchill, Sister May Paul.
1969 "Systems Concepts in Casework Theory and Practice." *Social Casework* 50, no. 2: 74–82.

Jayaratne, Srinska and Levy, Rona L.
1979 *Empirical Clinical Practice.* New York: Columbia University Press.

Kadushin, Alfred.
1959 "The Knowledge Base of Social Work." In Alfred J. Kahn, ed., *Issues in American Social Work.* New York: Columbia University Press.

Marx, Melvin H.
1963 "The General Nature of Theory Construction." In Melvin H. Marx, ed., *Theories in Contemporary Psychology.* New York: Macmillan, pp. 4–46.

Meyer, Carol.
1970 *Social Work Practice: A Response to the Urban Crisis.* New York: Free Press.

Miller, James G.
1955 "Toward a General Theory of the Behavioral Sciences." *American Psychologist* 10: 513–31.

Pincus, Allen and Anne Minahan.
1973 *Social Work Practice: Model and Method.* Itasca, Ill.: F. E. Peacock.

Reid, William and Laura Epstein.
1972 *Task-Centered Casework.* New York: Columbia University Press.

Roberts, Robert W., and Robert H. Nee, eds.
1970 *Theories of Social Casework.* Chicago: University of Chicago Press.

Turner, Francis J., ed.
1974 *Social Work Treatment: Interlocking Theoretical Approaches.* New York: Free Press.

GENERAL PRACTICE AND
SPECIALIZATION IN PROFESSIONAL SOCIAL WORK

Herbert H. Aptekar

Social work is a profession built around one of the inherent dilemmas in society. A principle which has long been recognized in the practice of social work is that there are two opposite trends in individual, group, and societal life: one which makes for change and development and another which is perhaps best described by the term *system maintenance.* On the one hand we wish fervently for change in the status quo. On the other we want to keep things as they are. As social workers we must live with this inherent dualism, and if we examine what it is that social workers do, we will find that we ally ourselves sometimes with one and sometimes with the other of these forces with which we are always confronted.

If we were to ask most professional social workers which of these two forces they prefer to be allied with, the answer almost uniformly would be with the forces making for change. But in taking such a position, do we not deny that we too are like the people with whom we work, the people who are subject to all that goes into system maintenance, and in many instances, at least partially responsible for it? In other words, while we like to think of ourselves as *change agents*, are we really and completely that? Do we possess the power to change any and all social systems, the family, the neighborhood, the larger community, the society as a whole? One needs only to raise the question in order to see that we possess no such power and that indeed no other profession does.

Our powers as change agents are very limited, which of course does not mean that we have no power at all to participate in the processes of change and development. Like the members of all other professions, however, what we can do is partial rather than total. Doctors, lawyers, educators, and others can master a *part* of their respective professions, but in no instances can they master the totality of the field in which they work. Does this mean, then, that in social work, specialization as in other professions is called for rather than general practice and that our professional educational system should be geared to specific

areas and types of social work, rather than to the development of what we sometimes refer to as the social work *generalist?*

The professions of law, medicine, and education each have a rather high degree of specialization. However, none of them can start and stop with specialization alone. In training and in actual practice, each of these fields requires a generic point of departure, a generic orientation to which the specialist must return repeatedly. In each of the three fields, there are practitioners who may be considered generalists, but they must know when their knowledge and skills are sufficient and when to turn to the specialist. Similarly, in each of the fields there is a rather staggering number of specialties, and the specialists too must be able to judge when general and not special knowledge or skill is sufficient. All three are becoming more and more social and psychological in their orientation. All are learning to respect and to utilize sociological and psychological insights. None of them, however, is likely to develop as a completely generic field in which specialization will have no value.

MODELS OF THE
SOCIAL WORK GENERALIST

In social work a variety of models currently operating emphasizes the need to redefine the generalist characteristics of the profession. The first model is one that is applicable to all social workers. The proposition to which we would want to give attention here is that social work in its very nature is a generalized profession. Perhaps this very fact suggests one reason why we have had so much trouble "finding ourselves" as a profession. If in its very nature social work differs from certain other professions in its lack of specific focus, then obviously defining the profession in terms of a single specific center of interest would be difficult if not impossible.

However that may be, we should like to suggest

Source: This article was specially prepared for this volume by the author.

that as members of a generalized profession we are all generalists. But what do we mean by a *generalized profession?* We mean a profession dependent upon societal need, which seldom remains stable for any great length of time in modern societies. We mean a highly changeable profession—almost an extemporaneous profession—and a profession, whether we like it or not, which doesn't quite try to be all things to all people but which certainly does see itself as painting on a broad canvas, so to speak. It wants to be in politics. It is dependent on economics. It certainly is concerned with social relations. It wants to be of service to the individual, the group, organizations, communities, societies. It gives priority to problems of the poor, but it believes that it has something to offer to others, too. It has not yet played the kind of international role which it probably will eventually take on, but many of us do feel that it should be an internationally oriented profession.

Is there one among us who does not have all of these different types of interest? Our knowledge in one area or another may seem inadequate to us, but we certainly do have the interest, and we see the interest which comes out of this broad an orientation to all of social life as a kind of prerequisite for the practice of social work. It may not be for the practice of psychotherapy, although even that is doubtful these days, or for the practice of medicine, dentistry, engineering, and other professions, but it certainly is for social work.

In this sense, then, we are all generalists and probably all want to be. Our starting point is our identification with humanity and our recognition of the fact that all people are subject to exigencies of life. If our interest is not international in character, it certainly is one which looks to the improvement and development of our whole society and not just the segment of it which makes up our own particular "professional life space." We are on the side of that which we see as being for the good of the society and against that which we believe to be contrary to the best interests of the society. At this stage of our development we cannot claim a body of incontrovertible scientific knowledge of what is good for society and what is bad for it. Nor can anyone else. We can perhaps agree on what our values are, however, and on our readiness to act professionally on the basis of those values, if not on a basis of scientifically established factual knowledge. We are ready to affirm that our values are egalitarian and societally oriented ones. Even though we recognize that at a given time

they may not be majority values, we believe they are values which ultimately must prevail in modern social and individual life. We are and must be cause oriented, and we are and must be part of a historical stream in which we contribute what we can to change the character and course of the stream.

Our number one model of the generalist may be one then which is applicable to all of us. We recognize that we are in *outlook and orientation* a very general type of profession; perhaps more like what education is and what the ministry may become, rather than what is true of some of the older and better-established professions. We see ourselves, in other words, as very much of an "open-minded" profession, a taking-on rather than an excluding profession, one willing to be used for a great variety of societal and individual purposes. If the individual member of the profession represents in microcosm what the profession itself does in macrocosm, then it follows that we are all generalists, that we all must be and that we all want to be.

Let us turn now to a second view of the generalist—one based not upon orientation and outlook, but instead upon *method, skill, and practice.* There was a time in the history of our profession (a history which of course continues into the present day) when our concern with method was a concern with methodological specialty. We were caseworkers, group workers, or community workers and few of us wanted to be anything other than what we were. The fact that these methods have much in common with one another was of little concern to us and we, in fact, wanted to exploit for all it was worth what we saw as distinctively characteristic of our own particular methodological specialty.

This view continues to be evident in recent years in the outlook of some people, especially in the field of social work education where it is held that at least a *two-track system*—one concerned with the so-called clinical operations of social work and the other concerned with social planning and community organization—should be established. Some see a need for even greater specialization and would increase the tracks to three, four, or five. It is even held sometimes that since we live in an age of specialization where, in some fields, the specialist can talk and be understood only by another specialist, social work too must follow the specialty route.

If what we said about our first model, however, is true then some doubt must be cast on the validity of a dichotomous view of social work or even on the validity of greater emphasis on the need for special-ization, and a question must be raised as to whether what we have *in common* with one another with re-spect to method is not greater than what we see as distinctive in the specialties. Is there such a thing as social work practice, rather than casework, group work, or community organization practice? Many of us know that there is and are prepared to demon-strate it. We may not have been able to do so just a few years ago, but we can now.

Many of our social work materials are taken from the large cities where social work is more apt to flourish on a broad scale and in specialized ways. Per-haps the big cities can learn something, however, from small ones and from rural settings, too. For many years well-trained social workers have gone into small communities—sometimes as the only so-cial worker in the community—and they have had to serve, literally, as fund-raisers, administrators, case-workers, group workers, and community organizers. Is the job that such people have done any less social work or any less skilled social work than that of the big city specialists? Is it possible that in some ways it was more skilled? Certainly in familiarity with and utilization of community resources, the creativity and capacity to innovate on the part of such people is challenged in the extreme.

Regardless of what one might think about de-gree of skill, however, the fact is that such people have had to be methodological generalists. It is neces-sary to raise the question as to whether the work that they do should not be carefully studied from the standpoint of its possible contribution to our under-standing of skill in social work practice rather than specialized skill. Are they less able caseworkers, group workers, or community organization workers; or are they perhaps more capable ones *because* they are familiar with *related* skills in the other fields? For example, caseworkers are known for their "in-terpretations" of behavior, and skillful caseworkers know enough about the timing of an interpretation to recognize that if given at one time it will be mean-ingless, whereas if given at another it may have great value for the client. Does such a person, when con-fronted with a community situation where a different type of interpretation may be in order, carry over his understanding of interpretation from the one field to the other? Recognizing that it is a different type of interpretation, does he nevertheless retain some of his casework adaptability?

This is not to argue, of course, that caseworkers

make better community organizers than non-caseworkers. What is being said is that in both fields one must interpret, that such interpretation requires skill, that whether transferable or not skill in one area of social work is not unlike skill in another area, and that the worker who has had to exercise skill in both areas may be able to tell something about it to those of us who have had to use it in only one. We are first beginning to build up our knowledge of gen-eralized social work practice. Those who have been necessarily unspecialized in their working situations might contribute much to our understanding of the problems and the skills required to practice in a gen-eralized way.

A third model, or perhaps we should look upon it as a variation of model two, which we have just discussed, is one *concerned with method also but instead of emphasizing the work of the person who must do every-thing, it concentrates on the one who works efficiently across, let us say, two methods but not necessarily all.* The caseworker who works with groups in a family agency might serve as an example, or the group worker whose point of entry into a community situa-tion is the interest of a group with whom he has been working. He sees himself primarily as a caseworker or group worker, as the case may be, but he does not feel that he should limit the scope of his activities be-cause of this fact.

Many such people, in fact, find themselves quite comfortable in extending the scope of their work, and some younger workers who have actually been trained to work in this manner feel that the job they are doing is one which is whole in character. It is so-cial work and the element in it which is practice and skill is social work practice and skill. Because one has a greater number of cases and a lesser number of groups in one's field placement does not mean that one knows more about cases and less about groups. One has learned something about how to act with both, and both are in a sense part of the same package.

A fourth model of the generalist is that of a worker who functions within an agency framework where *a broad range of problems* are brought. The point of emphasis in this particular one is on the character of the agency rather than on the worker himself. The agency's broad function and its form of organization makes it necessary for the worker to operate on a generalized basis rather than a specialized one. Exam-ples might be public welfare agencies, community mental health installations, certain types of programs providing for social aspects of medical care, and certainly all of the community agencies operating on a "saturation" basis. Many of these agencies, particularly the medical ones, employ specialists; but their social work staffs are in large part oriented to social services in general—those set up for children, for youth, for young adults, for the aging; those based upon monetary or economic need; those which are educational in character; those which must be administered individually; those which lend themselves to a group approach; those which require neighborhood organization; those requiring interagency cooperation; in fact, nearly every type of social service one can think of.

What is it like to work in such an agency? How different is it from working, let us say, in a child placement agency or a home for the aged? Does orientation to a multiplicity of services, or an attempt on the part of one person to render many services or at least coordinate them, affect the fundamental character of the job to be done? Multiservice agencies, especially those which are not departmentalized, may provide an example of one type of generalist. In examining the activities of workers in such agencies, however, we may find that there are significant enough similarities in practice to warrant the use of the term *generalist* for many of them and to make the term *specialist* quite inapplicable in their case.

A fifth model which we might want to examine is the generalist within a specific field of practice, that is to say, *the worker who does many things although he may be limited to a very special group of people.* An example might be the worker in an institution or a service for the retarded. Such a worker might work directly with the child, individually or in groups; he might work with parents in a similar manner; he might be actively engaged in the promotion of noninstitutional forms of care for the retarded child; he might be engaged in education of the community to the problems of retardation. In short, while concentrating on a special problem and a special group of people, his activities are still wide enough in scope to warrant the use of the term *generalist.*

A sixth model might be that of *the generalist within a specialized method.* There are many community organization workers, for example, who despite the wide scope of community problems are necessarily limited by the special type of problem with which they are concerned. Here an example might be the worker in a community council, let us say, as contrasted with the one who functions on a retarda-tion planning commission. There are specialized workers, of course, within community councils—those concerned with health care, recreation, and other fields—but many council workers are not identified with a single problem, or if they are, it is often for a limited period of time.

The identifications of the generalist within a field such as community organization might be said to be identified with the field of community growth and development, and whatever pertains to it is his concern. He is not so much interested in, let us say, better health care as he is in the development of a better community—one which might be expected to have better health care and better programs of all types. Many of the professionals who have gone into the field of what is now known as urban development are generalists of this type. They are promoters of social welfare rather than of specific programs. In former days many of them would have been called social reformers. Their fundamental interest is in institutional change, and anything which is innovative in character holds a kind of special interest for them. Being a generalist, in their case, is often equated with being an innovator. The two are not necessarily connected, and it must be recognized that there can be innovation which is antithetical—or even detrimental—to community growth and development. The measure of any program for a generalist of this type, however, is its contribution to community change.

A seventh and final model for our purpose is the person who may be called a generalist by temperament or evolution. This type would come close to our first one, which was the generalist by professional orientation. The person who is a generalist by temperament must also be a generalist by orientation, as indeed we all are. But this person adds a special fillip. He may be a specialist in a particular method—casework, group work, or community organization. But if he is, one will often find him a person who cannot be satisfied with limited interests. Such a person often goes into social work because of what he sees as the wide scope of the profession, and he finds confirmation and support, sometimes, in his professional education and in his membership in a profession which permits breadth of interest. Many of us are generalists by temperament although in the course of a professional career we have gone from one specialty to another. We have been caseworkers, supervisors, case consultants, administrators, educators, and goodness knows what else as far as level of operation is concerned. Most of us have shifted from one field of interest, such as child care or family welfare, to another substantive field. And some of us have shifted in our methodological specialties. One of the most common of such shifts is from casework or group work, via the administrative road, to community organization.

At this point it might be desirable to restate a proposition which is implicit in the above comments, namely, that there probably is no such thing as a pure generalist. The word is a descriptive one and, like many such words, it simultaneously says too much and too little. It doesn't fit anybody in any precise way. It is a kind of loose-fitting garment which any of us can put on when we wish to do so. We can also take it off, put it aside, and for a special occasion put on a made-to-measure or at least a specially gratifying garment. What this implies is a thought which was expressed by our committee in its first report, which is simply that while we are all generalists of one type or another, most of us are also specialists. The two terms do not set up an inherent dichotomy. They merely describe what is most evident in a given situation, and in so doing, they necessarily leave unsaid what becomes manifest on closer inspection. What we really need is a term which would not be quite so awkward as "generalist-specialist," but the English language, which is so inherently dichotomous, doesn't seem to permit that.

GENERALIST-SPECIALIST DILEMMA

In social work there are still many who feel that if we could just get rid of specialization and do whatever we do under one general rubric, we might serve society better and develop faster as an influential profession. I do not agree with this view, which I see as quite an uncalled-for return to a preprofessional state. Nor do I agree with the many critics of social work who would substitute political action for professional knowledge and skill which must be developed through long and hard effort. In taking this position I certainly do not want to maintain that social work can divorce itself from politics. What I am saying is that students who choose social work as a profession have chosen one of the most difficult of professions and not one of the easiest. In politics one can enter high positions with no direct training for them. Unlike politicians social workers cannot become instant general practitioners nor instant specialists. The road to professional status and performance lies in the difficult realm of simultaneously acquiring a generic understanding and practicing in a specific area. It is

somewhat like the student of music who cannot become a musician and a musician only. He must become both a musician and a pianist, a violinist, or master of some other musical skill. He must acquire a great deal of understanding of music, while acquiring specific skills applicable to certain instruments.

Thus in social work, as in other professions, the generalist must be something of a specialist. Just as the general practitioner of medicine in a rural area or a small community must know how to perform, let us say, certain emergency surgical procedures, so must the social work generalist think of himself as being at least somewhat knowledgeable in special fields of social work. Likewise the specialist should think of himself as having the requisite *generic* knowledge in his specialized practice.

What is requisite knowledge in professional social work today and how much of it can be subsumed under the title of generalist? How much of it is necessarily specialized? Let us consider a few areas of general knowledge, some of which are obviously common property of all the helping professions. First, it would seem to me, might be an understanding of the nature of the professions. In ordinary, everyday life it is not often necessary for people to think in terms of what is professional and what is not. If one is going to *be* a professional, however, it is important that one know something about what it means to be professional. Degrees and titles do not make one's behavior professional in character, nor does the mere possession of professional knowledge. But disciplined and knowing behavior does. In social work, no matter what the method, the realm of service, or the age group with which one is working, the behavior of the professional must always be exceedingly observant. The response of the person or persons with whom one works must be a guide to subsequent behavior of the professional himself in the professional interaction. Truth and honesty, to the degree that both are possible, should permeate professional communication. The social worker as a professional person must be able to subordinate his own personal needs and desires to the objectives and interests of those whom he tries to help, which means that self-understanding in terms of one's own needs, desires, and capacities is called for. Knowledge of the history and sociology of the professions is desirable, but not so important as knowledge and possession, so to speak, of one's own self.

Social work is a behavior-oriented profession. This means that the professional social worker must focus much of his attention on the behavior of others and of himself. Social work practice of any kind should be introverted and self-examining as well as extraverted and responsive to the needs and claims of others. This does not mean that professional social work behavior is self-effacing. Instead it is always cognizant of human differences, understanding of human weaknesses, but assertive in relation to human strengths. One's own opinions need not be withheld, but neither will they be imposed or forced on others. In short, professional social work is a behavioral art, and one is not a social worker until one becomes master, in his own self-development, of that art.

Does this mean that every social worker must be a clinician? I do not think that it does. There are many types of social work which cannot be described as clinical in character—social planning, community development, legislative action, and others. What is important from a professional social work standpoint, however, is that none of these forms of social work can be carried out effectively without significant knowledge of one's own self, without the ability to observe and adapt to the behavior of others, or without an understanding of the *processes*—by which we mean *step by step procedure*—of human interaction, with modifications introduced in one step after review of what took place in the preceding one.

If what we are saying here is true, then perhaps it does not matter so much whether one thinks of one's self as a generalist or a specialist. The behavioral requisites of the profession will permeate all of one's professional activity, regardless of whether one practices as a psychiatric social worker in a mental hospital or as a social planner working on mental health programs. The problem of generalist versus specialist diminishes—if it does not vanish altogether—and social work becomes a *whole* behavioral profession instead of a split one.

In recent years there has been much talk about a two-track system in professional education for social work. In some cases this has meant that there are two types of student: one a more assertive type, capable of activities such as social planning, administration, and policy making; and the other a more accepting and receptive type, capable of establishing one-to-one relationships such as may be required in clinical social work, institutional care, and so forth. If the thinking presented in this paper is correct, then the two-track system, splitting the profession into two as it necessarily does, is based on a fallacy. Planners, admin-

istrators, and policymakers are not inherently aggressive and incapable of understanding or working with other people in an observant, accepting spirit. Nor are clinical social workers incapable of self-assertion or the expression of difference of opinion with other people. In fact, some of the best clinical workers are highly regarded by their clients *because* they are open and honest in their expression of difference of opinion, and this proposition, in my judgment, must be true too of the planner, administrator, or community organizer.

The generalist-versus-specialist dichotomy thus becomes more of a semantic problem and less of a real one in the professional education of social workers. This does not mean that specialized knowledge and skill is unnecessary or undesirable, or that all that one needs to learn is how to get along with people. Quite the opposite in fact is true. Specialized knowledge regarding types of social work practice, types of service, types of social problems and types of behavior is possible, desirable, and in fact necessary. What is important, however, is that it be complemented by generalized knowledge and general professional development. Both should go hand in hand. Unless they do, something exceedingly important will be missing and we will have social workers who are half-trained rather than whole professional persons.

Learning about the whole profession of social work and its specialized areas can take place simultaneously. It can be integrated learning which enables the student to see the whole instead of concentrating only on a part; and it can be deepened, specialized learning with implications for the whole profession, when instructors are willing to think of what the objectives of their teaching should be. Do we wish to produce young professionals who have a firm grasp on and an identification with the profession as a whole, or do we wish simply to produce technicians? If the latter is our objective then we need not trouble ourselves about integration of the generic and the specific. If it is the former, then the instructor will be concerned with what the student is learning in other classes, in the field, and on his own. How contradictory is his thinking and is that what we want to substantiate? How cohesive is his thinking and what are we contributing through our monitoring of his total educational process? Are we contributing an awareness of where he starts in understanding and in competence for practice at any given period in time? There must be way stations in every educational process, a time and place for looking back and looking forward. Social work educators should man these way stations and they should take a good hard look at what is taking place in the student's classroom experience, in the field, and especially where the student stands in integrating both. This should be done with the student himself, as well as with his other instructors. It should be done as a way of evaluating how much conceptual learning he has acquired and how much "practice wisdom." The two sides of the social work coin are the generic and the specific. The learning of some students will be greater on the one side than it is on the other. Our objective, however, should be to have the student encompass both.

The reason students should be educated in this way is that as practitioners they will always have reason to try to balance their generic understanding and their specific responsibilities. Social work cannot yet claim to be a scholarly profession. There are scholars in it, but many practitioners derive their satisfactions from direct practice rather than from keeping up in a scholarly way with developments in the profession. In this respect, I am afraid, we lag behind other professions.

It is likely that in social work our knowledge, our efficiency, and our capabilities will gain great momentum during the years to come, when the students of today will be professional workers in a greatly altered society. The advances in other professions suggest that there will be similar strides in social work and that they are likely to be accelerated as time goes on. One facilitating factor in the acceleration will be a resolution of the conflict between the generic and the specific in professional social work education, a resolution that will carry over into practice. This facilitation will be unlikely to occur, however, if we persist in dichotomizing the profession. We need not do so. What will be necessary is recognition of the fact that generalists and specialists are not inherently opposed to each other in social work any more than in other helping professions. They may be in our language, but the English language has been known to cause trouble in fields other than social work. Let us not be trapped by our language and made immobile. Social work is inherently a mobile profession, and it will be more so if we can avoid false distinctions and concentrate on what the so-called generalist has, or should have, in common with the so-called specialist. Let us pool our resources, integrate them to the greatest possible extent educationally and in practice, and the growth of our profession will take care of itself.

RATIONALE FOR A GENERALIST APPROACH TO SOCIAL WORK PRACTICE

Edwin G. Brown

RECOGNITION OF THE NEED FOR ORGANIZATIONAL CHANGE AND NEW DELIVERY SYSTEMS OF SOCIAL SERVICES

The social climate that has evolved over the past decade has placed social work in the position of creating new practice approaches and services as a part of society's efforts to resolve human problems and suffering. As problem-focused agencies providing multiple services to neighborhood areas or total communities have developed, the traditional boundaries between casework, group work, and community organization have been strained. Social workers employed in these agencies have found that it is insufficient to work exclusively with individuals, groups, or communities in responding effectively to the needs of particular clients. Similarly, the profession and members of economically disadvantaged minority groups have noted that social work practitioners have often ignored the organizational structure of welfare institutions as they have proceeded to work on major social problems. The context of prac-

Source: This article was specially prepared for this volume by the author.

tice was taken for granted. The deliverer of services did not view tasks directed toward organizational development and change as being a part of his role. Social work services developed for one client population were offered to different clienteles under the assumption that they were sufficient or automatically transferable. The worker's primary orientation to helping was a practice specialization of either casework, group work, or community organization. The worker's plan for action was made from the context of one's method specialization. In other words, client problems were usually defined by, delimited by, or forced to conform to, the parameters of a given practice method. As a result, the profession has been accused of defining client needs in terms of the professional services available rather than the other way around. They have charged social workers with serving institutions—as agents of social control—instead of serving clients or being agents of social change. With respect to these charges, NASW has acknowledged the conflict and taken the following position:*

Traditionally, social work has been performed in agencies, with the result that self-serving public and private bureaucracies have been created. On the one hand, social work strives for professionalism, yet on the other, the members are found in social agencies in traditional employer-employee relationships. It is for this reason that many have labeled social workers as "semi-professional."

Social work must move away from such centralized agencies that are downtown, impersonal, and nonfunctional in relation to the constituencies that they are to serve. As long as social workers are located away from those it serves, the participation in policy of the organization by those who are served is effectively minimized. To be successful in the future, social work must be community based. In order to do this, it must be located within institutions and settings that are responsive to the community. Not only are social work organizations often self-servingly distant, and unresponsive to the needs of consumer, but also they often thwart or fail to enable the client to achieve the very task for which he originally sought service. Examples include the "treatment" of problems, which have their roots in social situations, within the walls of a social agency without ever venturing

beyond the individual and his problem. Another example includes institutional settings which purport to assist in the resocializing of people while only encapsulating them in a social system totally unrelated to the reality of the real world. The new result is system induced failure. [NASW 1971]

Yet social services are essentially bound to one type of organizational structure, namely the bureaucracy. This type of organization was never designed to be responsive to individuals. Therefore, the social work practitioner is placed in a bind between the context for his practice and the goals of his profession. The indications from practice for changes in policy and procedures and the press of the organization for sameness and consistency become polar issues for the social worker. Essential characteristics of a bureaucracy such as central administration and decision making, hierarchical structure, stability, uniformity of response, and the like, can no longer be seen as the sole organizational virtues for social workers' support. Rather, they are not infrequently impediments to the profession's commitment to individualization, humanization, and needed changes (Berkley 1971; Bennis, Benne, and Chin 1969; Etzioni 1964; and Toffler 1971).

Feedback from practice has begun to demonstrate the necessity of social work practitioners working with the organization per se to make it supportive of the solution-seeking activities of the client-practitioner partnership as they deal with complex and ever-shifting social problems (Wax 1978). This type of organizational development is achieved through the active participation of all staff in an ongoing process of change-maintenance assessment of agency services. Just as agency rules are initially established to support the meeting of specific needs and to provide services, it is necessary for them to be manipulated and altered over time in the interest of clients. The worker thus functions in relation to organizational structure, policy, and procedures as a sort of "outsider" within the agency. In this capacity the worker delivers direct services while maintaining open questioning as to continued relevancy and effectiveness. This two-way focus of professional responsibility and activity should avoid the creation of employment contexts that render the social worker unable to serve people. It is not a matter of opting for either complete organizational maintenance or complete organizational change. The ongoing challenge and professional responsibility is to strike the appropriate balance in each individual situation.

---

*Reprinted with permission from NASW. Glasgow, Douglas and Nancy Humphrey, "Proposal for the Future Delivery of Social Services: Position of the Western Coalition," NASW Delegate Assembly, 1971, mimeo. Copyright 1971, National Association of Social Workers, Inc.

Rapid Change

Heightened awareness of the social lag between client needs and the potential for services prompted a group of faculty at the School of Social Service Administration (SSA) to undertake an experiment dealing with social work methods of practice. Recognizing that the source of change comes from forces outside an organism or system (Swanson 1971), we decided to cast our work in circumstances that would require us to respond as maximally, freely, and as relevantly as possible to some of the stresses being felt by the profession. We were encouraged, therefore, to approach this effort inductively, i.e., the leads for practice theory would be generated from field work.

Some students of change (Swanson 1971, p. 18) posited that the *first response* to the press for change is a crucial focal point for study. The first response is believed to reveal the potentialities for change and also to call attention to the situational conditions that activated those potentialities (Swanson 1971, p. 18). Adapting this concept to social work education, we tried to develop the practice theory course content entirely from the practice experiences of our students. This focus on field work placed us in the position of noting the indications for changes in the curriculum (first responses) for the practice theory course.

Another factor guiding our approach was the insistence by minority and inner city clients that the effectiveness and relevance of social services be enhanced. SSA, being located on the edge of an urban ghetto, felt this force directly. Nathan Wright, Jr., has compellingly outlined a pragmatic, if not humane, reason for giving heed to the voice of the minorities. He observed that marginal people are in a system but not a part of it. Because of this position, they perceive clearly and can add a sense of rationality in the same way that marginal actors, on the side of the stage, interpret the action to the audience. In this role minority people represent a creative potential for all of society by being able to "tell it as it is!" (Wright 1967).

This idea has been elaborated by others (Said 1971) to explain a change function of any minority group:

The function of stereotyped behavior and distinctive subcultures in stable societies is conflict reduction and simple survival. Given this function, it is clear that the true social transformation requires the creation of new social stereotypes ... the newly emerging, expectant subculture is perhaps a real "vanguard" of prospective social change and the identifying characteristics of a particular subculture may

tell us more about the future of a society than the beliefs of the current elite or all kinds of silent majorities. By focusing on these emerging groups whose visions and expectations are at significant variance with the national norm of a given society, we wish to draw attention to their critical role in adaptation, and we are suggesting that social differentiation and the appearance, growth, and expansion of expectant subcultures is, itself, a better index of development than the usual standards. [Said 1971, p. 7]

It was reasonable, we hoped, to expect that practice methods and social services developed in response to a minority client population could project an across-the-board picture of major difficulties, as well as possible alternatives for action in social work practice more generally.

Inductive Leads for a Revised Approach to Practice

Three themes soon emerged from the field experiences of our students:

1. Social work methods specialization, used as the sole framework for defining practitioner roles, did not consistently lead to practical or logical interventions. Nor did a methods orientation provide students with a complete perspective on goals, values, or the full potential of the profession for producing change;

2. Agency structure, policy, and procedures frequently prohibited or, at best, failed to support "professional" or "relevant" practice and their accompanying worker activities;

3. The problems encountered in the community and the services being offered were frequently incongruent.

These pragmatic leads pointed the way to the development of a generalist approach to practice that is a solution-seeking orientation to the problems confronting clients. They also signaled the urgency for educating social work practitioners who are able to effect changes in organizational structure and the delivery systems of social welfare. They indicated the need to instill the practitioner with a sense of responsibility and to equip him with the knowledge and the skills for working toward professional goals within existing social work agencies or systems of agencies. To accomplish this end practitioners would have to lead out with indicated organizational change.

The generalist model was developed to approach this two-fold task. Our goal became the education of social workers who would be prepared to undertake simultaneous responsibility for the development, maintenance, and enhancement of individual and community well-being and to contribute to the responsiveness of society. Such an approach would combine the micro-macro elements in society that have all too often functioned independently of one another.

Recognition of Need for Combined Methods

Traditionally social work has defined its methodology in relation to the "size" of the client system served. In recent years, however, this conceptualization has been severely criticized as one that limits workers to a practice approach which fragments social problems, clients, and service delivery systems. Since social problems cut across client systems of different size and often involve multiple systems at the same time, social workers in traditional practice have been faulted for not addressing in a coordinated fashion the basic problems with which they should be concerned. Instead, they have been accused of trying to mold client problems to fit their individual method specializations. Schwartz has said:

The single variable embodied in the number of people one works with at the same time is simply not significant enough to be endowed with the designation of "method." Not significant enough, that is, if we reserve the term "method" to mean a systematic mode of helping which, while it is used differently in different situations, retains throughout certain recognizable and invariant properties through which one may identify the social worker in action. In this light, to describe casework, group work, and community organization as methods simply mistakes the nature of the helping process for the relational system in which it is applied. [Schwartz 1961, pp. 148–49]

Perlman, speaking to the same problem states:

Maybe the way to go about identifying social work practice activities is not within the traditional boundaries of casework, group work, and community work at all, but across lines by asking ourselves what kinds of problems call for what kinds of services and actions. It is possible that the ways we perceive a situation, define it, and go about treating it are shaped a priori by the particular methods to which we have allegiance or in which we have skill. [Perlman 1966, pp. 94–5]

The common elements of social work practice have been the topic of considerable concern for years. It appeared in the development of the "generic" curriculum (American Association of Social Workers 1929; Bartlett 1959; Perlman 1949) and emerged again in the fields of practice concept (Bartlett 1961).

Bartlett's efforts to define the common base of social work practice are yet another aspect of this prolonged work to define the profession and thereby maximize its contribution:

Instead of placing primary emphasis on social work's response to the setting or social institution in which it is practiced, the motion of the common base emphasizes social work's contribution as a profession. [Bartlett 1970]

Encouraged by the clarification of these major practice issues along with the explication of new directions to explore, we proceeded to define a generalist form of practice. An important distinguishing characteristic of a generalist approach to practice is its *solution-seeking emphasis* as opposed to the methods orientation of traditional practice or combined methods. A generalist practice could be developed, we concluded, by: (1) being responsive to the leads from practice; (2) utilizing a problem-solving approach as the major organizing principle; (3) turning to the practice literatures and skills of all three practice methods for intervention planning and implementation; and (4) focusing on the change maintenance considerations that are germane to each problem situation.

RATIONALE FOR THE GENERALIST APPROACH TO SOCIAL WORK PRACTICE

As previously explained, this particular approach to generalist practice evolved first in response to a renewed and changing awareness of the dynamic interrelationship of the individual to his total environment; secondly, to an increased awareness of the limitations imposed on the worker's role. We contend that a strict adherence to a methods orientation limits the perceptions and activity of social work practitioners. This viewpoint gave us a new feeling for the long-held social work principle that human problems are multicaused, multifaceted, and result in far reaching cause-effect spirals. Likewise agency structure, policy, and procedures too often hinder problem-solving activity rather than encourage or support it. It is the nature of the problem that is the crucial determining factor of interventions and other respective organizational support systems. It followed, therefore, that solutions and prevention of problems frequently require a multiplicity of methods in the interventions and that multipurpose agencies and expanded community effort are essential to support this kind of practice. These observations logically seem to require that social workers be prepared to understand and to work with the many levels of problems in which people are involved, as well as to deal with selected aspects of the cause-effect ramifications.

Given the foregoing viewpoint, our conception of generalist practice involves assisting individuals, families, small groups, and larger social systems to work on change which promotes the best possible relationship between people and their environment. In this process, all social work methods—traditional and innovative—are utilized, singly or in combination, to meet reality needs and to alleviate stresses in ways that enhance or strengthen the inherent capacities of client systems. Generalist practice is addressed to the solution and/or prevention of problems at all levels of intervention: intrapersonal, familial, interpersonal, organizational, community, institutional, and societal. Commonly, more than one problem unit is handled simultaneously. There is an effort to establish and review the necessary balance between the change-maintenance efforts of intervention relative to the targets for change and with regard to the specifics that need to be maintained to produce the desired change and safeguard its survival.

The generalist social worker is a practitioner who usually initiates the problem-solving process across individual or group services to persons who are having problems with social functioning. *Social functioning* refers to the life tasks required of people and their efforts to cope with them (Bartlett 1970, pp. 84–117). The exploration of these problems focuses on those social, cultural, and institutional antecedents in the larger social system that are adversely influencing the client's life along with the client's coping efforts. This process of problem identification and definition is the joint endeavor of client and worker. Plans are also formulated collaboratively, outlining interventions leading to solutions. In these two stages of the problem-solving process (problem identification and problem assessment) the worker has two judgments to make. One is the level(s) at which intervention should take place. The other is the individualized plan of action at that level to guide the actual interventive efforts. The assessment outline to guide the first decision is an open-system format that helps to avoid premature closure on the object of change (problem) and the means to be employed. This assessment will also assist in the determination of the social problem context in which the problem solving will be done.

The individualized assessment and plan for action may be drawn from any one or combination of the practice methods. Each practice method is seen as consisting of a repertoire of specific approaches or models. To analyze and address each problem situation, the worker attempts to match models with the needs of the problem. Eclecticism is used when a particular model is deemed to be insufficient in and of itself. In this way, already established knowledge is utilized and additional modes can be developed to meet new challenges to the profession. The generalist may or may not offer the specialized services. But he will know of their potentiality. Therefore, he can either obtain such services elsewhere, learn them personally, and/or work toward acquiring them in the community. Two guides for assessing the level of intervention were developed. They are outlined as follows.

OUTLINE FOR A BROAD-BASED ASSESSMENT OF PROBLEMS USING A COMBINED METHODS APPROACH

A.   Value of norms (relative to the specific problem or issue at hand)

1. Of the prevailing culture and of subgroups or minority groups
2. Of the support base of the services being offered
3. Of the individual worker
4. Of the client
5. Of the profession

B.   The basic assumptions that underlie the established service or proposed service (that respond to the problem)

C. The client

    1. Who is the client?
    2. Client workability (motivation and capacity for problem solving or prevention)
    3. The client situation (opportunity)

D. Dynamic forces operating to maintain the status quo (assessment of potential for change)

    1. Individuals or family
    2. Group processes
    3. Political and power considerations
    4. Self-interest concerns
    5. Resistances and defenses
    6. Enabling and restraining forces juxtaposed

E. Economic factors

    1. Causal factors
    2. Cost of alternative solutions or actions
    3. Prevailing economic trends

F. The worker

    1. Sanctions (existing and need to acquire new or more sanctions)
    2. Knowledge and skills vis-à-vis the problem
    3. Resources at his disposal
    4. Availability (time and other demands)
    5. Worker values and what he can commit himself to do (including worker motivation)

G. Research findings and practice observations (cumulative)

    1. The typical modal response of persons with the crisis or problem
    2. The specific steps leading to successful coping or problem resolution
    3. Specific interventions and their effectiveness

H. The service system

    1. Service goals or intent
    2. Agency policy and procedures (formal and informal)
    3. Client entitlements
    4. Allocation of manpower
    5. Interacting parts of service (coordination; systems analysis)

FRAMEWORK FOR PROBLEM IDENTIFICATION AND ASSESSMENT IN GENERALIST PRACTICE

Below is a series of questions to be used in thinking about and undertaking the assessment process in social work practice, specifically, generalist practice.

I. What is the current situation as it is first presented?

    A. In what context does the current situation exist?
    B. How is it manifested?
    C. How is it involved?

II.   Is there concern about the situation?

        A. Who is concerned? Why?
        B. How is the concern manifested?
        C. What, if anything, has been done about the concern?

            1. By whom?
            2. With what outcomes?

III.   Are there problems in the situation?

        A. If so, what are they?
        B. Who identifies them?
        C. Who is involved in them?
        D. How do the persons involved view the problems?
        E. How do *you* view the problems?
        F. What, if any, is the difference between your view of the problems and the view
           of others involved in the problems?

IV.   What are the various elements in the problems?

        A. Consider the following elements whenever identifiable and relevant:

            1. Individual conditions and situations
            2. Interpersonal conditions and situations
            3. Community conditions and situations
            4. Organizational conditions and situations
            5. Societal conditions and situations

        B. What elements are not identifiable or relevant? Why not?

V.   What does all the above mean?

        A. What is the meaning of the problem(s) and the situation in which the problem(s)
           exist to the people involved?
        B. What is the meaning of the problem(s) and the situation in terms of resources
           available to work out the problems?
        C. What is the meaning of the gaps in resources for the people, problem(s), and
           situation?

VI.   What assessment can be derived from all the above? Construct our assessment of the
        people-problem(s)-situation interrelationships, using an *appropriate* assessment
        framework from the various social work methods.

VII.   What are the alternatives for resolution of problems to be worked on?

        A. What priorities do you derive from these alternatives?
        B. What are your reasons for the priorities chosen?

VIII.   What intervention possibilities do the problems and priorities suggest?

        A. In relation to what goals?
        B. Why those goals?
        C. Who would be involved? Why?

In some instances, the generalist practitioner may initiate change in institutional systems apart from specific involvement with clients. At such times the generalist defines the problem, using various exploratory methods, and undertakes to engage individuals and/or groups to work collaboratively to bring about needed changes in institutional systems. In function then, the generalist serves as a bridge between the gaps in existing services. He also assists in developing the full potential (intent) of agency policy and procedures to adequately meet the client entitlement or need. To maintain a solution-seeking stance, the practitioner must be tuned in to a conception that exceeds: (1) his individual activities, (2) particular practice methodologies, or (3) agency services and setting. For this purpose, we suggest a social problem context for generalist practice which includes the accumulative body of existing knowledge, services, sanctions, etc., of the total interdisciplinarian and societal effort.

Focus must be on the social problem, for too frequently a beginning mode with a concern for people shifts quickly to a concern for the agency and the profession. [Nathan Cohen 1964, p. 385]

Viewed in another way, the guiding principle which activates and clarifies the generalist role is the constant search to narrow the difference between the services and opportunities that exist and what is needed to maximize client growth. It is this interface between the individual and the delivery system of services that comprises the arena of professional activity for the generalist and out of which interventions are developed and applied. The exploration and definition of the problem(s) [and] the organization and implementation of collaborative work on the total continuum of change require that the generalist work carefully to establish and maintain the sanctions necessary to support the change process.

In essence the practice methods to be utilized and their corresponding level(s) of intervention for generalist practice are prescribed by the nature of the problem to be solved. The practice examples from field work that follow illustrate generalist practice as it evolved. The setting for all the situations was a public aid office.

Coping on Old-Age Assistance (OAA).   In group supervisory sessions, it became clear to the students that the individual old-age assistance clients they were working with had a common concern: isolation. It was further clarified that this problem for the aged in general was exacerbated for persons receiving old-age assistance because of their limited financial resources. A single-method approach (in this instance, casework) was insufficient. The clients wanted contact with other people but the purposes and time limitations of the caseworkers were not conducive to meeting the need. At the onset, small group activities

seemed to be an appropriate service. This service approach was explained to the agency administrator who gave the necessary sanction to further explore the matter both within the agency and in the community. Existing local programs for the aged were found to be limited and inaccessible. The client population (all the OAA recipients of the district office) was polled to determine interest and to recruit client participation in the planning. Approximately fifty individuals requested that the agency organize social groups where they could meet for recreation and friendship. The respondents were grouped geographically to minimize transportation needs. Another survey was conducted to identify neighborhood meeting places. Churches proved to be the best resource. Six groups were established. Each group elected its own leaders, defined its own rules, and set the meeting times. Their orientations differed: arts and crafts; study; fun and games; or a round robin of activities. The final stage of this development consisted of trying to establish the groups as a regular service of the agency. All the while, the individual casework services traditionally offered by the agency were rendered by the same students.

School Lunches.   In working with individual ADC (Aid to Dependent Children) families on food purchasing and budgeting concerns, students began to question the adequacy of the grants. At the same time, the local welfare rights organization raised the same issue. The two groups met to study the matter further. They learned that the state welfare allotments for a child's lunch were inadequate to purchase a subsidized school lunch. Just as this fact was to be brought to the attention of the agency as a demonstration of the need to increase the food budget, the National Free School Lunch Program was announced. The program provided for nondeduction of free lunches from welfare budgets. The group perceived this policy as a welcome confirmation of their contention about the unrealistic food grants. The leadership of a local community organization chose to interpret the free school lunch program differently. They contended that it was an attack on poor families, which implied that local families were not properly feeding their children at home. Rather than support the public schools to take the new program to the people to decide for themselves, they pressured the school principals not to publicize the free school lunch program. The welfare rights organization and the students conducted a city-wide survey of the implementation of the free school lunch program. These data showed the implementation lag for the school district of concern. This information was presented in a community meeting where pressure was exerted on the schools to conduct a comprehensive family canvassing which would inform them of their entitlements. The same coalition of students and welfare recipients continued to meet and study the school lunchroom situation. The expanded use of the facilities posed real difficulties. The assistance of the university business school was enlisted to study the costs of alternative means of supplying lunches, such as catering in classrooms. This information was used locally and later served to assist the governor's office in planning for statewide implementation of a catering approach.

Multiproblem Families and Mother's Day. During the course of the first quarter in the agency, twelve multiproblem or hard-to-reach families were referred to the student unit. In trying to assist these families, the students sensed the implied message which the families experienced in their daily contacts with many of the agencies and institutions of the community: "You are unfit to be a mother; yours is not a 'real' family." Yet families they were, with all the responsibilities for socializing their members, but too often without encouragement or support. They were left to themselves—alienated and in conflict with agencies and their neighbors. It was decided that more impact needed to be brought into the lives of the clients to support their efforts to achieve their stated objectives and to stabilize their ambivalently expressed desires to be better parents. The reassurance offered individually by the student workers was not enough to offset the tide of disapproval. Two ideas were creatively joined to plan a more impactful intervention: (1) the concept of the ego ideal as a means of motivating a person to change through the acquisition of desired attributes; and (2) Mother's Day as a specific group utilization of this construct to influence behavior through the establishment of norms: The attributes of mothers are enumerated and honored in community-sponsored ceremonies; mothers and children, from their respective positions, review their lives; tears of both happiness and regret are shed in the process, accompanied by the resolve to do better. The mothers in the families being served by the students were being excluded. In an effort to reverse this situation, it was decided to involve the children from these families (eighty-nine in number) in giving a Mother's Day party. The children wanted to make gifts and have a program. The boys' club and a home

for the aged agreed to provide facilities and materials for the gift making, which took place over a six-week period. Invitations were personally delivered by the children two weeks in advance to ensure attendance. The families turned out en masse. A program of songs, poems, and stories told of the children's love and appreciation for mother. This was followed by a presentation of the gifts by each individual child before the entire group. Portraits were taken of each family group. Community singing followed, along with refreshments. The local newspaper covered the social event, complete with pictures. New self-concepts began to emerge as mothers told of feeling accepted for the first time in their lives. In the months that ensued, discouragements were assuaged with fond recollections of the Mother's Day party. Some of the children joined the regular groups at the boys' club through their exposure to them. A foster grandparent program to assist children with difficulty in reading was started at the home for the aged.

Groups for Youth Involved with the Law. Caseworkers were required to contact the families in their case loads whose youth received a station adjustment (a police station arrangement for a minor infraction of the law). The respective workers routinely visited the home to discuss the incident and to offer counseling to the family. A review of the station adjustment cases revealed that the youth were from nine to eighteen years of age and that for most of them this was their first formalized conflict with the law. These factors were held to be significant reasons for seeking agency approval to explore the possibilities for providing direct services to the young people themselves. Here were youths with a common concern and of an age when peer relationships are highly significant. Planning sessions between the Public Assistance and Juvenile Correction Agencies resulted in defining a recruitment system and arranging for goal-oriented, time-limited groups on a volunteer basis. The youth responded favorably, utilizing the peer groups: to examine the meaning of the station adjustment in their individual and collective lives, to explore the part they could play in their respective situations, and to discover and utilize the recreational facilities of the extended community.

Implications

The preceding vignettes portray generalist practice. Collectively they illustrate the following points:

1. Practice interventions are situation centered; i.e., focused on people's problems with social functioning;

2. Professional values and knowledge are drawn upon in assessment to review the relevancy of existing services and in planning interventions (rather than a methods orientation);

3. The total potential of the profession is tapped through the worker's utilization of all three practice methods: singly, serially, or collectively. The worker has competence in all three methods;

4. Agency potential, intent, and operations are constantly reviewed both within and among agencies;

5. All problems brought for service are continuously assessed for both their micro and macro components. To do this, two types of judgments are made: (a) the level for intervention, and (b) the specialized intervention plans which draw upon practice methods and the context of practice in terms of the social problem framework;

6. The worker assumes leadership responsibility for solution seeking at all levels of intervention;

7. Sanctions and resources are reviewed and/or acquired throughout the problem-solving process;

8. Knowledge of agency policy and procedures is used to acquire sanctions and in the process of organizational development;

9. The worker must be concerned with the effectiveness of the interventions used in his own practice;

10. The effectiveness of interventions is used as the backdrop against which to assess the differences between the reality and the ideal in services;

11. Both change and maintenance factors must be evaluated by the worker.

Thus, the generalist social worker is a problem-oriented change agent. As such, he must analyze all relevant systems, including the change-agent system. He does not accept traditional "givens" but he is a challenger and questioner of basic premises.

Generalist social work implies a revolutionary change in the nature of the service delivery system just as it implies a revolutionary change in the intervention matrix. The generalist concept implies moving beyond traditional concepts of "agency function" and reminds us that the agency, after all, was in-stituted to intervene in certain stressful and conflictual individual-societal connectives. Just as it is myopic to define problems a priori in terms of method, so it is also myopic to define intervention only in terms of present institutional "givens." The generalist concept implies that sanction for intervention comes from the entire gestalt of client/problem/environment/service system and not just the latter.

The main problem with this implication of the generalist concept is that the generalist often does not have the sanction to intervene where intervention is most desperately needed. The traditional social work response to this state of affairs has been to try to attain sufficient social authority as a profession to get sanction. But the social authority has often been given only at the price of compliance. The effort to achieve social authority must not be dismissed lightly, but it is quite clear that it is today woefully inefficient and insufficient. The generalist social worker must constantly be concerned with presenting the need for the increased or different sanction required for the problem solving (Wagner 1972).

ORGANIZING PRINCIPLE OF GENERALIST APPROACH

This problem-oriented approach to generalist practice is a solution-seeking stance that provides the worker with: (1) the means for assessing a given problem in its "social problem" context and its impact at various levels of society, from the individual to the community level; (2) guidelines to determine the level at which it is feasible to intervene; (3) the full range of social work interventive procedures indicated for problem solving; (4) the responsibility to assess the effectiveness of interventions; and (5) the basis to determine the direction of the next steps in the intervention process and the new tasks to be undertaken.

Intervention develops from the requirements of the problem rather than from the procedures of a practice method. The focus of joint client-worker solution seeking may occur at different levels of intervention. The levels-of-intervention concept designates the practice method(s) to be utilized and the client system(s) with which the problem-solving efforts may be accomplished; namely, individual, family, small group, community, organizations, institutional, and/or societal. It likewise assists in clarifying the social problem context of each particular problem-solving effort.

Major Assumptions of the Generalist Approach

The basic assumptions that support this generalist approach to practice are explicated as follows:

A. Assumptions related to social work practice:

1. People's problems in social functioning have their roots and their solutions at all levels of society simultaneously. Therefore, social work/interventions must also reflect this total view in an ongoing systemic way

2. The area of observation (assessment) will dictate the area of work for the generalist practitioner.

3. A problem-solving (solution-seeking) orientation directs the practitioner to all three methods as potential resources for intervention planning and implementation.

4. Assessment in generalist social work should consist of a broad-base formulation that exceeds the scope of a single method.

5. The practice methods of casework, group work, and community organization can be used singly, serially, or in combination in a direct-service approach. This approach to practice usually begins with individuals, families, or small groups and may extend through all levels of intervention contingent upon the particular problem with social functioning.

6. Social work practitioners have the responsibility of engaging in organizational development as a part of their total professional contribution.

7. Generalist practitioners must support both the change and maintenance functions of the organizational structure where they work.

B. Assumptions related to social work education:

1. The generalist approach to practice is a way of perceiving (assessment) as well as a way of doing. The generalist perspective draws upon the values and knowledge of the profession and utilizes the full interventive repertoire of social work.

2. All three social work methods have a common problem-solving base which makes the tasks in learning and practice manageable.

Existing practice theory and principles are therefore applicable to a generalist approach to practice.

3. The three direct practice methods of social work correspond with different levels of social intervention; i.e., individual, family, small group, neighborhood institutions, community organizations, and societal.

4. The individual social work practitioner is responsible for knowing the full range of interventive modes within the profession as a whole and has the responsibility to select among them in intervention planning and implementation.

5. It is possible for a single social worker to understand and use all three social work methods in his practice.

6. Ongoing organizational development is essential to fully utilize the profession's potential and to maximize the contribution of the practitioner.

7. Specific professional knowledge and skills are transferable and generalizable to new situations and circumstances.

8. Generalist social work practice maintains the orientation of the profession, i.e., to focus on the interplay between human coping and the demands of the environment and their dynamic effects on the growth of people.

9. The social work methods share professional values and knowledge which can be used in the assessment process to guide intervention planning and implementation.

10. The generalist practitioner contributes to the development of professional knowledge and the development of social services in being a communication link between the micro and macro components of social welfare.

REFERENCES

American Association of Social Workers. *Social Casework, Generic and Specific.* (New York: American Association of Social Workers, 1929).

Bartlett, Harriet. "The Generic-Specific Concept in Social Work Education and Practice." In Alfred J. Kahn (ed.), *Issues in American Social Work.* (New York: Columbia University Press, 1959, pp. 159–90).

———. *Analyzing Social Work Practice by Fields.* (New York: NASW, 1961).

———. *The Common Base of Social Work Practice.* (New York: NASW, 1970).

Berkley, George. *The Administrative Revolution: Notes on the Passing of the Organization Man.* (Englewood Cliffs, N.J.: Prentice Hall, 1971).

Bennis, Warren; Kenneth Benne; and Robert Chin. *The Planning of Change,* 2nd ed. (New York: Holt, Rinehart and Winston, 1969).

Cohen, Nathan (ed.) *Social Work and Social Problems.* (New York: NASW, 1964).

Etzioni, Amitai. *Modern Organizations.* (Englewood Cliffs, N.J.: Prentice Hall, 1964).

Gardner, John W. *Self-Renewal: The Individual and the Innovative Society.* (New York: Perennial Library, Harper & Row, 1971).

Glasgow, Douglas and Nancy Humphreys, "Proposal for the Future Delivery of Social Services: Position of the Western Coalition." (NASW Delegate Assembly, 1971 [mimeographed]).

Perlman, Helen H. "Generic Aspects of Specific Casework Settings." *Social Service Review.* (September, 1949, pp. 293–301).

———. "Social Work Methods: A Review of the Past Decade." *Social Work.* (Special Edition: Trends in Social Work Practice and Knowledge, Vol. 10, no. 4, 1965).

Said, Abdul. *Protagonists of Change.* (Englewood Cliffs, N.J.: Prentice Hall, 1971).

Schwartz, William. "The Social Worker in the Group," *The Social Welfare Reform, 1961, Proceedings of National Conference on Social Welfare.* (New York: Columbia University Press, 1961, pp. 151–56).

Swanson, Guy E. *Social Change.* (Glenview, Ill. and London: Scott, Foresman, 1971).

Toffler, Alvin. *Future Shock.* (New York: Bantam, 1971).

Wagner, John. "The Generalist Social Worker as Change-Agent." (4 pp. mimeographed).

Wax, John. "Developing Social Work Power in a Medical Organization," *Social Work.* (Vol. 13, no. 4, October 1968, pp. 62–71).

Wright, Nathan, Jr. *Black Power and Urban Unrest.* (New York: Hawthorn Books, Inc., 1967).

SOCIAL WORK PRACTICE: A LIFE MODEL

Alex Gitterman, Carel B. Germain

Over the years of its development, social work practice has had difficulty integrating two historical traditions: the emphasis on knowledge and skills to effect change in persons, and the emphasis on knowledge and skills to effect change in environments. Similarly, there has been difficulty in integrating method specializations of casework, group work, and community organization. In the past decade, new social conditions and new knowledge propelled social work to reexamine its formulations of practice and its technical interventions. Most efforts to reconceptualize the profession's practice manifest some common features: a view of human phenomena through a systems perspective, an emphasis on institutional and environmental structures, and the identification of various "target systems" as the loci for professional intervention.[1] Yet, quite naturally, a gap exists between the new knowledge and its use in everyday practice.

The life model integrates the treatment and reform traditions, by conceptualizing and emphasizing the dysfunctional transactions between people and their social and physical environments. Through an ecological theoretical perspective and a reciprocal conception of social work function, people and their environments receive simultaneous professional attention. Needs and issues are reconceptualized from "personality states" and "environmental states" to problems in living.

Within the ecological perspective, human beings are conceived as evolving and adapting through transactions with all elements of their environments.

Source: Reprinted from *Social Service Review,* Vol. 50, Dec. 1976, pp. 601–610, with permission of the University of Chicago Press. © 1976 by The University of Chicago Press.

In these adaptive processes the human being and the environment reciprocally shape each other. People mold their environments in many ways and, in turn, must then adapt to the changes they create.[2]

Increasingly, industrial society has posed complex adaptive tasks to human beings at all stages of the life cycle. The structures and functions of familial, organizational, and other environmental systems have undergone dramatic change. The family's capacity for fulfilling its integrative functions has been taxed by its members' divergent opportunities, needs, responsibilities, and interests. At the same time, institutions are experiencing serious problems in managing their intended service functions. These dramatic changes and disjunctions between adaptive demands and the resources available for meeting the demands generate stress. People's styles of coping with stress emerge from their perceptions of environmental demands and resources and of their own response capabilities.

Social work's distinctive functions and tasks arise from its social purpose: to strengthen coping patterns of people and to improve environments so that a better match can be attained between people's adaptive needs and potential and the qualities of their impinging environments.[3] Professional action is directed toward helping people and their environments overcome obstacles that inhibit the development of adaptive capacities. Assessment upon which action is based derives from a nonlinear view of causality. Assessment requires an understanding of the functions served by current transactions for the person and for the environment. In helping a person defined by self or others as depressed, for example, professional concern centers on the function of the depression for the person and his primary groups and on how it affects their reciprocal perceptions and transactions. Intervention then takes on the character of natural life processes that alter, use, or support properties of the environment, the coping qualities of the person, and the nature of the transactions between them.

Within this transactional focus, problems in living faced by individuals, families, and groups are further specified as: (1) problems and needs associated with tasks involved in life transitions, (2) problems and needs associated with tasks in using and influencing elements of the environment, and (3) problems and needs associated with interpersonal obstacles which impede the work of a family or a group as it deals with transitional and/or environmental tasks. Social work processes are directed to client problems and needs within one or more of these areas.

While these problems of living are interrelated, each comprises distinctive client tasks and professional interventions. For example, a sixty-five-year-old person may experience interrelated stresses arising out of the transition from employment to retirement, tensions within the immediate family, and unresponsive environmental institutions. The client and worker might contract to focus on the life transitional tasks, or the environmental tasks, or the maladaptive interpersonal processes among the family (or group) members. The focus might be on two or all three areas.[4] While the worker must pay attention to the complex interrelationships among these life forces, both the worker and the client must be clear at any given moment as to the specific problem-in-living receiving attention.

Emerging from the contracting process through which problems or needs are mutually defined, identified, and partialized, a division of labor evolves between client and worker.[5] The client focuses on his life tasks; the worker seeks to assure the conditions necessary for the client to achieve the tasks.[6] The worker remains continuously in tune with shifts in the client's concern from one area to another, drawing on knowledge and skill in the use of communication processes, actions to restructure situations, and environmental processes and resources.

TRANSITIONAL PROBLEMS AND NEEDS

Individual development occurs when internal, age-specific maturational phases transact with phase-specific environmental nutrients.[7] Thus every developmental stage represents mutual tasks for the individual and for his environment. The individual must meet maturational and social demands that may require shifts in self-concept, new ego skills, and the relinquishment of customary coping patterns for novel strategies. At the same time, the environment must provide the required opportunities and resources. Incomplete or thwarted task resolution at one stage tends to create difficulties in task resolution associated with a later stage.

Similarly, there are status-role changes that occur over the life span, such as a new job, migration to a new environment, marriage, and parenthood. Some status changes coincide with developmental stages, as in retirement or entry into junior high school. Some do not necessarily coincide with developmental phases, for example, migration or a new job. These changes, too, pose demands for new ego skills, the replacement of familiar adaptive patterns by new coping mechanisms, and shifts in self-concept.

There are also changes to less-valued and to stigmatized statuses when one becomes a foster child, a mental patient, a parolee or probationer, a welfare client, or a physically handicapped person. The tasks associated with these changes, however, are of a different order. In some instances, they are directed toward escaping the status, although the more stigmatized statuses have limited legitimized exits in our society.[8] In other instances, these changes place heavy coping demands in maintaining a positive self-image, controlling anxiety and depression, and taking effective action to escape the boundaries of these statuses. Moreover, occupants of these statuses are also dealing with the same developmental, status, and crisis tasks as other citizens. Hence they carry an enormous adaptive burden, but with far less environmental nutriment.

Finally, there are the expectable and the exceptional crisis events of life, the threats and natural losses that come to everyone over time and those catastrophic threats and losses that come too early, or too "unfairly," or too profoundly to be considered expectable in all lives. Such situational crises have an immediacy and enormity of demand that distinguish them, in part, from the developmental and role transitions previously discussed.[9] They often require immediate mobilization of the environment and of the individual in order to prevent collapse.

It is not only the individual, however, who experiences such transitional challenges. Families have a life cycle of their own. They also move through identifiable stages of development, status changes, and crisis events, such as a new marriage, the birth of a child, unemployment, or illness, posing tasks for the collectivity that may not always mesh with the transitional tasks of individual members.[10] Similarly, groups proceed through interactional phases of development,[11] status changes, and crisis events which threaten the life of the group.

In attempts to help individuals, families, and groups with developmental, status-role, and crisis tasks, certain practice principles become particularly relevant. Worker activity is directed toward exploration and mutual clarity of problem definition. People's stresses are legitimized as "normal" life processes appropriate for helping attention. The worker partializes problems into smaller, more manageable elements. At the same time, he searches for patterns of behavior and for connections between past and present patterns. At times, it may be difficult for the worker to invite this elaboration. The content may be quite painful (e.g., loss), or may touch upon social taboos (e.g., sexuality), or may trigger the worker's own unresolved developmental issues (e.g., ethnic identity). It becomes essential for the worker to sustain the content, carefully avoiding premature reassurance or interpretations. The worker and client together seek and use information, scan alternatives, and weigh costs and benefits. A central concern is to provide opportunity for resolution of life tasks in the life situation appropriate to the client's sense of time and space, his lifestyle and aspirations. (Real life action, or even role play, can be helpful in working on adaptive tasks.)

In families and groups, the worker also helps members to separate out their individual developmental goals and tasks from the expectations exerted by the collectivity and by environmental forces. At the same time, the worker encourages family and group members to be responsive to one another as they seek areas of common developmental expectations and tasks. And people are always encouraged to use family, peer group, and environmental supports in pursuing their transitional tasks.

ENVIRONMENTAL PROBLEMS AND NEEDS

This area of help is concerned with adaptive issues arising from the nature of the social and physical environments. The *social* environment, which man has created and to which he must then adapt, includes institutions, organizations, and social networks. The *physical* environment includes both natural and man-made structures and objects, and time and space.

A distinct feature of contemporary urban society is the existence of complex organizations and their impact on people's daily lives. As they become larger and more complex, organizations are more difficult to administer and coordinate. Out of necessity, they become preoccupied with the standardization of policies and procedures. Institutional homeostasis and administrative "peace and quiet" often take precedence over people's individualized service needs.

Within this context, people turn to organizations for essential services (health, education, welfare). At times, their contacts add to their distress instead of mitigating or alleviating it. Their encounters with organizational representatives may lead to a sense of personal inadequacy and stigma. While many organizational representatives are motivated to carry out their specialized functions at least initially, they sometimes build defenses against dehumanizing and frustrating conditions and a sense of failure. They may then become blind to the injustices and social inequities within their own and other organizations, and withdraw affect, zeal, and commitment to their service. Others may become overidentified with organizational need at the expense of client need. Still others may develop and rely on stereotyped characterizations of client behaviors.

Stigmatized by their client status and unaware of their rights and privileges, people often accept and resign themselves to these conditions. Hence, the social worker has a particularly critical function in helping people to use and to influence elements of their organizational environment. Knowledge and assessment[12] of organizational structures, functions, and processes provide an important basis for professional influence.[13] Interventive strategies of influence[14] include differentially invoking or appealing to the formal organizational objectives, structures, roles, and policies favorable to the client's request but circumvented; the formal organizational and environmental accountability and sanctioning mechanisms; the organizational or individual representative's self-interest and self-esteem; the professional service ethic supportive of individualization; and the informal system in which favors are collected and exchanged.[15] The effectiveness of these collaborative strategies are dependent on the worker's professional competence, credibility, zeal, and resilience. Within a host setting especially, professional visibility and reputation for competence provide an essential means for organizational involvement and influence. If these collaborative strategies prove ineffective, the worker may turn to more adversarial behaviors, for example, petition, public criticism, and use of mass media.

The concept of *social network* refers to important figures in the environment, including relatives, friends, neighbors, and peers. Such a network often meets the needs of human beings for relatedness; provides recognition, affirmation, and protection from social isolation; and offers the means for identification and for socialization to the norms, values, knowledge, and belief systems of the particular culture. It serves as a mutual aid system essential for adaptation and for coping with stress. Some networks, however, may reinforce deviance, be subject themselves to maladaptive interpersonal processes, or undermine the client's sense of identity and autonomy. Some social networks are too loosely organized and integrated to serve as a source of support. Some clients may be without any social network at all.

Since attachment behavior in the human being has adaptive importance across the life cycle, the social network is an important dimension of the social worker's attention. Client and worker action can be directed toward mobilizing or strengthening real life ties between the client and significant others in the life space, finding new linkages or reestablishing old ones. In the absence of natural networks, worker and client may consider the possibility of relational experiences through the use of other levels of social work personnel, volunteers, and friendly visitors. Together, worker and client may consider the use of organized groups (Parent-Teacher Associations, Parents without Partners, tenant councils, consumer groups, etc.) to meet relationship (and task) needs, or the construction of mutual-aid systems to meet adaptive requirements and to exchange resources. All of these actions are close to life processes and hence are likely to be of more adaptive value than major reliance on the time-limited relationship with the worker.

We are beginning to understand how people organize and use space in the physical environment and how, in turn, spatial variables affect behavior. Ward geography, for example, is an important factor in the social interaction of residents of a geriatric facility or patients in a mental hospital. Spatial arrangements in classrooms and treatment cottages may invite or discourage particular behaviors in children. Space, design, color, and decoration in social agencies communicate to users of services their differential statuses.[16] Social work interventions directed to spatial variables or to providing experiences in the natural world are used to enhance relatedness and increase the nutritiveness of the environment.

Whatever interventive strategies are used in helping people to deal with their social and physical environments, the worker must take into account the consequences and implications of his actions on clients. At times clients can be hurt by professionals with benign intentions but dysfunctional interventions. Users of service need to be fully involved in the assessment and intervention processes. Through their full participation, users of service become educated to environmental structures, functions, and processes. They develop greater competence in negotiating their environment and in exerting control over achieving their life tasks.[17]

MALADAPTIVE INTERPERSONAL PROBLEMS AND NEEDS IN FAMILIES AND GROUPS

As the family or group works on the tasks associated with life transitions or with using and influencing the environment, it sometimes encounters impediments posed by maladaptive communication processes and relationship patterns. Such impediments may be poorly understood or altogether outside the members' awareness. Behaviorally they are expressed through patterned scapegoating, power struggles, interlocking hostilities, mutual withdrawal, double binds, and other distortions. While these patterned behaviors often serve a latent function in maintaining the family or group equilibrium, the consequences are usually maladaptive for some members. Thus, these interpersonal obstacles to individual and collective growth and adaptation become a third area of help.

Practice interventions, then, include an assessment of the factors which generate the specific transactional obstacles. Our experience suggests that there are several repetitive sources of interpersonal conflict: (1) discrepancy between an individual's and the collective's life transition tasks: A family may be preoccupied with its survival and maintenance, while its young adult member is striving for separation. Or a group in a late stage of its development may experience serious difficulty incorporating new members; (2) dysfunctional accommodation to environmental pressures and inadequacies: In response to a hostile environment, some members may develop apathy that then interferes with mutual problem solving. Others may cope by scapegoating one another; (3) discrepancy among members' orientations to "power and love": One spouse may seek intimacy while the other requires emotional distance. Or the parents may disagree on matters of authority; (4) normative conflicts among members, such as differing generational perceptions of right and wrong, attractive and unattractive, good and bad; (5) compositional problems within the collective: A family or group may experience strain as a member leaves or a new or former member enters. Or a family or group may isolate a member because of deviant descriptive or behavioral characteristics.

When the focus is on helping families and groups to deal with such transactions as patterned scapegoating[18] or double-bind modes of communication,[19] the worker invites and encourages the members to view the obstacle through a systemic perspective. The worker encourages mutuality among members by helping them search for common concerns and self-interests. At the same time, the worker reaches for and encourages the elaboration of differential perspectives. Strategically, it is often easier for members with the greater power and personal strength to begin the exploratory process. As work on the obstacle proceeds, the less powerful and more insecure members often require special support and encouragement to risk their perceptions and interpretations. Expression of members' divergent, discrepant perceptions needs to be partialized and the associated affect encouraged. If members attempt to avoid the content, the worker focuses, mediates, and guards the conditions of their agreed-upon contract. Throughout, the worker provides relevant facts, interpretations, and perceptions and lends professional strength, support, and faith in members' capacity to move beyond the painful obstacle.

In a similar way, interpersonal barriers can arise between worker and client(s) manifested in distorted communications and maladaptive relationship processes. Frequently such barriers are defined as client resistance when, in fact, they are transactional in origin. They arise from incongruencies in perceptions and expectations; feelings related to age, sex, race, and ethnic differences; transference and countertransference; and ambivalences, cognitive discrepancies, and ambiguities. The worker has the responsibility for continuous vigilance concerning the possible existence of such barriers and for bringing them into open discussion so that mutual work on them may take place, including assessing their source, nature, and consequences.[20]

SUMMARY

The profession's social purpose has always referred to a dual interest in people and situations, but the lack of knowledge about their reciprocity made the practice application of social purpose difficult. This paper has attempted to present an integrated perspective on social work practice based on that reciprocity. The ecological perspective provides a means for capturing the transactional processes between human beings and their environments. The conceptualization of people's needs into three interrelated areas of problems in living transcends former methodological distinctions among casework, family therapy, and group work, and provides a life model for intervention.

NOTES

[1]See, e.g., Carol H. Meyer, *Social Work Practice: A Response to the Urban Crisis* (New York: Free Press, 1970); Allan Pincus and Anne Minahan, *Social Work Practice* (Itasca, Ill.: F.T. Peacock, 1973); Howard Goldstein, *Social Work Practice* (Columbia: University of South Carolina Press, 1973); Gale Goldberg and Ruth Middleman, *Social Service Delivery: A Structural Approach to Social Work Practice* (New York: Columbia University Press, 1974); and Max Siporin, *Introduction to Social Work Practice* (New York: Macmillan, 1975).

[2]Carel B. Germain, "The Ecological Perspective in Casework Practice," *Social Casework* 54 (June 1973): 323–30.

[3]See, e.g., William Gordon, "Basic Concepts for an Integrative and Generative Conception of Social Work," in *The General Systems Approach: Contributions toward an Holistic Conception of Social Work*, ed. Gordon Hearn (New York: Council on Social Work Education, 1969); and William Schwartz, "Social Group Work: The Interactionist Approach," in *Encyclopedia of Social Work*, ed. Robert Morris (New York: National Association of Social Workers, 1971).

[4]In these situations, it is essential that the client and worker work on the same problem in living at any moment in time. Otherwise one might, for example, focus on an environmental definition while the other might focus on a psychological identity definition.

[5]For discussion and illustration of the contracting processes, see Alex Gitterman, "Group Work in the Public Schools," in *The Practice of Group Work*, ed. William Schwartz and Serapio Zalba (New York: Columbia University Press, 1971), pp. 45–56; Alfred Kadushin, *The Social Work Interview* (New York: Columbia University Press, 1972), pp. 105–40; Anthony Mallucio and Wilma Marlow, "The Case for the Contract," *Social Work* 9 (January 1974): 28–37; and Brett Seabury, "The Contract: Uses, Abuses, and Limitations," *Social Work* 21 (January 1976): 16–21.

[6]Eliot Studt, "Social Work Theory and Implications for the Practice of Methods," *Social Work Education Reporter* 16 (June 1968): 22–24, 42–46.

[7]See Erik Erikson, *Identity and the Life Cycle*, Psychological Issues Monograph no. 1 (New York: International Universities Press, 1959), for the epigenetic development of the autonomous ego.

[8]Even though the formal role may be vacated, the person is assigned a similarly stigmatized status such as ex-mental patient or ex-prisoner.

[9]Developmental and social transitions occasionally take on the nature of crisis when the tasks are perceived by the person or the environment as insurmountable.

[10]Patricia O'Connell, "Family Developmental Tasks," *Smith College Studies in Social Work* 42 (June 1972): 203–10.

[11]For an elaboration of stages of group development, see James A. Garland, Hubert E. Jones, and Ralph L. Kolodny, "A Model for Stages of Development in Social Work Groups," in *Explorations in Group Work*, ed. Saul Bernstein (Boston: Boston University School of Social Work, 1968), pp. 12–53; W. Bennis and H. Sheppard, "A Theory of Group Development," *Human Relations* 9 (November 1956): 415–537.

[12]The depth and scope of an organizational assessment are dependent on such factors as client need, whether the worker is employed by the agency being negotiated, and previous contacts with the specific representative.

[13]Brager makes an important distinction between "helping" and "influencing" an organization (George Brager, "Helping vs. Influencing: Some Political Elements of Organizational Change" [paper presented at the National Conference on Social Welfare, San Francisco, May 1975]).

[14]Prof. Irving Miller has been particularly helpful in identifying various practice strategies (e.g., Miller's speech before the Alumni Conference of the Columbia University School of Social Work, November 3, 1973 [mimeographed]).

[15]See Alvin Gouldner, "The Norm of Reciprocity," *American Sociological Review* 25 (April 1960): 161–68; and Gene W. Dalton, "Influence and Organizational Change," in *Organizational Change and Development*, ed. Gene W. Dalton et al. (Homewood, Ill.: Richard D. Irwin, and Dorsey Press, 1970), pp. 250–58.

[16]Brett Seabury, "Arrangement of Physical Space in Social Work Settings," *Social Work* 16 (October 1971): 43–49.

[17]Group services have a unique potential for achieving this objective. They possess an inherent advantage in that: (1) people can gain strength, security, and relief from being with others in a similar situation; (2) perceptions of personal, psychological problems can be transferred into perceptions of collective, social problems; (3) collective action can gain greater

institutional responsiveness; and (4) groups can be linked with other groups, thus representing a source for significant political action.

[18]See, e.g., Lawrence Schulman, "Scapegoats, Group Workers, and Preemptive Intervention," *Social Work* 12 (April 1967): 37–43; and E. Vogel and N. Bell, "The Emotionally Disturbed Child as the Family Scapegoat," in *A Modern Introduction to the Family*, ed.

E. Vogel and N. Bell (New York: Free Press, 1968), pp. 382–97.

[19]See, e.g., Jay Haley, *Strategies of Psychotherapy* (New York: Grune & Stratton, 1963).

[20]For elaboration and illustration, see Alex Gitterman and Alice Schaeffer, "The White Professional and the Black Client," *Social Casework* 53 (May 1972): 280–91.

THE INTEGRATION OF INDIVIDUAL AND ENVIRONMENTAL CHANGE EFFORTS: A CONCEPTUAL FRAMEWORK

Charles Garvin, Paul Glasser

Any review of major writings on social work practice will reveal efforts to relate individual to environmental change to enhance the social functioning of persons. Harriet Bartlett, for example, states that the profession's focus is "at the most abstract level, the interaction of people and environment." She criticizes the profession for failing to bring ideas about people and environment together and one of her major points is to press for an understanding of the "active exchange" between these two entities.[1]

Recently writers have sought to resolve the individual-environment issue through the use of system,[2] organizational,[3] or other social-psychological or sociological concepts.[4] One problem with these efforts for practitioners and teachers of practice has been the level of abstraction required to sustain this type of theory building. To develop models which link person, problem, and situation across the spectrum of social welfare intervention is a necessary conceptual task but requires the generation of more specific practice principles.

One way to operationalize abstract models is to develop classifications of areas of practice without doing a disservice to the individual-environment exchange process within the area. Clear and testable propositions can then be generated which articulate with the broader framework but which are informed

by differing substantive matters. For example, this was the approach taken by Perlmutter in her development of the concept of functional fields, which she defined as "a system of service fulfilling a societal mandate to improve the life of the individual."[5] This paper takes a different route by generating a classification of the functions of social welfare organizations. This "organizational-environmental model" makes it possible to identify similarities and differences in practice procedures across a wide range of situations. It is specifically interested in specifying, however, a model for direct practice with individuals, families, and groups and does not claim to have created an approach useful for the full range of social work activities. But it is also interested in providing the interpersonal change practitioner with an orientation that enables him/her to provide service based on client need rather than a limited range of worker skills and techniques.

CHARACTERISTICS OF AN ORGANIZATIONAL-ENVIRONMENTAL MODEL

In this model, the individual with his or her knowledge, attitudes, feelings, and behavior is viewed not only in the context of the treatment situa-

Source: Charles Garvin and Paul Glasser, "The Integration of Individual and Environmental Change Efforts: A Conceptual Framework," *Contemporary Social Work Education* 1, no. 1 (1977): 13–23. Reprinted by permission of the publisher and authors.

tion, be it one-to-one, family, or group, but also in the context of the social environment. It is this environment which has either placed the individual "at risk," thus requiring preventive activity; or has actually elicited and maintained problems requiring rehabilitative activity.

SOCIAL FUNCTIONING

The task of social work from the point of view of this orientation to practice is to help individuals improve their social functioning. Social functioning refers to the ways individuals carry out their social roles. Roles are conceived as subcategories of socially defined positions, and of particular interest to workers are such positions, as patient, inmate, parent, employee, spouse, and student.[6] Some positions, like delinquent, school dropout, or psychotic patient, are often the focus of the practitioner's attention because he or she is asked to help such persons move out of these positions into others which are normatively acceptable. Effective performance of roles frequently requires the individual to integrate appropriate values, knowledge, and interpersonal skills. Certain emotional responses, such as dysfunctional anxiety or anger, may hinder appropriate role performance and also may be the focus of change efforts.

Alterations in role performance are sought through changes in the social structures and processes relevant to particular roles, changes in the person's behavior in response to environmental expectations, or as is frequently the case, both. However, social functioning is seen in highly specific terms. Whether it be with regard to individual behavior or the situation related to that behavior, or the prevention of or changes in problematic functioning, the change orientation must be clearly defined. The actions of clients or those in their environments, and modifications of these, are to be characterized in observable behaviors.

Thus, this notion stresses that the intervention agent focuses on helping each client modify his/her environment or his/her own behavior by making use of the interpersonal change experience. The worker facilitates the creation of specified interpersonal change conditions as one means to achieve individual or terminal goals. Group work may be most useful for some clients; individual contacts or family therapy for others. An activity program may be most useful for some clients; discussion for others. In each instance, however, the worker's primary attention is on how he/she can aid clients to change social roles or learn new ones in particular positions they hold or would like to occupy in the social environment.

Therefore, assessment requires specification of client behavior in the context of the life-space relevant to particular positions and roles in the social environment, and goals must be expressed in precise operational terms. Goals refer to a condition or state of a client or family or the situation of the client or family which the worker would like to see changed at the end of the intervention sequence. In marital or family therapy, goals may be stated in interpersonal or system terms, but also must be stated in such a way that there are observable indications that change has taken place. One of the practitioner's primary responsibilities is to account for and improve his/her practice as well as the practice of colleagues; therefore, goals must be sufficiently concrete to measure their achievement when the change process has been completed. Often it is necessary to establish [multiple] terminal goals, each related to one or different social positions and roles in life. This requires the worker to establish priorities among them for attention.

Since worker planning and individual accomplishment may best proceed through successive approximations to a terminal goal, proximate goals or steps along the path to a final goal may need to be specified. For example, to increase a couple's marital compatibility, it may be necessary to help them to accomplish more effective communication by learning to listen to each other with greater attentiveness and understanding before they can move on to attempt to achieve more consensus through problem-solving techniques.

INTERVENTION
IN THE ENVIRONMENT

The physical and social environment can serve as both the source of personal problems and as a powerful tool for individual change. In this paper the environment is conceived of in three ways.:

1. As the life-space in which an individual carries out roles which are part of particular positions;

2. As the organized institutional context in which professional change efforts take place;

3. As the social situation in which intervention approaches are made by the worker to influence client attitudes, knowledge, feelings, and behavior.

Clients may often be at risk or experience problems because of deleterious social circumstances. Worker or client intervention in the environment alone rather than one-to-one or group involvement with a practitioner over time may often be sufficient to achieve satisfactory change for adequate role performance. Actions to change a client's life situation may have to precede interpersonal practice. Experience has taught that adequate food, clothing, shelter, and medical care are prerequisites for effective psychological counseling.

Even when basic needs are met, social structures and processes may be problematic to role performance. There may be conflicting expectations for a position a person holds (role conflict), ambiguous expectations and insufficient reinforcement for fulfilling role requirements, or lack of resources and opportunity structures to carry out roles successfully. Normatively desired role performance may elicit punishing responses, and this may have to be the focus of change activity.

The organizational context of social work intervention can be supportive of professional work or sometimes, without intent, hinder or even prevent the achievement of legitimate individual goals. This will be given major attention in the material that follows.

This orientation, then, seeks to generate intervention methods derived from a comprehension of persons in terms of their personality and behavior as well as in terms of the social situations which contributed to their need for service. This requires a clear understanding by the worker of external forces which have created or are likely to create problems. The worker becomes a mediator then between the client, other clients if the individual is in a family or group work intervention situation, and the individual, family, or group and its social environment.[7]

AN ORGANIZATIONAL TYPOLOGY

The specific mediational issues are related to the functions which the agency fulfils in the broader community and the types of clients, therefore, who are likely to be referred to or attracted to the agency. These functions are conceptualized in this paper as falling into a limited set of categories, which have been derived from an understanding that all organizations serve as society's agents for either social stability or social change. This is true of education and welfare organizations as well, and the functions they serve are reflections of this dichotomy. While there

can be an exclusive emphasis in these agencies upon either social stability or social change, many try to achieve both. It is the particular emphasis or combination of emphases which establishes its practice climate.

Related to this dichotomy are the social functions organizations fulfil. Some provide services to people in the process of *transition* from one position to another; others provide services to people in the midst of *social conflict*. One function of transitional organizations is to help individuals to choose among alternative and often ambiguous norms in an anomic environment. The other function is to facilitate entrance into new positions. We will identify these organizations throughout this paper as fulfilling the functions of *anomic reduction* and/or *socialization*.

With the rapidity of social change in our society and the consequent normative conflicts, almost all social welfare organizations must, to some degree, help clients cope with problems of anomie; but some are more likely than others to focus on this kind of help. Many have been founded relatively recently in response to these new social demands and are important for the prevention of more serious personal problems. They have come into existence to aid individuals who are either unable to identify choices open to them or to make decisions among available alternatives. Among the options dealt with are the selection of lifestyles, vocational careers, and belief systems. More specific issues often considered have to do with sexual behavior, gender identity, and ways of relating to others. Examples of agencies which offer this type of service are teenage "rap centers"; some drug programs; women, minority, and gay consciousness-raising organizations; and counseling programs associated with universities.

In the second type of transitional function, socialization, are agencies which help clients move from one developmental level to another. Their emphasis is on anticipatory socialization, frequently building on already present knowledge and skills. Welfare and education agencies engaged in this function are schools, community centers, settlements, family life education programs, geriatric facilities, and preparation of retirement organizations.

Social conflict organizations also are seen to be of two types, although many agencies include both functions. Some primarily act as agents of *social control*. They are created through societal processes—usually legislative in nature—which provide sanction to the organizations involved to limit behavior classified as deviant. Examples are training schools for delinquents, prisons, as well as mental health programs which are custodial in nature. It should be emphasized that this is a classification of the functions of organizations and *not* of the tasks of the social workers they employ.

The second type of social conflict organization refers to those engaged in *resocialization*. There may be difficulty in classifying socialization as compared to resocialization functions. The former involve clients who are not likely to be in conflict regarding their present development. The latter emphasize resolving conflicts between previous behaviors and attitudes and those sought through agency services. Resocialization-oriented agencies include those devoted to skill development for the physically handicapped, retraining for the unemployed, and psychiatric treatment for mental patients. The last is included here because its purpose is to help clients to replace dysfunctional behaviors with those that lead to attaining personal goals.

The distinctions among these types of agencies is not always clear in the minds of the public, the employees of the organization, or the clients it serves; yet each creates a different context for practice. As ideal types, few may be exclusively oriented to transition or social conflict or the subcategories of each; yet it is possible to trace many problems experienced by workers to ambiguities in goals related to the aforementioned functions. Even when ambiguity is not present, specific programs within organizations may have different functions, and this may be a source of strain for the agency board and administrator, their employees, and their clients.

An example of such a strain is that of a worker who sought to help a client make a choice between homosexual and heterosexual orientations, thus reducing his feelings of anomie. Yet the agency implicitly brought pressures for heterosexual behavior, thus exerting social control. Another worker wanted to help clients secure career training which is a form of socialization. Agency resources were limited, however, and clients were only helped to make career choices, thus reducing worker activities to those related to anomie.

INTERVENTION

Social work intervention will differ in settings devoted to anomic reduction, socialization, social control, and resocialization. In all circumstances, however, the worker attempts to accomplish a series of planned tasks by carrying them out in ways which are specifically relevant to each setting. We will first describe these more general tasks and subsequently illustrate how they are executed under different organizational conditions.

1. Initial Assessment. As noted above, the worker mediates among individual needs, the conditions of the intervention context (individual, family, group) and the external environment. Yet, because individual or family goals are paramount, the worker must engage in an individualized assessment. This includes specification of actual or potential problems and study of their causal circumstances. These are found within the history, behavioral repertoires, and personality patterns of the individual as well as the dysfunctional situations in which he or she is located.[8] These situations may include primary group affiliations within the agency or other organizations as well as in institutions beyond the agency such as the family, place of employment, and community. While agency function establishes limits for services, a good deal of diversity is still possible.

2. Decisions on Contexts for Change. After the problem is identified and assessed, the worker and client must determine whether social work intervention is needed at all and whether individual, family, group, or other type of service should be a part of this. An important factor in the decision to make use of any modality is the client's informed choice about such services. The client should be given an accurate description of the service options and an opportunity to consider how these relate to his or her past experiences and current needs. Unfortunately, there is a dearth of definitive research for the worker to use as the basis for the recommendation for the choice among individual, family, or group work intervention. An example of a useful exception to this statement is recent research which concludes that clients with certain characteristics are likely to drop out of groups before receiving help.[9] It is quite clear, however, that selected clients in all social welfare settings can profit from group services.

3. Composition of the Action Situation. By this we mean the choice of worker and the selection of family members or group work members to participate if one of these modalities has been chosen. The major task is to determine how agency function and environmental stress articulate with the needs of individuals in terms of compositional issues. We have written previously about these concerns.[10] From the organizational and environmental perspective of this paper, however, some of the following issues come to mind in addition to our previous formulation: (a) What kinds of worker expertise are required for the anticipated individual *and* environmental change efforts? (b) What kinds of worker attributes (e.g., age, sex, ethnicity) will most enhance the attainment of *both* individual and environmental change goals? (c) What kinds of structures (e.g., roles, tasks, communications) are likely to emerge and how will this affect individual *and* environmental change goals? (d) What is the possibility that intervention situations of varying composition will appropriately affect selected individuals, families, subcultures, organizations, and communities as primary or secondary targets?

4. Initiating the Action System as an Intervention Context. The first sessions with the action system are vitally important as these experiences determine whether clients will remain in the intervention situation, how much they will trust the worker (and one another if they are part of a family or group), and the issues likely to be emphasized. The worker's efforts will be directed at enhancing the relationship of clients to him or her and to each other,[11] facilitating the clarification of purposes, and establishing ground rules for meeting times, places, and procedures. When group work is employed, this phase nears a close when clients achieve a "secondary treatment contract" in which their responsibilities to each other and to the worker are specified in a mutually satisfactory manner.

5. Worker Interventions for Change. The worker is continually in the process of making decisions regarding interventions. This complex process consists of worker and client selection of: (1) intervention targets, (2) intervention strategies, and (3) intervention techniques. As a result of this analysis, the worker can integrate his/her activities to promote changes in the individual, group, or family intervention context and environmental factors.

a. *Selection of intervention targets.* The decision here is which aspect of client behavior (i.e., affect, attitude, cognition, role performance) and/or which environmental conditions require modification in order to attain client or family goals. When environmental change is sought, it must be decided whether the client, *with* the help of the worker and/or other clients, or the worker *on behalf of* the client, will be the instrument of change.

Client environment is viewed here in terms of the opportunity structures it provides for each person to attain his or her objectives. At times these structures are present but require modification, as when a teacher fails to offer adequate reinforcement to a student or a prison fails to admit an inmate to a desired training program. At other times these opportunities are absent, as when a school does not have available remedial reading aid or a prison lacks vocational training programs.

b. *Selection of intervention strategies.* After selection of targets, a strategy of change is chosen. This comprises a series of activities aimed at attaining the desired result. Some strategies, such as the introduction of a nonverbal activity or of a reinforcement contingency program, place the worker in an "expert" position. Other strategies, such as those of task-centered work, place greater responsibility upon the client to select an appropriate means of change.[12] The employment of problem-solving approaches is clearly a mutual effort. Strategies to change environmental opportunity structures range from educational approaches to the creation of social conflict.[13]

c. *Selection of intervention techniques.* Techniques are worker behaviors derived from the strategy and enacted in each worker's personal style. One technique, for example, for enhancing problem solving is a "force field analysis"; another is signaling clients when they are "on" or "off" topic. A technique for teaching a skill is to model it; a technique for resolving ambivalence is "double chairing."

As noted above, these tasks will be enacted differently under varying organizational conditions. Space does not permit an exhaustive treatment of each condition, although illustrative material will be offered in a later section.

6. Termination and Evaluation. In one-to-one treatment the individual may leave, and in group or family work an individual may leave while the group or family continues or the entire group or family may terminate. The decision to discontinue may be made by the worker, the client, the family, or the group; feelings regarding termination may differ widely.

Ideally, termination occurs when the intervention goals have been achieved. The worker's task, then, is to reduce the nonfunctional attachments that clients may have formed which prevent them from realizing their new potential. The worker may also attempt to strengthen the changes that have occurred. Evidence that the termination decision was correct lies in the higher value the client places on leaving than on staying, as well as data indicating that he or she can transfer the new and more useful behavior into contexts other than the intervention situation.

When terminal goals have not been achieved, it is the responsibility of the worker to encourage clients to seek aid from other sources if this is required or may be helpful. For example, they may obtain alternative services from the same agency, or different services from other community institutions. At times an entire group is terminated when the group has developed sufficient resources to conduct its own activities. The group may also be referred to community institutions—such as community centers—for less intensive service.

It is incumbent upon the worker to evaluate the effectiveness and efficiency of services periodically throughout the change process as well as at termination. This allows for modification of goals and intervention plans and rejection of ineffective technologies.

We will now move on to illustrate how these tasks may be performed in agencies sharing a common function. For this purpose, we have chosen the resocialization function.

INTERVENTIONS IN ORGANIZATIONS WITH SOCIAL CONFLICT FUNCTIONS: RESOCIALIZATION

General Perspectives. Organizations engaging in resocialization are oriented toward helping persons develop new values, knowledge, and skills to replace dysfunctional ones. Clients who hold these attitudes and behaviors sometimes have psychiatric or other labels attached to them which can obscure the interactional nature of the problems. Marital and family counseling, medical social work with the physically handicapped and their families, and job training for technologically displaced, unemployed, and dissatisfied workers are all services related to this function. While there may be considerable environmental pressure on clients to seek help, they usually seek it because of personal discomfort.

Under these circumstances, clients are less re-sistive to change than under social control conditions and their motivation for resocialization is often high. They may find change difficult, however, because lifelong patterns have been upset. When some organizations, such as mental hospitals, drug programs, and prisons, focus on both social control and resocialization, it may be difficult to ascertain whether the agency is oriented more toward the former or the latter, and this may be confusing to workers and members alike.

Initial Assessment. The difference between socialization and resocialization functions is the conflict experienced by clients in resocialization between old and new role requirements. The emphasis in work with clients being resocialized, then, is to identify such conflict and the personal and social forces maintaining it. How the individual copes with conflict is also important to understand. Other assessment variables parallel those for socialization and include the client's awareness of socialization requirements and his/her skills, knowledge, and motivation to fulfil these. Resocialization, to be successful, often needs the encouragement and reinforcement of the client by groups in his/her environment. This is one reason marital and family therapy and social group work are often the preferable means of intervention. In some types of service, opportunities to put new knowledge and skills to work must be found. This necessitates careful evaluation of the environmental context for change.

Intervention Context. Depending on assessment indications, individual, family, small and large group contexts may be used. The individual who is in crisis or who requires immediate reinforcement to embark on a nondeviant career may require one-to-one work. The client whose family has been instrumental in maintaining his or her problematic behavior may require active involvement of that family in treatment. Work with community networks, ward groups, or institutional cottages may be required to create or enhance new opportunities for the client.

Composition of the Action System. The nature of the resocialization goal frequently suggests whether a client ought to be seen alone, with his spouse and/or other family members, or with peers who are pursuing similar aims. In group work it is useful for members to be committed to similar resocialization goals and, therefore, it is desirable that such groups be homogeneous in this respect. A group like Synanon that replicates in some way the division of labor of a small society—such as carrying on economic activities—

will require members with appropriate skills to perform a variety of relevant tasks. When family work is utilized, involvement of the broadest aspects of the family network may be required to support new client roles.

Initiating the Action System. In resocialization the worker builds upon the strong client motivation to change to establish rules for the intervention situation which will hasten and reinforce the change process. This often includes identification of intermediate goals and providing appropriate structured opportunities to deal with obstacles to progress toward agreed upon ends. In contrast, in social control settings, the worker must frequently begin by finding means to motivate the client to change, or even to join an intervention situation.

Intervention Targets. As in socialization, the targets for personal change will include modification of knowledge and skill. In addition to solving problems related to inadequate situations for change within the family, place of employment, or community, it is often necessary to diminish broader dysfunctional aspects of these systems, such as labeling, inappropriate discharge procedures, and client powerlessness.

Intervention Strategies. The major strategies for resocialization are education, problem solving, anticipatory socialization, and enhancing reinforcements for change. Problem-solving work is devoted to the reduction of stresses brought about by discrepancies between old and new lifestyles. The worker will also enable group members, when groups are employed, to help one another to cope with institutions which punitively identify them with their former behaviors and positions. In fact, effective work for resocialization will frequently require the social action potential of clients in conjunction with other clients and worker. Agency rules may have to be changed, job or training opportunities may have to be created, and resources to support use of training may have to be secured. Advocacy procedures may have to be employed.

Intervention Techniques. Depending on the nature of barriers to resocialization, different techniques will be used. Conflicting value orientations may sometimes be resolved through value clarification.[14] Another technique for helping the client achieve his or her goals is coaching.[15] This includes establishing short-term goals, closely observing performances to know when reinforcement is needed, and offering advice. Role play techniques are also useful as a form of rehearsal. Behavior modification techniques such as token reinforcement and group contingencies are applicable. Opportunities to observe other members or outsiders as models can be created. Another helpful approach is the development of a buddy system, consisting of pairs of clients who may meet each other through a group experience and who can support each other in completing resocialization tasks. The worker as well as other members may make assignments to individuals for completion between sessions. Approaches chosen must help individuals, singly as well as with others, to work for modifications in social situations in the agency and the community.

Termination. Ideally, in resocialization activity the client is reintegrated into his family, the employment market, peer group, community, etc. However, follow-up activity by the worker himself, others in the agency, or other agencies may be required to help the client or the family maintain the gains achieved. Sometimes new goals are sought as more pressing problems are solved, and new contracts are required with the same or different workers in a different intervention situation.

ORGANIZATIONAL PREREQUISITES

This orientation to practice, in which individual, group, and environmental conditions are all targets for change, requires an agency conducive to such an approach. It is not that social work cannot be practiced without this; rather, the worker must strive to bring about the kind of organizational environment required to maximize effective practice.[16]

1. Intake in the agency must be open to a broad range of clients. When groups are to be used, this must be sufficient to ensure: (1) adequate referrals, and (2) a sufficient heterogeneity of clients so as to meet compositional criteria.

2. The worker must be part of and have influence in the referral process. Workers doing individual work often refer their "failures" to groups and retain all clients who are likely to be therapeutic successes, thus limiting treatment options. A stigma must not be attached to participation in any change-oriented situation. Group composition may require that in some closed institutions members be recruited from differing residential subunits, and agency procedures should permit this.

3. The organization must provide necessary resources. These include meeting places suitable for individual, family, and small and large group activity and furnished accordingly. Funds for program equipment, refreshments, and transportation may be required for all forms of intervention. Another resource issue is sufficient worker time to do an effective job with family, group, or individual clients.

Opportunity to Work in the Social Environment Is Essential

4. Organizational rules must enhance treatment processes. Organizations tend to make rules *for* their subunits. These sometimes include prohibition of some activities useful for positive change, like family visits or some types of group programs. The worker must strive to change rules and procedures which prevent clients from making appropriate autonomous decisions about their own behavior or about creating environments more conducive to optimal social functioning.

5. The organization should be open to change processes initiated by clients. They are likely to point up needed modifications in agency rules, staffing patterns, and opportunities for client involvement in the organization and the community.

6. Team cooperation among workers should be encouraged. For this purpose informal channels are as important as formal ones. Clients should not be hindered unnecessarily from attending intervention sessions or fulfilling assignments.

7. The clients and worker should have access to the relevant environments outside of the organization. This is particularly true for closed institutions in which the client is likely to return to a negatively reinforcing environment unless change is initiated there before discharge. Even in open settings, however, workers should not be required to limit their activities to the confines of the agency.

Central to all of these conditions is the worker's power within the agency. The influences which the worker exerts through the organization's formal rules as well as its informal procedures are crucial in facilitating the helping process. This is particularly true for the types of people social workers help, who are likely to be among the most disadvantaged and oppressed within the society.

FUTURE DEVELOPMENTS

A major requirement for the further development of this orientation is more research. This must include intensive analysis of single cases as well as comparisons involving [a] larger number of persons. Since the intent of the model is to interrelate individual, family, group, and community environmental strategies, how these systems are actually acted upon in effective practice is of prime interest.

A second major task is to continue to identify findings from social and behavioral science theory and research applicable to this approach to practice. Practitioners and researchers must then devise and test interventions in social work settings based on these findings.

The above goals of research and utilization of social science findings will be enhanced by a more sophisticated typology of worker interventions. This can be based on the framework we offer here, which integrates environmental change efforts with interventions with a client system.

Finally, the authors are aware of the value of continually seeking to identify common elements among various practice models. A related concern is to strive to develop concepts which make it more feasible to train and employ workers who can work with individuals, groups, families, and environmental systems in a systematic and specifiable manner so that more comprehensive and effective services are available to all those who need them.

NOTES

[1]Harriett M. Bartlett, *The Common Base of Social Work Practice.* (New York: National Association of Social Workers, 1970). pp. 99–106.

[2]Gordon Hearn, ed., *The General Systems Approach: Contributions toward an Holistic Conception of Social Work.* (New York: Council on Social Work Education, 1969). Also:

The most widely read social work text using a systems model is Allen Pincus and Anne Minahan, *Social Work Practice: Method and Model.* (Itasca, Illinois: F. E. Peacock, Pub., 1973). An extension and revision of this approach can be found in Phillip J. Boas and Jim Crawley, *Explorations in Teaching Generic Social*

Work Theory. (Bundoora, Victoria, Australia: Preston Institute of Technology Press, 1975).

[3]Paul H. Glasser and Charles D. Garvin, "An Organizational Model," in *Theories of Social Work with Groups,* eds., Robert W. Roberts and Helen Northen. (New York: Columbia University Press, 1976). pp. 75–115.

[4]For a discussion of this approach, along with others, see Charles Garvin, "Education for Generalist Practice: A Comparative Analysis of Current Modalities," in *Teaching for Competence in the Delivery of Direct Services.* (New York: Council on Social Work Education, 1976). pp. 18–30.

[5]Felice Davidson Perlmutter, *A Design for Social Work Practice.* (New York: Columbia University Press, 1974).

[6]Bruce J. Biddle and Edwin H. Thomas, eds., *Role Theory: Concepts and Research.* (New York: John Wiley and Sons, 1966). See particularly the first four chapters.

[7]The specific term "mediation" has been used extensively by William Schwartz. See "Social Group Work: The Interactionist Approach," in *Encyclopedia of Social Work,* 2 vols. (New York: National Association of Social Workers, 1971). Vol. 2, p. 1258. Another discussion of this process can be found by Saul Bernstein in "Conflict in Group Work," in *Explorations in Group Work: Essays in Theory and Practice,* Saul Bernstein, ed. (Boston: Boston University School of Social Work, 1965). pp. 54–80.

[8]For an excellent discussion of this type of assessment, particularly in terms of dysfunctional situations, see Max Siporin, *Introduction to Social Work Practice.* (New York: Macmillan Publishing Co., Inc., 1975). pp. 219–50.

[9]For a summary of such research, see Irvin D. Yalom, *The Theory and Practice of Group Psychotherapy,* 2nd ed. (New York: Basic Books, Inc., 1975). pp. 222–35.

[10]Charles D. Garvin and Paul H. Glasser, "The Bases of Social Treatment," in *Individual Change through Small Groups,* eds. Paul Glasser, Rosemary Sarri, and Robert D. Vinter. (New York: The Free Press, 1974). pp. 495–99.

[11]A good deal of useful material on enhancing relationships may be found in Irvin D. Yalom, *Theory and Practice of Group Psychotherapy, op. cit.,* pp. 45–69.

[12]William J. Reid and Laura Epstein, *Task Centered Practice.* (New York: Columbia University Press: 1977).

[13]Paul H. Glasser et al., "Group Work Intervention in the Social Environment," in *Individual Change through Small Groups, op. cit.,* pp. 292–306.

[14]Sidney B. Simon, Leland W. Howe, and Howard Kirschenbaum, *Values Clarification: A Handbook of Practical Strategies for Teachers and Students.* (New York: Hart Publishing Co., 1972).

[15]Anselm Strauss, "Coaching," in *Role Theory: Concepts and Research,* pp. 350–53.

[16]For a program based on some of these principles, see George W. Fairweather et al., *Community Life for the Mentally Ill: An Alternative to Institutional Care.* (Chicago: Aldine Publishing Co., 1969).

LOCATING AND USING POINTS FOR INTERVENTION

Charles R. Atherton, Sandra T. Mitchell, Edna Biehl Schein

One of the most persistent problems for social workers in direct service is the lack of an economical, useful, and generally accepted terminology that locates a focus for intervention in the life situations of clients without the implications inherent in terms derived from a disease model. Obviously, social workers not wishing to use a disease concept can locate and describe points of intervention in commonplace ways, but this type of communication neither is economical nor has it led to a professional nomenclature for the kinds of problems that social workers confront. This article suggests that a promising alterna-

---

Source: Abridged and reprinted from *Social Casework,* Vol. 52, No. 3, 1971, pp. 131–41, and *Social Casework,* Vol. 52, No. 4, 1971, pp. 223–33. Reprinted with permission of the Family Service Association of America.

tive can be found by using terms associated with the concepts of social role and social system.

In recent years, considerable attention has been given to the conceptual and descriptive possibilities of *role* and *system* ideas. An abundant and formidable amount of terminology has been accumulated. Although this terminology has generally been used to guide research or theory construction, it can also be used to classify the interactional problems of people with other people, the conflicts between individuals and social systems, and the functional problems of social systems themselves. By this time, a considerable number of social workers have shown an interest in the use of role and system concepts for practice theory, organizational analysis, or the description of professional efforts.[1] This article, in offering an embryo classification of role and system problems, seeks to extend this interest in a form useful to practitioners. Before presenting the classification scheme, it may be helpful to consider some issues.

PRELIMINARY CONSIDERATIONS

The first of these considerations is the inherent value problem in any system of classification of disorders. Someone has to make an evaluation of a given state of affairs and decide whether that state of affairs is "good" or "bad," "functional" or "dysfunctional," "acceptable" or "unacceptable." This decision is not value free. There is no universally known and universally acceptable set of standards to follow in defining the most desirable state of being for people or societies. Some arbitrariness is, therefore, unavoidable as the social worker examines his client's life situation and tries to evaluate it. The social worker (or psychologist, counselor, or psychiatrist) neither can make his decisions on the assumption that "community standards" of behavior are always definitive of "normal" behavior, nor can he always assume that the client's standards are adequate.

The writers of this article believe that the social worker should assume a somewhat neutral stance and use as a standard the notion that the most desirable state of affairs for people is one that allows maximum freedom of the individual in his personal affairs as long as he harms neither himself nor others. The most desirable society is one whose norms allow freedom and in which whole role performance requirements are clear and acceptable to the individuals in that society, and the society's structure is open so that each individual can realize his legitimate aspirations

to the extent of his talent and ambition. This open view permits problems to be viewed as: (1) situations in which the individual is hampered, disadvantaged, or prevented from performing legitimate roles, (2) situations in which the individual performs roles harmful to his own freedom and development or to that of others, and (3) situations in which the social system is incompatible with the needs and goals of its component participants.

In other words, the ideal state of affairs would exist when persons live with each other in a state of mutually satisfying interdependence in which these persons are able to achieve the maximum goal attainment and personal sense of satisfaction in their relationships with each other and their institutional systems. This concept, which sees accommodation and interdependence as desirable, does not rule out competition or innovation. There is no intent to see differences and uniqueness of individuals and cultural groups dissolved. This view does, however, reject open conflict as a desirable state on the grounds that it is symptomatic of a breakdown in the basic interdependence of people who should have, in the ideal state of being, legitimate and rational ways of accommodation.

This view of a societal system, then, is the value base from which this scheme is developed. It avoids the implications of disease and narrow morality and focuses on genuine problems of the structure of the social system and the functioning of interdependent individuals on the basis of utility and mutual interests to achieve goals and aspirations that can be legitimated in a free and open society. Thus, behavior is "appropriate" or "inappropriate," "functional" or "dysfunctional," according to a standard that is explicit and can be broadly acceptable. Problems of the society can be evaluated by a standard that is also explicit and acceptable over a broad range of value positions.

The second preliminary difficulty concerns the problem of labeling.[2] By focusing on a label that identifies a faulty role pattern or performance rather than on a faulty personality, the writers hope to avoid some of the negative effects of labeling. This problem may never be resolved satisfactorily, but it is worth the attempt.

The third difficulty involves the vagueness and looseness of the concepts with which the writers are dealing. Although role and system concepts have promise, it is recognized that even the most common terms lack sharp outlines. The writers, therefore, have defined their terms as reasonably and clearly as they can. Where possible, they have borrowed and acknowledged good definitions. In some cases, the definitions represent a synthesis. In other cases, they have supplied original terms or definitions. The writers do not delude themselves by thinking that this set of terms is final and complete. Their chief aim is to provide for the clinician a set of terms and some way of conceptualizing a place to start, based on how things appear to the social worker in the immediate situation he faces.

THE CLASSIFICATION SCHEME

Any attempt to classify problems is open to question. The writers, therefore, can defend this scheme only on the grounds that it is reasonable and has a certain degree of validity. The notion behind this scheme is that some kinds of problems seem to be centrally located in the individual's immediate, personal relationships, whereas others are located more distantly. There is no intent, however, to order the problems in any hierarchy of importance because a distant problem, such as the closing of a factory one thousand miles away, may be more crucial for an individual than a chronic marital problem. Three major categories will be used: (1) problems related to performance of legitimate and acceptable roles, (2) problematical roles, and (3) problems in the structure of social systems that affect the behavior of individuals. Each of these categories will be defined as it appears; all terms within each of these categories will also be defined.

One additional caution requires emphasis. This classification system does not deal with the question of etiology. It seeks only to describe the way things appear to the practitioner in a particular situation. Much of the terminology is inelegant, partly because the terms available have neither the precision nor the clean distinctions that might be desirable. They are intended only to identify a place or places to start working. For example, *lack of motivation in role performance* is a vague term at best because the term *motivation* is only a construct for some variables that are not clearly understood. Nevertheless, motivation, whatever it means, may be the basic quality that the practitioner seizes upon as appropriate in his attempt to make an influential contribution to the worker-client relationship. The term, despite its lack of technical precision and refinement, may be useful only as a beginning point.

The writers have agreed to use the following definition of *role:* Role means a set of behaviors expected of an individual in relation to the behaviors of other persons or social objects in a given social situation. The expectation may be either on the part of oneself or others. The point is that there is no role in a vacuum. There are only roles in relation to other social objects.

Problems Related to Performance of Legitimate and Acceptable Roles

In this category, the assumption is that for some clients who use social work services, the major difficulty lies in the performance of a role (or roles) that is legitimate for both the client and the social system. There is little or no controversy about the role itself.

1. Impairment of Role Performance because of Illness.
This term denotes a condition in which the individual is hampered in the performance of a role (or set of roles) because of either an acute or a chronic illness. For the social worker the crucial point is not the cause of the impairment, since that is the physician's focus of interest, but the social implications of the impaired role performance. Some writers use the term "impaired role" or "role impairment." These terms are rejected here because there is nothing wrong with the role—the *performance* is the thing that is impaired.

2. Incapacity for Role Performance. This term describes the apparent lack of capacity for performing a legitimate or ordinary role under even favorable circumstances. It is intended to apply to situations in which the individual aspires to or attempts roles that are not within his talents or limits even though he is functioning well. An example of this situation might be that of a very frail boy who wants to be a tackle on the football team but could never make the weight. Care must be taken in using this term because so many people have the potential to achieve almost unbelievable goals, given favorable inputs to their situation.

3. Lack of Motivation in Role Performance. In this instance, the role is available, clear, and performable. For some reason that cannot be accounted for some other way, however, the individual simply is not willing to achieve the performance of which he is capable. Care must be taken to avoid confusing this situation with one in which the individual is prevented from role performance by some external factor. The term is intended to cover only situations in which motivation simply seems to be the only reasonable explanation for failure in performance.

4. Inadequate Role Perception. The problem is that the client is failing to perform a role because he does not understand what is involved in it. If he were aware of the implications he might accept the role (or he might reject it), but he is not really cognizant of the role's requirements.

5. Role Rejection. This familiar term is used to designate a situation in which a client rather actively refuses to play a role that significant others in his social system believe they have a right to expect. The assumption here is that the rejection is something creating a problem that would not exist if the role were accepted.

6. Role Abandonment. Henry Maas considers role abandonment as a mode of adaption and adjustment.[3] It is used in this article, however, to indicate problematical behavior. The definition offered here refers to a passive giving up of a role without apparent anxiety or hostility about it. It differs from role rejection in this sense. Role rejection implies a much more active posture of the individual, whereas role abandonment refers to an extremely indifferent sort of role performance.

7. Inadequate Preparation for Role Performance. This term describes a problematical situation in which the person lacks the necessary preparation for playing a role that he accepts or wants to accept. There is nothing wrong either with his capacity or with his health. Rather it is simply a lack of adequate social, educational, or technical skill that causes his unsatisfactory role performance. The use of this term assumes that resources are available either within the person or in the society to remedy the inadequacy of preparation.

8. Deficiency in Role Performance because of Inadequate Resources. Helen Harris Perlman discusses various types of deficiencies that affect a person's ability to perform a role effectively.[4] In this article the term is used to describe interactional situations in which an individual has been unable to achieve satisfactory role performance because his immediate social system lacks the resources to allow him to perform adequately. This condition is hard to distinguish from the previous condition of inadequate preparation but differs in that, in the previous situation, the resources were available but the individual had not been satisfactorily connected to them. In the present situation the immediate lack of resources is the major problem acting as a barrier to role performance.

9. Intrarole Conflict. Intrarole conflict describes the difficulty resulting from incongruent demands imposed by a given role.[5] An example of intrarole conflict might be that of the parental role requiring that one love a child and also discipline him. Sometimes these conflicting demands within a single role contribute to poor role performance. Obviously, this term, like the others, only applies when a perceived problem results.

10. Interrole Conflict. This term denotes the conflict and the resultant problem that occurs when one person is expected either by himself or by others to play two roles that have different norm requirements. An example of this conflict is that of the young man who wishes to be a serious college student and at the same time to be thought of as a very convivial good fellow. This problem differs from that of role separation, described later, in that here the possibility exists that some accommodation is possible.

11. Interposition Conflict. Maas actually uses the term *interrole conflict* in this instance. However, although the writers wish to preserve Maas's definition, they have attached it to a different term. Interposition conflict "is a stressful condition for two or more persons in related positions when the expectations for these positions do not complement each other as they should but rather overlap or are at cross-purposes."[6] The point here is that the conflict and the difficulty arise because each of two persons has a different definition of the other's position with respect to himself. Maas gives as an example the possible conflict in relations between physicians and other professionals ancillary to medicine in the care of patients. The expectations of one person may be radically different from the expectations of another person for himself.

12. Problem of Role Separation. This term describes the difficulty experienced by some people separating two or more legitimate, nonconflicting roles. Unlike role conflict, there is no juxtaposition of norm requirements. Under normal circumstances, the person plays a number of roles satisfactorily. Sometimes, however, one role seems to merge inappropriately with another. For example, a man can be a military officer and a husband at the same time. If, however, he cannot keep these roles separate, he may try to treat his wife and family as quasi-military subordinates—a treatment that would be entirely inappropriate and create a problem in role separation.

13. Incompatible Roles. Maas uses this term to cover situations in which a person is faced with two roles that are mutually exclusive and wholly incompatible.[7] This term is not the same as role conflict because in role conflict the notion is that some norm requirements of the role are mutually exclusive to norm requirements of a second role. In the case of incompatibility, the entire role is diametrically opposed to the other role. For example, one cannot be a mother and a virgin at the same time. There is no hint of norm conflict here, as much as it is the totally opposite definitions that are built into the role structure itself. The difference may be academic, but this term is included because it may make a practical difference that practitioners would want to recognize.

14. *Problems in Role Transition.* This term is used to designate those problems that occur when an individual is making a transition from one role to another and is having difficulty in so doing.[8] For example, a wife whose husband is advancing in his business or professional work may discover her situation problematical because different role behavior is expected of her in the role "wife" because of the husband's social mobility.

15. *Difficulty in Role Innovation.* This term is employed to identify the difficulty of a person who is attempting to change either the structure or the performance of a given role, but is having difficulty with the actual effort and mechanics of making the change. It differs from the previous term because the motivation for changing is within the person himself. The problem in role transition is caused by the individual's having difficulty because of the change in status or position or performance of a significant other. Role innovation identifies the shade of difference involved when the individual himself is attempting to make a significant change in role structure or performance, such as the difficulty encountered by the alcoholic, not because of his alcoholism, but because of his attempt to practice sobriety.

16. *Excessive Internalized Role Expectations of Self.* Sometimes people expect more of themselves than they are capable of delivering in some area of role performance. This excessive self-demand creates its own peculiar kind of role problem and failure in performance.

17. *Frustrating Role Expectations.* Although Maas uses this term,[9] the writers' definition of it is slightly different from his definition. It is used here to describe the personal sense of frustration and annoyance that an individual may feel because he is not able to fulfill the role expectations of another; there is no hint here about his capability of performing the role under a different set of expectations. The problem at which intervention is necessary is at the level of the expectations of the other in the case of a person who is sufficiently motivated to perform a role and is capable and prepared to do it under a different set of expectations.

18. *Disturbance in Role Performance because of Situational Crisis.* This term is designed to cover the situation in which the person is unable to perform as he normally would because of some immediate crisis in his social situation. The term is not designed to include difficulty in role performance because of the person's illness or lack of preparation but is limited to the kind of situation in which some critical incident has occurred in his immediate set of social systems or relationships and over which he has no direct control. An example of this problem is that of the person whose role performance is no longer satisfactory to himself or to others because he is out of work because of the failure of the company that had employed him. The crisis does not directly involve the person in its causative aspects, but the reaction is private and personal because the external incident has occurred. This definition is more limited than the initial description given by Perlman in the article cited.[10]

19. *Role Confusion.* It is intended here to conceptualize the role performance problem of the individual who is unable to sort out the roles he is expected to play or wants to play. This term is probably deficient in the confusion not of the role but of the individual who seems not to be able to sort out the requirements of a given role.

20. *Role Performance Retrogression.* Role retrogression is the term Maas uses for "slipping back to an earlier and, hopefully, more comfortable role when a current role is stressful."[11] Maas considers role retrogression as a mode of adaption, whereas the writers prefer to consider it a performance problem. It is true that it is an adaptive process, but it is so faulty and so filled with difficulty that it must be regarded as a point for intervention.

21. *Role Reversal.* This term is used here in a familiar and traditional way to indicate the problem that occurs when two persons in an interaction situation have exchanged roles in an inappropriate manner that creates trouble for them.

22. *Role Violation.* Here, the intention is to describe on a personal level the violation of one or more pre-

scriptions of a socially legitimate role. It is not intended to regard role violation as a condition in which deviant behavior is present, but rather to limit this term to those situations in which the individual performs a role that is considered legitimate, but does it in such a way that he violates important norm requirements in so doing. For example, the father who neglects to provide for his children according to the generally accepted beliefs and knowledge about the needs of children is performing his role as father, but he is violating the normative concepts of it in such a way to endanger the survival and development of persons dependent upon him. The role of father is not a deviant role, but is of course legitimate. The necessity for intervention is created by the violations of the prescriptions of the legitimate role; the father is not following a deviant role.

23. Role Shock. This term is used by Professor Donald Lathrope of the Jane Addams Graduate School of Social Work at the University of Illinois to describe a psychological shock that comes from realizing that one is unable to perform adequately in a specific role. This term thus covers the anxious or disturbed person facing some personal crisis, such as retirement, that will result in the individual's no longer being able to play a desired role and suffering as a consequence.

Problematical Roles

In this category a series of roles that in themselves seem to be problematical will be listed. The difference between this category and the one preceding is that there is not the difficulty of performance of a legitimate role but that a person is confronted with a role that is likely to cause him considerable difficulty. Liberty has been taken with the definitions of the terms in this category. Some of them have been borrowed and are used here in a sense different from that which their originators envisioned. This liberty has been taken simply to suit the convenience of the classification system and cannot be defended in any other way. The writers recognize the danger of this procedure because the terms used may have acceptable and broadly known definitions in another context. The alternative to borrowing a term and not using its original definition would be to create a new term. The difficulty with this procedure is that in the instances used here no other term seems to lend itself to the description of the problematical role being discussed. We have, therefore, taken the more dangerous alternative as the only realistic way to proceed.

1. "Roleless" Role or Rolelessness. This term has been used by E.W. Burgess for the role that lacks any definition at all.[12] The lack of a set of norms constitutes a unique role prescription by itself and certainly the person who is roleless has a doubtful status indeed. An example of rolelessness is the aged person with no significant interactions with his social situation.

2. Inadequate Role Modeling. Inadequate role modeling describes a condition in which the client—probably a child or adolescent—lacks a relevant adult role model. The problem is with the entire role identification process for the client. This condition may not seem to fit in this general overall category, but it has been placed here because it refers to a kind of inadequate total role configuration that goes beyond a simple problem in role performance.

3. Anomalous Role. This term is used to refer to persons caught in roles that are poorly shaped and whose norm requirements define a role that is outside the usual and generally satisfying modes of behavior. It probably should be parenthetically explained that this role, like some of the succeeding roles, does not adequately describe the total functioning of the person but centers on a problematical role as a point for intervention. It is the problematical role that the social worker must pay attention to as the focus for effort. It is not implied that everything the person does in some other aspects of his interactive life is faulty. The anomalous role is one that does contain some behavioral norms and expectations, but they are not as clear as they might be and, as a consequence, the role itself is shaped in a relatively unique way for the person performing it.

The situation of the divorced person in Western society may be considered an example of anomalous role. For this role, norms that can be clearly perceived and followed either do not exist or are so circumspect that a person cannot always dependably know what behavior is expected of him in social situations. This person is not "roleless," but simply often faces problematical situations because of the varying expectations of performance associated with a role that can only be regarded as an anomaly.

4. Illicit Role. This term describes a role that, although not necessarily illegal, is nevertheless clandestine and disapproved of to some degree. It is not intentionally implied that the social worker necessarily accepts the social disapproval of this role as a moral imperative, but he must take into account the problems of relationship that are created. Promiscuous behavior is an example of an illicit role.

5. Outsider Role. This term has been borrowed from Howard S. Becker. After considering the alternative of choosing another term, the writers have decided to use Becker's term with redefinition because it suits the notion to be expressed here very well. Becker uses the term to refer to a fairly large category of deviance. In Becker's definition, the outsider is simply a deviant from group rules.[13]

It is used in this taxonomy in a much more limited fashion. The outsider, as used here, refers to those roles of persons who are outside the general norms of a culture but only to those positions to which one must somehow make a commitment of himself. It is not intended to use it in the broadest sense to describe all who are outside the pale, but only those whose roles as outsiders involve some degree of personal choice. An example of the outsider is the young person who uses drugs. A case can be made for the idea that any youngster who turns to narcotics does so because of factors in his environment. In this article the writers have rejected an unadulterated behaviorism and have postulated the notion that some degree of choice is present. The individual may have a selection to make among drugs, alcohol, suicide, or some other form of self-destructive behavior. The outsider, in the sense used here, has made a more or less conscious choice to identify himself as a specific kind of violator of customary norms, and in so doing he has accepted another set of norm requirements that he more or less actively follows. This situation is problematical in the relationship of the outsider to significant others. The social worker is agreeable to seeing outsiders, as they are viewed here, at the request of parents, husbands, wives, and other significant others.

6. Deviant Role. The term deviant role is to be reserved for those roles in which the person plays a more severely disapproved role in connection with some significant others than is true for the outsider. The deviant pursues an individual course rather than one adhering to group norms. The deviant also appears to have less conscious choice of his problematical role than does the outsider. Admittedly, the distinction between the two may often appear academic, but it is included in the belief that it may have practical usefulness. The writers consider the voyeur a deviant rather than an outsider because the voyeur behaves primarily as if he were under some compulsion. He also generally operates as an individual rather than as a member of an outside group with a set of norms followed by a number of his fellows.

The actual nature of the deviant behavior does not seem important to the writers. There is a certain common element that would be the focus of the social worker's interest; namely, the deviant will have problems with significant others as a consequence of his individual behavior rather than as a consequence of membership in an outsider group. This term is not entirely clear and there might be instances in which it would be difficult to make the distinction. For example, the solitary drinker who consumes much more alcohol than his system can tolerate might be considered a deviant, whereas the convivial drinker who has attached himself to a group that has drinking as a central activity, may in fact be an outsider. The writers are not altogether satisfied either with this distinction or with this and the preceding terms; however, they believe they can be useful at this time.

7. Offender Role. This role has been used by a number of writers in an entirely different context. It is the purpose of this article to restrict the use of the offender role to those persons who have more or less permanently adopted a chronic set of norms that have as their central focus the frequent breaking of legal norms. The habitual criminal and the professional criminal are both examples of the role performance elements included in this classification.

8. Stigmatized Role. This term has been borrowed from Erving Goffman.[14] It is used here to refer to that role in which the person senses a great deal of disapproval to the point of revulsion. He recognizes that people are sickened or frightened by his behavior. The behavior may or may not be illegal, but the emotion evoked as a result of the value structure of society is one of extreme distaste. The reason that the writers state this definition in this way is that it would be the stigmatic aspects of the role that would probably be the focus of social work attention. The cause of the problem is the person's image that is reflected from significant others. It is not suggested that the stigma is appropriately placed on this person, for it probably is not. The suggestion is made simply to accept the fact that there are some behaviors or conditions that most people consider so frightening or horrible that they react in a way that makes living difficult for the person possessing the stigma.

It must be recognized that a number of the roles previously described have some degree of stigma attached to them. However, the difference lies in the ways a social worker would deal with the nature of the problem. For example, in the case of the offender, it is the offensive behavior with which the social worker would try to cope. In the case of the deviant, it is the nature and type of the deviance with which the social worker would deal. In the case of the role that would be considered stigmatized, it is the stigma itself that would receive the major part of attention. In other words, the social worker would be more concerned with the behavior of significant others to the person than he would be with the behavior exhibited by the person in the stigmatized role. As an example of the kind of role that the writers believe should be included here, mention should be made of the mental patient whose symptoms are bizarre and eerie. Social work's primary role would not be to work with the symptoms themselves, but rather to try to do whatever is reasonable to help the individual receive acceptance from his family or his peers and a certain amount of understanding, rather than stigmatization.

9. Ritualistic Role.   This term is intended to describe a role that seems to be totally devoid of meaning. There is practically no goal that can be reached by playing the role. Nevertheless, a person seems to continue to play the role as if it had some kind of meaning. This acting is similar to the idea expressed by the term, "ritualistic behavior," used by sociologist Robert K. Merton. An example can be suggested by the rather meaningless kind of role played by the chronically unemployed man who habitually makes attempts to look very busy and very committed to a set of norms that keeps him constantly in motion but produces limited goal attainment. The individual continues to play a very busy kind of part, but nothing ever happens as a consequence.

Problems in the Structure of Social Systems

This category includes various structural problems that seem related to difficulties faced by people in various roles. In some cases it appears that the structural problem mainly affects people as individuals, whereas in others it appears the major effect is on the group life of individuals. It is presumed that if the problem of a client or group of clients can be identified in one of the subcategories in this larger category, then the major social work role is that of advocate, broker, or social change agent. In any case, the reader is reminded that this particular category does not attempt to describe the characteristics of all social systems but only those problematical aspects of structure that seem to have interest and reference for social work.

1. Unfilled Status.   This condition exists when a crucial status in a social group is not filled by an occupant. It is assumed that the status in question is crucial for the operation of the group. For example, lack of adequate leadership would seem to threaten the adequacy of a group's functioning and, therefore, a group's lack of an adequate leader would be a problematical situation in a social system.

2. Disapproved Group Norms.   This category has an elusive "catchall" quality that is not entirely satisfying. It is intended to denote a set of group norms ranging from mildly illicit to destructively antisocial. Sometimes the social worker, particularly one working with groups, needs to recognize that the central fact for some groups is their nonconformity to legitimate cultural norms. Again, the social worker operating from the value position taken in this article has to decide how harmful these norms are in relation to the freedom and development of the group and its members.

3. Role Discontinuity.   Role discontinuity exists when there is an absence of clear and orderly developments in the training or patterning of people within the culture as these people grow into maturity. This term, which originates in the work of Ruth Benedict, is useful in describing the ambivalent position of some adolescents in the industrial society.[15] It probably should be pointed out that this problem is a system problem and therefore is included here rather than in the section dealing with problematic roles.

4. Nonavailable Roles.   This difficulty can be seen in those situations where there is a lack of role or status opportunity caused by the existing structure of the social system. Quite obviously it is crucial for the existence of the social system because no system can operate without providing roles and statuses for the people that comprise it and still remain a system.

5. Excessive Role Expectations.   This term can be used to explain those situations in which occupants of various statuses within the social structure make excessive demands upon other people, particularly when these demands cannot possibly be met.[16] For example, the extremely domineering wife expects her husband to be a great lover, financially successful, highly intelligent, and handy around the house without recognizing that he lacks the potential to do so. This term corresponds roughly to excessive internalized role expectation of self at the individual level, but it locates the difficulty in a social system itself and does not consider the effect on the individual on whom the excessive demand is made. The social worker, confronted with this situation, has to make a judgment about whether the focus of his intervention is in support of the person with a role performance difficulty or whether he should attack the excessive demands by another person in the client subsystem. If the second decision were made, this term would be descriptive of the problem. If the social worker did not have access to other persons in the original client social system, he would have no other choice than to consider it an individual problem in role performance, thus focusing his interventive efforts on the role performance level, rather than on the level of the system.

6. *Damaging Role Expectations.* This term differs from that of excessive role expectations by suggesting that there are some instances in which the social system or subsystem demands or expects role performance that would be damaging to the person of whom such performance is expected. This damage is not due to an excessive demand, but to the nature of the demand itself. The person can in fact meet these expectations, but it would be damaging for him to do so. A crude example is that of the alcoholic wife who expects her husband to go drinking with her. Although he may be capable of drinking with her, if he is also an alcoholic, the expectation is damaging to him. It seems better to provide this separate category than to have to see this kind of system expectation seen only as excessive. This category, therefore, has been added to the previous one.

7. *Lack of Purposive System Orientation.* This category includes problems of social systems that occur when a system is dysfunctional because of the lack of a focus that might encourage the commitment of members and enhance group solidarity. One can argue that under these conditions a system ceases to exist. However, it is preferable to consider it as a disorder of systems on the grounds that, when a social system or group loses its purposive orientation, the system continues to operate for a time, although entropy will probably set in. By the time a social worker views such a group or system, it should be possible to be aware that the group lacks any kind of purpose or goal direction before the system shuts down.

8. *Status Conflict.* This term refers to conflict within a social system over the occupation of some important status to the degree that the functioning of the system is seriously threatened. An example of status conflict might be the case of an interacting group whose leader leaves the group and conflict ensues among the other members over the status of leader. Some of this conflict may be healthy, but there is a time when the conflict among members who are seeking status that only one can actually attain will be harmful to the group.

9. *Status Rejection.* In this case, a social system has reached a state of dysfunction because a member with potential for filling a status within the system actively rejects such a status. The difference between this category and that of unfilled status is that in unfilled status there is no occupant. In this instance, there is a potential occupant, but he has rejected the status actively.

10. *System Resource Deficiency.* This term designates a number of problems in which the social system itself lacks the resources to meet the needs of persons who occupy statuses within the system. It is not implied that resources cannot be created or provided, but at the moment at which the social worker views the situation a deficiency exists. This problem would probably be viewed as a system problem by a community worker but as a role performance problem of an individual by an agency serving individuals.

11. *Intersystem Conflict.* This condition probably relates more to the subsystems than it does to total systems. It is used to refer to the kinds of problematical situations in which two social systems are in harmful conflict because of differing values or norms. This term is borrowed from Jessie Bernard,[17] but the definition has been altered to suit the purposes of this article. The intention here is to describe the situation in which social movements or interest groups are engaged in a competitive struggle for recognition, domination, or status.

12. *Intrasystem Conflict.* This term has been coined to cover what Ödd Ramsoy calls normative conflict.[18] Intrasystem conflict occurs when the norms of a given social system are contradictory and persons within the system are forced to make choices of following norms that are in opposition to other norms. An example of this conflict is the case of the man who by law must file an income tax return, but who by custom is encouraged to cheat on it. This problem is not an individual one, but is obviously a difficulty in the structure of the social system.

13. *Role Rigidity.* Role rigidity is a system problem in which the social system has so narrowly or strictly conceived a role that it can hardly be accepted by

people, or it causes problems for them when they do accept it. It is the problem of a system that often establishes some kind of perfect behavior that a person cannot comfortably use as a role model. It could be argued, for example, that the concept of the American mother as a selfless, giving, martyr-like figure is an example of this type of system problem. No woman could possibly meet the norm and yet some women appear to accept this norm as one that they should meet in actual living. The consequent difficulty that they experience in their personal lives, then, is not necessarily a role performance problem, but a discrepancy between the role as the social system conceives it and the actualities of human performance. Role rigidity, therefore, has been classified as a structural problem rather than a role performance problem. When the problem is highly individualized, it would probably be considered one of excessive internalized role expectations of self.

14. Role Failure. This condition involves a role that formerly existed in a social system but is no longer viable or no longer in existence. The condition is not role performance failure, but actual failure in a role to persist in a social system. A commonplace example of role failure would be the technological unemployment of a young man who chose to be a steam engine mechanic in the early years of this century and now in mid-life finds himself completely without a viable occupational status. He has done nothing to warrant this situation, but the invention of other forms of transportation have made the role to which he aspired no longer available in the society. This category is considered different from the nonavailable role category in which roles have never been in existence in sufficient quantity for persons to occupy them.

ROLES TAKEN BY THE SOCIAL WORKER

The preceding material illustrates the way in which role and system concepts can be integrated into social work practice. It appears to the writers that this type of practice lends itself to finding points at which to begin the intervention process without resorting to a medical model using a disease metaphor. In order to complete the description of the use of the points for intervention material, consideration will now be given to the roles that can be taken by the intervenor once he has determined on a suitable point for intervention.

A number of roles have been attributed to the social worker and offered as if those roles represented the totality of social work activity. It is probably more helpful to speak of the social work *role-set*[19]—a range of role relationships peculiar to the position of social worker. Accordingly, it is assumed that what must be related to the points for intervention categories is a set of roles that the social worker should be prepared to play. The assumption is made here that the social worker should be able to assume any role that is appropriate as he perceives the nature of the presenting problem, rather than to play only one role despite the differences in the presenting problems. It is usually not helpful to a client's problem for the worker always to play the role of psychosocial therapist or always to play the role of advocate. It is not helpful either for the worker to shift between the roles of therapist or social activist.[20] The social worker's role-set includes a wide and varied range of roles.

In Table 15–1 an attempt has been made to suggest a central role that should be taken by the social worker for each term in the points-for-intervention scheme. The worker's assuming a particular role does not exclude the possibility that certain facets of other roles would also be called into play. Some of the material may seem to be oversimplified, but it allows a set of rules to be located and made available for discussion. The chart attempts to include all possible roles that can be assumed by any social worker, regardless of setting or field of practice. Clearly, the chart must be read selectively, and the social worker should easily be able to select the roles appropriate to his setting; some imagination, however, may be required.

Table 15-1. Central Roles of Social Workers in Intervention Scheme

Points for Intervention	Social Worker's Role	Appropriate Activity
Problems related to performance of legitimate and acceptable roles		
1. Impairment of role performance because of illness	Broker (or referral agent)	Refers client to appropriate medical or rehabilitative service as needed
	Interpreter	Interprets (puts in symbols meaningful to client) the social implications of illness or treatment
	Psychosocial counselor	Offers empathy, encouragement, allows ventilation of feelings, and otherwise follows traditional, well-known role of psychosocial counselor
2. Incapacity for role performance	Resource person	Suggests alternative roles that client could perform and helps client find alternative goals that allow him to attain his goals of status, achievement, or performance
3. Lack of motivation in role performance	Sociobehavioral counselor	Shapes appropriate behavior by providing positive reinforcement for behaviors consistent with the person's desired performance (See Edwin J. Thomas, "Selected Sociobehavioral Techniques and Principles: An Approach to Interpersonal Helping," *Social Work* 13:12–26 [January 1968].)
4. Inadequate role perception	Interpreter or educator	Interprets details and implications of a given role that client wants or is expected to play; teaches role components, such as how to be a good mother
5. Role rejection	Sociobehavioral counselor	Reinforces behavior that increasingly approximates the desired behavioral components of the rejected role
	Mediator	Helps the client find a dignified and minimally damaging way out of the system that expects role acceptance; helps the client explain his role rejection to the family or other group in which he is rejecting the role in terms that they can accept; acts as a mediator (See William Schwartz,

Table 15-1. (continued)

Points for Intervention	Social Worker's Role	Appropriate Activity
		"The Social Worker in the Group," *Social Welfare Forum 1961* [New York: Columbia University Press, 1961], pp. 146–77.)
6. Role abandonment	Mediator	Acts as a negotiator between the client and the system in which he is unable to participate freely and creatively
7. Inadequate preparation for role performance	Educator or broker	Teaches skills for role performance or refers to appropriate social resource that, through training in skill, knowledge, or art, can prepare the client for the desired role
8. Deficiency in role performance because of inadequate resources	Advocate or service developer	Acts as the client's agent in trying to persuade or force the community to provide an appropriate resource or, if feasible, to develop the service within existing frameworks (See Mary J. McCormick, "Social Advocacy: A New Dimension in Social Work," *Social Casework* 51:3–11 [January 1970]; and Francis P. Purcell and Harry Specht, "The House on Sixth Street," *Social Work* 10:69–84 [October 1965].)
9. Intrarole conflict	Crisis intervenor	(See Martin Strickler, "Applying Crisis Theory in a Community Clinic," *Social Casework* 46:150–54 [March 1965]; and Martin Strickler and Jean Allgeyer, "The Crisis Group: A New Application of Crisis Theory," *Social Work* 12:28–32 [July 1967].)
10. Interrole conflict	Crisis intervenor	Same as in *intrarole conflict*
11. Interposition conflict	Mediator	Mediates the problem involving two persons with differing expectations of each other's position
12. Problem of role separation	Interpreter	Interprets to the client the inappropriate merging of roles that cause his difficulty

Table 15-1. (continued)

Points for Intervention	Social Worker's Role	Appropriate Activity
Problems related to performance of legitimate and acceptable roles		
13. Incompatible roles	Crisis intervenor	Same as in *intrarole conflict*
14. Problems in role transition	Crisis intervenor	Same as in *intrarole conflict*
15. Difficulty in role innovation	Crisis intervenor	Same as in *intrarole conflict*
16. Excessive internalized role expectations of self	Psychosocial counselor	Uses the traditional insight development counseling that social workers universally used to apply to all problems
17. Frustrating role expectations	Psychosocial counselor	Relieves the situation by helping to develop insight on the part of the significant other who is making frustrating demands on the client
18. Disturbance in role performance because of situational crisis	Crisis intervenor	Plays an assertive role to give direction and specific help to relieve the problems of client's situation, such as a new job, a place to live, money (See David Hallowitz et al., "The Assertive Counseling Component of Therapy," *Social Casework* 48:543–48 [November 1967]. Hallowitz uses his approach in emotional crisis, but it clearly is adaptable to the situational crisis.)
19. Role confusion	Psychosocial counselor or crisis intervenor	Clarifies the roles that are confused, allowing the client to make a more informed choice
20. Role performance retrogression	Sociobehavioral counselor	Same as in *lack of motivation in role performance*
21. Role reversal	Mediator	Attempts, through what can best be described as a bargaining process, to induce a reasonable compromise between the parties involved
22. Role violation	Sociobehavioral counselor	Uses behavioral norms as goals; in the context of family counseling, uses sociobehavioral techniques to help with problems of child neglect, marital infidelity, or some other violation of a legitimate role (See Thomas, "Selected Sociobehavioral Techniques"; and David Hallowitz, "The Problem-

Table 15-1. (continued)

Points for Intervention	Social Worker's Role	Appropriate Activity
Problems related to performance of legitimate and acceptable roles		
		Solving Component in Family Therapy," *Social Casework* 51:67–75 [February 1970].)
23. Role shock	Crisis intervenor	Attempts to cushion the shock by enabling the client to find alternate meaningful roles
Intervention in problematical roles		
1. Rolelessness	Broker or referral agent	Helps to find some facility or group in which roleless people can find meaningful roles (For the best resource, see Frank Riessman, "The 'Helper Therapy' Principle," *Social Work* 10:27–32 [April 1965].)
2. Inadequate role modeling	Role model or broker	Serves as a role model himself or refers the client to a facility, agency, or group that offers role models
3. Anomalous role	Catalyst	Uses David Hallowitz's "problem-solving" method as the best approach to the person suffering from the difficulties of an anomalous role (See Hallowitz, "The Problem-Solving Component.")
4. Illicit role	Group counselor	Serves as group counselor to offer services to persons ensnared in illicit roles
5. Outsider role	Broker	Refers client to a "helper" group, such as Alcoholics Anonymous and Synanon
6. Deviant role	Sociobehavioral counselor	Same as in *role violation*
7. Offender role	Sociobehavioral counselor	Same as in *role violation*
8. Stigmatized role	Advocate	Represents the client in dealing with significant others
9. Ritualistic role	Sociobehavioral counselor	Helps on the behavioral level, rather than through insight development, those who, according to the old medical model, are classified as character disorders

Table 15-1. (continued)

Points for Intervention	Social Worker's Role	Appropriate Activity
Problems related to performance of legitimate and acceptable roles		
1. Unfilled status	Catalyst	Same as in *anomalous role*
2. Disapproved group norms	Sociobehavioral group counselor	Adapts Thomas's ideas to working with the group whose norms are causing them trouble
3. Role discontinuity	Agent of social change	Focuses attention on the inconsistencies and discontinuities in society; must use creativity to perform the major professional role in a social change or social action framework (For an excellent discussion of the issues and problems involved in this professional role, see Charles S. Levy, "The Social Worker as Agent of Policy Change," *Social Casework* 51:102–8 [February 1970].)
4. Nonavailable roles	Advocate or change agent	Same as in *role discontinuity*
5. Excessive role expectations	Advocate or mediator	Gives the client faced with excessive demands support and direct help in defending himself psychologically; relieves the pressure on the client by using mediation techniques
6. Damaging role expectations	Advocate or mediator	Same as in *excessive role expectations*
7. Lack of purposive system orientation	Catalyst	(For a discussion of the role of catalyst, see David Hallowitz et al., "The Assertive Counseling Component.")
8. Status conflict	Crisis intervenor (with group skills)	Uses the methods and strategies usually discussed under the banner of crisis intervention
9. Status rejection	Catalyst	Creates enough tension in the system for galvanizing a potential occupant into assuming the status that he has been rejecting
10. System resource deficiency	Collective bargainer	(For an excellent discussion of the potential of this role, see George A. Brager and Valerie Jorrin, "Bargaining: A Method in Community Change," *Social Work* 14:73–83 [October 1969].)

Table 15-1. (continued)

Points for Intervention	Social Worker's Role	Appropriate Activity
Problems in the structure of social systems		
11. Intersystem conflict	Mediator	Same as in *role rejection*
12. Intrasystem conflict	Agent of social change	Brings conflicts to society's attention and offers means for bringing about change that reduces the contradictions
13. Role rigidity	Agent of social change	Works toward changing the social definition of the problematical roles so that they are not as rigidly defined and consequently hard to play
14. Role failure	Broker	Directs people to other roles or to training that will equip them for other roles

NOTES

[1]See, for example, Helen Harris Perlman, "The Role Concept and Social Casework: Some Explorations, I. The 'Social' in Social Casework," *Social Service Review,* 35:370–81 (December 1961); idem, "The Role Concept and Social Casework: Some Explorations, II. What is Social Diagnosis?," ibid., 36:17–31 (March 1962); Herbert S. Strean, "Role Theory, Role Models, and Casework: Review of the Literature and Practice Applications," *Social Work,* 12:77–87 (April 1967); Bruce J. Biddle and Edwin J. Thomas, eds., *Role Theory: Concepts and Research* (New York: John Wiley & Sons, 1966); and Henry S. Maas, "Behavioral Science Bases for Professional Education: The Unifying Conceptual Tool of Cultural Role," in *Proceedings of the Interdisciplinary Conference on Behavioral Concepts Which Can Be Applied to Education for the Helping Professions* (Washington, D.C.: Howard University School of Social Work, 1958), pp. 11–22.

[2]See Thomas J. Scheff, *Being Mentally Ill* (Chicago: Aldine Publishing Co., 1966).

[3]Maas, "Behavioral Science Bases," p. 19.

[4]Perlman, "What Is Social Diagnosis?," p. 25.

[5]Alfred Kadushin, *Child Welfare Services* (New York: Macmillan Co., 1967), p. 17.

[6]Maas, "Behavioral Science Bases," p. 16.

[7]Ibid., pp. 16–17.

[8]Ibid., p. 17.

[9]Ibid., p. 15.

[10]Perlman, "What Is Social Diagnosis?," p. 26.

[11]Maas, "Behavioral Science Bases," p. 20.

[12]E.W. Burgess, "Aging in Western Culture," in *Aging in Western Societies,* ed. E.W. Burgess (Chicago: University of Chicago Press, 1960).

[13]Howard S. Becker, *Outsiders* (New York: Free Press of Glencoe, 1963), p. 3.

[14]Erving Goffman, *Stigma: Notes on the Management of Spoiled Identity* (Englewood Cliffs, N.J.: Prentice-Hall, 1962).

[15]Ruth Benedict, "Continuities and Discontinuities in Cultural Conditioning," *Psychiatry,* 1:161–67 (May 1938).

[16]Maas, "Behavioral Science Bases," p. 14.

[17]Jessie Bernard, *Social Problems at Midcentury* (New York: Rinehart & Co., 1957), p. 480.

[18]Ödd Ramsoy, *Social Groups as System and Subsystem* (New York: Free Press of Glencoe, 1963), p. 30.

[19]See Robert K. Merton, "The Role-Set: Problems in Sociological Theory," *British Journal of Sociology,* 8:111–16 (January 1957).

[20]The writers are deliberately excluding such positions as administrator, supervisor, and social work educator because their focus is on practice.

EVALUATING THE EFFECTIVENESS
OF SOCIAL WORK INTERVENTION

Stuart A. Kirk

Social workers are involved in a wide variety of attempts to alter or transform social conditions and processes. Over time the targets of change and the tools for change vary. With experience, however, the ability of the profession to effectively induce change should steadily increase as the principles of effective intervention are established. These principles of effective intervention can only emerge if attempts to induce change are carefully monitored and evaluated. Hence, evaluation of social work intervention is a cornerstone of the profession.

To evaluate in its most general sense means to determine or fix the value of something, to examine and judge it. People routinely make casual minor judgments about their acquaintances, their jobs, their clients, and the products they purchase and use. Evaluation in this casual sense is a ubiquitous, subjective, social phenomenon. But evaluation concerning the effectiveness of social work intervention, in the context of this paper, refers to *the objective and systematic gathering of information about planned social work intervention in order to assess its effects.*

Three aspects of this definition need to be emphasized. First, the information gathered in an evaluation is not primarily impressionistic or casual, but rather the result of carefully used scientific research techniques or methods. Second, the data gathered are pertinent to a conscious and deliberate attempt to intervene in some situation with the explicit intention of changing it in some respect. Third, the assessment of the intervention is primarily concerned with the effects of that intervention, both the intended and the unintended consequences. When an intervention achieves its intended effects, we say that it was effective, while the unintended effects both positive and negative are usually referred to as side effects. This definition of effectiveness evaluation does not make any assumptions regarding the nature of the intervention, the phenomenon to be changed, or the nature of the intended consequences. But evaluation, or evaluative research as it is often called, encompasses other forms of assessment as well.

TYPES OF EVALUATION RESEARCH

Evaluation research encompasses *evaluation of structure, evaluation of process,* and *evaluation of outcome* (Zusman and Rieff 1969; Fox and Rappaport 1972). *Structural evaluations* consist of attempts to describe the dimensions and organization of services. These studies are often based on assumptions about the ideal structure for intervention and measure existing services according to these. Evaluations of structure are primarily descriptive and focus on such service characteristics as staff-client ratios, organizational staffing patterns, and the size and quality of the physical plant. For example, in the case of residential facilities, factors such as the size and number of rooms per resident, the number and adequacy of the bathroom facilities, kitchens, and fire escapes and the level of training of the staff are noted. This information can be used to assess the extent and distribution of agency resources and uncover various structural deficiencies. But structural evaluations are of limited use in assessing the actual quality of service or in estimating its effectiveness. Their main purpose is to ensure a minimum level and quality of service for the purposes of accrediting or licensing the agency.

Studies of the process of intervention focus on the operations of the agency and the intervention methods. These studies generate descriptive data about the characteristics of the clients being served, the service activity itself, and the interaction of the operation of the agency and the movement of clients in the system. These studies examine both the extent of the efforts made to induce change and the processes through which these efforts were carried out. Included here are the various techniques of administra-

Source: Reprinted with permission of the University of Kansas School of Social Welfare from the *Journal of Social Welfare*, Vol. 1, No. 2, (Winter 1974), pp. 65–79.

tive monitoring of the operation, fiscal accounting of the flow of monetary resources through the agency, social accounting regarding who was serviced and how, and various forms of time and motion studies (Tripodi, Fellin, and Epstein 1971). But included also are studies of the intervention process itself, for example, the nature of the interaction of client and social worker in an interview situation. Process studies provide information about the operation of the program or intervention, but they do not assess the effectiveness or efficiency of it. This is left for the third general type of evaluation—evaluation of outcome.

Outcome evaluation, often referred to as the evaluation of accomplishment or effectiveness, focuses on the consequences of the intervention, particularly on whether the intervention produced the effects that were intended. Effectiveness studies examine the outcome of change efforts in terms of changes in the client's behavior, personality, or feelings, changes in group or family functioning, or changes in the occurrence of community problems. In addition, outcome studies can be used to study the efficiency of the intervention if cost-analytic techniques are combined with the effectiveness evaluation (Tripodi et al. 1971). Outcome evaluations are by far the most important type of evaluation, since it is on the basis of information about an intervention's success that program decisions are often made.

WHY EVALUATE?

Why evaluate the effectiveness of social work intervention? There are professional as well as practical reasons for being concerned about the effectiveness of social work intervention. First, social workers are called upon to use their professional skills to induce change; they offer services with the explicit or implicit promise that their interventions are effective in dealing with the problems brought to them to resolve. It is an integral part of the professional-client relationship that the one providing the service be accountable to the client, regardless of whether the client is an individual, a group, an organization, or a community. The client commits his time and resources to the worker because he expects that he will be given effective help with the problem at hand. The only way for social workers to ensure that their help is effective is to continually, vigorously, and objectively evaluate that service. Second, the information provided to the worker by evaluation research serves as a source of feedback for the improvement

and refinement of his interventions. Third, the availability of objective data on the effectiveness of interventions may promote rational decision making and inhibit the use of personal or political biases from influencing the assessment of social interventions. What differentiates a good (effective) from a bad (ineffective) program can be determined by facts rather than by political whims. This is not to say that evaluation research may not be shaped or used for political purposes, because it can be. Evaluation can be used to postpone program decisions, for ducking responsibility for program decisions, as a public relations gimmick, or simply to fulfill grant requirements (Weiss 1972, pp. 11–12). But evaluation, done with the intent of providing objective information, can be an aid to rational decision making and to the improvement of professional intervention.

Also, there are survival reasons for being concerned with evaluation. The effectiveness of social work interventions is being called into question by government officials, by committees that fund social work programs, and increasingly by social workers themselves (Mullen and Dumpson 1972; Fischer 1973). The increasing salience of the issue of effectiveness probably springs from many sources, including: (1) the increasing numbers and costs of major social welfare programs; (2) the growing suspicion that many of these programs (e.g., Head Start, community mental health, the poverty program, social services in public welfare programs, the rehabilitation of criminals, etc.) may not be reaching their intended objective; (3) the fact that many social welfare interventions which originally focused on the very poor and deprived (e.g., mental hospitals, public assistance) now are likely to involve a broader group of citizens (e.g., community mental health programs, income maintenance programs); and (4) related to many of these, the rise of consumerism and the recognition that the recipients of services have rights and can make demands on the service providers. These and other developments have undoubtedly accelerated the demand for social workers to be accountable to their clients and the tax paying public. There is a general move at all levels of government to make funding decisions contingent on evidence of intervention effectiveness. In short, social workers are increasingly asking and being asked to demonstrate that their efforts on behalf of change do indeed bring about change.

In order to meet this demand and their professional responsibilities, social workers need to be familiar with the evaluation enterprise in order to understand it and to contribute to it. The evaluation of social work intervention requires attention to four central and interrelated issues: (1) the definition of the problem to be changed; (2) the determination of the goals to be sought, (3) specification of the interventions used, and (4) the structure of data gathering, i.e., the design of the research. The basic components of each of these will be briefly described.

Defining the Problem

Whether the change agent is a caseworker helping an individual or a policymaker developing a new program, the first task is an analysis of the problem or situation to be changed. Although at first it may seem that the definition of the problem is relatively simple, it can be a difficult task. Furthermore, a faulty or inaccurate problem analysis may lead to the selection of inappropriate goals, incorrect interventions, and consequently, an evaluation will show that the intervention was of little or no benefit (Twain, Harlow, and Merwin 1970, p. 34ff).

The first step in problem analysis is to determine the nature and scope of the problem. Who is affected by the problem? How are they affected and by how much? How did the problem get recognized and initially defined? What other problems is it related to and how? Is it really a single conceptually distinct problem or many, and how are the parts of the problem related? What is the history of the problem? What are the known or presumed causes of it? This list of issues regarding problem analysis is as appropriate for microsystem problems of individuals as for macrosystem problems concerning the entire society. Problem analysis is not only necessary for the person planning the intervention, but equally important for the person who has the task of evaluating the change efforts. The evaluation must begin with a description and analysis of the phenomenon to be changed.

For example, take the problem of delinquency. Any intervention attempting to reduce delinquency must first specify what is meant by delinquency and analyze the problem for clues about effective points for intervention. If delinquency is conceptualized as the product of faulty personality development, interventions may be addressed to facilitating the personality development of those who are adjudicated delinquents. In contrast, if delinquency is seen as a "normal" response of certain youths who are denied access to legitimate careers or roles, then interventions may be addressed to providing or altering the opportunity structures for these youths. Alternative problem analyses can likewise be given for poverty, pollution, mental illness, mental retardation, and so forth. Thus it is important for the evaluator in conjunction with the intervenor to be clear about the definition of the problem.

Specifying and Measuring Goals

Evaluating the effectiveness of social work interventions requires that one know what goals the intervention sought to achieve and have methods of determining to what extent the goal was accomplished. It would be possible, of course, to measure the effects of an intervention without knowing which effects were the intended objectives, but this appears to be a rather inefficient approach to evaluation. In order to assess whether the intervention was successful in inducing change, the goals of the intervention must be clear, specific, and measurable (Weiss 1972, p. 26).

The specification of the goals of intervention is rarely easy. First, the goals of many interventions may be hazy, ambiguous, and hard to pin down (Weiss 1972, p. 25). For example, an intervention may attempt to increase the ego strength of the client, raise the general welfare of the population, improve the quality of life, achieve equality, improve family life, or make a person better adjusted to his circumstances. What exactly do these goals mean? How would one know if they were achieved or not? With what indicators could these goals be measured?

Second, every organization has covert or latent goals as well as the manifest or publicly enunciated ones. Achievement of which of these goals will constitute success? For example, in addition to attempting to help families, a family agency will have latent organizational maintenance goals—it must attend to its own survival as an agency. If an agency achieves its stated goals, but fails to maintain financial backing from its constituency, it may disappear from the scene. This would be an example of an agency that is successful in achieving some goals but a failure in terms of organizational survival goals.

The third possible barrier to specifying goals is that some interventions may have different goals over time or even contradictory goals. Hoshino (1973, p. 377) cites the example of AFDC programs which profess to be trying to strengthen family life, but actually have an antifamily bias. Or, similarly, welfare programs which purport to promote the recipient's well-being may at the same time strive to minimize expenditures. Is success to be measured in terms of the recipients' well-being or the size of the welfare department's budget?

The fourth problem frequently encountered in determining the goals of interventions occurs when there is an absence of goals. The goals described may actually be an aspect of the process of intervention. This occurs, for instance, when a social worker states that his objective is to "work with the client" or to "develop a relationship" with him. This pertains to the process, not what the end result is expected to be. Likewise, when a policymaker or an administrator describes the purpose of his program as "to provide service to a given population," he is specifying the nature of the intervention input and not the goals, output, or the benefits which are thought to derive from the services given.

Finally, a problem in specifying goals occurs when the stated goals are too grandiose in relation to the intervention. If the stated goal of a small community action agency is to eliminate poverty in its city, for example, the objective, however laudable, does not provide a very useful yardstick with which to measure the outcome of the agency's efforts. The goal needs to be grounded. What aspects of poverty are to be attacked? Among what specific local population? How long might it take to know whether the program succeeded?

Even though the goals of a program or intervention may not be explicit or offered in useful form, the evaluator, if he is not a direct participant in the intervention, can engage in a variety of activities to tease out or determine the de facto goals. If the intervention is a broad-scale one that has its origins in legislative or administrative policies, the enabling legislation or the administrative guidelines should be examined carefully for statements of goals. Interviews with key policymakers, administrators, and staff may be necessary in order to reach a firm sense of the major and minor objectives of the intervention. But interviews will often uncover divergent claims regarding the program or the intervention's purposes, and it may be useful to have group discussions with staff to resolve some of these conflicting opinions. In addition, goals can be inferred from close observation of the intervention activity and intimate knowledge about it. Regardless of the process of determining what the actual goals are, the precise content of them should be made as clear as possible.

In order to specify the content of the goals of the intervention, attention needs to be paid to at least three issues: (1) the target unit, (2) the existence of multiple goals, and (3) the causal sequencing of goals.

The first consideration in specifying the content of goals is to determine the target unit to be changed. Is the element to be changed an attribute of a person, a family, a group, an organization, a community, or a nation? Attributes of persons include attitudes, values, personality, behavior, knowledge, or various skills. Group characteristics include various sociometric variables, group cohesion, decision making, or task performance. Changing organizations might entail altering rates of productivity, client populations served, or other organizational characteristics such as administrative efficiency and coordination, resource accumulation, or independence. And finally, intervention at the community level might be for the purpose of changing the rate of crime, illness, child abuse, per capita income, unwanted pregnancies, patterns of racial segregation, or the distribution of political power. The first task in specifying the content of intervention goals, then, is to specify the unit that is the target of change efforts.

Change efforts often have multiple goals. A social worker helping a family may be attempting to improve the school performance of the children, lessen the mother's depression, assist the father in finding a job, and secure other resources for the family—all at the same time. Similarly, an enriched preschool program may aim to increase a child's motivation and ability to learn, detect and seek help for his medical problems, increase future school performance, and strengthen the entire family's ability to function as a unit. Or an effort to organize tenants in a poor area of the city may be geared toward bringing about a change in the landlord-tenant laws, achieving better enforcement of the housing codes, and creating a new sense of unity and power among the residents in the neighborhood. In all these instances, the change efforts are directed at multiple goals and the evaluation of outcome must take into account the variety of goals and how they are related to each other.

In a situation of multiple goals, the goals may be of equal importance to the intervention or they may fall into [a] hierarchy of goals ranging from major goals to minor ones. For instance, in the example above, organizing tenants may have the primary goal of bringing about better enforcement of the housing codes and only secondarily the objectives of changing laws and building a self-interest political group. Thus the achievement of the first goal may mean success for the intervention, even though the other secondary goals were not fully reached.

A more complicated context of multiple goals occurs when the multiple goals are seen as causally linked. An intervention may have the immediate objective of providing more information to a given population with the assumption that this information will lead to certain changes in behavior and that these in turn will benefit the community. Thus goals may be viewed as linked over time in a presumed causal sequence. When goals of the intervention are viewed as linked, it is important in the evaluation to make explicit the theory of causation or change that is employed and the assumptions that underlie it. For example, an obesity clinic may have the immediate goal of reducing the food intake of its clients, which is seen as leading to a loss of weight, which in turn is viewed as reducing the probability of heart disease (Suchman 1967, p. 51). The presumed validity of the causative assumptions that are made will significantly affect the goal against which the effectiveness of the program must be measured. For example, if past research has established that reduction of food intake will lead to a loss of weight and that such weight reduction lowers the probability of heart disease, then an evaluation of program outcome can concentrate only on the immediate goal (reduction of food intake) and assume that if that is achieved the other goals will also be reached.

On the other hand, if there is reason to doubt the causal assumptions, then the evaluation should not only examine the success of the program in achieving its immediate goals, but if possible, should examine whether such success does indeed lead to the intermediate or long-range goals. For example, a social caseworker may view his immediate goal as maintaining the participation of a client in a therapeutic relationship. The assumption might be that such participation increases the likelihood that the client will gain insight into his problems and that this insight will lead to changes in the client's problem behavior. If this theory of change is correct, one could use length of time in therapy as a sufficient outcome measure. However, if the theory of causation is suspect, it behooves the evaluator to examine not only participation, but also the relationship of participation to insight gained and of insight to behavioral change. In this way, the evaluation contributes both to the knowledge about the effectiveness of specific social work interventions and to the general knowledge regarding how various activites are related. But even

when an evaluation cannot critically examine the validity of the causative assumptions linking the multiple goals, it can at least make those assumptions explicit.

Once the goals of an intervention have been defined and their relative importance and relationship to each other made explicit, it is necessary to develop methods of measuring those goals. How exactly will the social worker know whether his efforts made the client happy, improved the family's functioning, reduced the incidence of mental illness in the community, or improved community relations? By what signs or indicators will it be apparent whether the intervention was a hit or a miss? Criteria for goal achievement must be selected and these criteria become the operational definition of the goals. Goal achievement is then measured in terms of these operational criteria. Measures of these criteria must either be selected from existing and available measures, or new measuring methods must be developed and tested. For example, a program designed to increase a child's school performance (immediate goal) may define that performance in terms of reading and mathematical skills and assess those skills by a battery of standard achievement tests (operational definition). Whenever possible, it is desirable to use multiple measures to assess goal achievement, since change is often multidimensional and may be evident on some measures but not on others. Similarly, as wide a variety of the available research techniques that are appropriate to the evaluation should be used: observation, interviewing, paper and pencil tests, examination of physical evidence, or the content analysis of available documents. Attention should be given to both the reliability of the measures (i.e., the extent to which the differences they measure reflect real differences and not inconsistencies in the measuring instrument), and their validity (i.e., the extent to which they measure what is supposed to be measured) (Herzog 1959, p. 37ff).

Specification of the Intervention

Once the problem to be changed has been defined and the goals of the intervention set, one might think that the next task is to observe whether the goals are achieved after the intervention has occurred. But first the exact nature of that intervention should be specified so that it can be either replicated or avoided. What precisely was the nature of the intervention used in the situation? And what aspect of that intervention is responsible for the results?

Social work intervention, as Breedlove (1972, p. 58) has so correctly emphasized, is not a homogeneous, unitary, or single activity; and it therefore needs to be specified in any evaluation. For example, to describe an intervention as "casework" or "community organization" is inadequate. Casework as an intervention needs to be specified in terms of the techniques actually used (positive verbal feedback, advice, nonverbal expressions of support, interpretations of the client's problem, etc.). Likewise, intervention at the community level may include holding public meetings, gathering factual information, speaking with community leaders, attending and participating in city council meetings, placing political advertisements in the media, or developing a new service for clients. In assessing the effectiveness of an intervention and refining that intervention to become even more successful, the outcome must be examined in relation to each of the component parts of the change effort. Specification of the intervention process, then, is an integral part of outcome research.

It is possible to do what has been called *black box* evaluation research in which change is measured both before and after an intervention, but where the nature of the intervention is not considered or detailed. This type of outcome research may be useful for legislators or funding bodies who are only concerned with results and not with the means by which they are achieved (Mogulof 1973). But the professional social worker, whether a clinician, program planner, or administrator, needs to know what specific procedures are effective and under what conditions. In short, he needs to develop some theoretical understanding about the principles of intervention that are generalizable to other situations, and for this purpose, attention must be paid to the nature of the intervention.

Specification of the intervention should include a description of the input activity, the intervenors, and the clients or problem situation. What was the nature of the intervention actually attempted as distinct from the intervention that may have been originally planned? What type of service was given, how frequently, and for how long? Who conducted the intervention? What were the numbers and training of the staff involved in the change efforts? What were their feelings and expectations regarding their efforts? What was the organizational context of the activity? What was the nature of the problem or the composition of the target group in terms of age, sex, socioeconomic status, race, attitudes toward the pro-

gram or problem, their expectations, motivations, and aspirations (Weiss 1972, p. 46)? All of these factors should be known and considered in any outcome evaluation so that the reader can replicate the intervention or properly generalize the findings.

Designing the Data Collection

A social worker offers marital counseling to a young couple and their marital problems decrease. Some delinquents lessen their involvement in criminal activity after participating in a community recreational program. A city council passes some policies favorable to a low income neighborhood during the time when a social worker has mobilized many poor people and had them attend city council meetings. A health education campaign is undertaken shortly before a drop occurs in the community's incidence of venereal disease. In all of these instances an intervention appears to be associated with some change in a problem situation. The question is, however, was the intervention effective?

The intervention would be effective if these consequences were indeed the desired goals of the intervention, and if it can be demonstrated that the intervention was responsible for the changes. There are three conditions for determining causality between two events (usually referred to as the independent and dependent variables) and all three must apply. First, there must be some evidence of covariation of both the variables. It must be evident that the occurrence of the independent event or the event thought to produce the change is associated with the occurrence of the effect desired, the dependent variable. For example, if a couple's marital problems remain unchanged after counseling, the criterion of covariation is not met; intervention was initiated, but the problem did not vary. Second, it must be established that the intervention occurred prior in time to the change in the dependent variable. If the delinquents had lessened their involvement in crime even before their participation in a recreational program, one could not argue that the program was responsible for this prior reduction in delinquency. Only their behavior following their program contact could be viewed as a possible result of the program. Finally, it must be established as convincingly as possible that the changes observed in the dependent variable or problem situation are not due to some variable other than the planned intervention. How do you know that the action of the city council was due to the presence and activity of the neighborhood activists and not the result of a long-term development of social programs in that city or the recent receipt of a federal grant, or a court order? How can one attribute responsibility for the change to one variable (the planned intervention) when a number of other variables were occurring at the same time?

Inferences of causality are made possible through the structure or logic of the data collection, what is commonly called the *research design*. It is through the design of the data collection procedures that an evaluator can establish covariation, time order, and control for important extraneous variables. Campbell and Stanley (1963) present an excellent discussion of the threats to the validity of evaluation efforts and how a variety of the most common research designs deal with these threats.

The choice of research design depends on many factors, including the target of the change effort, the nature of the intervention activity, the desired or intended objectives, the organizational context of the intervention, the degree of control over the situation that the evaluator may have, the extent of cooperation of those people participating in the program, ethical considerations, and the amount of time, money, and effort that one is willing to commit to an evaluation. Thus, there is no research design that is most appropriate to all evaluation efforts. Nevertheless, some research designs are probably the most useful and adaptable to social work intervention. Of these, three prototypical designs will be discussed. These are the *control group experimental design*, the *single-subject clinical designs*, and the *time-series design*.

The classic experimental design is the *pretest-posttest control group design* (Campbell and Stanley 1963). This design is most adaptable to situations where the targets of the intervention are individuals or small groups, and where the person conducting the intervention or the evaluator has considerable control over the process of intervention. Thus many "treatment-oriented" change efforts directed at individuals or families and sponsored by local clinics and family agencies could utilize this procedure. This design consists of three steps: (1) randomly assigning some clients to an experimental treatment in which they receive the service that is being evaluated, while the other clients are randomly assigned to serve as a control group in which they are either denied service or receive the regular service; (2) pretesting all clients before the change effort is initiated to determine their level of functioning; (3) posttesting or measuring all the clients following the treatment experience. Assuming that the randomization was successful in developing two comparable initial groups, the effectiveness of the intervention is determined by the degree of positive change observed in the experimental group in relation to the degree of change observed in the control group.

It is often not possible or appropriate to use an experimental group design. This is especially true in the case of the individual clinical practitioner who wants to be able to monitor, evaluate, and improve his own practice, but who cannot generate a large group of clients and assign them to separate treatment conditions. For this instance, one of the single-subject designs may be helpful (Stuart 1971, p. 1114; Howe 1974). The most basic of these designs and one frequently used in evaluating behavior modification programs with individual clients is the *A-B-A-B* or *reversal design*. Since the practitioner does not have access to a control group against which to measure his results, the A-B-A-B design uses the client to serve as his own control. The evaluation consists of observing the client's problem behavior prior to treatment and establishing the extent or rate of that behavior, called the *baseline*. Then the treatment is initiated and the magnitude of the problem is continually measured.

If a change occurs in the client's problem it may be due to the treatment, but it could conceivably be caused by other factors as well. As a way of controlling for these extraneous variables, or more precisely, as a way of demonstrating that the association of treatment and behavior change is not spurious, the treatment is withheld for a time and the client's problem behavior is observed. After this period of no treatment, the treatment is administered again and the problem or behavior is observed again (hence the A-B-A-B name). If the problem behavior decreased during the initial treatment period and increased with the withdrawal of treatment, but then declined again with the second administration, it is substantial evidence that the intervention was indeed responsible for the change.

There are other intervention situations involving changes in social conditions where individuals alone are not the target of change and where the evaluator does not have the benefit of forming a control group or of administering and withdrawing the intervention at will. Many instances of planned policy changes or social reform designed to affect some macrolevel phenomena are of this type. If one wants to increase an organization's efficiency by changing its administrative structure, it may not be a change that can be easily reversed, withdrawn after a time, or administered only to an experimental group. If the organization's efficiency is observed to increase immediately following the change, one is faced with the task of determining whether to attribute the increased effectiveness to the administrative reorganization or to other factors. For example, the efficiency increase could be part of a long-term trend in that organization that would have occurred anyway. Or, the efficiency rate may be constantly fluctuating, and the intervention took place when efficiency was at a low point and could have been expected to rise. One methodological approach to evaluation of this type of intervention is the use of a time-series design.

A *time-series design* is a quasi-experimental design which consists of taking periodic measures of the unit to be changed (the dependent variable) and then introducing the intervention and continuing to take periodic measures of the variable. What one is looking for is a discontinuity in the measures occurring at the time of the intervention. The design is thus similar in many ways to the A-B-A-B (Campbell 1969; Campbell and Stanley 1963). By observing the phenomenon for a period of time prior to and subsequent to the intervention, one is able to determine whether the observed change, if any, between the measure immediately preceding the intervention and the measure immediately following it was part of a long-term trend, a normal fluctuation, or a genuine discontinuity probably caused by the intervention.

The time-series design can be strengthened by introducing an equivalent control group that is not subject to the intervention and making observations over the same time period on that unit (Campbell and Stanley 1963). For example, if a state mental health department wants to initiate a statewide community mental health program and wants to evaluate the impact of that reform on the psychiatric hospitalization rate, it could examine its own hospitalization rate over a number of years, introduce the reform, and continue to monitor the hospitalization rate thereafter. At the same time, it could select another state that is similar in terms of population characteristics and other relevant factors but which is not undergoing such a reform and observe its hospitalization rate over the same time period. Any change occurring in the experimental situation could then be compared not only with its own preintervention measures, but also with the measures of the control situation, thus lending greater validity to the inferences drawn from the data.

CONCLUSION

Social workers take on awesome responsibilities. They offer their services to change the lives of individuals, the conditions of communities, and the quality of life in society. In order to be accountable to their colleagues, their clients, and their communities they must be able to demonstrate that they possess the knowledge and skill to induce those changes that they are attempting to bring about. Such accountability requires that social workers continually attempt to build their knowledge of the principles of effective intervention and refine their skill in implementing those principles. Both tasks require that evaluation of intervention effectiveness be made an essential component of social work practice.

This paper has outlined some of the major elements in evaluating social work interventions. The problem situation to be altered must be clearly specified and carefully analyzed. The goals of the change effort should be systematically delineated and operationalized. The intervention itself needs to be precisely documented and measured. And finally, information about the change observed must be collected in such a way that it can be used to make sound inferences regarding the actual impact of the change effort. These elements are by no means exhaustive nor have they been fully detailed. Nevertheless, they constitute the first steps that must be taken on the road to developing effective social work interventions.

REFERENCES

Breedlove, James L. Theory development as a task for the evaluator. In J. Mullen and J. Dumpson (Eds.), *Evaluation of social intervention*. San Francisco: Jossey-Bass, 1972, pp. 55–70.

Campbell, Donald T. Reforms as experiments. *American Psychologist*, 1969, 24, 409–429.

Campbell, D. and Stanley, J. *Experimental and quasi-experimental designs for research*. Chicago: Rand McNally, 1963.

Fischer, J. Is casework effective?: A review. *Social Work*, 1973, 18, 5–20.

Fox, P. and Rappaport, M. Some approaches to evaluation of community mental health services. *Archives of General Psychiatry*, 1972, 26, 172–178.

Herzog, E. *Some guide lines for evaluative research.* Washington, D.C.: U.S. Department of H.E.W., 1959.

Hoshino, G. Social Services: The problem of accountability. *Social Service Review*, 1973, 47, 373–383.

Howe, M.W. Single-subject research in social work education. Paper presented at the Annual Program Meeting of the Council on Social Work Education, Atlanta, Georgia, March, 1974.

Mogulof, M. Elements of a special-revenue-sharing proposal for the social services: Goal setting, decategorization, planning, and evaluation. *Social Service Review*, 1973, 47, 593–604.

Mullen, E. and Dumpson, J. (Eds.). *Evaluation of social intervention.* San Francisco: Jossey-Bass, 1972.

Stuart, R.B. Research in social work: Social casework and social group work. In *Encyclopedia of social work*, Vol. II. New York: National Association of Social Workers, 1971, pp. 1106–1122.

Suchman, E.A. *Evaluative research.* New York: Russell Sage, 1967.

Tripodi, T., Fellin, P., and Epstein, I. *Social program evaluation.* Itasca, Ill.: F.E. Peacock, 1971.

Twain, D., Harlow, E., and Merwin, D. *Research and Human services.* New York: Research and Development Center, Jewish Board of Guardians, 1970.

Weiss, C. *Evaluation research.* Englewood Cliffs, N.J.: Prentice-Hall, 1972.

Zusman, J. and Reiff, E. Evaluation of the quality of mental health services. *Archives of general psychiatry*, 1969, 20, 352–357.

PART IV

Illustrations of Practice

Social workers are members of a profession that by its very nature—that is, its unique emphasis on the dignity and worth of the individual—requires a *flexibility* of response to situations, problems, and events at various levels of intervention, from microsystems to macrosystems. A position stressed throughout this book—in fact, the book's *raison d'être*—is that the social worker must and can be prepared for a practice that is characterized by constant change. The term employed in this book to describe a social worker so prepared is the *social work generalist*. In other words, social workers should be social workers first—equipped with a core of skills, values, and philosophy—and then, depending on the need, focus on work with individuals, families, small groups, communities, or broader systems.

This latter idea is meant to suggest that while social workers have the knowledge and skills to respond flexibly to a variety of problems at different levels of intervention, they may also have in-depth, highly specialized skills with selected problems. Thus, a social worker might very well be "only" a generalist (or may specialize in general practice); or a social worker might be a generalist first, and a specialist second. Most social work settings contain numerous examples of practice where, at initial contact, the social worker responds to a client or client system by using a number of different roles encompassing both direct and indirect interventions. Then, over a somewhat longer period of time, the worker might place special emphasis on one role and one set of problems.

For example, a client or group of clients coming to a family service agency or to a settlement house might be aided through a variety of initial interventions that employ such roles as advocate, broker, and provider of concrete services. Then, after assessment has clarified the dimensions of the case/situation, the worker might decide to place major emphasis on a clinical role and its set of interventions or on a community development role and its interventions. However, even if one role and set of interventive procedures is given primary attention, the worker, by virtue of the generalist perspective, will still be attuned to the need for, and will follow through when indicated, with intervention in different roles and at different levels.

In fact, as the reading selections in Part IV illustrate, no matter what the role or level of intervention, social workers need and use a variety of generic skills: skills at making comprehensive assessments and in problem solving, skills in building relationships, skills in locating resources, skills in working with individuals and groups, skills in evaluation, and so on. Indeed, whether individual social workers consider themselves basically caseworkers or basically community organizers, much of the knowledge and many of the skills they use overlap. Community organizers, for example, rarely "work with" entire communities. Usually, the target system is the community, but the basic process involves working with individuals and small groups in, or relevant to, that community. Thus, those generic elements of knowledge and skill, plus the sharing of a common value orientation and a focus on social functioning, form the basis for considering social work practice from the generalist perspective.

The purpose of this part of the book is to illustrate some of the problems and situations with which social workers are concerned and a number of the interventive strategies and skills used by social workers. It obviously would be impossible to illustrate all of the possible combinations and permutations of the situations, strategies, and skills with which social workers are involved, and no claim is made that this is intended here. Many of the case illustrations involve social workers in *direct practice*—working with or on behalf of clients—but at different system levels. A variety of problems, situations, and social work roles were selected to illustrate the range and breadth of social work practice. Not all of the illustrations can be considered generalist practice per se, but several do illustrate the social worker functioning in multiple roles or at multiple levels of intervention; for example, caseworkers engaged in advocacy, community workers providing concrete services, and so on. These illustrations might be read most profitably by considering them in light of the material presented in Part III of this book; for example, the points-for-intervention schema (reading selection 15), which relates various assessment criteria to numerous social work roles. Further, the material in Part III is also intended to provide a framework for analyzing practice from a holistic, systems-oriented point of view and can be applied to each illustration in Part IV as a means of evaluating the judiciousness, efficiency, and perhaps effectiveness of the intervention as described in each situation.

As noted above, social workers are concerned with and provide services to clients in a broad range of situations and in numerous problem contexts. The core commitment of social work is to fight against poverty and racism both at the societal level and in terms of the pernicious effects of poverty and racism on individuals. Similarly, social workers are committed to working to obviate the effects of oppression on a wide range of groups, including the aged (Brody 1971), the sexually oppressed (Gochros 1972; Gochros and Gochros 1977), women (see *Social Work* 21, no. 6 [November 1976], entire issue), battered wives (Schuyler 1976), and people suffering from drug abuse (Brill 1971). In addition to the traditional settings in which social workers provide services—hospitals, mental health clinics, family service and child welfare agencies, schools, and so on—social workers increasingly are providing services in innovative settings; for example, working with lawyers (Scherrer 1976), with the police (Roberts 1976), and in private industry (Skidmore, Balsam, and Jones 1974).

READING SELECTIONS IN PART IV

Again, it would be impossible to illustrate all of the settings, problems, and total range of skills used in each case or situation in this book; however, the reading selections in this part were chosen to illustrate a cross section of the above, including a number of basic social work skills, intervention at several levels, a variety of problem areas, and several different settings. Two articles illustrate generalist practice, per se; another describes practice with major preventive implications; one describes the social work role and functions in lobbying, a practice with major implications for instituting social change; another describes the practice of social workers attempting to overcome racism in the schools; one describes the practice of social workers in an innovative setting: private industry; another describes the importance of understanding the distinctive characteristics of the ethnic group with which the social worker is working so that techniques may be varied accordingly; one describes social work practice in a secondary setting (public health); and the last article describes delivery of mental health services in a Black ghetto using a systems approach.

"The Broome Street Network: An Ecological Approach to Systems Intervention" by Hetrick and Hoffman tells how a community-based health team worked to relocate (when that seemed the only alternative) members of a long-standing network of friends and neighbors. The focus in this case was on a specific environmental manipulation—the relocation—but it illustrates how this intervention involves dealing with change processes on many levels: from individual change to changing of entire social systems. This article also illustrates the functioning of a multidisciplinary team and the use of *systems intervention*, which weaves naturally back and forth from one level of change to another.

"New Dimension to Family Agency from Family Life Education" by Carder illustrates the social worker engaged in activities with both preventive and remedial overtones. The program was an outgrowth of the very successful project ENABLE, a nationwide family life education and neighborhood action program (Manser, Jones, and Ortoff 1967). The program described by Carder was an outreach program involving individual, group, and community skills. Eight groups were formed: Some focused on parents, some on mothers alone, and some on teens. The leadership skills used by the workers, plus some of the basic concepts involved in family life education, are discussed by Carder. In addition to the important preventive implications of family life education, the author reports that the groups opened lines of communication between neighborhood residents and the power structure that resulted in improved use of community services.

Mahaffey's "Lobbying and Social Work," while not a case illustration per se, does examine the crucial role of lobbyist for all social workers. The article reviews the rationale for the social worker as lobbyist and provides important step-by-step guides for social workers functioning as lobbyists. The intent of this article is not to isolate lobbying as a separate job, but rather to spell out for all social workers—whether caseworkers or community workers—the ways in which they can work toward achieving some of the goals of the profession. In other words lobbying and, by extension, social action are not the sole province of community organizers, but, first and foremost, are the province and the responsibility of all social workers.

"Confronting Racism in Inner-City Schools" by Prunty, Singer, and Thomas discusses the recent increase in school integration efforts in some communities, which has highlighted the prevalence of racial friction in some public schools. Given social work's major commitment to working to eliminate racism, this article is an illustration of efforts in that direction. Of course when viewed in the global sense, the elimination of racism may seem an overwhelming task. But when the issue is dealt with in a particular institution and when sound principles of social work practice are used, the efforts of such intervention can be significant. In this article the authors describe how a mental health consultation project confronted the issue of racial and cultural differences in an effort to bring about social change in the schools. The article describes the step-by-step approach of the consultants: from development of the project, to its initial implementation based on careful assessment, to implementation of an intervention program (workshops on interracial relationships), to project evaluation. Although the project could not lay claim to having completely eliminated racism in the schools, its positive effects (based on research evaluation of outcome) and its careful use of a systematic approach to practice can stand as an important model for social work practitioners to examine in the continuing search for guidelines for more effective practice.

Foster's "How Social Work Can Influence Hospital Management of Fatal Illness" is an important contribution to the literature on general social work practice. The social worker in this article—a medical caseworker—performed many of the traditional roles expected in working with individual clients. But her focus on the entire system—in this case the hematology service of a large hospital—led to intervention to change the ward culture. The way this change was carried out, working with both staff and clients, is described. Foster acknowledges that maintaining positive system changes may be a never-ending job, but she clearly illustrates the way an initial focus on individualized services (a focus, incidentally, that continued) led, through use of a social work assessment, to a change encompassing several system levels.

"Industrial Social Services: Linkage Technology" by Weissman describes an interesting approach to practice in a rather innovative setting for social work: a major industrial plant. The approach to practice is grounded in task-centered practice (Reid and Epstein 1972, 1977) and basically involves a comprehensive orientation to the broker/mediator role of social work. The linkage strategy and technology involves three stages: (1) locating and selecting an appropriate community resource, (2) providing access to and connecting a client with the resource, and (3) evaluating through follow-up contacts with the client the quality of the resource and the effect of the linkage on the client's problem. This article illustrates the important benefits that social workers can provide outside of traditional settings through the creative development of approaches to practice that are based on sound social work thinking, but that expand conventional approaches to practice in innovative ways.

"Dimensions in Social Work Practice with Native Americans" by Lewis and Ho focuses on a crucial aspect of social work practice: work with ethnic minorities, in this case, Native Americans. Lewis and Ho highlight the importance of thorough understanding of Native American culture before attempting to intervene in problems affecting Native Americans. They provide a framework for understanding the unique needs and potentials of Native Americans, as well as a number of suggestions for enhancing social work services to Native Americans. Although this article focuses on Native Americans, its key points are generalizable to any ethnic group with which social workers may be working: understand the needs, potentials, and culture of that group before initiating any intervention plan. Otherwise, social work efforts may be doomed to failure.

"Social Work in the Field of Public Health" by Hall and Young describes the roles and skills of the social worker functioning in a public health setting. Since it obviously is impossible to include in this book illustrations of every setting in which social workers work, and because many social workers do work in settings in which they are not the primary service providers, this reading selection was prepared and included in the book in order to illustrate a number of points that may be generalized to other situations: (1) work in a secondary or host setting, (2) need for a variety of social work roles and skills, (3) need for generic social work training, coupled with additional knowledge and skills that relate to a specific field—in this case, public health, and (4) interdisciplinary team work. The authors describe both the range of social work functions that are incorporated in a public health setting and the integration of theories and methods used by social workers with other professional practitioners and provide some information about the field of public health per se. The focus of this reading selection—changes in the delivery of human services and the perspectives of the public health social worker—may also, as the authors suggest, be valuable in several other settings, such as schools, residential programs, community mental health programs, and welfare programs.

Taber's "A Systems Approach to the Delivery of Mental Health Services in Black Ghettos" describes an ecological systems approach to social work practice in which naturally existing systems of support within the community were utilized to maximize the impact of social work intervention. Two social groups in the community were identified and intervention was carried out in such a way that the "natural mental health functions" of these systems were enhanced. Several examples of this approach to practice are provided whereby the worker, again functioning in several roles but primarily as a mediator between the natural group and the external system, focused on mutual support and competence rather than on pathology. Thus, these clients or consumers received and participated in the services without any necessity for labeling them as patients or as "sick."

In summary, Part IV of the book presents a number of reading selections illustrating social work practice at various levels of intervention—with individuals, families, groups, neighborhoods, communities, and larger collectivities. The workers engage in numerous roles and varied activities, including advocacy, brokerage, therapy and behavior change, consultation, organizing, planning system-change, lobbying, provision of concrete services, and community and locality development. The agencies or auspices of these services include a hospital, a family service agency, a mental health center, a community-based health service, a school, an industrial plant, and a community antidelinquency program. Throughout this part the emphasis is on assessment of problems and situations from a social work perspective, which calls for the worker to respond differentially in terms of the uniqueness and specific characteristics of each case. Several of the reading selections also show one worker performing a multitude of tasks, again, often at different levels of intervention. While every social worker cannot be expected to be an expert at every task, the extent to which social workers can be expected to respond flexibly to the specific needs of each problem or situation is the extent to which our profession can be considered to have integrated its knowledge into a generalist perspective. And that may also relate to the extent to which social work as a profession can be judged relevant to the human condition.

REFERENCES

Brill, L.
    1971   "Drug Abuse Problems—Implications for Treatment." *Abstracts for Social Workers* 7, no. 1:3-9.
Brody, E.M.
    1971   "Social Work Practice with the Aging." *Abstracts for Social Workers* 7, no. 3:3-8.
Gochros, H.L.
    1972   "The Sexually Oppressed." *Social Work* 17, no. 2:16-23.
Gochros, H.L. and J.S. Gochros.
    1977   *The Sexually Oppressed.* New York: Association Press.
Manser, E.P.; J. Jones; and S.B. Ortoff.
    1967   "An Overview of Project ENABLE." *Social Casework* 48:609-15.
Reid, W.J. and L. Epstein.
    1972   *Task-Centered Casework.* New York: Columbia University Press.
———, eds.
    1977   *Task-Centered Practice.* New York: Columbia University Press.
Roberts, A.R.
    1976   "Police Social Workers: A History." *Social Work* 21, no. 4:294-300.
Scherrer, J.L.
    1976   "How Social Workers Help Lawyers." *Social Work* 21, no. 4:274-78.
Schuyler, M.
    1976   "Battered Wives: An Emerging Social Problem." *Social Work* 21, no. 6:488-91.
Skidmore, R.A.; D. Balsam; and O.F. Jones.
    1974   "Social Work Practice in Industry." *Social Work* 19, no. 4:280-86.
Social Work.
    1976   21, no. 6 (November), entire issue.

THE BROOME STREET NETWORK:
AN "ECOLOGICAL" APPROACH TO SYSTEMS INTERVENTION

Emery S. Hetrick, Lynn Hoffman

Ecology—n. (Gr. Oikos, house; + -logy, the branch of biology dealing with the relations between living organisms and their environment. (Webster's New World Dictionary of the American Language 1963)

This paper describes an experiment in which a community-based health team attempted to relocate members of a long-standing network of friends and neighbors that came to be known as the "Broome Street Network." The team is a Mobile Crisis Unit attached to a hospital serving New York's lower East Side, which will be called the "Health Center." Conceived by Dr. Edgar H. Auerswald, the team was designed to provide on-the-spot aid and consultation for a limited number of situations needing intensive effort that were referred to its attention by Health Center staff or by people in selected "listening posts" (such as a school, a precinct station) in the community. At the time this article was written, the team included a psychiatrist (Dr. Emery Hetrick), a social worker, two community case aides, a driver of the team's microbus, and an office manager.

The theoretical model on which the idea of the mobile unit is based follows the "ecological systems" approach developed by Dr. Auerswald,[1] but owes much to the type of crisis therapy research represented by Langsley and Kaplan's project in Denver,[2] and the work of therapists like Ross Speck with kinship and neighborhood networks.[3]

In line with this thinking, the mobile unit was set up so that it could look two ways: within the individual, to take into account the biological systems whose malfunctioning may be contributing to his distress; and beyond the individual, or even his family, to take cognizance of the social-environmental structures he inhabits. The model of an ecological field is useful here because it suggests the complicated interlock of factors that mesh together to produce a given behavior, situation, or event. The mobile unit staff attempted to understand any situation it encountered in terms of such a field, and to plan interventions accordingly.

The narrative below shows how the unit was able to use a particular environmental manipulation—relocating two elderly people from Broome Street—to deal with change processes on many levels. These levels have here been singled out and emphasized but in real life are interdependent and sometimes inseparable. The story of Mrs. Bercowits demonstrates a process of culture change: how to move a person from a simpler way of life to a technologically more complex one. The story of Miss Sadie describes a far more difficult feat: that of bringing a recluse back into a world she left twenty years before and working briefly with her, without any attempt at extensive personality revision.

The relocation project, during which the mobile unit enlisted the aid of focal members of the Broome Street Network, as well as the formal helping groups in the community, shows how it is possible to go beyond individual change to a level where entire social systems can be influenced. Of course, any one of these points could be the take-off for a separate study. Simplicity was sacrificed in favor of showing how the activity of a community health team weaves naturally back and forth from one level of change to another. In particular, we wish to demonstrate the difference between the new type of systems intervention and the traditional type of therapy that focuses on processes within the individual, prefers talk to action, and never ventures into the field.

Mrs. Pearl. The mobile unit stumbled accidentally on the Broome Street Network through an encounter with a fringe member of it, Mrs. Pearl. Mrs. Pearl had come to the Health Center with many complaints: some medical, some emotional, some to do with living problems. Her medical condition was taken care of, and this, together with a demonstration of sympathy and interest, calmed down the feelings of desper-

Source: This article was specially prepared for this volume by the authors.

ation and fear that at times overwhelmed her and made her seem "crazy" to Health Center staff. As part of their normal procedure, the team made a home visit. They found that Mrs. Pearl and her husband lived in a building that was being torn down to make room for a new expressway and that they were unable to locate new living quarters.

The couple's impasse about housing led the team to the local office of the Department of Relocation. While discussing the Pearls' situation, the relocation social worker brought up the plight of a number of other old people in the area who were going to have to move and whose situation looked problematical. There was Mrs. Bercowits who had been living in the streets since her building had been vacated. She had refused six perfectly good apartments and was in the process of turning down a seventh because it was "too high up." There was old Mr. Klugman who was afraid of living in the projects. He was thought to be incapable of living alone anyway and was being pressured to move to a nursing home. And finally, there was Miss Sadie.

Miss Sadie. This lady was a recluse who had not set foot outside her apartment for twenty years and who had not allowed any garbage to go out for five. The relocation people felt that she would hardly accept—much less survive—a transplant, and they were looking for the services of a psychiatrist who would route her to an appropriate institution. The team was intrigued and told the relocation social worker that they would like to find out more about her. The worker gave them the address of a Mrs. Klosky, the wife of the owner of the grocery store across the street from Miss Sadie. On going to this address, the team found the store boarded up, but they finally located Mr. and Mrs. Klosky in their apartment next door.

Mrs. Klosky was a pleasant, sharp-witted lady of about fifty-five. Once reassured that the team had Miss Sadie's best interests at heart, she was quite willing to talk about her. She had known Miss Sadie for many years. Miss Sadie was the daughter of a very fine and respected rabbi. When her mother had died, some twenty years before, she had sat shiva* according to the Orthodox Jewish rite. However, she had been somewhat more Orthodox than usual and had continued to sit shiva. Her father knew this was not right, but had not been able to get her to leave the

house. For the next ten years she stayed at home, caring for her father and watching TV.

One day, her father came into the Kloskys' grocery store and ordered ten dollars worth of groceries. He was apparently sick, for he took himself to Bellevue—without telling his daughter where he was going—and shortly after, died. Mrs. Klosky, who knew the grocery-buying habits of most of her customers, was alerted to an unusual situation by the rabbi's large purchase; never before had he shopped for more than two or three days at a time.

When his death became known, the neighbors began to wonder what to do about his surviving daughter. In order to force her out of seclusion, it was decided to adopt the harsh tactic of not bringing her any more food. Days passed, and Miss Sadie did not appear. Finally, Mrs. Klosky broke the well-meant siege. She went to Miss Sadie's house and found her lying in bed, limp with hunger, but refusing to believe that her father was dead. Indeed, since she never saw her father's body, there was no evidence that could have brought the reality home, and she eventually settled on the explanation that he had been spirited away by a sister in Brooklyn.

Mrs. Klosky took pity on her and brought her food. She also got her on welfare, something of a feat considering that Miss Sadie refused to appear for an interview. From this time on, Mrs. Klosky managed Miss Sadie's life for her. She cashed her welfare checks, even getting a new mailbox lock so that she could take the check out of the box and bring it to Miss Sadie to sign. She took Miss Sadie's shopping lists and filled her orders. Mr. Klosky brought up her supplies and carried down the garbage. After he became infirm and could no longer negotiate stairs, Mrs. Mandelbaum, who lived with her retarded daughter down the street, took up the groceries. Mrs. Klosky arranged with the iceman to take out the garbage until the icebox was replaced by a refrigerator and the iceman stopping coming. After that Miss Sadie collected the garbage and stored it. She resisted all efforts to have it removed, saying that she was collecting it for a "prize."

However, in spite of her peculiarities, Miss Sadie was no fool. She had held a good office job before her mother's death, and she was still very good with figures. "People are not so stupid or crazy as you think they are at first encounter," Mrs. Klosky told the psychiatrist. "Sadie knows what she's about. I once made a mistake in her favor and she wrote down, "Shame, shame, you made a mistake." So I wrote back to her,

---

*A week's ritual of mourning.

"To err is human." She answered me, "To forgive is divine."

The Meeting with Miss Sadie. By this time the psychiatrist was determined to visit this unusual person and asked Mrs. Klosky if she thought Miss Sadie would consent to see him and some members of the team. Mrs. Klosky said she would try to arrange an entree and took them across the street to the building where Miss Sadie lived. Miss Sadie's window was on the second floor facing the street. Mrs. Klosky called up to the window and soon a face framed by long, messy hair peered out. Mrs. Klosky told Miss Sadie that she had some visitors. Miss Sadie raised the window. Mrs. Klosky explained that this gesture meant that Miss Sadie was receiving.

"Tell her you're from the 'Office,'" Mrs. Klosky suggested. "She thinks she's employed by the FBI, and if you tell her that, she may feel better about you." The psychiatrist followed this advice. When he announced himself in this fashion, Miss Sadie looked through the door and remarked, "Well, I guess you must be from a *different* office." She then let her visitors in.

At first glance the apartment seemed crammed full of garbage and trash; the smell was overpowering. However, a second look showed that it was far from disordered. The garbage and refuse were placed neatly in grocery bags that were stacked against the walls to a height of four to five feet. The bags contained only garbage that would not decompose, bones that were picked clean, and empty tins. The only refuse-free room was the front room, which was filled with broken, dust-covered furniture and was apparently never used. The rest of the apartment could only be described in terms of available space: the narrow passage down the garbage-lined hall; the hall windowsill, which served as Miss Sadie's larder and held a jar with bits of gefilte fish and two milk cartons; a passageway to the bed; and a passageway to the bathroom where only the toilet was accessible: the sink was covered up and the bathtub was filled with garbage except just under the tap.

As might be imagined, Miss Sadie's appearance was in harmony with her surroundings. To quote the psychiatrist's report:

Miss Sadie was a heavy, dumpling-shaped woman with hair hanging in loose strands over her shoulders. She was wearing a torn and dirty sweater, an ancient black skirt, and a blouse of some filmy, rotted material. When she smiled, she showed wide-gaped, yellow-stained teeth. Her manner was guarded and quite suspicious, an impression reinforced by the fact that she squinted and that only one eye focused on the person she was talking to, while the other veered off in the opposite direction. Nevertheless, she seemed quite willing to talk....

During their conversation the psychiatrist tried to find out whether Miss Sadie understood that she would have to move. She understood, but she stated that she was not going to do anything until she received her "instructions." "The Office," she said, was preparing an apartment for her and would let her know when it was ready. The psychiatrist translated this to mean that she knew that the Department of Relocation was finding her an apartment and that once it was fixed up, she would be willing to move in. This turned out to be a slightly generous interpretation, but the psychiatrist took it back to the social workers at the Department of Relocation. He recommended that preparations be made to find Miss Sadie a temporary apartment in Mrs. Klosky's building, which was not being torn down right away, while working to get her in shape to live in an apartment by herself.

Mrs. Klosky. Meanwhile, the psychiatrist began to realize that he had stumbled upon a treasure in Mrs. Klosky. She had a long and intimate knowledge of the neighborhood in which she lived. He went back to see her in order to get from her as much lore as he could and also to get her help in planning Miss Sadie's future.

To begin with, he found that she knew not just the people the Department of Relocation had mentioned, but at least fifteen other old people in the neighborhood who were going to have to move. This group was a remnant of the predominantly Jewish community that had settled on the lower East Side in the teens and twenties. The lucky and successful had moved out, leaving those who were less mobile behind. Mrs. Klosky, by virtue of her position as grocer's wife as well as her natural talents, had become a kind of unofficial mayoress of this small social network. Her constituents—all of whom she knew by face, although not all of them knew each other—looked to her to mediate for them with social systems like housing and welfare, to distribute gossip and information, and to keep a watch over their little world.

As these people got older, Mrs. Klosky's function became more important. Not only could someone's nonappearance at the store tell her that something unusual was happening and cause her to inquire among that person's friends, but the shopping lists themselves provided clues to people's lives. In the case of the illness of Miss Sadie's father, it was Mrs. Klosky who alerted the neighbors and took over the situation. Mrs. Klosky had aides—like Mrs. Mandelbaum and her daughter—and knew who to call upon for a particular piece of help. She was also sensitive to what kind of help would be useful. Asked whether another lonely lady in the neighborhood would spend time with Mrs. Pearl, who led a very isolated life, she explained that most of the neighborhood people felt that Mrs. Pearl was extremely hard to be with, let alone be friends with. Mrs. Klosky did support the idea of having Miss Sadie moved into her building; but this could not be for long, as her building was also coming down and Mrs. Klosky was then going to live with her daughter's family in Brooklyn. She suggested that a final disposition might be made of Miss Sadie by putting her into a common apartment with the Mandelbaums, who were also about to be moved. The Mandelbaums should be given an apartment in the project where Mrs. Mandelbaum's ex-husband lived, because even though his ex-wife never saw him ordinarily, she would go to care for him when he was sick.

As Mrs. Klosky talked it became clear that the informal helping system of which she was the focal figure had roots that went back to the days of the newly arrived immigrants and the communal practices that came out of their struggle to survive. In telling of the early days after she first moved to the East Side, Mrs. Klosky described the kind of sharing that would take place among the families who lived in her building:

We came to this country in 1921, from Poland, right after the pogroms, and we like escaped to America. My father was here six months before. He came here and he lived on M Street; on one side were the horses that pulled the garbage trucks, and on the other side were three buildings that a Hungarian-Jewish man bought and he rented out to these people—apartments were very hard to get in 1921, they didn't have much building because it was right after the first World War. All these people came from all corners of the earth. They were Hungarians and Russians and Polish and all kinds of mostly Jewish people in those three buildings. I'll never forget it as long as I live. We were six children and parents in three rooms: two bedrooms, and in the kitchen the girls slept at night on a bed that you opened up. In the dining room my brother slept on an open-up bed, and that's how we managed.

But Fridays—they baked! One had a rolling pin because they had just come over, one had the pans, one had the board, and they waited for one another and borrowed from each other, and Jewish people, they have to know whether this one is kosher enough and that one doesn't mix her dishes. And the wonderful baking smells would permeate the whole house. And they would bring it out in the hall: "Taste my cake," "Taste my kugel," "Taste my fish." And it was immaculate, when you washed up the house Friday toward evening, washed up your piece of the hall—you washed up the communal toilet in the hall—and that's how we lived. And we were very, very happy.

What was remarkable was that though all the arrivals and departures and the vicissitudes of the time the old communal structure had not died out. The more fit took care of the less fit, and many a socially or physically disabled person was kept quietly out of sight of authorities and enabled to escape the nursing homes and hospital wards that might otherwise have been their lot.

The team began to plan procedures that would avoid these solutions, so likely once the colony's protective casings—seen so differently by the authorities as "slums"—were torn away. In particular they tried to think about the problem of moving these people in such a way that they could keep or replicate the environmental and social webs that sustained their lives. Where this was not possible, the team hoped to teach them how to manage in the new environment, realizing that for some of them, going into a high-rise apartment meant going for the first time into the technological age.

Mrs. Bercowits. Moving Clara Bercowits was an example of this problem in an extreme form. The story also illustrates the beginning stages of the team's attempts to mesh with people from a different agency, thus setting the stage for the interagency collaboration that was so important in Miss Sadie's case.

Mrs. Bercowits was living in the streets. She had been sleeping on cold nights at the home of a neighbor, Mrs. Sokol. Mrs. Sokol was part of the helping network, but it must be said that her help did not come for free. She charged Mrs. Bercowits only seventy-five cents a night, but extras could be excessive; for instance, a cup of hot water and a tea bag cost Mrs. Bercowits fifty cents.

Mrs. Bercowits worried the social workers at the Department of Relocation, not only because she insisted on living in the streets, but because she cut such a strange figure. She ran a constant risk of being picked up by some authority who would feel she was too odd-looking to go wandering around like that. Tiny and thin, she piled clothes on herself as though she were a clothes rack. Actually she was. She had no closet to put her things in at Mrs. Sokol's. But in spite of her weird appearance, she was organized and very much in command of herself. As one of the relocation social workers put it:

Even on the hottest day she usually wears a blouse and four or five sweaters, a scarf around her neck, a woolen hat, dresses that are incredibly long, very old shoes, stockings and socks, and she always carries her two little shopping bags in which are clothes, her keys, her welfare card, string, yarn, what she considers important. But she does have a system—if you ask to see her welfare card she usually can go into the paper shopping bag and with a minimum of effort she can find it.

The relocation social workers asked the mobile unit for advice about how Mrs. Bercowits could be persuaded to take an apartment they had just offered her. The team psychiatrist suggested that they tell her they were furnishing it for her and that when it was ready, she would just have to move in. This plan was adopted and the social worker who got the apartment ready thought up a bit of strategy of her own. Although Mrs. Bercowits had signed the welfare forms requesting furniture, she was still insisting that she would not set foot on the eleventh floor. The worker got the welfare investigator to put pressure on her. Apparently he said to her, "Look, Mrs. Bercowits, you signed this paper and as far as the Department of Social Services is concerned, this is your legal address. If you're not there, your money will be, and if some of the checks are returned to us, that'll be it." Mrs. Bercowits said, "I'll go live there." As the worker explained, "She's a hard-headed, practical woman."

The day of the move, the worker, her supervisor, and the housing manager took Mrs. Bercowits over to her new place. As they went into the lobby of the housing project, Mrs. Bercowits asked for her keys, but objected to the paper clip the worker had used as a key chain because it was "ugly." The worker went across the street and bought her a key chain. From that time on Mrs. Bercowits led; her escort mostly followed. She proved to be a remarkably apt learner and stopped at every new piece of equipment until she was sure she knew what it was and how to work it. She refused to go up in the elevator until she had been shown her mailbox and then she said, "Put my

name on it so that I can get my checks." She also opened and closed it several times herself. The elevator made her nervous, but she watched carefully how to push the buttons that operated it. When they got out on her floor, she went up and down the hall investigating and, when she discovered the incinerator, asked to be taught how it worked. The apartment door was another problem; she spent some time on that. Finally she was willing to go inside the apartment itself. The rest of the story is told in the words of the relocation social worker who accompanied her:

After we went inside, Mrs. Bercowits walked around the whole apartment without putting down any of her bags. She looked around and she felt the bed and said, "Nice, very nice." She looked out the window and said, "Too high. It makes me sick." So we said, "Don't be silly, Mrs. Bercowits. We came all the way over here now and we're very tired." So the three of us just sat down at the table and chairs and let her kind of walk around.

She was delighted with the kitchen, though she had never seen a refrigerator and didn't know how to work it. The pilot light on the gas stove was new to her, too. Then she went into the bathroom, and this was it, this was what clicked. Right away she wanted to know if the three of us would stay while she took a bath. We said, "No," because we didn't want to give her any more support than she really needed, but she begged us, so we said, "All right, we'll stay." She went into the bathroom and for one hour—this was incredible—the splashing and the humming and the singing that went on! She was very happy in that bathroom.

Another interesting thing, she doesn't seem to get the concept of the one faucet—you know, she's apparently used to two faucets—so what she does is run the hot water and then she turns that off and runs the cold water. She called out to us that she really didn't like the color of the towels we'd selected but that was all right, she'd put up with this. When she finally came out, she was dripping wet, her hair was all stringy—I don't think she really dried herself—so I said to her, "You can't go out now, Mrs. Bercowits, you're sopping wet." She says, "No, if you're leaving, I'm leaving, it's too high, I'm afraid to stay here."

We didn't want to push it because we thought we'd accomplished a lot for one day, so we said, "Okay, Mrs. Bercowits, are you coming back tonight?" So she said, "Maybe." I suggested that we leave the light on. She said, "Oh, no, you don't burn electricity. I could find my way back again. No lights."

Before she crossed the threshold, she went and she tried every window to make sure it was locked. We explained to her that it was impossible for anyone to get in, she is on the eleventh floor, there are no ledges. But she said, "No, every window must be locked." Knowing how attached she is to her possessions, I felt that if I could get her to leave something, she'd come back, even if it were just to get that. So she let me take off a couple of her sweaters and she left them in a drawer and again said that the bedroom was "Nice, very nice."

When we came out, we locked the door, and then she wanted us to open it again so she could lock it herself. And she stood and looked at the door and the number, you know, and she read it to herself. And she looked up and down the hall to get her bearings. And she asked if she could ring for the elevator, which she did. When she got on the elevator she said, "I know how to do it," and she pushed the first floor button and we came down.

Mrs. Bercowits finally did move in after arranging to have a lady companion stay with her. This was against a department regulation, but the social workers chose to overlook that. As the companion was a former cook, this took care of Mrs. Bercowits' nervousness about the stove and the refrigerator. The entire episode was enlightening, showing that for many old people a move to a modern building is the opposite of an improvement. For Mrs. Bercowits the lovely new apartment was full of things that were strange, fearful, alien; it was an environment that she literally didn't know how to manipulate. Her sharpness in picking out the bits of technology she needed to master and her resolution in applying herself to learn them impressed her escorts. For her part, Mrs. Bercowits was not insensible to the patience and forbearance shown her. Before leaving the apartment she cast about to show her guests some parting gesture of hospitality. In the social worker's words:

She didn't want to make us a cup of tea, afraid of the stove you know, so she asked each one of us if we would like to use her toilet: "Please use." I went in to use it, you know, and I said, "That's really lovely, Mrs. Bercowits." And when I came out she asked the supervisor, who said, "Not now, but can I come back and use it some other time?" "Anytime." So this was her way of being nice.

The Relocation of Miss Sadie. Preparations for this event took place over a period of two months. The mobile unit staff met several times with the Department of Relocation, figuring out plans and strategies. However, the total amount of time the mobile unit spent on the entire project—including the initial visits to Mrs. Klosky and Miss Sadie—did not exceed ten hours. To a large extent, the details of the plan were carried out by social workers from the departments of relocation and social services; the unit acted mainly as consultant and only took active control on the day of the move.

First of all it was arranged to on-site Miss Sadie temporarily in Mrs. Klosky's building, and an apartment was found there for her. Then came the matter of getting the Department of Social Services to supply furnishings. The psychiatrist felt that careful thought should go into the choice of items, as the apartment would be Miss Sadie's total world. He had noticed that the only mirror in her old apartment was in the unused front room and completely covered with dust. Thus she had no way of seeing how ragged and filthy she looked. He made sure that a mirror would be in the bedroom of her new domain. She would need a radio and an electric clock in order to be more clued in to the rhythms and events of the outer world. In particular, the psychiatrist wished to make up for the one deficiency of the new place from Miss Sadie's point of view: It had no window on the street. As a replacement the psychiatrist decided to get a mechanical window: a TV set. He requested one from welfare on somewhat dubious medical grounds and the request was granted, although the department refused to buy it until the move was assured. The welfare workers quickly got into the spirit of the event and contributed many details of their own, like a brightly colored housecoat, pretty nightgowns, and a modish black dress for Miss Sadie to wear on moving day. In one respect they went beyond the call of duty: Going through an abandoned apartment in Mrs. Klosky's building, they discovered a dining room suite of fine mahogany Chippendale and promptly diverted it to Miss Sadie's use.

During this time an incident occurred that disproved the myth that Miss Sadie was totally helpless. Mrs. Klosky had gone for a visit to her daughter in Brooklyn, and Miss Sadie had no one to get her groceries up to her. According to the relocation workers who were keeping watch on her, she had leaned out of her window and commandeered the help of a couple of boys playing in the street. Until Mrs. Klosky returned, they brought up her supplies.

The date set for the move, July 18, finally came around. Mrs. Klosky came back the night before and agreed to lend her presence and influence. Another old friend of Miss Sadie's—a woman the mobile unit had not previously known about, called Mrs. Hirsch—showed up, too. Also on hand were eight people from four agencies: Department of Relocation

(2); Department of Social Services (2); the Mobile Crisis Unit (2); and the police department (2). Two unofficial visitors—a social worker from the British West Indies and an additional psychiatrist from the Health Center—came along with the mobile unit and acted as temporary team members.

It was a very hot morning. Bets on the move were being taken at the departments of relocation and social services. The team psychiatrist, Mrs. Klosky, Mrs. Hirsch, and the social worker from relocation went up to fetch Miss Sadie. They found her sitting on her bed. She refused to move, saying that they would have to wait till Monday. A two-hour period of negotiations followed, while everybody took turns trying to dislodge her. The worker did get her to put on the new dress by pointing out that her usual ensemble, which showed her bare, dirty midriff, was a bit immodest to go out in, but her cooperation ended there. Mrs. Klosky, with a rare display of sternness, ordered her to stop her foolishness and go across the street. She still refused. The "Office" was fixing her a place in the Bronx and she was going to sit where she was until it was ready. The psychiatrist gave her a deadline of ten minutes and three options: (1) to call up the "Office" to see if it would come across with alternate lodgings before the deadline was up, (2) to sit where she was until the workmen came to demolish the building, and (3) to walk across the street. This exhortation didn't move her either. The people in the apartment were hot, discouraged, and nearly suffocated from the smell of garbage.

Finally the psychiatrist gave up and went to phone the local precinct station, asking them to send an ambulance to take a lady to Bellevue. But before they arrived the social worker, arguing with Miss Sadie on the bed, fell on the clue that saved the day. She heard a remark pass Sadie's lips: "You can't make me go, only if you should carry me across the street." The worker interpreted it to mean that as long as Miss Sadie did not have to go on her own legs, she would not resist. She went out to confer with the psychiatrist and ran into the two policemen. They had just learned that the psycho they were expecting to take to Bellevue was only an old lady who was going across the street. The worker explained that, on the contrary, this was a poor, feeble soul who needed a wheelchair and a gallant escort. The two cross policemen immediately turned into two cheerful boy scouts.

In the meantime the psychiatrist had been clued into the new strategy. Since the police car had no

wheelchair, he ran down to call the Health Center ambulance service and asked for one. It arrived shortly and was placed in the hall outside the apartment. One of the policemen called from the doorway to Miss Sadie, who was standing in the bedroom, "Hey, Sadie, come out here, I've got something to show you." Miss Sadie walked toward him and stepped across the apartment threshold for the first time in twenty years.

After that there was no further problem. Miss Sadie was placed in the chair. Since it had no arms, the policemen strapped a belt around her waist and tied her arms and upper body to the chair back with a necktie so that she would not fall out. It was only at this point that she gave a low cry. The policemen carried her down the steps, out the door, and across to the new apartment.

Once set loose from the wheelchair, Miss Sadie went over and sat down on her new divan, looked around at the attractively furnished living room, and broke into a smile. By this time, many people had tears in their eyes, and Mrs. Klosky and the social worker were openly weeping. A celebration seemed in order. The psychiatrist dashed out and got a bottle of champagne and a prayer shawl as housewarming gifts; Mrs. Klosky brought up seltzer water. Mrs. Klosky had remembered to rescue the mezuzahs from the door of the old apartment and now placed them on the door of the new one. Then Mrs. Klosky said that she had to go downstairs because she was cooking for the Sabbath. In explaining the religious significance of this to the psychiatrist, she observed that Miss Sadie may have been resistant to moving that morning because it was so close to the Sabbath. Even though there was no infringement of Orthodox law in moving before sundown, Miss Sadie had been known to stretch a point of ritual before in order to rationalize her wishes.

The Aftermath of the Move. In the days after the move, Miss Sadie began to respond to her changed circumstances. A later visit revealed that she must have taken a look into the mirror, because her face and her arms up to the elbows were clean. She also asked the welfare workers to buy her two new housedresses. Most impressive of all, she was taking her garbage out into the hall and dumping it in the incinerator. The psychiatrist, discussing with her the next move to an apartment in one of the projects, reported that she seemed quite accepting of the idea, once she was assured that a home-care person would be available to see to her needs.

Oddly enough, it was not Miss Sadie but Mrs. Klosky who was most upset by the move. When one of the team members called her later to ask how Miss Sadie was doing, she at first seemed distant and unwilling to talk. Miss Sadie, she said, wasn't too happy. She had never received the promised TV set and badly needed the electric clock and radio. However, Mrs. Klosky felt that Miss Sadie shouldn't be given a telephone—as had been planned—because she was not used to having people telephone her and, when the phone rang, would only worry that it was somebody who wanted to break in; furthermore, she should be moved to the projects before her housekeeping had time to degenerate again to the point of jeopardizing her eligibility.

Mrs. Klosky also complained that the relocation people had called to ask for her help in moving some other old people. She wanted the team to tell them to stop bothering her; she didn't want to get mixed up in any more operations like that. It had angered her to see Miss Sadie treated with disrespect. She described how the policeman, who had tied her to the wheelchair, had said to Mrs. Klosky, "Are you her friend?" When Mrs. Klosky said, "Yes," he said, "Then why don't you tell her to wash and get clean?" Mrs. Klosky retorted, "Young man, if my friend did wash and get clean, you wouldn't be tying her to a chair!"

Finally, Mrs. Klosky came out with the real hurt. After the move she had gone to see Miss Sadie, and Miss Sadie had accused her of "going over to the Enemy." Mrs. Klosky, always ready with a tart reply, said, "Well, if I'm the Enemy, perhaps you don't want me to bring your groceries." Miss Sadie quickly answered that she didn't mean that. But the barb had stuck.

Mrs. Klosky ended the conversation with a rather startling remark. She said that she had met a lady acquaintance in the street who had asked her about the mobile unit psychiatrist everybody had been hearing about. Mrs. Klosky said to the team member, "I told her I didn't know him." This was a curious and sobering reaction; it led the team to realize that what was for them an occasion for rejoicing—namely, Miss Sadie's move—did not necessarily have the same meaning for everybody else. In a network where some are caretakers and others are taken care of, a change toward more independence for one of the cared for may have a profoundly disturbing effect on one of the caretakers, whose life has just as surely been altered.

The Other Systems. The story of the Broome Street Network did not end there. As a result of the moving of Miss Sadie, the Commissioner of Relocation wrote a letter commending the teamwork between the Mobile Crisis Unit and the social workers on his staff. In this letter he said:

To my knowledge, it is the first time my department has ever faced the relocation of an absolute twenty-year recluse. The successful transfer of this withdrawn person into a viable apartment rather than a hospital ward is something at which we wonder and applaud. . . . The fact that three tenants so far in the area have been brought to the level of relocation with the unit's help gives pause for thought about possible new dimensions in relocation.

The "new dimensions" the letter was referring to was more than an empty phrase. It was a plan—based on the experience the mobile unit had shared with the relocation social workers—to start moving people with greater reference to the social worlds they came from. In meetings held between the Department of Relocation, the Mobile Crisis Unit, and the Department of Housing, possibilities were discussed of renovating small older buildings and using them for relocation so that networks of long-standing neighbors, such as the Broome Street Network, could be moved virtually intact. Another idea was to reserve sections of new public housing for such groups. In planning these settings an effort would be made to design facilities so as to respect the preferences and needs of the particular groups who would inhabit them. In regard to the process of relocation itself, the members of the relocation staff who had worked with the mobile unit continued to expand techniques for moving people that took into account their circumstances and lifeways. To sum up, there had been a shift in thinking on the agency's part toward a more *ecological* approach to relocation.

It is now time to close the story of the Broome Street Network. In ending it might be appropriate to go back to the person who introduced us to it: Mrs. Pearl. Here is an excerpt from a letter she wrote to one of the psychiatrists on the Health Center staff. It was written on a child's lined note pad in a large, primer-book hand. The letter, although it was not intended for this purpose, is included as a reminder of the pious and communal way of life that is about to vanish from the city along with Broome Street's abandoned tenements.

This 9th Day of April, 1968

To precious Dr. ———

When I first met you And asked if I may take a few minutes, To tell you of my difficulties, You did not refuse, And this is the real reason why I take time now, Before Passover, When everything has to be cleaned so Matzohs have to be on the table, I cannot wait, but wish for you With all my heart, "A Healthy, long life." I had a song for you, while I was putting up my cooking at an early hour, 3 a.m. I average from 2 to 4 hours of sleep. And read the following:

My brother had a wonderful voice. Two of them took vocal lessons, Papa with a big hammer and chisel used to make "Itzchaims" for Synagogue. There are two at the House of the Sages at Broome and Willett Streets which we held for about fifty years. He made them in a large city of Russia, Odessa, where Papa was born, Forks, spoons, knives, all by hand.

And I keep up my life, and like to stand and look at the painting of Mother and Father together on the wall, one cannot miss when I enter the door of my so-called dinette. I have only two rooms. The melody is what my brother sang: Sunset, Sunrise, Sunrise, Sunset (not these words) My room here is quite dark. Thank the Lord I have an attick, So I could see early, the Sunrise.

I get ready for the Synagogue, And proudly take the prayer-book in hand. To the Synagogue I am going, Dressed in black from toe to neck (imagination). And the Torah is my love and life, The Talles* is a precious shawl, Which I put on my bent shoulders, And this is my life, and my joy.

On my table I see a Talles, Skull Cap, Prayer Books, and all, the Tvillen,** And there's always a candlelight, In memory of those innocent, who fell . . . And now you know the kind of girl I am. This is my reference.

NOTES

1. Auerswald, Edgar H., "Interdisciplinary versus Ecological Approach," *Family Process* 7, no. 2 (September):202–15, 1968.
2. Langsley, D.G. and D.M. Kaplan. *The Treatment of Families in Crisis*, New York, Grune & Stratton, 1968.
3. Speck, R.V. and D.L. Attneave. *Family Networks*, New York, Vintage Books, 1973.

---

*Prayer shawl
**Phylacteries

NEW DIMENSION TO FAMILY AGENCY FROM FAMILY LIFE EDUCATION

Joan Haley Carder

This article is a report on the beginning of an outreach community program which added diversification to the Family Service Agency of Pulaski County. This voluntary agency in North Little Rock, Arkansas, a community with a population of 287,000, seized upon an opportunity to work with other organizations and a variety of groups without any guarantee of success. The agency was willing to take this risk, which has proved successful both for the agency and the community.

Family life education is a term used interchangeably with *parent education* or *parent group discussion*.[1] However, for the purposes of this article the term *family life education* is preferable because it is more comprehensive and includes groups of individuals who are not parents. The term *education* in connection with the groups discussed in this article takes on a broader meaning than just the intellectual capacities of the participants. It coincides with Peter B. Neubauer's description of education which "recognizes the importance of feelings and attitudes, and uses emotional mobilization as well as intellectual stimulation."[2] Within this framework the process of learning is dynamic. The members of each group contribute from their own interests and experiences. They learn from each other by verbalizing and assessing attitudes and feelings about day-to-day family living.

Source: Joan Haley Carder, "New Dimension to Family Agency from Family Life Education," *Social Casework*, Vol. 53, No. 6, June 1972, pp. 355–60. Reprinted with permission of the Family Service Association of America.

BACKGROUND

The Family Service Agency of Pulaski County remained small and relatively static for the first twenty-four years of its existence. It offered a valuable service to those in the community who came into the agency for counseling services, but there was no plan for reaching out into the community. The staff and board of directors were limited by funds from the community United Fund campaign and were hesitant to consider the use of federal funds.[3] In March 1966 the agency decided to take steps toward involvement with social action and federal monies by establishing a community program called Project ENABLE—Education and Neighborhood Action for a Better Living Environment. This project, a component of the federal Office of Economic Opportunity (OEO), was sponsored jointly by the Family Service Agency of Pulaski County and the Urban League of Greater Little Rock. Project ENABLE was developed nationally by the Family Service Association of America (FSAA), the National Urban League, and the Child Study Association of America (CSAA). The following statement seems to sum up Project ENABLE:

Expertise in parent education through small group discussion, casework knowledge of individual behavior and family relationships, and skill in community organization were joined in a team approach to help parents discover the strengths within themselves and the resources in their communities to change the situations in which they live and rear their children.[4]

Project ENABLE was not re-funded nationally because of shifting priorities. However, because of the success of the program in Little Rock, this program received continued OEO funds. Because ENABLE had a low national priority, the name of the Little Rock program which did continue was changed to PECO—Parent Education and Community Organization. Although the name was changed, the philosophy and approach remained the same. Concrete, positive changes were occurring within the poverty communities as a result of the group discussions and community action. Consequently, the host agency became interested in a similar approach as an integral part of its regular program, which includes work with middle-class as well as with poverty communities.

The first discussion group within the family life education program was formed in October 1967. This group was designed for mothers of handicapped children. There were two different series during the next nine months, and a number of the same mothers participated in both series. The handicaps of the children varied from birth defects and physical limitations to mental retardation and emotional problems. All the handicaps were considered severe, and, although the mothers were from varied backgrounds, they found a commonality in having a special child.

Time was not available for the group leader to conduct the necessary follow-up and recruitment for continuing groups. Consequently, there were only a few sporadic family life education groups during the next three years. In October 1970 the agency's staff and board decided that they were treating a potentially valuable program in a shortsighted manner and were not taking the necessary steps to make it an integral part of the agency. The commitment was made to assign a full-time staff member with the necessary interest and special training to develop the family life education program.* A special committee of the board was appointed to work with the staff person in establishing policy and promoting the program.

RECRUITMENT IN THE COMMUNITY

Three months were spent in making key contacts with individuals and groups within the community. These contacts had a twofold purpose: to assess the needs for the program and to interpret the program to the community. Most people were interested in this new outreach program aimed at prevention of individual and family breakdown through group education discussions; however, a few persons were skeptical about the recruitment of middle-class parents in this community. Nearly fifty different contacts were made during this assessment stage. There was also radio, television, and newspaper publicity about the program. The goal was continual public exposure for the group leader, the agency, and the new family life education program.

The staff of this family service agency had always given talks to community groups. In an effort to complement the philosophies of the family life education program, the board wanted the project policy to include a discussion period; even in a single meeting there is potential for learning when people

---

*When one considers that the total agency staff consisted of four full-time and two part-time social workers, this was a strong commitment.

are emotionally involved through discussion in accordance with their own interests. During the next five months of the program, January through May 1971, the staff conducted thirty-eight single meetings with a total attendance of nine hundred and thirty-one people. This figure does not include the seventeen performances of "Plays for Living," another part of the family life education program in which a thirty-minute live drama is presented, followed by a thirty-minute discussion period.

One of the original groups in this expanded program emerged from nine months of single meetings with a women's church circle. This was the most successful group because the women were able to get to know and trust the leader as well as each other. This kind of recruitment is not possible for every group. In this group, a depth of discussion was promoted that was similar to that experienced in a group meeting for a protracted period. There were fourteen women enrolled in the series. Five had not been members of the original group. An evaluation form was sent to each member several weeks after the conclusion of the series. Members were asked not to sign the forms so that they would feel free to give negative as well as positive comments. There were a few negative comments including the fact that three women wanted a more intellectual discussion of articles or books. Most of the comments were positive: "I feel I gained a great deal"; "The course made me stop trying to please everyone and start being honest with myself and others about how I feel"; "In many ways I feel as if I'd been freed from the cage I had myself in." One form was not returned, but the other thirteen indicated that the members liked the series and would enroll in the next series.

Recruitment is vital to the success of any family life education group, but it would not be humanly possible nor feasible for the leader to recruit every group. ENABLE found a method of using indigenous neighborhood members to interpret the program and to recruit the neighborhood residents for the group discussions. The agency capitalized on this idea by interpreting the program to the key people in each group or organization and allowing them to recruit the group members. In the four groups which were sponsored cooperatively with the Pulaski County Social Services (Public Welfare), the recruitment was carried out by the individual caseworkers. After the caseworkers were convinced that the group discussions would be helpful to their clients, they became enthusiastic about recruiting. Many of these busy,

dedicated caseworkers arranged day-care and provided transportation for the group members each week. Without the efforts of the caseworkers, most of these mothers would not have been able to attend the sessions.

STRUCTURE OF THE GROUPS

A discussion series of eight weeks seemed ideal, but the agency experimented with shorter and longer series. The shortest was five weeks, and the longest was twelve weeks. An eight-week series has been generally accepted in other agencies also. The sessions were on a weekly basis and lasted ninety minutes, except for one group for which the session was sixty minutes. To offer structure and continuity, the same facility was used each week for the group. Coffee and soft drinks were available for the members, and day-care was provided for young children while their parents attended the meetings. Refreshments were more important in the non-fee-paying groups; the members took turns in bringing cakes and cookies, and thus they felt that they were contributing to the group. The socialization afforded in this procedure was a meaningful part of the group experience. The members of the fee-paying, affluent groups were only concerned that there was a coffee pot available during the group meeting.

The optimum number recruited for each group was fifteen to twenty people to ensure attendance of eight to twelve. Experiences of the group leaders in the ENABLE program indicated that with a lower socioeconomic population at least twice the feasible number for a group had to be recruited. This hypothesis was proved true in all of these groups. In one group of socially and economically deprived mothers, seventeen had planned to attend the first meeting, and only eight came. The general policy was to admit new members through the first three sessions but not after this point, because such late arrivals tended to be disruptive to the group.

Part of the first session of each series was spent in collecting a topic-agenda, commonly known as the "Go-Around," from the members. Each member was given an opportunity to suggest a topic relating to his daily living for discussion during the series. An effort was made to discuss each topic, although new topics could be brought up during the series and were often more significant than the original topics. No one was pressured to participate, and the approach was on a positive basis.

The assumption was that learning is more acceptable to adults when they are treated with respect and perceived as having the ability to run their lives. They are then free to weigh the pros and cons and to derive conclusions without fear of being unduly criticized or treated like children. Each group was organized with some homogeneity, such as parents with children of a certain age or teenagers. With some commonality there was sharing in learning.

Breakdown of Eight ENABLE Groups

Parent Groups
Parents from affluent community
Foster parents

Mother Groups
Mothers from affluent community
Mothers under Aid to Families with Dependent Children program
Mixed, socioeconomically and racially (Chinese, Filipino, Japanese, Negro, and Caucasian)

Teen Groups
Middle class, males and females
Foster teens, males and females
Middle class, females

The board of the agency was well aware that this program was not designed to make money or even to support itself at first. Thus, there was freedom to recruit the groups according to interest and need. There was an equal distribution of fee-paying and non-fee-paying groups, four of each. The agency has a sliding scale fee policy, and this philosophy was generally adopted for the family life education program. The fees for the paying groups ranged from two to sixteen dollars for the series. The breakdown of these eight groups shows the breadth and variation of the program.

LEADERSHIP TECHNIQUES

Leadership in any type of group varies with the individual leader's personality, knowledge, and skill, and this fact is true of the leadership of the family life education groups. Because there is no screening of the membership of these groups, it is imperative that the leader have knowledge of personality development and family life from a psychodynamic background. The leader needs to be able to assess and diagnose each member and his situation; he must also have knowledge of learning theories and group process.

Aline B. Auerbach discusses these criteria in more detail when she writes about [the] role of the leader.[5] She also describes the alternatives of activity and passivity and the need to be selective according to the purposes of the group. One general rule in family life education is that the leader needs to be more active in the beginning to demonstrate the importance and use of the members' interaction. As the group develops, many of the leader's functions are taken over by the members, who learn to ask questions, to assess the problem, and to understand it in the process of helping and learning from each other.

There are three general areas of responsibility in the role of the leader.[6] The first responsibility of the leader is to provide an atmosphere in which attitudinal learning can take place by accepting differences as well as similarities, maintaining a mood of challenge not defeat, and teaching the concept of ambivalence. The second responsibility of the leader is to develop the content for discussion by eliciting topics from the members and maintaining a group focus. The third responsibility is to serve as a role model in dress, manner, empathy toward people, and approach toward problem solving. The leader is encouraged to arrive thirty minutes early for each meeting and to remain after the meeting in order to be available to members of the group who need to talk on an individual basis.

Dual leadership may be indicated for certain reasons, such as teaching, but in the experience of CSAA, co-leaders generally have presented more problems than benefits. In a teaching situation this is not truly dual leadership because one person is the leader or teacher and the other person is an observer or learner.

One of the primary goals in leadership is the ability to be flexible and adaptable to the needs and purposes of the group. For instance, with parents who have read everything on child care from Benjamin Spock to Haim Ginott, the leader's role would be to guide the group in applying concepts on an individual basis. However, with a less well-informed parent group, this leader might need to use printed material on the stages of development and sex education.

CONCEPTS OF
FAMILY LIFE EDUCATION

Family life education is a method of service applicable to people from all socioeconomic levels and educational backgrounds. In each group the leader abided by the age-old social work concept—"Start where the client is." Some groups were not ready for learning about family dynamics or problem solving; the teenagers who lived in foster homes were one example. They were suspicious, distrustful, and hostile, and the goals of the group were limited to socialization and some group identity. Because discussion was not fruitful, the leader used games, role playing, and other similar techniques.

Most parents desire a better life for their children than they have had, and they hope to avoid the same mistakes made by their parents. These hopes and desires are present in teenagers. The presence of certain concerns that people have about themselves and their families is the concept of universality, an important one in family life groups. In addition to these universal concerns, there are also individual differences and responses to life which provide each group with its uniqueness.

Parental anxiety is alleviated through examining old ideas and replacing them with new understanding of the parents' feelings and reactions and the meaning of behavior. Strength is gained through understanding the differences in the developmental stages of children and families. Parents in the group discussions find comfort in realizing that, although there are no easy answers, they are not alone and that there is an opportunity to search for solutions which will work for them and their families. Often during the series, parents or individuals try new methods and report to the group on the outcome.

The goals of learning to assess and handle family problems, developing self-esteem, improving parental functioning, and enhancing the marital relationship were realized to some extent in most of the groups. One woman said she had learned that everyone has a choice; for example, with her children it might be either to "do something" or "get clobbered," but everyone does have a choice. Recognition that each person is an individual with worth was illustrated by a withdrawn woman who brought a beautifully home-decorated cake to a meeting and received recognition for this contribution, even though she was not able to contribute verbally. Another woman expressed relief that her feelings and reactions were similar to those of the other women in the group. A teenage boy discovered that he was able to relate to an adult woman without either being dominated and controlled or having to run away to escape. One couple realized that they had been avoiding inti-

macy in their marriage by being involved with projects and constant activity; they decided to learn to communicate with each other and develop closeness.

Learning from each other through group discussion may have more relevance for parents today than at any other time since CSAA had its origin in 1888. At that time a small group of mothers in New York City banded together for the purpose of becoming better parents. Margaret Mead has evolved an interesting concept which relates to parents of today. In *Culture and Commitment* she describes parents as immigrants in our present culture.[7] According to her, parents are being replaced by peers as the significant models of behavior in this "cofigurative culture." In the family life education groups, parents can learn from their peers and do not feel as alone as immigrants in this time of rapid change, decay, and breakdown of the family and society.

CONCLUSION

The family life education program is a valuable asset to the total agency's purpose of developing wholesome family life through education for family living and prevention of individual and family breakdown. It is not always an end in itself, but it is often a springboard for those who need further indepth counseling or referral for other specialized community services. The philosophy and method is flexible and can be effective with various types of community groups.

Because of the time-limited nature of the groups, they provide a valuable opportunity for training students and new workers in group process, child development, and family dynamics. The trainee can be involved in the group from its beginning through the end. This program is truly an outreach approach of taking the service to the people. Only one of the eight groups was conducted within the agency. The others were held in churches, community centers, state agencies, and institutions. The public relations work inherent in the coordination of the groups can only enhance the collaborative effort in providing services to people within the community.

The beginning was bright, and every effort is being made to ensure that the family life education program in the Greater Little Rock area does not burn itself out. Plans are under way to contract for other federal monies to be used in augmenting the program. The potential for another discussion series with the original groups is good. Double the original number of groups have expressed interest in a family life education series. There will be a continual need for keeping the program before the public through various avenues of publicity.

"Project ENABLE," or PECO as it is known in Little Rock, has been phased out by the federal government, effective September 1, 1971. The program did enable the parents in the poverty communities of Pulaski County, Arkansas, to provide better homes and community environments for their children. Lines of communication were opened between neighborhood residents and the power structure and resulted in improved utility services, health clinics, day-care centers, and so on. One group with a number of mothers rearing their sons without fathers was instrumental in the establishment of the first Big Brothers program in the county.

The original discussion leader for ENABLE incorporated these concepts in a statewide mental health project, Mental Health Education to the Family and Community, which was funded by the National Institute of Mental Health. Project ENABLE also gave impetus to [the] Family Service Agency of Pulaski County in the development of the family life education program about which this article is written. It did "enable" in this community.

NOTES

[1]See Aline B. Auerbach, *Parents Learn through Discussion: Principles and Practices of Parent Group Education* (New York: John Wiley & Sons, 1968), p. 4.

[2]Peter B. Neubauer, The Technique of Parent Group Education: Some Basic Concepts, in *Parent Group Education and Leadership Training* (New York: Child Study Association of America, 1953), p. 11.

[3]Alline del Valle and Felton Alexander, Effects of the Project on Family Service Agencies and Urban Leagues, *Social Casework*, 48:633–38 (December 1967).

[4]Ellen P. Manser, Jeweldean Jones, and Selma B. Ortof, An Overview of Project ENABLE, *Social Casework*, 48:609 (December 1967).

[5]Auerbach, *Parents Learn Through Discussion*, pp. 160–79.

[6]Leadership Training Institute, Little Rock, Arkansas, August 21–September 1, 1967, conducted by Alline del Valle, consultant, Family Life Education and Group Services, Houston, Texas.

[7]Margaret Mead, *Culture and Commitment: A Study of the Generation Gap*, paperback ed. (New York: Doubleday & Co., 1970), p. 51.

LOBBYING AND SOCIAL WORK

Maryann Mahaffey

How does a social worker influence the legislative and administrative process to achieve the profession's social policy objectives? The literature on social work—and other human service professions—is virtually devoid of materials delineating the discrete sequence of actions necessary.

What are the objectives of the social work profession?[1] Specific and immediate goals vary widely in the different fields of practice, but in general social workers consistently seek to expand social and rehabilitation services for those who are powerless, dis-

criminated against, shackled by circumstances, and deprived of opportunities to achieve their maximum individual potential. We also seek to change the environment in order to reduce the needs and to help people reach their individual potential.

In view of the increasing recognition of societal and environmental effects on personal well-being, systems theory should be helpful in analyzing the individual's needs, detecting problems that prevent realization of potential, and designing interventions to help. Most social workers seek those changes in sys-

Source: Copyright 1972, National Association of Social Workers, Inc. Reprinted with permission from *Social Work*, Vol. 17, No. 1 (January 1972), pp. 3–11. This paper is a revision of a version presented at the National Conference on Social Welfare, Chicago, Illinois, June 4, 1970, and published in *Social Work* Vol. 17, No. 1 (January 1972).

tems—individual, group, and societal—which will lead to better services for more people. In working toward this target, we should be aware that a system consists of many subsystems and that factors outside the system itself can influence its functioning.

Systems theory, however, inadequately reflects the past and scantily provides for future evolution. Moreover, it is static because it neglects to analyze power, conflict, and values and their influence on systems and events. Many sociologists are reexploring dialectical theory with the hope that they can use it to analyze current events, provide a base for interpreting change, and develop means to create change.

It seems clear that for some time to come this society will be governed by present political structures. Therefore, social workers should know how to use the existing political system for the benefit of the people we are committed to serve, the people with whom we are seeking to achieve a better world. As many of us are learning, we must influence the political process if we are to achieve change.

To influence the political process, it is necessary to understand it. Applying problem-solving procedures would be helpful. These involve: (1) defining the problem, (2) surveying the setting and participants' roles, (3) assessing forces concerned, including contradictory and countervailing forces, (4) determining goals and objectives, (5) implementing plans, and (6) feeding back information in order to evaluate the process and results to determine next moves in creating change.

Politics has been variously termed the art or science of government, the art of balancing, the art of compromise, the art of the possible, the art of dissimulation, and the exercise of power. The governmental system itself is a system of checks and balances based on the concept of multiple decision centers. Since the governed include disparate groups and individuals who have widely varying interests and objectives, those involved in the political process are inevitably concerned with dialectics. They are constantly seeking to identify forces that are dying or coming to life and to assess the new problems created by solving old ones. Thus politics and government embrace such strategies and tactics as struggle and confrontation, negotiation, compromise, coalitions, and gaining and utilizing power to move ahead step by step toward agreed-upon goals and objectives.

Struggle.   Through struggle and striving for reform, people learn to identify their self-interest and distinguish friends from enemies. They begin to understand what the real issues are and to avoid secondary concerns that deplete their energies and deflect them from major goals. They learn to work together and build power based on numbers that can counteract other kinds and levels of power such as money or position. For example, those participating in various liberation struggles—women, blacks, Chicanos, Native Americans, and other oppressed minorities—are learning that by working together they can exert power to reduce exploitation of any group or individual. Struggle often requires confronting the opposition and demands a willingness to fight for rights as well as privileges.

Negotiation.   Lobbying might well be compared to union negotiating. Both union negotiator and lobbyist have to deal with and come to terms with the boss in a small group meeting. The union negotiator must continually remember the constituents' fundamental interests, as well as the interests and power of the opposition. The negotiator must know the realm of the possible and continuously probe to expand the limits.

The same is true for the management negotiator who has to report to the board and stockholders—as the lobbyist must report to the employing organization. The negotiator or lobbyist who forgets the power of his/her supporters and the thrust of their goals cannot do the job efficaciously in the long run. In fact, constituents could be sold out.

COOPERATION

Perhaps the most telling political axiom is "union gives strength." The lobbyist knows little can be done alone. The cooperation of others is constantly sought in many aspects of the work. Colleagues are co-opted to expedite certain measures. Coalitions and alliances are deliberately formed to serve organizational ends.

Compromise.   The lobbyist must be prepared to fight for as much as he/she can get and often be willing to forfeit one provision to obtain another. Compromise should lead to long-term gains rather than loss. In negotiating the best that is possible at the moment, conditions may be accepted that do not favor the establishment of a basic principle advancing the major objective. For example, a lobbyist might support the president's Family Assistance Plan because it establishes the principle of federal responsibility for minimum income through grossly inadequate family allowances that include the working poor—though opposing the forced work subsidization of low wages and continuation of the means test. Before negotiating a compromise, the lobbyist should resolve three key questions: What principles are basic? Where is the line drawn between establishing a principle and selling out? What is acceptable to the sponsoring group?

In addition, the positions must be clear and argued out before the compromise is struck, rather than settling before positions have been firmed in anticipation of resistance.

Step-by-Step Progress. Once a principle is established, there is always the hope that a measure can be improved in the future. Amendments may relate, for instance, to expanding coverage, broadening services, or revising disadvantageous provisions. Small as well as big victories in the negotiating process strengthen massive demonstrations and protest movements. It is difficult to sustain a massive effort without periodic concrete achievement. Small victories build people's faith both in their ability to create change and in their change agent. The challenge lies in helping people see that the immediate success is a step along the way to the larger victory and to recognize that this step-by-step progress is a way of building power.

Use of Power. The political process inevitably involves strategies for using power. These range from simple persuasion—through bargaining and exchanging—to manipulation, dissimulation, and coercion. It is the wise lobbyist who so uses power that friends and allies are retained while objectives are obtained.

Sometimes those engaged in the political process become enthralled with the game, the means, and the power, developing an inflated pride in their own cleverness and skill with words and facts. It is a cardinal rule that the lobbyist must never lose sight of change objectives. She/he must always remember that the political process operates within a system, that the lobbyist is an agent for change, and that lobbying encompasses a methodology for creating that change. Lobbying is not an end in itself.

BARRIERS TO INTERACTION

Social workers have many illusions and misconceptions about the political process and politicians. Couple these with the public stereotypes of social workers and the barriers to effective social worker–politician relationships become evident. These barriers must be broken down if social workers are to achieve credibility and influence as lobbyists.

Limited Knowledge. Many social workers have limited knowledge about governmental structure and even the basic principles of civics and economics. Too few understand that a bill goes through a series of steps before it is voted on. Thus few bills can survive the total legislative process as originally written. While the bill is in process, the legislator proves she/he is on the job by proposing, supporting, or opposing—often with other colleagues—various deletions, revisions, and additions, taking whatever action seems most appropriate to protect one's own and the constituents' interests. Politicians serving as ombudsmen for constituents continually deal with the messes created by themselves, powerful interests, and bureaucracies in which "their people" were cheated or harassed by complicated regulations or inefficient administrators. They are under constant pressure to find immediate solutions to difficult problems. The politician knows that issues are embedded in feelings—including their colleagues' competitiveness for position.

Disdain. All too often social workers look on the political process with disdain and aversion. Many consider politicians as reactionary, venal old men who make deals and sell out their principles. These generalizations may sweep the social worker off course and deter actions social work training would indicate: to diagnose the politician's concerns and relationships, locate the people who could be helpful allies or supporters, and search for areas of common interest and consequent influence.

Impatience. Social workers sometimes become impatient with the prolonged time involved in creating change, and some lack the staying power to survive the compromises, twists, and turns of the political process. They perhaps forget that the larger the system, the more complex and difficult it is to change. Many of them consider that their rights of self-determination and individual decision making are eroded by the disciplined group effort necessary to remain in the political mainstream, keep track of the complex interplay of forces, and maintain effective coalitions.

ILLUSIONS

Much has been written about politicians' reactions to crises of the moment, but it is an illusion that all politicians lack values and long-range goals. One state senator, for example, measures every bill and governmental action by its effect on the poor blacks who make up his constituency. He is a supporter of government as the employer of last resort. He thinks the government subsidizes the rich and penalizes the poor and he wants to reverse that. Believing in accountability to those who elected him, he holds an annual legislative conference and monthly public sessions with constituents. He assiduously works to build support in his district.

Another state senator has introduced legislation to establish subsidized adoption and increase the assets elderly citizens can have and still qualify for Old Age Assistance; yet, he also introduced legislation to reduce the Aid to Dependent Children allotment called for by the state's governor. He is a businessman from a rural area concerned with preserving free enterprise, limiting the central government's powers, and if possible, reducing governmental expenditures.

Naiveté. Social workers are often incredibly naive about politicians and the political process. Some believe that politicians are so powerful that they are unapproachable. They forget that politicians usually want to get reelected in order to retain their position, move to higher office, or increase their power and influence. Therefore, politicians are vulnerable to voter pressure at selected points, especially by those in their own districts. They forget, too, that politicians are not always consistent. In addition, there are politicians who by virtue of their work to maintain a base in their district have been able to take advanced positions and continue in office. Congressman Dellums's support of national health care is an example.

There are social workers who view themselves as morally and ethically superior and tend to rely on individual moral suasion to influence the politician. They are not being realistic. Should a legislator's colleagues be trying, for example, to avoid raising taxes, the legislator knows that morality cannot be used to sway them even if the legislator believes strongly in the moral principle at stake. Politicians have long memories about casualties at the polls and recall all too vividly those who were defeated because they sponsored tax increases at the wrong time, although for altruistic reasons.

Politicians' Viewpoints. The social worker–lobbyist is one of many trying to influence politicians. She/he is not generally in a favorable position at the outset. Politicians often believe that the social worker lacks

political sophistication. They think social workers avoid conflict they cannot control—and consequently lack the will to join in long-term support of or sustained attack on a controversial position. Also, some politicians distrust "intellectual" professionals. Because of such negative attitudes, the social worker–lobbyist may not always receive a prompt and warm reception. Thus there is a need for a delicate balance—avoiding oversensitivity about oneself, keeping long-range goals in mind, but remaining sensitive to the legislator's feelings.

Yet the social worker's potential position can be advantageous. Rather than being the supplicants, we can be the suppliers of life-giving skills and coveted information. Politicians are perpetually concerned about getting feedback from varied sources to check their facts and impressions. They are constantly searching for reliable information about conditions and relationships in communities they represent. The social worker–lobbyist, with training in social relationships and specific knowledge about people's deprivations and needs and about the services existing to meet needs, should be perennially helpful. We will have to be persistent, however, and prove the value of our expertise.

Many politicians believe change could be created more readily and people helped more if social workers showed less concern for self-protection and greater eagerness to help clean up politics—including willingness to run for public office. Since the elected governing bodies of the nation represent major potential change sites, the stakes are high. They are especially high if social worker–lobbyists are ready to engage in the long, arduous, and time-consuming task of educating people in regard to their self-interest and organizing them to influence the political process. It is essential that social workers be elected to public office and that others support them with time and money.

LOBBYIST'S FUNCTION

The lobbyist is a person paid (and/or contracted with) to represent an organization officially with governmental officeholders, groups, and agencies. Most lobbying relates to special interest bills, is pursued with legislative and governmental administrative leaders, and does not ordinarily receive public attention. In recent years, citizens' groups on specific issues have been on the increase.

General Responsibilities. The social worker–lobbyist protects the organization's interests in the legislature and with administrative units, while endeavoring to present a personal image of tact, integrity, and discretion. She/he has primary responsibility for establishing contacts for the organization, ascertaining limits of action, and apprising the organization's leaders of findings so they can decide their course.

The Effective Lobbyist. The effective lobbyist must be a person of varied skills who can be depended on by client, organization, and legislator alike.[2] The agent is friendly, outgoing, articulate, logical, and persuasive. The good lobbyist can work independently, following the organization's general directives. She/he is flexible and willing to maintain irregular work hours if necessary. The lobbyist has the maturity to argue vociferously on one issue, be a friendly partner on another, and ignore personal rebuffs by either friend or foe. Above all, the good lobbyist knows when to talk and when to listen. The good lobbyist also knows how to wait. It's not necessary to buy lunches, but politicians do remember who supports them and who contributes money to their campaign. Campaigns are expensive and most politicians hate fund raising.

NEEDED SKILLS

The social worker–lobbyist should be skilled and experienced in the strategies and tactics involved in changing the political process, i.e., harnessing struggle, negotiating, compromising, cooperating, moving ahead step by step, and using power. A sophisticated sense of timing must be developed and a sense of appropriateness. The lobbyist must be perceptive about when to propose changes and know how to maneuver among the various interest groups. For instance, if there is to be a demonstration, she/he should be able to recommend astutely when and where it might be held, how many might participate, and what the target should be. If time and place are wrong, if too few or too many take part, if the target is poorly chosen, results may be psychologically damaging for participants, let alone the cause itself.

The lobbyist is familiar with parliamentary procedure, studies the structure of the legislature and other governmental bodies, and gathers helpful information about incumbent officeholders and legislators. She/he develops the skills needed to glamorize a specific issue and keep it alive with legislators who

are inundated with issues.[3] The lobbyist knows how and when to seize the initiative and put the pressure on through phone calls, letters, and meetings with constituents.

The lobbyist develops the ability to diagnose individual and group motivation, knowing how to analyze forces operative in the field and probe for areas of compromise. Strategies are suggested and ways to use them recommended. A good lobbyist becomes aware of the stresses and strains between houses of the legislature, various levels and branches of government, parties, factions, and individual officeholders. The lobbyist learns about the power of committee chairs and members—and their secretaries and their aides, who are sometimes the key to reaching them. The aides should be cultivated, for often the politician is too busy to go into detail and is buffeted by many issues. Therefore, the politician relies on aides to analyze and summarize, as well as to recommend action and strategy. Such is particularly true of administrators. A big part of politicians' work is constituent complaints so it is important to gear discussions to their constituent needs.

Most legislation is modified and defeated in committee and many times it is easier to defeat a bill than pass it.

A lobbyist may discover that the chair of a powerful committee is unshakable on certain issues but willing to compromise on others. A certain chair may lack leadership ability and be unable to twist arms, trade on bills, and get legislation through. Another legislator is a good diagnostician, is tough and willing to risk his or her own future for the fate of a crucial issue, knows his or her goals, and wields tremendous power through control over the agenda and skillful use of the rule of the gavel. That legislator may be the key to achieving the organization's objectives.

MAJOR TASKS

The duties of a social worker–lobbyist are many and varied. Major tasks may be summarized briefly as follows:

1. Offering the expertise of the social work profession to legislators, who find it impossible to study and understand all the numerous bills they must consider. The lobbyist volunteers support and information and in turn seeks support and data helpful to the employing organization.

The lobbyist offers technical assistance at the appropriate moment on one bill, provides research results before the crisis level is reached on another, and organizes and exerts constituent pressure on still another—maintaining bipartisan relationships on all. Sometimes the lobbyist organizes support for the politician, enabling the politician to "go out on a limb";

2. Keeping track of pertinent legislation, whether it is sponsored or opposed by the client organization. The lobbyist finds out who would be best for supporting certain legislation and works closely with that lawmaker, discovering who wants to amend the bill and how and why, checking on positions of administrative departments, the chief executive's office, and the others concerned. Amendments agreed to by the sponsoring organization are ready to be offered to legislators;

3. Paying special attention to committee votes, which are not publicized, are often difficult to ascertain, yet are vital in targeting organizational influence. The lobbyist seeks to know what is happening in party caucuses because positions are hammered out and deals often made in these important meetings;

4. Developing contacts with other lobbyists and sharing information with them, as the agent looks for common goals, and sounds out possibilities for potential coalitions;

5. Developing a liaison between the organization and the legislative body. The lobbyist pins down votes and follows up on why legislators voted the way they did. The lobbyist feeds information back to the client organization and its members. She/he may also be helpful in contacting the press and setting up press conferences, working with the organization's public relations director or committee;

6. Assisting the client organization to train and organize its members in influencing the political process, working with the organization, and planning and coordinating delegations, demonstrations, members' appearances at committee hearings, and presence when the vote is taken.

THE EMPLOYING ORGANIZATION

Political power develops when people are organized, united, and active. Social work organizations should organize their members and be able to mobilize them as necessary. Having a lobbyist may stimulate such action. In employing one, the organization clearly indicates the lobbyist's responsibilities and the person to whom the agent answers. The organization itself is primarily responsible for organizing its members, educating them on issues, keeping them informed about events, and unearthing those who know and have influence with legislators—including agency board members who have largely been unutilized and unorganized for political action. However, it may be part of the lobbyist's job to assist in this work.

The organization is also responsible for keeping issues alive among its members, which involves the constant struggle of competing with countless other demands. A piece of legislation can take five years or more to pass, and in the prolonged process, members can forget reasons for early compromises and priorities. When an organization is splintered at a crucial moment, it may lose the legislation because legislators will say, "If you are not together, we are not going to bother with the bill and your position on it." Alerting members to progress on major issues is vital. This can be done through newsletters or special bulletins which may cover questions raised, arguments used, and key opposition or support gained or lost. A "telephone tree" or network such as the NASW ELAN system is essential.

The social work organization should train its members in working with politicians so that they can take on tasks needed to push the legislation ahead. Members should be organized so that they can be tapped when a critical point in the legislative process is reached. This action includes a carefully timed phone-calling campaign (with messages left with the politician's secretary or aide), contacts in meetings, handwritten one-paragraph letters, presence in numbers (sometimes with signs) at hearings, testimony at hearings, and equally visible presence when the vote is taken, followed by written thank-yous or acknowledgments.

Electioneering and Party Work. Some social workers can help elect candidates of their choice. More must become candidates. Some members may work within the party structure preparing resolutions for party committees and building a base of party support. Thus social workers can be in situations conducive to developing the legislators' confidence and trust. Too many social workers are not familiar with their rights, nor do they know the extent of possible political activity even under legislation like the Hatch Act.

EXPERT KNOWLEDGE

Many social workers are relied upon by elected officials for expertise in their specific fields. They provide supporting data for bills in their area of competence, give requested advice, analyze bills, and draft legislative proposals or amendments. Those who are experienced in preparing such materials know that a premium is placed on brief, succinct statements. They learn to prepare one-page summaries that begin with a one-sentence statement of the problem, document needs, state pros and cons, furnish precedents and costs—and, above all, are honest. A trusted constituent may read a summary aloud to an official or point out its salient facts because elected officeholders do not have much time for in-depth reading. It is important to deal with one issue at a time—seldom more than three. Be willing to talk to the aides.

Constituent Pressure. At times the membership may be called upon to exert needed constituent pressure. Mass mailings, directed as the occasion warrants to legislators or chairs or members of committees, are sometimes useful; only, however, if there are unusually large numbers mailed in a concentrated time period. Constituents' praise for politicians and their thanks for their efforts—successful or not—are also important. At times the outstanding expertise, authority, or influence of a specific agency member or board member may be called for. For example, influential social workers may affect the committee assignment of bills, thus helping to save favored legislation.

Testimony at Hearings. The organization's members should be prepared to testify before committee. The lobbyist should hold an orientation session with them beforehand, telling them what may be expected of them, pointing out elements of an impressive presentation, and warning of pitfalls to avoid. Role playing would also be helpful. Members' appearances at hearings are coordinated through the lobbyist and the designated organizational legislative chairman. Common faults that create hazards for the testifier are issuing moral arguments without concrete accompanying proposals, making statements that are not backed up by adequate research and documentation, failing to touch base with others involved, and using confrontation tactics that can alienate the politician. Such attacks may win audience attention but turn off the politician and political colleagues. It is also important to be concise and short in presentations.

Unfortunately, some public hearings merely seek to document positions already determined. Realizing this, some legislators may not be influenced by

hearings, but they nevertheless serve several useful purposes. They provide opportunities to: (1) spotlight issues, (2) educate the public and arouse public opinion, (3) publicize the positions and proposed solutions of those testifying, (4) educate committee members, and (5) permit legislators to test public reactions to their positions. Hearings can create publicity for the politician and for the issue.

One group didn't want the hearing with the politician, for they didn't want to share the publicity; however, the press didn't know them and, without the politician, their hearing was not covered by the media. Politicians are often willing to share the spotlight and highlight the group in a hearing.

Priorities. The organization should establish priorities and stick to them. A lobbyist can work well on only a limited number of bills. A member can devote time and enthusiasm to a limited number of issues. The organization might be wise to concentrate on a few significant legislative measures that have some likelihood of passage, rather than scatter its efforts on a dozen or more minor measures and waste time on provisions that are perennially defeated. At the same time it is important to remember that one must always be on the alert to the sleeper, i.e., be ready to mobilize forces to defeat legislation or change legislation that may not be on the priority list but might suddenly develop strength in the legislative body.

MODEL FOR LEGISLATIVE ACTION

The target date is the January session of a state legislature.

Previous Spring. Discuss with key members of the organization the specific legislative propositions to be worked on, including areas of agreement and items that can be compromised if need be.

Previous Summer. Select an organizational steering committee and a coordinator with whom the lobbyist will plan and carry out the following activities to implement strategy:

1. Collect evidence providing the rationale of need for the proposed legislation;

2. Draft petition for social workers and community residents, to be addressed to legislators and signed according to legislative districts. (Social workers' refusals to sign may indicate opposition within the organization);

3. Arrange for the organization's members to form district delegations and name delegation chair-

persons. Hold district delegation meetings with lawmakers to explore support. If an election year, there should be meetings with all candidates to ascertain their positions on issues. Assign two member constituents to each legislator to get to know him or her before and during the session. Make appointments; outline in writing the issues (no more than three) you wish to discuss. Make your visit short; be succinct.

Previous Fall. Form a small committee representing a cross section of the membership. These people should have the enthusiasm and the available time to be part of periodic delegations to the government halls. Their work during the fall is exploratory; demands and pressure come later:

1. Arrange for an official visit with the chief executive by the committee to ascertain his viewpoints. Leave a brief written account of the points you want to make—solutions and documentation;

2. Meet with appropriate leaders of the organization to report findings as well as select and order priorities;

3. If not an election year, select sponsors of new legislation and meet with them. Tie the issue to their constituents' interests;

4. If an election year, arrange delegation meetings in legislative districts to meet with primary winners and assess their support on issues with high priority.[4] After the election, arrange for the committee to meet with the winners and obtain commitments;

5. Obtain commitments from allies and form coalitions when possible;

6. Discuss legislation with key administrators, ascertaining their level of support or opposition and the changes they may favor.

January. All important initial contacts should have been made previously. The beginning of the session is a time for consolidating positions with lawmakers, exerting preliminary pressures on major measures, and offering social work expertise on bills under consideration:

1. Arrange for a committee delegation to visit the chief executive and aides to obtain active support for desired legislation and bring letters from other members favoring it. Visits might also be arranged with key lawmakers and aides;

2. Present to each legislator lists of bills the organization supports and opposes;

3. Continue to collect and analyze background information about lawmakers; keep records of political contacts and actions;

4. Report to the organization's members via newsletter.

Throughout Session. After the legislative bodies have chosen their officers and their committee chairpersons and members—about mid-January—the work goes forward and continues throughout the session:

1. Make sure of promised support;

2. Work with legislators on introduction of measures;

3. Visit lawmakers to enlist allies and assess strength;

4. Send newsletters regularly to key members of the organization (perhaps weekly). Include district delegation chairs;

5. Send monthly report letters to the organization's total membership;

6. Hold organizational steering committee meetings regularly to decide about compromises, arrange members' visits to legislators, discuss coalitions, and so on. The feedback system is crucial to success in influencing the political process;

7. Thank legislators, administrators, and all others who provided support.

SUMMARY

Lawmakers will continue to be influenced by a variety of people and organizations. A growing number of social workers can be among the influencers. But if social workers are to serve effectively as lobbyists, they must have training in the political process and acquire increased political sophistication. The field as a whole must grow in the ability to use conflict, develop power, and be decisive and prepared to take risks while applying the art of compromise. Lobbying demands that social workers utilize to the fullest their diagnostic and organizational skills. It may well prove easier to train a social worker to be a lobbyist than to train a lobbyist to understand and represent social work goals.

The lobbyist must marry social action and practice. To achieve change the agent must have experience, skills, and knowledge so the lawmaker can be provided with needed authoritative information. The social worker–lobbyist can maintain commitment to social work philosophy and values only if she/he clearly defines the objectives, relates means to ends, and establishes proximate and middle-range goals consonant with and directed toward long-range goals. Compromise can establish a principle to be developed in future legislation. But the lobbyist must be willing to continue the fight to expand the principle and be clear about where to draw the line so that a sellout is avoided.

The late Whitney M. Young, Jr., said in his closing remarks to the 1969 NASW Delegate Assembly: "I think that social work is uniquely equipped to play a major role in the social and human renaissance of our society."[5]

There *are* social workers who are successfully influencing the political process, as well as social workers who have been elected to municipal, state, and national offices. The profession needs more of them.

NOTES

[1]For discussion of social work purposes and goals, see William E. Gordon, "A Critique of the Working Definition," *Social Work*, Vol. 7, No. 4 (October 1962), pp. 3–13.

[2]In 1960, 46 percent of the Michigan legislative lobbyists were college educated and experienced in government. The lawmakers looked to them for information, expertise, and most important, attitudes and opinions of constituents. The old-time lobbyists who openly buy their way are less in evidence as the caliber of legislators improves in Michigan. See Walter De Vries, "The Michigan Lobbyist: A Study in the Bases and Perceptions of Effectiveness." Unpublished doctoral thesis, Michigan State University, 1960.

[3]In Michigan, for example, some 3000 bills were introduced into the 1970 legislature, with the normal session running from January to June.

[4]A 1971 NASW Delegate Assembly resolution titled "Attack on the Social Welfare Profession and the Poor and Disadvantaged" calls on NASW members to "... move immediately on a program of holding elected and appointed officials responsible for their performance including becoming actively involved in the full range of activities designed to influence the political process, implying member participation in electoral politics and the defeat of those officials who attack the poor and disadvantaged and the profession of social work...."

[5]"Society Needs 'To Care,' Said Whitney Young," *NASW News*, Vol. 16, No. 4 (May 1971), p. 3.

CONFRONTING RACISM IN INNER-CITY SCHOOLS

Howard E. Prunty, Terry L. Singer, Lindsay A. Thomas

The community mental health movement has concerned itself with consultation to schools since the mid-1960s, when community demand for more accessible mental health services arose.[1] Although debates about methodology have taken place between advocates of the case conference and proponents of systems change, it is clear that the ideological thrust behind mental health consultation to schools has been toward primary prevention.[2] As the racial turmoil of the late sixties erupted, mental health consultation to schools could have taken a new direction.

Creative energies might have turned to the development of responses and activities that would reduce patterns of discrimination and segregation in the schools. Generally, however, school consultation failed to face the problem of racism, the major issue in question for most urban areas.[3]

Most studies of mental health consultation to poverty or inner-city agencies do not even mention racism, let alone attempt to formulate systematic responses to it. Although many researchers have found a high correlation between racial prejudice and men-

---

tal health issues, the problem of racism, as Willie, Kramer, and Brown have pointed out, is seldom a specialization area in state and local mental health departments.[4] Caplan's definition of primary prevention points up the need for a mental health specialty area concerned with racism and its effects. According to Caplan, primary prevention should involve:

identifying current harmful influences, the environmental forces which would support individuals in resisting them, and those environmental forces which influence the resistance of the population to future pathogenic experience.[5]

The Community Mental Health and Mental Retardation Center located in [the] Western Psychiatric Institute and Clinic in Pittsburgh pursued a new approach to school consultation by addressing the following concerns: (1) the prevention of mental health problems as it relates to the developmental stages of the middle-school child, (2) the development of the middle-school child as it is affected by cultural and racial differences in an integrated environment, and (3) institutional racism. This article traces the development of the approach, describes the project in which it was utilized, and discusses its implications for future consultative efforts.

PROJECT DEVELOPMENT

The Community Mental Health and Mental Retardation Center serves one of ten catchment areas in Allegheny County. The center is centrally located within Pittsburgh, in a triangular area bounded by two large rivers. The broad cultural and racial diversity of the area is striking. The presence of rivers, railroads, and other physical barriers tending to segment the city has contributed to its ethnocentricity; it remains one of the most ethnically diverse urban centers in the United States. The city's ethnocentricity influences the way in which its residents utilize mental health services. The Community Mental Health and Mental Retardation Center has therefore worked energetically to shape and plan services based on an understanding of the influences of culture and race on mental health and mental illness. Treatment services, consultative and educational programs, and outreach activities have been structured to reflect cultural, ethnic, and racial differences among the population through the use of satellite offices and mental health teams composed of staff members from different cultural groups.

The high degree of ethnocentricity found among Pittsburgh's population significantly affected the movement to integrate its public schools. Many individuals and organizations that supported integration became community allies. The Consortium, an informally structured coalition of community groups, city-wide agencies, parents, and school officials, was one such organization. The Community Mental Health and Mental Retardation Center joined with the Consortium to determine what role the center might play in easing racial tensions and improving intergroup relations in the schools. In addition to its concerns regarding the prevention of mental health problems in the schools, the center's staff was motivated by the recognition that the goals of school integration would be difficult to achieve unless the problems of racial friction and discriminatory practices in the schools were confronted openly.

Shortly after the formation of the Consortium in May 1975, a marathon series of meetings involving school officials, social agencies, and parent groups was held. With the help of a local foundation, in one month a package of proposals was developed and grant requests totaling $160,678 were submitted for approval. The foundation approved the grant requests in early July. The proposals had been developed to provide skilled mental health consultation that would assist school personnel in the following ways: (1) by increasing their understanding of social and cultural differences, (2) by improving their ability to handle racial conflicts, and (3) by expanding their knowledge of the developmental needs of children.

Designing a program to help school personnel cope with problems related to racial and cultural differences presented a unique problem: Should consideration be given to the race of the consultants themselves? Should they be white? black? Or should consultants of both races be sent to a school? The merits and disadvantages of the alternatives were discussed, and it was decided for the following reasons that a racially mixed team of consultants would be used:

It was necessary to demonstrate to school personnel that evenhandedness would be used in dealing with specific racial and ethnic problems in the school and with the developmental needs of the children;

The presence of a consultant from each race would initially reduce the anxieties, fears, and latent concerns of white school personnel;

The relationship between the consultants would serve as a model to demonstrate how positive contact between whites and blacks could be developed;

The interaction between consultants from different races and cultures and the sharing of insights, experiences, and perceptions would produce dynamic and effective methods of intervention.

Accordingly, two mental health consultants—one, a black woman, the other, a white man—were assigned full time to a middle school in the fall of 1975. The school had approximately 1600 students—51 percent of whom were white and 49 percent black—and approximately 100 faculty and other staff members. It was felt that the full-time presence of the consultants would help reduce staff resistance to the fact that they were not school personnel and would also facilitate the development of trust between themselves and members of the school staff.

IMPLEMENTATION

The first phase of the project was directed toward the introduction of the two mental health consultants to the school, toward their gaining visibility and credibility, and toward their implementation of consultative strategies regarding the developmental needs of children, and racial and cultural differences. By placing the consultants in the school four days a week to maximize their accessibility, their initial period of orientation and of observation of the school took place not only in classrooms and staff meetings, but also in hallways, lunchrooms, and teacher lounges. The consultants' accessibility allowed them to be seen as resources available when needed.

This early phase of the project was primarily a period of observation in which the developmental needs of the children in the classroom were examined and aspects of institutional racism in the school were assessed. The white male consultant assumed responsibility for personnel dealing with sixth-grade classes, physical education, occupational and vocational studies, and fine arts; the black female consultant assumed responsibility for staff dealing with seventh-grade and eighth-grade classes. Some of the concerns expressed by teachers during this early phase of the project were related to discipline, classroom arguments between black and white children,

and the tension resulting from those arguments. Many teachers requested some form of in-service training to address these issues; others continued to seek consultation for individual cases and concerns.

The consultants were able to establish a high degree of trust between themselves and the school staff during the initial period of the project. This trust blossomed into informal and often unspoken agreements between consultants and staff. At first, the consultants sought teacher permission to sit in on particular classes as observers. These early observations helped them construct an accurate frame of reference from which to view in perspective the problems they were beginning to detect. The observations also aroused the curiosity of the teachers observed. They began to seek feedback regarding the consultants' perceptions of classroom dynamics and of the children. In turn, the consultants responded by providing them with feedback that was nonjudgmental and essentially descriptive. The nonevaluative nature of the observations helped teachers feel less threatened by the consultants' presence.

Teachers soon began to request that certain children be observed. In most cases, these children had repeatedly been physically expelled from classes as disruptive to the classroom process. Most had been suspended more than once. Teachers applied various labels to these children, such as "socially and emotionally disturbed," "mentally retarded," and "brain injured," and a request for a consultative observation of a child often indicated the desire for confirmation of a label's applicability. Whenever this occurred, the consultants stressed the need for psychological evaluations of these children rather than the use of hastily applied, unreliable labeling.

INITIATION OF WORKSHOPS

Three months after the project's start, a two-month teachers' strike began. During this time the consultants met with the project's director to reevaluate objectives and discuss new strategies. From these meetings came the blueprint for a twelve-week workshop with the following goals: (1) to reduce racist attitudes, (2) to increase awareness of racial and cultural differences, and (3) to increase awareness of issues involving the sexuality of black and white youngsters. In recognition of the fact that institutional racism is a systemwide problem requiring a systemwide response, workshop sessions were to involve the entire staff of the school, including administrators, faculty, aides, secretaries, social workers, and nurse. Workshop goals had been developed on the basis of conferences with school personnel as well as the consultants' observations.

Concern for the success of the school's integration efforts prompted its principal to make workshop participation mandatory on the part of all staff. During workshop sessions, the consultants raised questions about what they considered to be indications of institutional racism in the school. The disproportionate number of suspensions of black children was one such indicator. A similar issue, noted by teachers and consultants alike, involved the frequent assignment of children to instructional units based on skill. This meant that the advanced group was inevitably white and the least advanced black: the school's enrichment program, for example, was disproportionately (90 percent) white. Some teachers questioned aspects of the statistical information brought forward, and some were shocked by the findings. Most, however, doubted that any relationship existed between the figures and the presence of institutional racism. The authors mention this last point to indicate the difficulty of confronting the issue of racism head-on.

The issue of cultural differences was also a problematic one for the school's staff. Many considered it counterproductive to focus on the differences between children, even though remarks were often made that black children seemed more aggressive or mentally slower than their white schoolmates. The comment that "kids are kids" was frequently overheard. In this regard, the consultants first attempted to help staff members develop an awareness and appreciation of cultural and individual differences and then create conditions to accommodate those differences. However, when they attempted to list and discuss differences between black and white children, staff reaction was hostile. One administrator expressed the opinion that such a listing parroted the racist theories of Jensen and Shockley.[6] Some teachers dealt with the sensitive issues that arose in workshop sessions only during individual conferences with the consultants. The combined use of workshop sessions and continuing consultant support helped facilitate awareness of racial issues among staff members.

Another issue, that of interracial sexual relationships, was particularly frightening to teachers and administrators. Two white female students began to follow two black male students aggressively wherever they went in school and after school as well. Teachers and counselors began to express their concern about the sexual relationships that they envisioned developing. A teacher informed the parents of one of the girls that she was "worried about the kind of friends she [the girl] was seeing." One of the consultants succeeded in getting the teachers to focus on the school-related offense, namely, the cutting of classes, that was taking place. At the suggestion of the consultant, the girls and their families were then referred to the school counselor for appropriate help. In this instance, the consultant was able to help the school's staff respond suitably to an issue that was for them overwhelming in its implications.

To complement this phase of the project and provide follow-up to the content and processes of the workshops, consultation to the school staff continued; in fact, the number of requests for individual consultations soon became overwhelming. The requests involved such issues as the acting out of children in classrooms and hallways, apparent confrontations between "aggressive" blacks and "passive" whites during classes, and confrontations and reciprocal namecalling between white teachers and black students. The consultants made use of case conferences, parent meetings, and teacher conferences and continued to develop staff trust and confidence—two important ingredients to successful mental health consultation—through informal gatherings in teacher lounges and lunchrooms.

Throughout the duration of the project, weekly meetings between the consultants and the project's director were held to assess progress continually as well as to maintain some outside perspective on the consultants' involvement. The Community Mental Health and Mental Retardation Center provided the consultants with supervision and guidance, and in conjunction with two other community mental health service units, it also supplied psychiatric facilities and backup services for ongoing diagnostic evaluation and treatment of referrals from the school.

In addition to these contacts, the consultants maintained close communication with those working on other special projects in the school. Since an experimental approach to integration was being undertaken at the school, the community and school board were both involved in providing it with certain resources. Knowledge of the progress and operations of other ongoing projects was often useful to the consultants in their planning. Knowing, for example, that another project had assumed responsibility for working with the children allowed them to concentrate on working with the school staff.

PROJECT EVALUATION

With regard to the project described, consultants could at best be expected to have only indirect effects in terms of creating an environment more favorable to the elimination of racist practices, fostering intergroup processes and relations that would heighten tolerance and sensitize one group to the feelings of another, and heightening awareness of children's developmental needs. However, when evaluation questionnaires intended to measure the effectiveness of the project were completed by the school's staff, they revealed that the overwhelming majority of staff members (80 percent) had found the consultation helpful. School personnel indicated that the consultants had facilitated interfaculty communication and had helped them develop an awareness of problems as well as learn to share the common experiences and difficulties of other staff members. Negative reactions were expressed regarding the mandatory nature of workshop participation, the time involved in such participation, the specific focus of the consultation on racism, and the fact that the consultants "refused to provide answers."

From September 1975 to June 1976, 1942 consultation sessions that encompassed 3823 contacts between consultants and individual staff members were held at the school. The total number of service hours involved in these sessions was 1688, and an additional 861 hours had been devoted to planning and preparation. The sessions took the form of individual case conferences, team meetings, parent conferences, workshop sessions, and other meetings with school personnel. Contact was made with every staff member in the school, and ongoing weekly consultation involved the entire administrative staff, 54 percent of the teaching staff, and 49 percent of the nonteaching staff. The continuous nature of the consultative relationships may indicate the value of the consultants to the school and the fact that certain intrinsic needs of the staff were being met by the consultations. What is not entirely clear at this point is the nature of those needs. On the basis of comments made by school personnel, the consultants believed that many of them derived a great deal of satisfaction from the presence of "someone who would listen and would not pass judgment."

CONSULTATIVE MODEL

In the opinion of the authors, the mental health project helped create an environment in the school conducive to improving both the quality of education and relations among children of different social backgrounds. At the same time, they believe that the project constitutes a model of mental health consultation for the inner-city middle school confronting the issue of racism. They would add, however, that further research is needed to assess fully the implications of this model for efforts toward integration in the schools. More specifically, implementation of the model involves the following:

One of the major issues of urban schools, the prevalence of racism, is addressed directly; most models do not deal with this issue at all;

The success of the model is contingent on three important factors: broad community support (such as that provided by the Consortium), collaboration with the school board, and adequate funding (in this case, supplied by a local foundation);

The consultants are not seen as an extension of the school board because of the adversary relationship that usually characterizes interaction between board and school personnel. Outside funding, such as that obtained through a community mental health center, is therefore used so that consultants will be independent from the board;

Racially mixed teams of consultants are employed. Selecting consultants from different races demonstrates an evenhanded approach, lessens anxieties of white school personnel, serves as a model of interracial cooperation, and provides the consultants themselves with opportunities to share a variety of perspectives;

The consultants are given full-time assignments in the model to accommodate the intensity of feelings that may emerge, to identify potentially explosive racial issues, and to provide continuity and follow-up consultation;

Since they are working with a diverse urban population with regard to a dynamic issue (racism), the consultants are flexible in their techniques, using both the case-conference and the systems-change approach. In contrast to other models characterized by this kind of flexibility, the model places strong emphasis on informal consultative relationships;

Contact is made with the entire school staff because of the pervasive nature of institutional racism;

Arrangements are made for the provision of psychiatric facilities and backup services for ongoing evaluation and treatment of school referrals;

Weekly collaboration with a project director sensitive to the issues of institutional racism is a characteristic of the model. Such collaboration provides additional perspective on consultative efforts and facilitates evaluation and the development of consultative strategies.

CONCLUSION

Achieving racial integration of the country's schools poses many problems. In classes that are no longer segregated, people from different races and different cultures are often brought together for the first time. If this encounter is to be positive in nature, community mental health centers must assume a leadership role in responding to what Goldin has described as "the dramatic call to action in addressing the Number 1 public health problem confronting our country today—racism."[7] This leadership role must include the development of research-based models that blend "innovative ideas and practices with proven bases for professional activity in such a manner that genuine social change is achieved."[8]

NOTES

[1]Samuel B. Sarason, *Psychology in Community Settings: Clinical, Educational, and Social Aspects* (New York: Wiley, 1966); and Emory L. Cowen, Elmer A. Gardner, and M. Zax, *Emergent Approaches to Mental Health Problems* (New York: Appleton-Century-Crofts, 1967).

[2]Emory L. Cowen et al., "The Primary Mental Health Project: A New Way of Conceptualizing and Delivering School Mental Health Services," *Psychology in the Schools*, 8 (1971), pp. 216–225; Emory L. Cowen et al., "The Prevention of Emotional Disorders in the School Setting: A Further Investigation," *Journal of Consulting Psychology*, 30 (1966), pp. 381–387; and L. Anderson, "The Mental Health Center's Role in School Consultation: Toward a New Model," *Community Mental Health Journal*, 12 (1976), pp. 83–88.

[3]Charles V. Willie, Bernard M. Kramer, and Bertram S. Brown, eds., *Racism and Mental Health: Essays* (Pittsburgh: University of Pittsburgh Press, 1973).

[4]Ibid.

[5]Gerald Caplan, *Principles of Preventive Psychiatry* (New York: Basic Books, 1964); p. 27.

[6]Robert A. Jensen, *Educational Differences* (London, Eng.: Methuen, 1973); and William Bradford Shockley, "On Black Genetic Inferiority," *Ebony*, 29 (July 1974), pp. 104–107.

[7]P. Goldin, "Preparing Mental Health Professionals as Race Relations Consultants," *Professional Psychology*, 1 (1970), p. 343.

[8]Ibid., p. 350.

HOW SOCIAL WORK CAN INFLUENCE HOSPITAL MANAGEMENT OF FATAL ILLNESS

Zelda P. Leader Foster

In recent years caseworkers in hospital settings have been urged to broaden the base of their practice and to assume greater responsibility for effecting needed social changes.[1] However, little has been written about how the caseworker can influence the organization in which he works to provide benign and therapeutic influences for all its clients or how he can deliberately effect such changes. This paper

---

will describe the steps and processes of a clinical social worker who intervened actively and purposefully to modify the ward culture for a group of hospital patients.

The setting is the hematology service of a veterans' hospital. The majority of the forty men in this service are married, fathers, and breadwinners and range in age from 25 to 40. They have been admitted for treatment for serious blood diseases: Hodgkin's disease, leukemia, or lymphoma. While periods and degrees of chronicity vary, life expectancy is drastically reduced for all patients. They are followed by the hospital, as inpatients and outpatients, throughout the course of their illness.

THE WARD THAT WAS

To understand why and how the social worker became engaged in a four-year process of ward-wide environmental intervention, it is important to understand the ward culture he encountered, joined, and ultimately challenged. By *ward culture* is meant the patterned ways staff, patients, and families regarded, responded to, and communicated with one another.[2] Of early significance to the social worker was the fact that this culture perpetuated a clearly defined patient role. The troublesome aspect was that this role seemed to prohibit free choices and decisions. Staff and patient culture interlocked to promote and maintain defined patient and doctor roles.

Staff Culture. The structure derived from the staff's commitment to protecting these patients from learning the names and nature of their diseases. Staff had long ago concluded that patients could not bear such knowledge without devastating fear and anguish. Substantiating this assumption was the traditional medical viewpoint that it is correct and humanitarian to protect the patient from unnecessary emotional pain. The psychological justification was that denial is an essential defense against unacceptable pain. This theory reinforced a role model for the doctor that attributed to him the responsibility for knowing what is best for the patient. In turn, the role of other staff members was to carry out the doctor's prescription, free of the burden of decision making. The coping patterns that developed out of the role ascribed to the doctor by his professional training and by society were not unusual. They were no doubt intensified because the staff was dealing with a patient group whose illnesses would be fatal despite their efforts.

Staff's reactions to the fatally ill patient, medical failure, and their own feelings of helplessness included the use of individual defense mechanisms. The composite of individual and corporate defenses was formalized into a group pattern that took definite shape and became ritualized.[3]

The doctors developed and acted out a stereotyped view of their behavior. They suppressed questions, offered evasive answers, and provided direct reassurance to offset any patient doubts. For his own good, the patient was not encouraged to express feelings, reactions, or doubts. Thus, staff culture defined how the patient should respond to his illness.

Patients' Responses. The patients readily learned what was expected of them. Those who deviated— who did not respond to their cues—were viewed by staff as problem patients and an effort was made to help them conform. The patients should not be viewed as helpless victims of this philosophy. They were also participants in the system and, in complying with staff expectations, promoted the philosophy. Most patients did not ask questions, did not insist on receiving accurate knowledge of their disease, and did not share feelings and fears with staff.

Families. The responsibility of sharing the secret diagnosis with the doctor and of protecting the patient from gaining knowledge about his disease was left to the patient's family. If the family had insisted on sharing the information with the patient, it would have been permitted, but they were never encouraged to do so. This arrangement initiated two important processes. (1) The family was left alone with their ambivalent feelings about this new role because the staff was so committed to protecting the patient that relatives could not be helped to weigh alternatives. Only when the family was determined that the patient should know would any information be revealed. Most families, while ambivalent, feared the patient's reaction and decided to spare him from what they felt would be painful to him. (2) Staff were relieved when relatives were apprised of the situation. Now by not informing the patient they were also carrying out the family's wishes.

A result of this system was that the family and doctor bypassed the patient and excluded him from decision making. Thus, the family became part of the ward culture and found the role of relative clearly prescribed. They saw patients as helpless, dependent, and incapable of self-assertion. Therefore, they must take action on the patient's behalf. Financial matters, future planning, and concerns of children were not referred to the patient. Since these patients were generally married men who until recently fully supported their families, role reversal occurred suddenly—husband and father roles were canceled out by the patient role.

The patients seemed to quietly accept that their families had taken over. This reaction was viewed as justification for staff philosophy. Staff did not recognize that they had created a self-fulfilling prophecy by requiring behavior that conformed to their own preconceived attitudes. Actually the doctor, patient, and family roles had been staged, and on the surface the performance seemed flawless. The players knew their parts and each part interlocked with and supported the others.

SEARCH FOR ALTERNATIVES

The social worker's function was similar to that in most medical settings—helping patients and families with the medical and social problems resulting from illness. Since the social worker shared the views of the staff culture, he hoped to help prevent patients from feeling the sorrow and pain of fatal illness. However, it is the nature of casework to study how social and external forces relate to inner feelings and how they impinge on each other. This approach forced the social worker to examine his role. If the patient role is viewed as the way the individual responds to and attempts to meet social expectations, it is clear that here role expectations solidified the kind of defense mechanisms that most people under great stress try to adopt. What was not clear was the extent of the strain on those patients who found only partial psychological relief and were only partially able to adopt the rigidly defined role offered them. At what cost was the patient excluded from sharing his needs, dilemmas, or wishes with his family? Would another type of ward culture offer patients a wider choice or better alternatives? The social worker's prime concern with each individual patient was his feelings, thoughts, and attitudes. As he began to explore the inner world of these patients, he opened to public view what had previously been unshared and even taboo. The strains that patients and families experienced as they attempted to play their parts became visible.[4]

Many patients described feelings of rejection, isolation, and abandonment. They felt cut off from other people and sensed the stigma attached to dis-

cussing their feelings and diseases. They were aware of questions brushed aside, brusque answers, and deliberate evasions and half-truths. These reinforced their disturbing fantasies and feelings of despair and hopelessness. Direct reassurance had failed to dispel the underlying anxiety. Instead, it was interpreted as evidence of staff disinterest and aroused the patients' suspicion and distrust.[5]

Estrangement from family was another common problem. Patients complained that they were not made aware of family problems and conflicts and were left out of family planning and decision making. Relatives appeared upset; their reactions seemed artificial. Patients pondered the meaning of these reactions, alone and afraid.[6]

Patients were ambivalent about what they wanted to find out. On the one hand, there was a need to be more connected with reality, and on the other, a wish to be defended against it. What type of help would permit the patient to resolve this dilemma? Pivotal to this question was the recognition that while it was the patient's dilemma, the existing ward culture attempted to solve it *for* him. The social worker utilized individual approaches to try to help the patient resolve the conflict, but this alone was not sufficient. It was also necessary to intervene in the ward culture, specifically in the communication system between doctors and patients.

CHANGING THE CULTURE

As a first step, the worker shared the patients' feelings with the staff. The staff's initial reaction was to deny that the patients had such thoughts. Then they modified their viewpoint and attributed the emergence of these thoughts to the act of casework exploration. They still held that the best way to handle these feelings was with reassurance and repression. Now the doctors reassured more and the patients accepted it less because a new element had been introduced into the ward culture. With better communication between the patients and staff, it became increasingly difficult not to hear or feel.

How the social worker was able to demonstrate the need for social change in the ward culture is illustrated in the following cases.

1. Mr. M, a 25-year-old patient with chronic leukemia, learned that his wife had melanoma. He requested help in planning for their infant child in the event that both died or one was left chron-

ically ill. The social worker presented the family situation to the doctors. They readily saw that this man's problems would not be alleviated by evasive reassurance. After an initial reaction of helplessness (they had "nothing to offer this dying man," they said) they were able, with the social worker's guidance, to help him do what he wanted to do—plan for his family. They saw and accepted their responsibility for giving him the facts about his illness. After frankly sharing with him the nature and prognosis of his disease, they waited. Everyone wondered what would happen to a patient who had been given the burden of knowing he would die.

Mr. M spoke frankly and calmly to the social worker of his poor prognosis. He sorrowfully imagined his child growing up and never knowing him. He feared for his wife—a dependent girl who strongly relied on him. Questions of why this had happened to them revealed his inner sense of outrage. At the same time he established a goal, or perhaps a defense—to be strong and remain intact so that he could emotionally support and plan for his family in this crisis.

The social worker encouraged the doctors to share their empathy and concern with Mr. M. A new phenomenon developed—a relationship between patient and staff, characterized by mutual trust, openness, and equality. The staff regarded Mr. M as a person to admire and proudly pointed to his independence, responsibility, and strength. Without recognizing it, the staff had modified the role image of a patient, and Mr. M was referred to as an "ideal" patient. For the first time ward culture offered rewards and approval for a different coping pattern. With this change in social expectations, Mr. M found a source of personal prestige and privilege. He lived his remaining one and one-half years constructively involved in making important decisions, developing relationships, and fulfilling his need to be integrated with himself and external reality.

For staff, this was a unique patient, and would have remained so, had not two others quickly come to their attention.

2. Mr. P, a 30-year-old engineer, was found shortly after admission to have leukemia. He had planned to be married in two months and the doctors advised his parents to tell the fiancée the truth so she could make her decision. The parents refused. Several weekly sessions of medical–social work ward rounds were spent discussing the moral dilemma of this case. The social worker explained that the dilemma existed because the patient was excluded from decision making. Unable to persuade the social worker to intervene with the parents, the doctors considered telling the fiancée themselves, but knew that this was not legal. The staff struggled, and the social worker encouraged the expression of their resistance and doubt. Emotions were intense. The doctors felt frustrated. This was an area in which they rarely had to make a decision because the ward culture had previously promoted a clear course of action. Moreover, the social worker challenged them by not insisting that the parents tell the fiancée. The doctors' feelings of helplessness and anger were not resolved. The patient was reluctantly told his diagnosis, simply because the staff had no other choice.

Mr. P immediately told his fiancée, who wanted to marry him in spite of his disease. After a series of interviews with the social worker, Mr. P decided that he could not freely marry under these circumstances. The staff reacted to his decision with sadness because the fiancée wished desperately and pathetically to marry him. However, they also felt a sense of relief, as if a burden had been lifted. The patient had, in effect, told them that he could accept and wrestle with his own problem.

3. Mr. K, 29, discovered that he had leukemia when he opened and read a slip of paper he was carrying to the laboratory. Prior to this, he had often questioned the social worker as to whether he had anemia or something worse. After reading the diagnosis, he immediately went to the doctor and demanded an explanation. The doctor told him it was a terrible mistake made by the secretary. Mr. K remained unconvinced and said that he had opened the lab slip in order to confirm his suspicions. He assured the doctor that it would be a relief "to know the score." Once the doctor admitted the diagnosis and answered Mr. K's questions about the probable course of his disease, Mr. K came to the social worker and freely shared his mixed feelings of shock, relief,

and sadness. Like Mr. M and Mr. P, he felt he must be involved with reality. In the course of work with him, he agreed to tape several interviews for teaching purposes with ward physicians. In these he explained how he felt about the period of life left to him and how important it was for him to know his prognosis. He saw this activity as an important contribution to helping others and derived considerable ego satisfaction from it. A highly social and sensitive person, he referred other patients who had shared their troubled thoughts with him to the social worker. Having developed a stake in the way his illness was being handled, he created a subtle impact on patient culture. Mr. M and Mr. P related primarily to and influenced staff culture; Mr. K related more to the patient group.

These three cases, which occurred in a relatively short period of time, had been handled differently but this did not result in disaster. The patients appeared to be functioning well, talking more freely with their doctors, and obviously liked and trusted them and showed new self-reliance. These patients were successful in bringing about significant social change in the ward milieu. For the first time it became a matter of ward policy to consider the willingness and capacity of each patient to know his diagnosis. Furthermore, the majority of patients were considered capable of understanding the nature of their diseases. The ward culture was influenced strongly by this expressive, questioning, assertive, and independent majority. The good patient was no longer one who silently submitted to his fate, but one who courageously faced his disease and continued in his role as husband, father, and breadwinner. The improved communication system between doctor and patient fostered a mutual respect that had not existed previously. Patients were able to view the doctor more realistically and had less of a need to invest him with magical, omnipotent powers.

MAINTAINING
THE CHANGED CULTURE

Some of the foregoing changes have become self-perpetuating. Natural carriers of the culture are long-term or readmitted patients, a relatively stable nursing staff, and a social worker who remained on the service for four years. The rotation of medical residents on a three-month cycle is potentially disrup-

tive. The social worker assumed that each new group of residents would require exposure to some of the processes other doctors had experienced in the early stages of ward change. Their willingness to be involved in a process involving examination of their own intense feelings and their acceptance of the right of another discipline to challenge their philosophy have naturally varied. It is possible that the social worker would not have been able to handle this process consistently if he had not himself been a solidly integrated part of the ward culture. Certainly this facilitated the development of skills that sped up the process of acculturating resident physicians, as well as providing him with an important knowledge of the ward power structure and significant leverage points.

Specialized skills are required to maintain a ward culture of this type, i.e., one that provides the patient with a range of choice in coping with his disease. Such a culture is highly dependent on the staff's willingness and ability to offer the patients consistent and stable support. It requires a continued openness of communication, respect for individual differences, belief that a person with a fatal disease can have a self-determining life, and a capacity for meaningful interpersonal relationships with patients. In such a culture, the patients tend to develop strong positive feelings for the service and the staff.[7] They feel and respond to the genuine and long-term investment and involvement with them, derive a sense of security from the knowledge that a relationship will be offered them throughout the course of their illness— one that is related to their individualized needs and feelings—and develop a stake in continuing or perpetuating such an ambience.

Another factor in maintaining the ward culture is related to the selection of casework methods to be utilized with this patient group. One aspect of this is especially relevant. It involves the management of ego defense mechanisms. The patients tend to share readily feelings of depression, anxiety, and discomfort if the caseworker is willing to hear them. However, these realistic feelings frequently mask more permeating and pervasive fears that immobilize and overwhelm them. Therefore, it is important to reach these underlying feelings and free the patient to share his more primitive and nightmarish thoughts. Fantasies of punishment and death frequently break through the ego defenses and leave the patient at the mercy of his unresolved conflicts and their concomitant anxiety. It has been shown that only as the patient is able to put his worst thoughts and fears outside himself is he able to relinquish the tormenting and fruitless struggle against a harsh and unrelenting reality and become engaged in a process directed at helping him plan and make decisions for his remaining life and his family's future. Most patients experience a feeling of relief and freedom in sharing deeper feelings. Recognition of the capacity to control their behavior, if not their fears, does much to reduce the feelings of helplessness and frustration.

It is recognized that modifications in ward culture inevitably raise new problems. Patients have varying capacities to recognize and integrate their poor prognoses, internalize their anxiety, and meet a complex of social roles. Although the new ward culture offers a broader range of coping patterns, it may not provide adequate protection for those patients in need of external supports to maintain essential defenses of denial. Experience has shown that many patients can make successful adjustments to fatal illness based on a well-developed connection with reality. Some cannot. Better techniques are needed to provide a ward social system that can meet the needs of all.

NOTES

[1] Harriett M. Bartlett, *Social Work Practice in the Health Field* (New York: National Association of Social Workers, 1961), pp. 50–51, 71, 276–278.

[2] Rose Coser, *Life in the Ward* (East Lansing: Michigan State University Press, 1962).

[3] Renee Fox, *Experiment Perilous* (Glencoe, Ill.: Free Press, 1959).

[4] Norman Polansky et al., "Determinants of the Role-Image of the Patient in a Mental Hospital," in Milton Greenblatt, D.J. Levinson, and R.H. Williams, eds., *The Patient and the Mental Hospital* (Glencoe, Ill.: Free Press, 1957), pp. 380–401.

[5] Rosalind Jablon and Herbert Volk, "Revealing Diagnosis and Prognosis to Cancer Patients," *Social Work*, Vol. 5, No. 2 (April 1960), pp. 51–57.

[6] Kurt R. Eissler, *The Psychiatrist and the Dying Patient* (New York: International Universities Press, 1955).

[7] Renee Fox, op. cit.

INDUSTRIAL SOCIAL SERVICES: LINKAGE TECHNOLOGY

Andrew Weissman

BACKGROUND

The Counseling Center at United States Steel–South Works (USS-SW) is available to all employees of the plant, as well as to members of their families. Funds for the program are provided by a contract between United States Steel–South Works and Human Affairs, Inc., a private social work consulting firm. The program provides comprehensive services: (1) counseling, which ranges from common sense advice to treatment based on the Task-Centered Model; (2) linkage services, which provide referrals to other community resources; and (3) emergency services, which have included a twenty-four-hour-a-day hot line.[1] Efforts are made to attract those eligible for the program through advertising and direct meetings with employees, management, and union representatives.

THE TASK-CENTERED MODEL

This article[2] proposes an organizational and intervention model for industrial casework service that differs from most existing industrial service programs. Drawing from the experiences of other programs examined,[3] the Counseling Center at USS-SW chose a modified version of the Task-Centered Case-

Source: Andrew Weissman, "Industrial Social Services: Linkage Technology," *Social Casework*, Vol. 57, No. 1, January 1976, pp. 50–54. Reprinted with permission from Family Service Association of America.

work Model as the basis for its program. A number of factors entered into this decision:

1. First, many people are served in relatively few interviews.[4]

2. Secondly, William J. Reid and Laura Epstein have stated that a focal construct of their model of casework is "the expressed, considered request" a person makes about the problems with which he needs help.[5] This premise may also serve as an organizational principle. Rather than presuppose the problems and services a given population may need, we have found it possible to construct programs aimed at satisfying the specific needs that the clients have brought to the attention of the center.

Thus Reid and Epstein's focal construct, translated organizationally into operation, becomes an offer of help to any employee or family member with any type of problem. We think this is a logical extension of the Task-Centered Model, providing an empirically supported method of serving large numbers of employees at their work site.[6]

LINKAGE STRATEGY AND TECHNOLOGY

The center at USS-SW provides linkage services in three pre-referral stages: (1) locating and selecting an appropriate community resource; (2) providing access to and connecting a client to the resource; (3) evaluating, through follow-up contacts with the client, the quality of the resource and the effect of the linkage on the client's expressed problem.[7]

Reid and Epstein state that "problems of resource needs that are simply referred to another agency, as is often the case, do not 'count' as target problems in our system of bookkeeping."[8] This position is not unusual, since linkage services or "brokerage" "is barely discussed in the professional literature. . . ."[9]

LOCATING AND SELECTING COMMUNITY RESOURCES

The emphasis of this program is on alternatives to simply referring people to other resources. If the staff are in fact to organize a service which aims to help anyone with any type of problem, then each worker must be armed with techniques to facilitate the client's use of additional resources.

1. The first stage in the linkage process involves worker and client in a joint effort to identify the specific problem. If the counselor can offer no remedies for the problem, he has an additional task—the location of appropriate community resources.

As the center's programs have developed, its target populations have presented the typical problems of people leading normal lives. As these varied problems have been brought to its attention, the center's task has been to devise solutions or to locate outside resources with the services most directly related to these problems. To do this, the staff have scoured the community and have become experts in areas where traditionally social workers rarely work: They have become familiar with bankruptcy proceedings, the Chapter XIII courts, the *pro se* court, consolidation loans, wage assignments, repossessions, consumer fraud, and legal problems of all types. In addition, staff are, of course, familiar with the problem areas most often encountered by social workers, such as mental health, drug addiction, alcohol abuse, child welfare, and health service needs.[10] They have compiled extensive lists of available community resources which complement existing social service directories.

As the counselors have become more knowledgeable in the newer areas, they have also had to evaluate the caliber of the available and relevant services. Surprisingly, the clients in the target population have brought few problems for which there are no resources within the community. More importantly, most community agency staffs have proven most cooperative in assisting the clients referred to them.

After determining that a client could benefit from another agency's help, deciding which resources to offer for his selection becomes a major focal point in the delivery of linkage services. To assist him in choosing a resource, the counselor must not only know what appropriate agencies are available; he must also be able to explain how each agency operates and evaluate the quality of its services.

2. In the second stage of the linkage process, the worker must explore with the client all the options available, explaining clearly but briefly the possible consequences of each option for the client. These options should be compared to the one option that is always available—doing noth-

ing. Through this comparison, the client will have a realistic idea of the potential benefits and liabilities of taking any specific action.

3. Thirdly, while this joint selection process should be encouraged, most often the client will want to know what the worker recommends and why. The worker has an obligation to give direct advice based on his professional assessment of the existing resources and of the client's problem. Throwing the decision back on the client is an abrogation of professional responsibility under the guise of "participation."

CONNECTING THE
CLIENT TO THESE RESOURCES

After locating and selecting a resource with the client, the next step is connecting the client to the resource. Little has been written about the techniques involved in this process. In the center's experience, it has been noted, however, that while many such connections are suggested, few actually occur.[11] Further, while a common complementarity of interest between a client and the resource to which he is referred is often assumed, it is more often an illusion than a reality.[12]

It should be emphasized that the worker, or the agency that employs him, serving a population in the manner described, must maintain continuous contact with those responsive resources in the community which provide services that the target population is likely to need. This type of ongoing contact averts the crisis of trying to ferret out a resource in an emergency.

CONNECTION TECHNIQUES

The following is a description of what the author terms *connection techniques* and *cementing techniques.* Far from being new to the profession, these tactics are an integral part of social work's practice wisdom. The author has merely provided a beginning systematization of them. The techniques are listed in order of increasing complexity. The first tactic encompasses the absolute minimum of successful linkage techniques. The succeeding tactics include all those which precede, providing supplements to the basic technique.

1. The simplest type of connection involves writing out the necessary facts: the name and address of the resource, how to get an appointment at the resource, how to get to the resource, and a specific explanation of what the client may expect to occur once he arrives. Here the initiative for contacting the resource, making an appointment, and following through with the appointment rests with the client. Experience indicates that this basic technique works extremely well when people already know what they need but have had difficulty in locating the appropriate resource.

2. The next step involves providing the client with the name of a specific person to contact at the resource. This tactic has one serious drawback: if the client contacts the resource and the person the worker has sent him to see is not there, very often the client gives up.

3. As the complexity of the client problem increases, it helps to provide the client with a brief written statement, addressed to the resource, describing in precise terms the nature of the problem and what the client would like done. The client should be involved in the composition of this statement.

   The techniques described up to this point may also be accomplished in telephone interviews with a client as well as in office interviews, with minor modifications.

4. At the next level, the client calls the resource to make an appointment while he is in the worker's office. Alternatively, the worker may place the call to ensure that the appropriate person is contacted, but the client then takes over the phone conversation. Here the worker is helping to pave the way for the client.

5. There are times when, after the techniques described above have been used, it is necessary for the worker to request a family member, relative, or friend to accompany the client to the resource; occasionally the worker himself will go with the client to the resource.

CEMENTING TECHNIQUES

The center has also found that there are some specific steps workers can take to make sure that the initial connections will work to the client's advantage; these are labeled *cementing techniques,* and are listed below.

1. *Check-back:* The client is asked to call the worker

after the initial contact at the resource to summarize what has been accomplished so far.

2. *Haunting:* The worker, with the client's approval, plans to contact the client by telephone after the initial contact at the resource and after each subsequent contact.

3. *Sandwiching:* A planned interview with the client before he goes for the initial interview at the resource and immediately after that interview.

4. *Alternating:* A planned series of interviews held intermittently during the period in which the client is involved in interviews at the resource.

These four tactics are used to help clear up any misunderstandings that a client may encounter at the cooperating agency.

The worker may also contact an untapped resource for future clients. Here the resource and the worker develop procedures that can help the resource better serve the populations that the worker represents. For example, a worker might help a resource recognize some of the organizational obstacles to serving a given population. Typically, it is hard for clients working swing shifts to have an interview at the same time each week.

5. Follow-up evaluation is essential for three purposes: to make sure that the client is getting what he wants; to determine that the problem is on the way to resolution; and to document information to guide further linkages to the cooperating agency.

FINDINGS

. . . [The following figures] present demographic data on 655 employees served by the United States Steel–South Works Counseling Center in its first eight months of operation (267 family members are excluded from these data).

Male	556(86%)
Female	95(14%)
Black	327(50%)
White	244(37%)
Latino	84(13%)
Hourly wage	545(83%)
Management and salaried	110(17%)

431 (66%) of these employees are married and 341 (52%) have been employed by the firm for more than five years.

Types of problems brought to the counseling service:

Social-environmental problems	247(38%)

(marriage, child, peer, housing, consumer fraud, drug addiction, mental retardation, education, homemaker service, secondary alcoholism, job training, day care)

Legal problems	126(19%)

(divorce, home closing, contempt, arrest, garnishment, nonsupport, delinquency, legal advice)

Financial problems	190(29%)

(debts, money management, insurance claims [medical and other])

Mental health problems	77(12%)

(alcoholism, psychosis, character disorder, neuroses)

Health problems	37(6%)

(location of medical resources)

Additionally, 30 percent of these problems were seriously affecting the employee's work performance.

Percentages are rounded.

CONCLUSION

The Center has just begun documenting the typology of problems that accompanies specific linkage techniques. The findings in that area are therefore mostly impressionistic.

The statistics gathered thus far, however, have indicated that people served for legal, financial, or health problems most often required only direct linkages to resources. Connection techniques 1 and 2 and cementing techniques 1, 2, and 5 have generally been employed with success. This group accounted for 22 percent of the total population served thus far.

At the other extreme, people with social-environmental and mental health problems more often required connection techniques 3 through 6, and cementing techniques 3 through 5. This often resulted in the employee's receiving a combination of help from a community resource and the center's counseling staff. This group accounted for 41 percent of the total population served.

Conscious use of these techniques has meant that about 75 percent of the linkages made to community resources succeeded in the sense that people followed through and used the resource. Further, 86 percent of the clients thought that they received a service they wanted and 84 percent believed that the problem situation they came with initially had improved. These later data were gathered from questionnaires mailed to a random sample of 350 employees, which yielded 269 usable replies.

The linkage techniques used in each case were those thought most appropriate by the worker involved, based on his professional judgment. At a later stage, as the center documents and refines the techniques outlined here, the author hopes to be able to differentiate and describe the results of the experimental manipulation of these differing techniques.

NOTES

[1]Carvel U. Taylor and Andrew Weissman, *Handbook for the Organization of an Employee Assistance Program* (Philadelphia: Human Resources Network, 1975) forthcoming.

[2]A different version of this paper was presented at the *Task-Centered Conference*, The School of Social Service Administration, University of Chicago, May 1975.

[3]Specifically we have based our services on the information available from: Rex A. Skidmore, Daniel Balsam, and Otto F. Jones, Social Work Practice in Industry, *Social Work*, 19:280–86 (May 1975); Hyman J. Weiner et al., The World of Work and Social Welfare Policy, mimeographed (New York: Industrial Social Welfare Center, Columbia University School of Social Work, 1971); Hyman J. Weiner, Sheila H. Akabas, and John J. Somer, *Mental Health Care in the World of Work* (New York: Association Press, 1973); Calvin P. Leeman et al., *The Job Improvement Service Demonstration Project* (Springfield, Va.: National Technical Information Service, 1972); Robert Noland, ed., *Industrial Mental Health and Employee Counseling* (New York: Behavioral Publications, 1973); Hans B. C. Speigel, *Not for Work Alone* (Springfield, Va.: National Technical Information Service, 1974); Elisabeth Mills, Family Counseling in an Industrial Job-Support Program, *Social Casework* 53:587–92 (December 1972); Paul R. Brooks, Industry-Agency Program for Employee Counseling, *Social Casework* 56:404–10 (July 1975).

[4]See for example, Weiner et al., *Mental Health Care*, p. 68. Seventy-nine percent of 393 people were served in twelve or fewer interviews. Brooks, Industry-Agency Program, pp. 408–09. The author states that the average number of interviews per case was 4.7.

[5]William J. Reid and Laura Epstein, *Task-Centered Casework* (New York: Columbia University Press, 1972), p. 35.

[6]The United States Steel Counseling Center, the CNA Counseling Service, and Kennecott Copper's Insight Program annually serve about 10 percent of the populations of their respective firms.

[7]Allen Pincus and Anne Minahan, *Social Work Practice: Model and Method* (Itasca, Ill.: F. E. Peacock, 1973), p. 18.

[8]William J. Reid and Laura Epstein, *Task-Centered Casework* (New York: Columbia University Press, 1972), p. 48.

[9]Ruth Middleman and Gale Goldberg, *Social Service Delivery: A Structural Approach to Social Work Practice* (New York: Columbia University Press, 1974), p. 66.

[10]Susan Roberts, Inflation, Recession—and Families, *Social Casework* 56:182–85 (March 1975). It is noted that nationwide the number of family service agencies offering financial counseling to clients has risen from 32 in 1968 to more than 100 in 1975.

[11]Stuart A. Kirk and James R. Greenley, Denying or Delivering Services? *Social Work* 19:443 (July 1974).

[12]Middleman and Goldberg, *Structural Approach*, pp. 39, 67.

DIMENSIONS IN SOCIAL WORK PRACTICE WITH NATIVE AMERICANS

Ronald G. Lewis, Man Keung Ho

Despite social workers' empathy with the social problems and injustices long associated with the Native American people, they have been unable to assist them with their problems. This lack of success on the part of social workers can be attributed to a multitude of reasons, but it stems, in general, from the following: (1) lack of understanding of the Native American culture, (2) retention of stereotyped images of Native Americans, (3) use of standard techniques and approaches.

The ineffectiveness of social workers in dealing with Native Americans can often be attributed directly to the methods and techniques they use. Naturally, social workers must work with the tools they have acquired, but these may have a detrimental effect on a Native American. For example, the concept of "social work intervention" may be consistent with much of the white man's culture, but it diametrically opposes the Native American's cultural concept of noninterference.[1] There is a great need for social workers to examine carefully those techniques they plan to use in treating their Native American clients. The purpose of these pages is to identify selected dimensions that are important in social work practice with Native Americans.

Although there is no monolithic Native American culture—because each tribe's culture is unique to that individual tribe, and no social worker could be expected to be familiar with the cultures of some two hundred tribes—the worker should familiarize himself with those customs that are generally characteristic of all Native Americans. Only after a worker has gained at least an elementary knowledge of Native American customs and culture can he proceed to evaluate the various approaches and techniques and choose the most effective ones.

NATIVE AMERICAN TRAITS

The concept of sharing is deeply ingrained among Native Americans who hold it in greater esteem than the white American ethic of saving. Since one's worth is measured by one's willingness and ability to share, the accumulation of material goods for social status is alien to the Native American. Sharing, therefore, is neither a superimposed nor an artificial value, but a genuine and routine way of life.

In contrast to the general belief that they have no concept of time, Native Americans are indeed time conscious. They deal, however, with natural phenomena—mornings, days, nights, months (in terms of moons), and years (in terms of seasons or winters).[2] If a Native American is on his way to a meeting or appointment and meets a friend, that conversation will naturally take precedence over being punctual for the appointment. In his culture, sharing is more important than punctuality.

Nature is the Native American's school, and he is taught to endure all natural happenings that he will encounter during his life. He learns as well to be an independent individual who respects others. The Native American believes that to attain maturity—which is learning to live with life, its evil as well as its good—one must face genuine suffering. The resilience of the Native American way of life is attested to by the fact that the culture has survived and continues to flourish despite the intense onslaught of the white man.

One of the strongest criticisms of the Native American has been that he is pessimistic; he is presented as down-trodden, low-spirited, unhappy, and without hope for the future. However, as one looks deeper into his personality, another perspective is visible. In the midst of abject poverty comes "the courage to be"—to face life as it is, while maintaining a tremendous sense of humor.[3] There exists a thin line between pathos and humor.

The Native American realizes that the world is made up of both good and bad. There are always some people or things that are bad and deceitful. He believes, however, that in the end good people will triumph just because they are good. This belief is seen repeatedly in Native American folktales about Iktomi the spider. He is the tricky fellow who is out to fool, cheat, and take advantage of good people. But Iktomi usually loses in the end, reflecting the Native American view that the good person succeeds while the bad person loses.[4] Therefore, the pessimism of Native Americans should instead be regarded as "optimistic toughness."

Those who are unfamiliar with the culture might mistakenly interpret the quiet Native American as being stoical, unemotional, and vulnerable. He is alone, not only to others but also to himself. He controls his emotions, allowing himself no passionate outbursts over small matters. His habitual mien is one of poise, self-containment, and aloofness, which may result from a fear and mistrust of non–Native Americans. Another facet of Native American thought is the belief that no matter where any individual stands, he is an integral part of the universe. Because every person is fulfilling a purpose, no one should have the power to impose values. For this reason, each man is to be respected, and he can expect the same respect and reverence from others. Hence, the security of this inner fulfillment provides him with an essential serenity that is often mistaken for stoicism.

Native American patience, however, can easily be mistaken for inactivity. For instance, the Kiowa, like other Native American tribes, teach their young people to be patient. Today, when the young Native American has to go out and compete in another society, this quality is often interpreted as laziness. The white man's world is a competitive, aggressive society that bypasses the patient man who stands back and lets the next person go first.

The foregoing are only a few of the cultural traits that are common to most Native American tribes, but they represent important characteristics about which the effective social worker must be informed. The concepts of sharing, of time, of acceptance of suffering, and optimism differ significantly from the white man's concepts. In dealing with a Native American client, the social worker must realize this and proceed accordingly. He must be familiar with the Native American view that good will triumph over evil and must recognize that Native Americans are taught to be patient and respectful. If the worker fails to do this, he is liable to make false assumptions, thus weakening his ability to serve his client effectively.

CLIENT-WORKER RELATIONS

A social worker's ability to establish a working relationship with a Native American will depend on his genuine respect for his client's cultural background and attributes. A worker should never think that the Native American is primitive or that his culture and background are inferior.

In the beginning, the Native American client might distrust the worker who is from a different race and culture. He might even view the worker as a figure of authority, and as such, the representative of a coercive institution. It is unlikely that he will be impressed with the worker's educational degrees or his professional title. However, this uncompromising attitude should not be interpreted as pugnacity. On the contrary, the Native American is gregarious and benevolent. His willingness and capacity to share depend on mutual consideration, respect, and noncoercion.

Because their culture strongly opposes and precludes interference with another's affairs, Native Americans have tended to regard social work intervention with disfavor. Social workers usually are forced to use culturally biased techniques and skills that are insensitive to the Native American culture and, therefore, are either detrimental to these clients or at best ineffective.

In an effort to communicate more fully, a social worker is likely to seat himself facing the client, look him straight in the eye, and insist that the client do likewise. A Native American considers such behavior—covert or overt—to be rude and intimidating; contrary to the white man, he shows respect by not staring directly at others. Similarly, a worker who is excessively concerned with facilitating the display of inner feelings on the part of the client should be aware of another trait. A Native American client will not immediately wish to discuss other members of his family or talk about topics that he finds insensitive or distressing. Before arriving at his immediate concern (the real reason he came to the worker in the first place), the client—particularly the Native American—will test the worker by bringing up peripheral matters. He does this in the hope of getting a better picture of how sincere, interested, and trustworthy the worker actually is. If the worker impatiently confronts the client with accusations, the client will be "turned off."

Techniques of communication that focus on the client—that is, techniques based on restating, clarifying, summarizing, reflecting, and empathizing—may help a worker relate to the client who sometimes needs a new perspective to resolve his problems. It is important that the worker provide him with such information but not coerce him to accept it. The worker's advice should be objective and flexible enough so that its adoption does not become the central issue of a particular interview.

For the Native American, personal matters and emotional breakdown are traditionally handled within the family or extended family system. For this reason, the client will not wish to "burden" the worker with detailed personal information. If the client is estranged from his family and cultural group, he may indirectly share such personal information with the worker. To determine the appropriate techniques for helping a Native American client deal with personal and psychological problems, the worker should carefully observe the client's cultural framework and his degree of defensiveness. The techniques of confrontation traditionally associated with the psychoanalytic approach and the introspective and integrative techniques used by the transactional analysts tend to disregard differences in culture and background between a client and worker. Additionally, the worker should be aware of the danger in overly identifying with the Native American culture. Some social workers see their task as encouraging pride in being Indian and reaffirming the clients' heritage and tradition. The worker cannot solve for the Native American this unique dilemma of being caught in two cultures. He can only serve as facilitator by pointing out the dilemma and helping the clients to work out their own identity. This is a unique struggle for the Native American client and pitting white culture against Indian culture conveys the idea of "either-or" when the choice might be "both-and."

FAMILY COUNSELING

In view of the close-knit family structure of Native Americans, along with the cultural emphasis to keep family matters inside the family, it is doubtful that many social workers will have the opportunity to render family counseling services. In the event that a Native American family does seek the worker's help, the family worker should be reminded that his traditional role of active and manipulative go-between must be tempered so that family members can deal with their problems at their own pace.[5] Equally important is the worker's awareness of and respect for the resilience of Native American families, bolstered in crisis by the extended family system. The example of the Redthunder family serves as illustration.

The Redthunder family was brought to the school social worker's attention when teachers reported that both children had been tardy and absent frequently in the past weeks. Since the worker lived near Mr. Redthunder's neighborhood, she volunteered to transport the children back and forth to school. Through this regular but informal arrangement, the worker became acquainted with the entire family, especially with Mrs. Redthunder who expressed her gratitude to the worker by sharing her homegrown vegetables.

The worker sensed that there was much family discomfort and that a tumultuous relationship existed between Mr. and Mrs. Redthunder. Instead of probing into their personal and marital affairs, the worker let Mrs. Redthunder know that she was willing to listen should the woman need someone to talk to. After a few gifts of homegrown vegetables and Native American handicrafts, Mrs. Redthunder broke into tears one day and told the worker about her husband's problem with alcoholism and their deteriorating marital relationship.

Realizing Mr. Redthunder's position of respect in the family and his resistance to outside interference, the social worker advised Mrs. Redthunder to take her family to visit the minister, a man whom Mr. Redthunder admired. The Littleaxe family, who were mutual friends of the worker and the Redthunder family, agreed to take the initiative in visiting the Redthunders more often. Through such frequent but informal family visits, Mr. Redthunder finally obtained a job, with the recommendation of Mr. Littleaxe, as recordkeeper in a storeroom. Mr. Redthunder enjoyed his work so much that he drank less and spent more time with his family.

Obviously treating a family more pathogenic than the Redthunders might necessitate that the social worker go beyond the role of mediator. Nevertheless, since Native Americans traditionally favor noninterference, the social worker will not find it feasible to assume the active manipulative role that he might in working with white middle-class families. The social work profession needs new and innovative approaches to family counseling that take into account social and family networks and are sensitive and responsive to the cultural orientation of Native American families.[6] The social and family network through which a Native American seeks help may be schematized as follows:

1. Individual

2. Goes to family first

3. Then to extended family (cousins, aunts, uncles, etc.)—social network

4. Religious leader

5. Tribal council

6. Finally, formalized health care delivery system

Generally speaking, when the individual has a problem, he or she goes to the immediate family. If the problem is not resolved there, the social network is then contacted: relatives, friends, a bar, anyplace where someone will listen.

Next, the spiritual or religious leader may be contacted.

He or she may go to the Indian Tribal council. The tribal council may help by using legal or political clout to solve the problem, such as getting a child into boarding school.

The last resort for a Native American to seek help is to go to the formal agencies, which to the Indian People represent mainstream society. Usually the circumstances necessitating this are the most extreme—the person seeking help [or one] of his relatives is dying, going to prison, etc.

For a worker to maximize the use of the natural network system, he must not be judgmental of a structure that may not be consistent with his value system and cultural background.

GROUP WORK

Groups should be a natural and effective medium for Native Americans who esteem the concept of sharing and apply it in their daily lives. Through the group process, members can share their joy, intimacy, problems, and sorrows, and find a means of improving their lives. Today's society tends to foster alienation, anomie, disenfranchisement, dissociation, loneliness, and schizoid coolness.[7] People wish for intimacy but at the same time fear it.[8] The new humanistic approaches to counseling and psychotherapy have developed a wide variety of powerful techniques for facilitating human growth, self-discovery, and interpersonal relations.[9] The effectiveness of these approaches in cutting through resistance, breaking down defenses, releasing creative forces, and promoting the healing process has been amply demonstrated. However, such approaches are highly insensitive to the cultural orientation of Native Americans. These people consider such group behavior to be false; it looks and sounds real but lacks genuineness, depth, and real commitment.

As the worker uses his skills in forming the group, diagnosing the problems, and facilitating group goals, he may inevitably retain certain elements of manipulation. However, if he is committed to recognizing individual potential and to capitalizing on the group model of mutual assistance, he should come close to meeting the needs of Native Americans who value respect and consideration for oneself as well as others.[10]

To avoid manipulation and coercion, a group worker needs to utilize indirect and extragroup means of influence that will in turn influence the members. Thus the worker may act upon and through the group as a mediating structure, or through program activities, for the benefit of his clients.[11] The success of the worker's influences and activities is related to his knowledge and acceptance of Native American culture, its formal and informal systems and norms.

Regardless of whether the purpose of the group is for effecting interpersonal change or social action, such Native American virtues as mutual respect and consideration should be the essential components of the group process. Using the group to pressure members who are late or silent will not only jeopardize and shorten the group's existence, but will cause alienation and withdrawal from future group activities.

In view of the vast cultural difference between Native Americans and other ethnic groups, especially whites, it is doubtful that a heterogeneous grouping of members will produce good results. Similarly, group activities that are action oriented may be contradictory to Native Americans who view the compulsion to reduce or ignore suffering as immaturity.

COMMUNITY WORK

Because of the Native Americans' experience of oppression and exploitation—along with their emphasis on noninterference and resolute acceptance of suffering—it is doubtful that a social worker, regardless of his racial identity, could bring about any major change in community policies and programs. The only exception might be the social worker who is accepted and "adopted" by the community and who agrees to confine himself to the existing system and norms. A worker's adoption by the Native American community will depend on his sincerity, respect, and genuine concern for the people. This concern can best be displayed through patience in daily contact with the community as well as through his efforts to find positive solutions to problems.

A worker who uses the strategy of trying to resolve conflict as a means of bringing about social change will undoubtedly encounter native resistance and rejection. On the other hand, a worker who shows respect for the system, values, and norms of the Native American eventually places himself in a position of trust and credibility. Only through mutual respect, and not through his professional title and academic degree, can the worker produce meaningful social change.

Obviously, social work with Native Americans requires a new orientation and focus on attitudes and approaches. The term Native American encompasses many tribes, and within these there are intratribal differences; furthermore, individuals within each subtribe may react differently to problems or crises. Therefore, it is impossible for a social worker always to know precisely how to respond to a Native American client or group. The worker must be willing to admit his limitations, to listen carefully, to be less ready to draw conclusions, and to anticipate that his presuppositions will be corrected by the client. The worker must genuinely want to know what the problem or the situation is and be receptive to being taught. Such an unassuming and unobtrusive humanistic attitude is the key to working with Native American people.

The social worker who can deal most effectively with Native Americans will be genuine, respectful of their culture, and empathic with the welfare of the people. By no means does the Native American social worker have a monopoly on this type of attitude. In fact, the Native American social worker who has assimilated the white man's culture to the extent that he no longer values his own culture could do more harm than good.

Recognizing the distinct cultural differences of the Native American people, those who plan social work curricula and training programs must expand them to include specific preparation for workers who will be dealing with Native American clients. Literature on the subject is almost nonexistent, and researchers and educators would do well to devote more study to how social workers can serve Native Americans. More Native Americans should be recruited as students, faculty, and practitioners in the field of social work. All persons, regardless of race, should be encouraged to develop a sensitivity toward Native Americans whom they may have the opportunity to serve. Social work agencies that deal primarily with Native American clients should intensify and refocus their in-service training programs.

A worker has the responsibility of acquiring knowledge that is relevant to the Native American culture so that he is capable of providing this effective treatment. A joint effort on the part of all those involved is required to give the service to Native Americans that they justly deserve.

NOTES

[1]For a detailed discussion of noninterference, see Rosalie H. Wax and Robert K. Thomas, "Anglo Intervention vs. Native Noninterference," *Phylon*, 22 (Winter 1961), pp. 53–56; and Jimm G. Good Tracks, "Native American Noninterference," *Social Work*, 18 (November 1973), pp. 30–34.

[2]Good Tracks, op. cit., p. 33.

[3]Clair Huffaker, *Nobody Loves a Drunken Indian* (New York: McKay, 1967).

[4]See John F. Bryde, *Modern Indian Psychology* (Vermillion: Institute of Indian Studies, University of South Dakota, 1971), p. 15.

[5]See Gerald Suk, "The Go-Between Process in Family Therapy," *Family Process*, 6 (April 1966), pp. 162–178.

[6]Ross V. Speck and Carolyn L. Attneave, "Social Network Intervention," in Jay Haley, ed., *Changing Families* (New York: Grune & Stratton, 1971), pp. 17–34.

[7]Rollo May, "Love and Will," *Psychology Today*, 3 (1969), pp. 17–24.

[8]Edward A. Dreyfus, "The Search for Intimacy," *Adolescence*, 2 (March 1967), pp. 25–40.

[9]See Bernard Gunther, *Sense Relaxation: Below Your Mind* (New York: Macmillan, 1968); Abraham Maslow, "Self-Actualization and Beyond," in James F. Bugental, ed., *Challenges of Humanistic Psychology* (New York: McGraw-Hill, 1967); H. Ohio, *Explorations in Human Potentialities* (Springfield, Ill.: Charles C.

Thomas, 1966); Carl Rogers, "Process of the Basic Encounter Group," in James F. Bugental, ed., op. cit.

[10]For further discussion of a reciprocal model, see William Schwartz, "Toward a Strategy of Group Work Practice," *Social Service Review*, 36 (September 1962), pp. 268–279.

[11]For further discussion of indirect and extra-group means, see Robert Vinter, *Readings in Group Work Practice* (Ann Arbor, Mich.: Campus Publishers, 1967), pp. 8–38.

SOCIAL WORK IN THE FIELD OF PUBLIC HEALTH

William T. Hall, Christine L. Young

Social factors have been recognized by American health care professionals as critical to the effective delivery of services since the early 1900s. However, with the beginning of large-scale public health programs, additional personnel were needed to deal with the social factors in the patients' families. Social workers became involved in programs for venereal disease and tuberculosis control and infant and well-child care.[1] Since social workers' first involvement in community health care, the social work role has expanded to include program consultation and education, administration, and research in community health care as well as clinical services.

At this point the scope of social work practice in health care is difficult to characterize because of the variety of organizational settings, client populations, and social work methods involved. Social work intervention may occur in hospitals, community health programs, and voluntary health and welfare organizations within the health care field. Social work intervention is also utilized with a variety of populations, such as infants, childbearing women, geriatric groups, and various categorical disease programs, such as alcoholism, developmental disabilities, and heart disease. Within the many organizational settings, social work intervention may take various forms, including clinical social work, consultation, advocacy, community organization, and research.

The increased involvement of the social work profession in the health field has been facilitated by both national growth of health care organizations and greater scientific knowledge about prevention and treatment of disease. However, the social work profession is confronted with the same dilemma as are other professionals in the health field, such as physicians and nurses, regarding the most effective education and training for a field that is constantly changing. The concern for social work education in the health field has led to a range of programs at the undergraduate, graduate, and post-graduate levels. At this writing there are more than thirty schools of social work planning or already implementing a "health specialization" sequence as part of the master's degree program. In addition, several schools of social work are planning with schools of public health toward a joint MSW-MPH curriculum. In at least one university (Pittsburgh), social workers with the MSW may pursue, simultaneously, the MPH from the Graduate School of Public Health and the Ph.D. from the School of Social Work. Social workers are also enrolled in doctoral degree programs in schools of public health. In addition to the degree programs, social work education has expanded the continuing education curriculum to include health care topics. Recently two new journals concerning social work in the health field—*Social Work in Health Care* and *Health and Social Work*—began publication.

The involvement of social work in the health field and the recognition of the needs in social work education and training in health care topics have led

Source: This article was specially prepared for this volume by the authors.

to an examination of the intervention priorities and the most effective educational process. This article will discuss the intervention priorities and the educational process for one area of social work in the health care field: public health social work. The purpose of the article is to examine the public health social work model as an example of the integration of the theories and skills of both the public health and social work professions and to discuss the application of this model for other areas of social work practice, particularly in the health care field.

PUBLIC HEALTH SOCIAL WORK

Although social workers have had long-standing involvement in medical social work, it is important to distinguish between medical social work and public health social work. Traditionally, medical social work concentrated primarily on clinical interventions with individuals and families. These interventions had to be complemented by a broader perspective of the patient, the organization, the community, and the particular health problems. Elizabeth P. Rice has indicated the need for a reexamination of the clinical focus of medical social work. She states:

Until we lift into our practice a broader understanding of the group we serve, until we contribute our thinking and our facts to the programming and planning in the particular agency in which we practice, until we widen our understanding of the individual to see him as he affects and is affected by his family and the community, and until we have a greater dynamics of the community—until this time, we will neglect the potentialities that exist for the more comprehensive practice of social work.[2]

Public health social work is the integration of the theories and skills that are useful in the effective health care delivery to the patient and his or her family. Social work intervention in health care can include clinical services, consultation and education, administration and planning, and research and evaluation. Examples of these interventions within the public health social work model include the following:

Clinical services include direct casework and group work services to patients and their families, coordination of services, health education, and development of an appropriate service plan for health and social needs;

Consultation and education may occur within the health care team or setting, within university and community settings of other health care professionals, within university and community groups such as parent groups, and professional groups—for example, teachers, police officers, and lawyers, and political groups, such as legislators;

Administration and planning include the development of appropriate and accessible health services, consumer involvement, the development of additional services as needed, and the evaluation of needs for existing services;

Research and evaluation include the identification of high-risk population for social and health needs, the particular health and social needs of these populations, and the evaluation of service programs.

These skills must be adapted to the health care setting, the population to be served, and the particular health problems. The social worker would be expected to establish priorities within his or her role that would be most effective for quality patient care. Quality patient care is defined as treating all patient needs—physical, psychological and social—within the context of the health care plan.

For effective functioning within the health care setting, it is important for the social worker to also have additional knowledge and skills that relate specifically to health care. These additional skills not only lead to the personal growth of the social worker; they are becoming increasingly necessary for effective functioning within the health care setting. Some important skills include the following:

1. Knowledge of the skills and values of other professionals involved in health care, such as nurses, physicians, physical therapists, and administrators;

2. Training in the biological sciences, particularly those related to growth and development, maintenance of health, and the early detection and treatment of diseases;

3. Training in the administration and management skills needed for coordination of programs;

4. Training in the use of statistics, computer science, and data processing, and the use of consultants in the information sciences.

Social workers with these additional skills ideally would be able to use both social work and public health principles effectively, define their role as so-cial workers more flexibly, and function indepen-dently as competent professionals within a wide range of health and social welfare settings. The social worker in public health does not relinquish his or her primary profession of social work; instead the so-cial worker adds the additional knowledge and per-spective of public health.

The integration of the social work and the public health professions represents one model for social work in the public health care field. The public health social worker, like other professionals who have training in two or more fields, can experience the dual perspective of the *marginal man*.[3] Although this dual perspective can lead to psychological and professional conflicts within the individual social worker, it can also foster independence and creativity. The public health social worker can act as the liaison between the social worker and other health care professionals. Through the use of skills in clinical social work and consultation, the social worker can contribute the knowledge and skills of the social work profession to other health care profes-sionals and community groups. Conversely, through the use of skills in public health practice, the social worker can contribute to the social work profession through program consultation, teaching, and research.

PERSPECTIVES OF THE PUBLIC HEALTH SOCIAL WORKER

The integration of the social work and public health perspectives can best be illustrated by an ex-amination of the key perspectives of public health so-cial work:

1. A primary focus on the population rather than the individual patient,

2. Use of an interdisciplinary approach for total pa-tient care,

3. Focus on the primary prevention of social and health problems,

4. Use of social work skills for casefinding and caseholding,

5. Reliance on quantitative measures for admin-istrative and research purposes.

Population Focus

Within public health social work, the individual is seen as part of a population with specific social and health care needs. Since no program is able to pro-vide services for all members of the population, pri-orities for services are established through the use of social and health data. Frequently populations have social and health problems because of the complex interaction of psychological and physical health. Al-though all persons have different attitudes and be-haviors regarding their health, some groups have greater needs for social work involvement because of their particular health and social needs. These popu-lations are labeled *high-risk* since they have social and health conditions that place them at greater risk for health problems than other groups. The purpose of social work intervention is to identify the social fac-tors that can be modified through clinical services, program planning, consultation, research, or ad-vocacy and to develop appropriate services for these high-risk populations. Some examples of high-risk populations include:

1. *Age groups* that have increased social and health needs, such as infants and young children and the elderly. These populations need additional social supports because of their physical depen-dence; their primary needs are accessible and continuous care of health needs in community-based settings;

2. *Handicapped persons*, such as the mentally re-tarded, psychiatric patients, and persons with limited mobility or chronic disease. These per-sons have difficulties using health resources and may not have adequate community programs for health care and rehabilitation;

3. *Cultural minorities* that may have language and cultural barriers to receiving health care. Their health status generally is lower than the rest of the population, and they may have a lack of in-formation about health care, resources, and inad-equate health resources in their community;

4. *Highly mobile populations*, such as migrant laborers and persons displaced due to wars, political tur-moil, or natural disasters, that have acute health problems due to the migration itself. A second-ary consequence is the difficulty of these groups in using preventive health care services on a continuous basis due to their mobility.

Interdisciplinary Care

The patient can only be provided total or quality care if a variety of professionals are available for treatment and consultation. The social worker can be uniquely qualified for interdisciplinary practice whenever he or she has additional training in health care and is able to use the social work skills of group work and consultation. Social work intervention can be utilized for consultation and training of other professionals involved in the health care plan and for direct and indirect services to the group of people being served by the health care plan.

The scope of social work involvement in health care has broadened due to the recognition by both behavioral and physical scientists that social factors have a critical influence on an individual's or group's health. Social factors such as poverty or the age of the group can affect many aspects of health, whereas other social factors such as a particular cultural practice or personal habits may affect health only in a minor way. The primary areas that are affected by social factors include:

1. *Health status:* the present state of health of the person or group. This includes history of treatment and rehabilitation of injuries or diseases, preventive health care such as adequate nutrition, dental care, and immunization, and the present state of personal health;

2. *Health care utilization:* the pattern of a person's or a group's utilization of services from a professional health care provider. This includes personal and cultural differences in attitudes toward: particular health care services, such as immunization, surgery, blood transfusion; particular methods of service delivery, such as hospital care, emergency services, or home care; or particular categories of service providers, such as physicians, nurses, or social workers.

3. *Health care resources:* the facilities, personnel, and financial and political support that are available to an individual or a group within a community. The resources must not only be present in the community; they must be available, accessible, and appropriate for the particular health and social needs of the individual or group.

It is important to recognize that the effect of any particular social factor can vary widely depending on the group of people to be served, the type of health problems, and the method of intervention. For example, cultural attitudes of a particular group toward hospitalization will probably not affect their usage of immunization programs or dental care, but will have significant effect on their attitudes toward such interventions as surgery, nursing-home care, and childbirth within a hospital. Within the interdisciplinary setting the social worker is able to analyze the social factors of the particular group of people that is being served. He or she can develop professional and programmatic strategies that will most effectively deliver the health services in a manner that is appropriate, accessible, and acceptable.

Primary Prevention

Primary prevention involves those efforts directed toward keeping an event (disease) from occurring in the first place. The impact of a program of primary prevention depends upon three variables:

1. The magnitude of the disease in the community as measured by incidence, prevalence, or mortality;

2. The potential effectiveness of the program in reducing the number of events;

3. The percentage of the population at risk that will accept the program.[4]

The ideal public health social work intervention is the primary prevention of the social and health problems. Primary prevention uses the social work skills of consultation, community organization, and professional education, as well as clinical skills when dealing with individuals and families. The goal of primary prevention is to provide adequate information and support so that the social and health problems can be prevented through changes in attitudes and behaviors related to psychological and physical health. The social worker relies on biology, epidemiology, biochemistry, and other sciences for a basis of identifying the psychological and physical characteristics that need modification. Social work skills are utilized to develop effective programmatic interventions in order to promote well-being and the prevention of health and social problems.

Casefinding and Caseholding

When the particular characteristics of a high-risk population have been identified, the public health social worker becomes involved in casefinding and caseholding. *Casefinding* can include a variety of social work methods such as community organizations and clinical skills that will facilitate the entrance of particular persons who are at high-risk for health problems into the health care system. Screening programs, health education, and epidemiological investigations are examples of public health methods used in case-finding. Frequently the social worker becomes involved in *caseholding* with patients who are presently in the health care system. Caseholding uses similar techniques as casefinding; however, its principal purpose is to keep these high-risk persons and groups in the health care system.

Quantitative Methods

The qualitative skills of social work are complemented by the quantitative skills that are becoming increasingly needed in all professions. Accountability is best achieved with the conjoint use of social work skills of analysis and conceptualization and the use of quantitative methods such as the computer sciences and statistics for research, evaluation, program planning, and administration. Quantitative skills are necessary due to the need to evaluate professional competence and to develop uniform professional standards such as the Professional Standards Review Organization (PSRO). It is important for the social worker to plan and evaluate both within the social work department and the total health care program. Legislative changes such as patient rights and the greater complexity of health care organizations have made health care professionals more accountable to the consumers, the funding sources, and the community. These legislative and administrative changes have markedly altered the need for all professionals in the health care field to develop quantitative skills for the most competent performance.

The perspectives of the public health social worker then may be characterized as an embodiment of the epidemiological approach. (*Epidemiology* may be defined as the science concerned with factors and conditions that determine the occurrence and distribution of health, disease, defect, disability, and death in populations.) Reeder states: "When the objective of the research is to study the role of *social* factors in the etiology of disease we refer to this as *social epidemiology.*"[5]

PUBLIC HEALTH SOCIAL WORK IN A COMMUNITY HEALTH PROGRAM: A BRIEF EXAMPLE

Leaders in the field of public health are generally agreed that significant advances in the battle against our major killers—heart disease, stroke, cancer, and accidents—are not likely to come about as a result of some dramatic biomedical breakthrough. Rather the focus of attention and effort must be on primary prevention: keeping the "disease" from occurring in the first place. And this will require changing the lifestyle of that particular group of people identified as a high-risk population.

Reeder states, "Although much is still unclear with regard to etiological mechanisms involved, preventive health actions can be taken based upon the contributions of social epidemiology to disease control. . . . In the 1968 statement of the American Heart Association, the personal attribute of 'certain personality-behavior patterns' and the environmental factor of 'emotionally stressful situations' are given official recognition for the first time as risk factors in coronary heart disease."[6]

A community health program in heart disease prevention serves as a good example of this strategy of changing lifestyles to prevent heart disease and the consequent severe psychosocial trauma to the patient and family.

This particular project identified a working class population at high risk for heart disease by virtue of their having high blood pressure readings and high levels of cholesterol and other fatty substances in the blood. It was believed that the behavior patterns of this population in terms of smoking, eating, and stress response contributed to these clinical precursors of heart disease—for example, high blood pressure—and put them at greater risk of having a heart attack. The primary objective of the project was early intervention to modify behavior and reduce the presence of the clinical precursors and thus prevent the heart attack.

The program involved a multidisciplinary team including physicians, nurses, epidemiologists, statisticians, nutritionists, health advisors, and social workers. Again, the objective was the primary prevention of a health problem. The public health social workers on the team contributed significantly to this effort. While their attention, too, was on the health problem they, from their professional orientation, were focusing on the psychosocial determinants of the unhealthy behavior patterns of smoking and eating. And their concerns carried beyond the physical trauma of a heart attack to the psychological and social consequences of the cardiac event to the patient—if the patient survived—and to the patient's family.

Starting with a population already identified as high-risk by way of certain physical signs, the social workers then screened this high-risk population for additional risk factors, such as dysfunctional family relationships, negative attitudes toward health care, and poor understanding and acceptance of their health status. This group might then be considered to be a particularly high-risk subgroup requiring more aggressive intervention. Much effort on the part of the social workers was directed toward caseholding; that is, toward dealing with those psychosocial problems that might result in the patient's dropping out of the project and greatly increasing the chances of experiencing a coronary. Caseholding efforts included the use of sporting events and other recreation that participants usually enjoyed as part of the counseling sessions, as well as the involvement of other family members in the health education program for nutrition, exercise, and smoking habits. The social workers adapted their techniques to the social and health needs of the participants by using already existing social supports such as family and friends to maintain the participants' interest in better cardiovascular health. Through social work intervention the participants were able to realize the means to good health within their own family and culture by modification of their lifestyle.

SUMMARY

The foregoing is not intended to propose that the public health social worker possesses skills unique in the field; rather it is the blending of these basic social work skills with the public health perspective that gives this model its individuality. The public health social worker proceeds from a perspective that:

Focuses on *causes* as well as consequences,

Appreciates the unique characteristics of client *populations* as well as the individuality of clients,

Includes a population focus that subdivides into *relative-risk* categories,

Pays attention to the *denominator* (those not yet ill but in danger of becoming so) as well as the numerator (those already ill),

Seeks to understand the forces that keep persons *well* in addition to the insults that make them ill.

In summary it is a perspective concerned with understanding the nature and the extent of the problem, since it is the nature and extent of the problem that must dictate the services to be provided.

We have discussed the changes in the delivery of health services. However, corollary changes have also occurred in the delivery of human services. These include the need to adapt to the changing patterns of service delivery, the increased participation of consumers and the community in service delivery decisions, and the need for accountability. Therefore, the perspectives of the public health social worker can be valuable in other social work settings, such as schools, residential settings, welfare programs, and community mental health programs.

NOTES

[1] E. Spencer, "Public Health Social Work," in A. Katz and J. Felton, eds., *Health and the Community* (New York: Free Press, 1965), pp. 451–65.

[2] Elizabeth P. Rice, "Social Work in Public Health," *Social Work* 4, no. 1 (January 1959):88.

[3] Myron Lefcowitz, "The Public Health Professional: A Marginal Man," *American Journal of Public Health* 54 (July 1964):1125–28.

[4] Irving S. Wright and Donald T. Frederickson, eds., *Cardiovascular Diseases—Guidelines for Prevention and Care* (Washington, D.C.: U.S. Government Printing Office, 1973), p. 43.

[5] Leo Reeder, "Social Epidemiology: An Appraisal," in E. Gartly Jaco, ed., *Patients, Physicians, and Illness*, 2nd ed. (New York: Free Press, 1972), pp. 97–102.

[6] Ibid., p. 98.

REFERENCES

Bartlett, Harriett. "A Professional Reminiscence," *Health and Social Work*, Vol. 1, No. 1, (February, 1976), pp. 6–10.

Bartlett, Harriett. *Social Work Practice in the Health Field*, New York: NASW, 1961.

Bracht, Neil F. "The Contribution of Public Health Social Work in Academic Departments of Community Medicine," *Millbank Fund Quarterly*, Vol. 47, No. 1, Part 1, pp. 73–89.

"Concepts of Mental Health and Consultation—Their Application in Public Health Social Work," Publication No. 2072. Washington, D.C.: Public Health Service, U.S. Department of Health, Education, and Welfare, 1970.

Hookey, Peter, Ph.D. "Education for Social Workers in Health Care Organizations," *Social Work in Health Care*, Vol. 1, No. 3, (Spring, 1976), pp. 337–46.

Insley, Virginia. "Health Services: Maternal and Child Health Services," *Encyclopedia of Social Work*, Vol. 1, Washington, D.C.: NASW, 1973, pp. 552–60.

Proceedings of Tri-Regional Workshop on Planning and Im-

plementing Social Work Programs in Community Health Services for Mothers and Children. Pittsburgh: Public Health Social Work Program, Graduate School of Public Health, University of Pittsburgh, 1968.

A SYSTEMS APPROACH TO THE DELIVERY OF MENTAL HEALTH SERVICES IN BLACK GHETTOS

Richard H. Taber

In our attempt to develop new and more effective models for the delivery of mental health services to children in a black lower socioeconomic community, we have found the concept of the ecological systems approach extremely useful. Using this model we have explored the ecology of our community in order to define naturally occurring systems of support within the community—systems which, when utilized as a target for special types of intervention, could maximize the impact of our work.

This paper will focus on the rationale for our selection of two small natural groups: a partial social network composed primarily of mothers of highly disorganized families with young children, and a peer subsystem of 14–17-year-old boys. The ecological framework provided significant direction to our attempts to approach and work with these indigenous systems in such a way that members of the natural groups were given mental health services without being required to perceive themselves as patients.

The Rebound Children and Youth Project is jointly sponsored by the Children's Hospital of Philadelphia and the Philadelphia Child Guidance Clinic. It is charged with providing comprehensive health, dental, mental health, and social services to children in the area adjacent to these two institutions.

The community is a black ghetto in which 47 percent of the families have incomes below $3000 and "only 38 percent of the 1131 children covered in our survey are growing up within an intact family unit" (5). The project enjoys a positive image in the

neighborhood because of the involvement of the community in ongoing planning and the sensitive work of indigenous community workers, as well as the provision of much-needed pediatric services on a family basis.

We began this project with the view that many children in the black ghetto live with several pervasive mental health problems, primarily poor self-image and the concomitant sense of powerlessness. There are three ways of conceptualizing this problem. One is the individual psychological approach, which would identify early maternal deprivation as a primary cause. This factor can be identified in numerous cases we see clinically. Many children in this population have experienced early separation, abandonment, or maternal depression.

A second is the sociopolitical point of view, which directs attention to the systematic oppression and exploitation of this population by a predominantly white power structure. It also identifies historical and current influences which have undermined the family structure in the black ghetto and points to white racism as the source of black feelings of inferiority.

The ecological systems approach—the third way—directs our attention to the transactions and communications which take place between individual members of the poor black population and the systems within and outside of their neighborhood—that is, what actually goes on between the individual and his family, the individual and the extended fam-

---

Source: Reprinted from Richard H. Taber, "A Systems Approach to the Delivery of Mental Health in Black Ghettos," *American Journal of Orthopsychiatry* 40:4 (July 1970), pp. 702–709. Copyright 1971 by the American Orthopsychiatric Association, Inc. Reproduced by permission.

ily, the individual and the school, the individual and his job, the individual and the welfare agency, etc. Our exploration of these transactions, or *interfaces between systems*, shows that most of the transactions which take place are degrading and demoralizing and are experienced by the ghetto resident as "put downs."

When the problems of poor self-image and sense of powerlessness are approached from the concept of ecological systems, pathology is seen as the outcome of transactions between the individual and his surrounding social systems. Because no one element of these systems can be moved or amplified without affecting other elements, the ecological approach to the delivery of services requires exploration of the ways in which "the symptom, the person, his family, and his community interlock" (2).

As an example, to plan effective services for a 15-year-old boy, we must explore not only the boy as an individual but also what takes place at the interfaces between the boy, his family, the school, and other formal institutions and at the interface with peers, adults, and other representatives of the larger society. Chances are that his family expects little of him that is positive except that he stay out of trouble. He may often hear that he is expected to turn out to be a no-good bum like his father. At the interface with adults in the neighborhood he meets with open distrust and hostility. If he should wander out of the ghetto into a white area, his blackness, speech, and dress quickly cause him to be labeled as a hoodlum and treated with suspicion. He sees the police or "man" as a source of harassment and abuse rather than protection. If he is still in school he has become used to not being expected to learn (3). He may not know that the curriculum was designed with someone else in mind, but he is certainly aware that his style of life and the style of learning and behavior expected in school do not mesh (8). If he is in contact with a social or recreational agency, chances are that its program is designed to "keep him off the streets" and control his behavior. Competence is not expected from him and cannot be demonstrated by him. However, his peer system, usually a gang, does give him an opportunity to demonstrate competence. He is needed by the gang in its struggle to maintain "rep" and fighting strength. Gang membership offers him structure, a clear set of behavioral norms, a role and opportunity for status—all essential elements in the struggle toward identity. He is, however, then caught up in a system of gang wars and alliances which he

has little or no control over and which limits the availability of role models.

Adults in the ghetto neighborhood have similarly limited opportunities for self-definition as persons of worth and competence. For reasons which have been dealt with elsewhere (6), a mother may not perceive herself as able to control her children's behavior outside of her immediate presence; yet she is expected to do so by a whole series of people representing systems within her neighborhood—her neighbors and relatives, the school, etc.—and outside her neighborhood—the attendance officer, the police, etc. Her transactions with people representing formal social agencies and other social systems are usually experienced as destructive. In the interface with welfare, legal, medical, and other services, she receives attitudinal messages which are critical or punitive or, at best, patronizing. If she goes for therapy or counseling in a traditional psychiatric setting, she must accept another dependency role—that of patient. One of the conditions of receiving such help is usually that she admit to a problem within herself. She may also perceive the therapist's interpretations of her behavior as robbing her of any expertise about herself. What may hurt her most are the verbal and nonverbal attacks she receives from moralistic neighbors.

One source to which she can turn for acceptance and support in dealing with personal and interfamilial crises is her social network of friends, relatives, and neighbors. An important function of the network is to offer her guidance in her contacts with external systems. A friend or relative may accompany her to an appointment. Often after an unsuccessful encounter at an interface, the group will offer sympathy from collective experience and suggestions for avoiding or coping with the system the next time the need arises.

Having identified the existence of these two social groups in our community (the social network and the gang), we began to wonder how to utilize our knowledge so as to intervene in these systems in a way that would maximize their natural mental health functions. Unlike members of an artificial group, members of a natural group have day-to-day contacts and ongoing significance in each others' lives. The effects of therapeutic intervention in them should be able to transcend a one-hour-a-week interview and reverberate through the ongoing system. Also, intervention with natural community groups fits with our point of view that the answer to the problems of ghetto residents must come from the emergence of self-help groups within the community. Sources outside the community will never be willing or able to pour enough resources into the ghetto to solve the problems there. And our recognition of the value of local self-help organization brings us to a point of substantial agreement at the interface between our project and emerging black awareness and black nationalism.

We sought to work with natural systems without requiring that the people perceive themselves as patients. The intervenor sought to define his role as that of advisor, rather than leader or therapist. We felt that this model would prove most effective for the promotion of indigenous leadership and help establish the self-help system on a permanent basis. Through successful task completion, people would have concrete reason to see themselves as worthwhile and competent.

In order to avoid making people patients, we chose to focus attention on transaction and communications at strategic interfaces rather than on individual problems. We find that this focus is more syntonic with the point of view of our target population, because members of the disorganized lower socioeconomic population tend to see behavior as predominantly influenced by external events and circumstances rather than intrapsychic phenomena (5, 8).

One advantage of an approach which does not require that people perceive themselves as patients is that the natural group and the intervenor's involvement are visible. This increases the potential of the group for having an impact on other individuals and systems in the community. And the individual, far from being shamed because he is a patient, feels the pride of being publicly identified as a member of a group which enjoys a positive image in and outside the community.

THE "C" STREET NETWORK

The social network we chose to work with was one of highly disorganized family units which had been observed in the course of an anthropological study of families in the neighborhood (4). The families which formed the core of this network lived on "C" Street, a street which has a reputation in the neighborhood as a center of wild drinking, promiscuous sexual and homosexual behavior, the numbers racket, and gambling.

The approach to the "C" Street network was planned by a project team which included a pediatrician and two indigenous community workers. Our plan was to seek to improve child-rearing practices and parent-child communication by raising the self-esteem and effectiveness of the parents. The indigenous community workers played a key role in introducing the mental health intervenor to members of the network and have played important ongoing roles as linking persons in the interface between network members and the white middle-class social worker.

Our approach to the system was through one couple in the network who in response to a survey question had indicated interest in participating in a discussion group on neighborhood problems. The worker introduced himself as a person interested in working with neighborhood discussion groups. It was agreed that such a group might be most effective if it were limited to people who knew each other well or who were related. Despite the expressions of interest by the network members, it was several weeks before the group began meeting formally. Before the members could trust the intervenor and before they could feel that meeting together might really accomplish something, it was necessary for the social worker to have many contacts with the members in their homes or on the street. In addition to discussions of members' ideas of what could be accomplished by meeting together, these contacts were social in nature, since it was necessary for the members to see the intervenor as a person who was sincerely interested and was not turned off by clutter, roaches, etc.

Initially we wanted to let the network define itself, but we were also committed to including the men of the community in our intervention program. Because of the sex role separation in this group, however, we had limited success in including men in formal group meetings, although the intervenor did have other contacts with the men in the network.

One critical step in the development of this program was that the network members, assisted by the community workers, needed to help the intervenor unlearn some of the anti-organizational principles of group therapy and to recognize the importance of ordered, structured communications. In other words, the group itself had to push "to stop running our mouths and get down to business." Once officers had been elected and rules had been developed for conducting meetings and a dues structure set up, the group became task oriented. The format was that of an evening meeting in the home of one of the members, the formal business meeting followed by a social time during which refreshments including punch and beer were served. The first main areas of concern were more adequate and safer recreation for the children and improvements in housing. Through group and individual activity, houses were fixed up and the street beautified. Recreation for the children included children's parties and bus trips, planned and executed by the mothers, and the sponsorship of . a play-street program.

One of the community workers is now working more closely with the group as the social worker begins to step back. The group plans to run its own play-street program this summer, as they are convinced that they can do a better job than the community house that ran it last year.

THE NOBLETEENS

The other natural group which we began to intervene with was a subsystem of the local gang. The boys initially contacted were still in school, although far behind; they did not have major police records. The intervenor discussed with them the idea of getting together with other boys to discuss what it's like to grow up black in a ghetto community. They were asked to bring their friends.

Letters and personal reminders were used for the first several weeks. The intervenor was frequently out on the street, available for informal encounters. Unlike the adult network, where almost all our contacts have continued to be in the group's neighborhood, the boys have had their meetings in the clinic from the outset. They still stop by almost daily to see their advisor.

The initial ten-meeting program was focused on current relationships with school, police, and community, on vocation and the development of black pride and awareness, on sex and parenthood. Use was made of movies such as the *Lonely One* and *Nothing But a Man* and dramatizations of written material such as *Manchild in the Promised Land*.

At an early meeting of the group one of the more articulate members referred to the tape recorder and asked if this was to be like a study of ghetto youth. The intervenor said that that was not the purpose, but that one project that the boys might be interested in would be to make tape recordings about life in the ghetto to educate "dumb white people." The group picked this up enthusiastically as an op-

portunity of showing people outside the neighborhood some of the positive things about themselves, since they thought that the papers usually talked about the bad things. The passive process of having discussions that were tape recorded turned into the active process of making tape recordings. From his position as a learner from a white middle-class background, the intervenor could ask questions and promote reflections. It became possible to highlight and underline examples of positive coping. The group became for the boys a place in which they could express the most positive aspects of themselves.

After the initial period, the group decided to become a club and the intervenor's role was then defined as that of advisor. (One of the club president's functions is to be a "go-between" between members and advisor.) The group structured itself and took a more active task focus—throwing dances, starting a basketball team, starting an odd-job service (which has since involved contracts to move furniture), writing articles for the Rebound Newsletters. Carrying on their "thing" about educating people outside their system, the boys made presentations to the staff and agency board of directors, spoke on a soul radio station, and wrote articles about themselves. Maximum use of these experiences was made by the intervenor in promoting recognition and development of individual assets and skills.

As a result, new opportunities for role experimentation and contact with role models have been made available to the boys. Through successful completion of tasks the group has won a "rep" in the neighborhood and gets positive reinforcement from adults. One development is that the Nobleteens have "quit the corner." As they became involved in the Nobleteens and began to see themselves as valuable people with futures, the boys spent less time hanging out with the gang and reduced their delinquent activities. This affected the fighting strength of the gang in the balance of power with other gangs, and so the gang challenged the Nobleteens' existence by beating up several members. The next day, a member of the gang happened to be stabbed by a member of a rival gang, but when a runner came to enlist the Nobleteens for revenge, they refused to fight.

A black male community worker is now co-advisor to the Nobleteens. His focus with the group will be to further promote positive black identity through involvement in activities such as a Black Holiday marking the date of the assassination of Malcolm X. He will also be helping the boys take on a business venture of benefit to the community. The present intervenor hopes to develop a program in which a subgroup of the club will be hired as big brothers to younger boys who have been clinically identified as needing a relationship with an older black male.

THE ROLE OF THE INTERVENOR

Because the intervenor or advisor is in frequent contact with group members, often on a social basis, he enters into and can influence the social context on their behalf. He also stands in a unique position in the group in that he is conversant with external systems. He can therefore provide a linking function by bringing the systems together, promoting what is hopefully a growth-producing transaction for the group member and an educational one for the representative of the external systems. In terms of communication he can act as a translator for both sides. Because accommodation has taken place between him and the group members, he is better able to use their language and they, his.

Several examples here may illuminate the therapeutic possibilities of the intervenor's role in the interface between the natural group and the external system.

Example 1. In the first several months of the Nobleteens, Rick, a 14-year-old boy, visited as a guest, a cousin of a member. He was known by the nickname "Crazy" because of his impulsivity and lack of judgment. He impressed the worker as a depressed, nonverbal youngster. He then stopped coming.

During the summer the advisor was approached by Rick's mother to act as a character witness. Rick had been arrested for breaking into a parking meter and she was panicky because he had already been sent away once. The advisor talked with Rick while they cleaned paint brushes. Rick convinced the advisor that he really didn't want to be sent away again, and the advisor convinced Rick that it wasn't going to be as easy to stay out of trouble as Rick pretended it would be. They finally agreed that the advisor would recommend Rick's inclusion in the club and would report his impressions to the court.

Rick was known to the boys in the Nobleteens but usually hung out with a more delinquent subgroup. When the advisor recommended his inclusion in the club, one of the members (who happened to be retarded) questioned why Rick should have prefer-

ence over the boys who were waiting to get in. He then recalled seeing the advisor coming down in the elevator with Rick's mother, realized that it was about the trouble Rick was in, and quickly withdrew his objection.

Beyond this there was no discussion of Rick's problem, but the message was clear. The club members included him in their leisure activities and protected him when trouble was brewing. Eventually the charge was dropped, and he has not been picked up for delinquent behavior since that time. He has responded positively to the feeling of group inclusion, appears noticeably less depressed, and is more verbal. The payoff came for Rick when he was unanimously elected captain of the basketball team.

Example 2. A well-known child psychiatrist was brought to a Nobleteen meeting to consult with the boys in writing a speech for influential people in the health and welfare field. His goal was to argue for more flexibility on the part of youth-serving agencies. The intervenor's only role was to bring the two together. The psychiatrist was familiar with the boys' language, and they were experienced in discussing topics which focused on their relationships with external systems. Tape-recorded material from the meeting was included in the speech, and the boys gained a great sense of competence in verbalizing their concerns and points of view.

Example 3. At one meeting of the "C" Street network club, two members informed the advisor that Mrs. White, the club president, was having an extremely severe asthma attack. The group discussed this informally and came to the conclusion that it was really her "nerves" and that she should go into the hospital. Mrs. White had been hospitalized several times previously and was diagnosed as a borderline schizophrenic. Mrs. White's main supports—her sister and her closest friend—were extremely anxious, their own fears of death and separation coming to the surface. This placed them in a real approach-avoidance bind. The advisor agreed to visit Mrs. White after the meeting.

Mrs. White was lying on the couch coughing in uncontrollable bursts. The advisor soon labeled the coughing (which was panicking her and the other two women) as a "good thing" and encouraged it. He sympathetically listened to Mrs. White recount her dramatic collapse on the hospital's emergency room floor and her subsequent hallucinations. While she talked, the two network members busied themselves cleaning up the house and attending to the children. Once the advisor had listened, he began exploring areas of stress with her. The most recent crisis was that she was being threatened with eviction for non-payment of rent. She had contacted her relief worker, who had promised to contact the landlord. The advisor promised to talk to the relief worker. He also learned that in desperation she had gone to a different hospital. She had confidence in the treatment she received there, but did not see how she could go back for an early morning clinic. The advisor agreed that Rebound could provide her with a cab voucher.

Then the three women and the advisor sat and discussed the events of the club meeting. Mrs. White's coughing subsided, and she became calmer as she related to outside reality. The friend's and the sister's anxiety was also reduced. They could then respond in ways which reduced rather than heightened Mrs. White's anxiety.

The significance of this intervention lies not so much in the availability of the professional to meet the immediate dependency needs and to manipulate external systems on the woman's behalf as in his being in a position to repair her system of significant supports. A member of her own system would thenceforth be able to remind her that her rent was due when she got her check and remind her about the attendance officer if she became lax in getting her children off to school. The program continued to meet her dependency needs and support her medical care through the cab vouchers. Initially the vouchers were obtained for her by the professional; later she took responsibility for reminding him about getting them; eventually she went to the clinic's business office to get them herself. She has not suffered a severe attack or psychotic episode since the intervention.

Our commitment was to develop models for the delivery of services which multiply our therapeutic impact by bringing about change in existing systems. By focusing on competence and mutual support rather than on pathology, we have experimented with a model for the delivery of services to people who do not wish to perceive themselves as patients.

REFERENCES

1. Attneave, C. 1969. "Therapy in tribal settings and urban network intervention." *Fam. Proc.* 8:192–211.

2. Auerswald, E. 1968. "Interdisciplinary vs. ecological approach." *Fam. Proc.* 7:202–215.

3. Clark, K. 1965. *The Dark Ghetto: Dilemmas of Social Power.* Harper and Row, New York.

4. Leopold, E. 1969. "Hidden strengths in the disorganized family: discovery through extended home observations." Paper presented at meeting of Amer. Orthopsychiat. Assn.

5. Leopold, E. 1968. "Rebound children and their families: A community survey conducted by the rebound children and youth project." Mimeo.

6. Malone, C. 1966. "Safety first: Comments on the influence of external danger in the lives of children of disorganized families." *Amer. J. Orthopsychiat.* 36:3–12.

7. Minuchin, S., et al. 1967. *Families of the Slums: An Exploration of Their Structure and Treatment.* Basic Books, New York.

8. Minuchin, S. 1969. "Family therapy: Technique or theory." In *Science and Psychoanalysis*, J. Masserman, ed. 14:179–187. Grune & Stratton, New York.

9. Minuchin, S., and Montalvo, B. 1967. "Techniques for working with disorganized low socioeconomic families." *Amer. J. Orthopsychiat.* 37:380–887.

10. Rabkin, J., et al. 1969. "Delinquency and the lateral boundary of the family." In *Children against the Schools*, P. Graubard, ed. Follett Educational Corp., Chicago.

PART V

Issues

The subject of issues and their implications for the future of social work brings together and synthesizes for the reader the major themes of the text. Foremost among these themes is the belief that a generalist approach to practice is relevant to the times. Relevance implies a fit between the presenting issues and the profession's response. An issue is defined as a *societal concern*. This concern is differentially defined by the many individuals, groups, and organizations that have a stake in its resolution. To illustrate, care of the elderly may be regarded as a medical problem by the medical care system; for the elderly it is perhaps more of a problem in securing the essential services that make it possible to live independently in the community. Thus, for the elderly, it is not a medical problem so much as it is a problem of securing adequate housing, income supports, and personal support services, such as homemaker help. This is not to suggest that the elderly do not have medical problems and needs. Illness management is a major area of need and concern. However, in many instances it is not their overriding concern. Old age can be an emotionally healthy and satisfying time of life with a minimum of physical and mental impairment provided that sufficient basic social resources are available (Butler and Lewis 1973). The point in this discussion is that issues can be viewed differently by the service user—sometimes called the patient or the client—and the profession serving as caregivers.

Another dimension to the discussion of issues needs to be made explicit. Societal values and accompanying belief systems shape and determine society's definition of what is problematic. The student engaged in the study of social issues must become aware of the fact that every society maintains an *ordered variation* in their value orientation (Kluckhohn and Strodbeck 1961).

Success, achievement, and progress are dominant themes in the American value structure. A subdominant theme is humanitarianism, which explains the ambivalence over the support of social programs that come into conflict with the dominant themes of achievement, success, and progress. For example, the tragedy of old age in America—demonstrated by our failure to provide a decent existence for millions of elderly—becomes understandable but certainly not acceptable with the realization that this sector of society no longer can look to achievement and progress. For all practical purposes their life-goals are behind them. They are no longer regarded as the doers in society. The elderly have no future as future is regarded in the dominant value theme of America. (Butler and Lewis 1975).

The final part of this book, Part V, examines some of the issues—that is, the areas of societal concern—that have been developed in the preceding reading selections of the book.

The reading selections examine, in order, a variety of social concerns: population and technological changes, the role of the social worker in the future, prospects and problems for the generalist perspective in social work, and finally, the crucial issues of effectiveness and accountability of social work practice.

"Meeting Human Needs—An Integral Component of Public Policy," by Hauser, addresses four major areas of societal concern or issues: population explosion, population implosion, population displosion, and techniplosion. These four developments have profoundly affected societal values, institutions, and behavioral responses. The specific consequences that emerge from these developments have been identified by Hauser as follows:

1. Population explosion: A predicted population growth in the magnitude of 300 million by the year 2000 raises serious questions about quality of life for the nation;

2. Population implosion: In a relatively short period of time, the nation has shifted from a rural society to an urban world. The primary issues generated by population implosion are the changes in values, institutional changes, and behavioral changes required to live effectively in an urban world. Hauser suggests that the Constitution of the United States add another ten amendments and a Bill of Urban Rights to properly address human needs in a twentieth-century demographic and technological world;

3. Population displosion: The diversity or polyglot character of world communities is growing. Heterogeneity and diversity, when coupled with rising expectations and new belief systems, heightens conflict and tensions;

4. Techniplosion: The fourth development refers to the vast technological change in present society. Technology has produced a better environment; yet it poses the single greatest threat to the very survival of civilization.

There are several principles and concepts that need to be understood in considering the issues identified by Hauser and in assessing their impact on social work practice. First, it is essential to understand the high degree of interrelatedness of population explosion, implosion, displosion, and techniplosion. The totality of their impact on societal values, institutions, and behavioral responses has, to a large extent, helped to create the conditions that the profession now identifies as social problems: permanent structural unemployment for millions, large-scale substance abuse (alcohol and drug), decaying inner cities, racial and ethnic conflict, environmental pollution, traffic congestion, and the many other urban dilemmas.

Second, the concept of *cultural lag*—defined as the difference in response of societal institutions and their representatives to change; or more succinctly, some things change more rapidly than others—is a major issue for the profession. A profession that fails to recognize the implications of the changes identified by Hauser and consequently fails to make the necessary changes can be charged with cultural lag.

The reality is that change is constant, making cultural lag an ever-present danger and requiring constant review and flexibility in professional response. A generalized approach to practice, as conceptualized in the text, provides a more relevant and adequate professional model for coping with societal complexity and change and offers a more comprehensive approach to problem solving in an urban world.

Hauser's analysis of demographic and related issues and their relationship to the etiology and duration of social problems provides the necessary backdrop to "The Professional Worker and the Year 2000" by Walz and Hoffman. Hauser's thesis that man has created a twentieth-century technological world and is struggling, albeit unsuccessfully, to live in it parallels and reinforces Walz and Hoffman's premise that the new forms of technology have produced a postindustrial cybercultural society. The authors identify the central issues and role demands for an emerging new social work perspective:

1.   The need to master the new tools, particularly the computer, in a technologically oriented society;

2.   The need to redesign and rebuild the existing social welfare programs and institutions;

3.   The need to develop new managerial, administrative, and policy analysis knowledge and skills;

4.   The need to grasp the essence of a much broader field of social problems and systems of interventions;

5.   The need to build an adequate data base, clinically and epidemiologically;

6.   The need to humanize the agency environment, in essence, to create human-size and human-quality organizations;

7.   The need to develop the skills for effective participation in the political arena: lobbying, presentation of effective testimony, assistance in the design of public policy;

8.   The need to develop expertise in the use of mass media for serving a large diverse population, particularly in the task of resocializing people into new energy conserving and consuming roles.

Rebuilding a way of life and restructuring its institutions imply a new synthesis and redefinition of social work. The emerging trends identified by Walz and Hoffman include: a multidisciplinary approach to training and practice; a greater willingness on the part of professionals to share their knowledge and skills with the service receivers; and a more global vision that fits with the emerging global ecology that is important for social work participation in multinational developments.

Walz and Hoffman's reading selection prepares the reader for fully understanding and incorporating the concepts of "Generalists in Human Service Systems: Their Problems and Prospects" by Yessian and Broskowski, which addresses the related issues of internal integration of human-service organizations, interactions among organizations, and the responsiveness of organizations to service-receiver needs. Fragmentation, inaccessibility, discontinuity, inadequate response to presenting problems, and lack of accountability have become a litany of charges directed at much of social programming developed in the past several decades (Mullen and Dumpson 1972; Gilbert and Specht 1974; Rosenberg and Brody 1974).

The authors identify a new generalist in the human services, a professional who can more effectively meet the challenge of planning, designing, developing, and administering social programs. The *organizational generalist* in contrast to the *clinical specialist* will have the following attributes and assignments:

1.   Take a more holistic view of the total program mission;

2.   Exhibit a concern for multipopulation groups as contrasted to a concern for one sector of the community;

3.   Have staff responsibilities in contrast to line responsibilities. Staff responsibilities include managerial, supervisory, planning and policy formulation and analysis, and program designing responsibilities.

A number of professional roles are identified for the organizational generalist in human-services delivery: broker/affiliator; mediator/integrator/coordinator; general manager; educator; and analyst and evaluator.

Several factors are identified by the authors that have limited the growth and influence of the organizational generalist to date. These dilemmas are exceedingly important to understand, for they refer to the basic conditions and limitations of a cybercultural society as noted in the Walz and Hoffman reading selection. These factors include:

1. The greater influence of differentialization and specialization as basic processes in responding to the complex needs of urban society;

2. The difficulty experienced by generalists in demonstrating the effectiveness of their contributions. The effectiveness of specific gains or changes in policy planning and administration are hard to measure empirically;

3. The higher prestige accorded the specialist in society;

4. The continued dependence on selective, categorical approaches to legislation and funding. The reasons are political, fiscal, and administrative.

"Expectation, Performance, and Accountability," by Tropp, brings the discussion of issues and their implications for the generalist in social work full cycle. The public is more informed and sophisticated, with higher expectations; the imperialist position of not questioning the performance of the professional is no longer acceptable. Tropp reminds us that social workers need only to view themselves in the role of taxpayers or consumers to get an idea of the performance and accountability expected.

Profound changes in the total environment have brought all professions into a period of time that rightfully could be termed the *decade of accountability*. Tropp makes explicit a standard of accountability that includes: (1) provision of services to the public as claimed within the scope of the particular professional knowledge and skill; (2) delivery of services to those who contract for their use; and (3) education of social work practitioners and certification that they are qualified to practice their professions responsibly.

Expectation, performance, and accountability form a triad of reference points for examining the influence of the many variables that serve to define the conditions and criteria for their application to social work practice. Clarifying the expectations of service on which the user and provider agree is a starting point in the process of accountability. Yet, as Tropp reminds us, studies of social work effectiveness reveal a recurrent theme: Social agencies do not deliver what is expected of them. The question is raised whether the expectations for service were initially unrealistic. There is ample reason to believe that considerable disparity does indeed exist between expectations of providers, users, and sponsors of programs. What seems to block the congruence of perception of problem, need, mission, and application of the appropriate intervention? These are the hard-core issues that must be addressed by the profession.

REFERENCES

Butler, Robert, N., and Myrna T. Lewis.
  1973   *Aging and Mental Health*. St. Louis, Mo.: Mosby, p. 16.
Gilbert, Neil, and Harry Specht.
  1974   *Dimensions of Social Welfare Policy*. Englewood Cliffs, N.J.: Prentice-Hall.
Kluckhohn, C., and Strodbeck.
  1961   *Variations in Value Orientation*. New York: Row Peterson.
Kahn, Alfred J.
  1969   *Theory and Practice of Social Planning*. New York: Russell Sage Foundation.
Mullen, Edward S., and James Dumpson & Associates.
  1972   *Evaluation of Social Intervention*. London: Jossey-Bass.
Tropman, J. E.; M. Dluhy; and W. Vasey.
  1976   *Strategic Perspectives on Social Policy*. Elmsford, N.Y.: Pergamon Press.

MEETING HUMAN NEEDS—
AN INTEGRAL COMPONENT OF PUBLIC POLICY

Philip M. Hauser

Man, or a very close relative to man, has been on this earth for perhaps four million years. Man is the only complex, culture-building animal on the globe; he has generated four developments, which without question have more profoundly affected his attitudes, his values, his institutions, and his behaviorisms than anything else to which you might refer.

These four developments may be referred to as the population explosion, the population implosion, the population displosion, and the techniplosion. To prove that I am a professor of sociology, I should say that I regard these four elements as elements of the sociomorphological revolution. The *population explosion* refers, of course, to the remarkable acceleration of the rate of world population growth, particularly during the three centuries of the modern era.

By the *population implosion,* I refer to the increasing concentration of people on a relatively small portion of the earth's surface, a phenomenon better known as urbanization.

The *population displosion* takes an archaic word out of the dictionary to refer to the increasing heterogeneity of people who share not only the same geographic locale, but increasingly the same life-space— social, political, and economic activities. By heterogeneity, I refer to the diversity of people by culture, by language, by religion, by value systems, by ethnicity, by race, by lifestyle, and so on.

The *techniplosion* or tremendous acceleration of the rate of technological change certainly requires no further elaboration. These developments are interrelated. The explosion has fed the implosion; both have fed the displosion. Technological change has generally preceded social change and has been both antecedent and consequent to it. From the standpoint of quick-time perspective, I would like to point out the population explosion, out of four million years on this earth, as an event of only the past three cen-

turies. The population implosion worldwide is less than two centuries old. And the displosion, in the sense in which I am defining it, is as recent as the end of World War II.

The United States is the most dramatic example of the form of these developments, and I shall focus on them with relevance to human needs.

My thesis is that man as the only complex culture-building animal on the globe has developed a twentieth-century demographic and technological world. He is still trying to learn how to live in it— thus far not too successfully. This twentieth-century demographic and technological world has precipitated unprecedented problems, including human problems in the transition from what the anthropologist Robert Redfield called a middle community—the agrarian small-town type of society—to what Karl Mannheim has called a mass society—the urban and metropolitan order. These human problems have intensified and worsened, even as our traditional means of dealing with them have diminished, as human bonds have weakened, and as the twentieth-century demographic and technological world has delivered us into a highly interdependent and greatly vulnerable society.

The next segment of my thesis is that the problems which afflict us include the human problems— on the economic side: unemployment, underemployment, poverty; on the personal side: delinquency, crime, alcoholism, drug addiction, the revolt of youth, the revolt of women, the revolt of minority groups; on the political side: problems of the relation between central and local government in the United States, and for that matter, throughout the world, problems of political corruption. These are simply a superficial listing of the problems, many of which add up to dire human problems. These problems are going to grow considerably worse before they grow

Source: Philip M. Hauser, "Meeting Human Needs—An Integral Component of Public Policy," *Public Welfare* 30(1972):8–14. Reprinted with permission of the American Public Welfare Association. © 1972 American Public Welfare Association.

any better, the basic reason for which is that we are attempting to deal with these twentieth-century problems with nineteenth-century, eighteenth-century, and prior century ideologies, values, and institutions, including forms, structures, processes of government.

Our problems, our human problems—including welfare problems, with which all of you are identified—are going to grow considerably worse as long as we live in a nation where national priorities call for supersonic transports while efforts are made to diminish funds available for school lunches for underprivileged children; for antiballistic missiles, for new welfare schemes, while simultaneously vetoing legislation and appropriations for education, job training, and job opportunities.

Our problems are going to grow considerably worse on a human front. We are going to fail to meet human needs to a point where I think the very viability of the American society may be in question over the next several decades, as long as we have an administration in which the presidential spokesman, presumably making the viewpoint of this administration perfectly clear, is quoted as saying that the people on welfare are obviouly lazy, stupid miscreants whose rooms should be wallpapered with newspaper want ads to inspire them to rugged individualism and self-support. As long as we have these nineteenth-century attitudes, obviously ignorant of the requirements of the twentieth-century demographic and technological world, in administrative control—whether it is in Washington or in the state of California—our human problems are going to grow considerably worse before they grow any better.

THE POPULATION EXPLOSION

When the first census was taken in 1790, we were a nation of fewer than 4 million people. When the nineteenth dicennial census results were made available of population as of April 1, 1970, they indicated that we have become a nation of 205 million inhabitants. Now the number exceeds 208 million. Looking to the rest of the century, it is a virtual certainty, short of anything catastrophic and despite some predictions in the press that "zero population growth" is around the corner, that by the year 2000—a little more than a human generation from now—the U.S. population will be between 280 million and 300 million people. As a matter of fact, the Commission on Population Growth in the American Future, now concluding its final report for the president and the Congress, has taken it for granted that we shall reach 300 million, and it is raising basic questions about whether there really may be a fourth 100 million and whether or not such numbers of people may interfere with the quality of life in this nation. That's the explosion.

THE POPULATION IMPLOSION

When the first census was taken in 1790, 95 percent of the American people lived in rural places—on farms, or in small towns having under 2500 persons. There were only 24 urban places in the nation; only 2 of them had populations in excess of 25,000—New York and Philadelphia. This was the agrarian setting in which the Constitution of the United States was written, and it should create no wonderment on anyone's part to recognize why the Constitution of the United States is inadequate from the standpoint of meeting human needs. I would like to suggest that what we need is another ten amendments and a Bill of Urban Rights designed to meet human needs, because human needs of the type facing us today were unknown in the agrarian America in which our constitution was written.

A prerequisite to understanding many of the human problems confronting us today, many of which are encapsulated in what we call the Urban Crisis, we must know that this nation did not become an urban nation—in the sense that more than one-half of its people lived in urban places—until as recently as 1920. This means that in the year 1970, the United States marked the completion of its first half-century as an urban nation. A half-century is a very small period of time in the life of a nation and less than one lifetime.

It may be implied that most of the leadership in the Congress of the United States—particularly those leaders from the South with a one-party system and with seniority rules that determine power in the Congress of the United States—were born in an agrarian America. Most of them acquired nineteenth-century and even eighteenth-century ideologies and values. It is small wonder that many of them give evidence of never yet having entered the twentieth century in urban and metropolitan America.

Another implication is the generation gap—the complete inability of a generation, born into an agrarian society [and] having inherited the shibboleths and the values of the dead past, . . . [to] even communicate with the younger generation, born into a metropolitan America [and] having an absolutely different set of values. There are parents and children who are no longer able to speak to one another. They speak right past one another; they are not in the same universe of discourse. If we look ahead to the remainder of this century, it is a virtual certainty that practically all of the increase we experience in population will go into urban America.

For two consecutive decades and for the first time in the history of this nation, the increase in the urban population has exceeded the increase in the total population. It signifies that for the first time in our history the rural population is actually diminished in absolute size. This may continue. Looking ahead, the increase will become an urban or metropolitan increase, because with present trends, perhaps 85 percent of the total increment of population we experience by the year 2000 will go into metropolitan United States, defined by the government as cities of 50,000 or more and the counties in which they are located. That's the population implosion.

THE POPULATION DISPLOSION

Everybody in the United States, of course, comes from somewhere else. We are among the most polyglot of all nations. President Roosevelt one time incurred the undying enmity of the Daughters of the American Revolution when, having been invited to address their annual conclave, his salutation was, "Fellow immigrants. . . . "

As recently as 1900 without tracing the whole story, 49 percent of the American people were either foreign-born, children of foreign-born (that is, second generation immigrants), blacks, or members of other races. As recently as 1960 (the most recent census result on this subject) 30 percent of the American people were either foreign-born, children of foreign-born or of mixed parentage, blacks, or members of other races. By the population displosion, I have in mind not only the heterogeneity of people sharing the same geographic locale and the same life-space— social, political, and economic activities—but ... something new that has been added since World War II. Since that time, the world has been swept by the revolution of rising expectations.

This means that this is the first generation in the history of mankind in which there are virtually no peoples left anywhere on the globe who are willing to settle for second place or to do without freedom and independence that they have not yet achieved; there are no minority groups anywhere that do not insist on full equality in fact as well as in theory and

law. Antiquity was characterized by heterogeneous peoples. Ancient Rome had quite a diversity of peoples, but in previous societies diversity was accompanied by rigid stratification, by caste system, by slavery. We say under these conditions, each of the peoples knew their place.

But in a world swept by the revolution of rising expectations, where minority peoples have a view of a form of egalitarianism in a pluralistic society, something new is added to the situation. That something new is evident in frictions throughout the globe. This is the basis for understanding what is going on, for example, in Northern Ireland in the bitter conflict between Catholics and Protestants; in the conflict between India and Pakistan, or, for that matter, in that which has raged among the diverse linguistic groups within India; in the fratricidal battle between West and East Pakistan, which among other things is a horrible tribal conflict between the Punjabi and the Bengali; between the Chinese and the Malays in Malaysia; among the tribal groups in Africa; between the blacks and whites in the Union of South Africa, Rhodesia, the United Kingdom, and the United States of America. All of these may be better understood as frictions and transitions still under way into a twentieth-century demographic and technological world in which man has not yet learned how to live.

In this country let me focus on the blacks as a symbol of the problems that arise from a population displosion. In 1790 there were about 800,000 blacks in this nation, somewhat fewer than there were in the city of Chicago in 1960, but they then made up 20 percent of the American people, which percentage remained until about 1820. Then, under one of the great compromises of the Constitutional Convention, the slave traffic stopped. White immigrants continued to come. The proportion of blacks continued to dwindle to less than 10 percent by 1930. Since 1930 they have held their own or grown more rapidly than the white population, so they are up to about 12 percent again. As recently as 1910, 89 percent of blacks were still concentrated in the South, largely in the rural slum South, or approximately 3 percent less than the concentration as reported in the Census of 1860, the last census before the Civil War.

At present, almost one-half of the nation's blacks are in the North; sometime during the 1980s the proportion of blacks in the North will exceed the proportion in the South.

Another basic fact is that as recently as 1910, when 89 percent of the blacks were in the South, 73 percent lived in rural places, those with populations under 2500 people. By 1960 those percentages became reversed. The blacks have been transformed from 73 percent rural to 73 percent urban in a half-century, less than one lifetime. As recently as 1960, according to the 1960 census results, 78 percent of black adults (those 25 years of age and older) had not completed high school; 23 percent were functionally illiterate; that is, they had no education beyond the fifth grade, usually in Southern schools, and were unable to read a metropolitan newspaper. This was their share of the American way of life. This was their preparation for one of the most dramatic transformations in the history of man, in less than one lifetime. I stress this feature because there are societies in America called SPNGE—Societies for the Prevention of the Negro's Getting Everything, usually made up of immigrant white ethnic groups who say they started in the slums; they had to work their way up and out; and question why all these special things for the blacks. What they do not understand is that when they came to this country with nothing but strong backs, the nation was still building railroads, factories, the urban interstructure, and with a strong back you were able to make a living.

When the blacks entered the mainstream of American life after having been here for three and one-half centuries with nothing but strong backs, they came in when America was so technologically advanced that there was little demand for unskilled labor. Our blacks have come to the mainstream of American life in a situation which doesn't permit them even to make a living. This is a pretty fundamental difference, among other differences.

THE TECHNIPLOSION

These developments—the population explosion, implosion, and displosion—have precipitated unprecedented problems. There is no point in listing before this group the problems which concern public welfare, the problems of human need. In the transition by reason of these developments, from the little community to a mass society, new human needs have emerged. The kinds of needs are represented, for example, by the need for pure air, pure water; the elimination of the slum; acquiring the basic skills, the civic skills which enable one stand on his own feet in our society; by the problems of unemployment, underemployment, and consumer exploitation; the problems of inequality and lack of opportunity for minority groups, and so on. These problems will grow considerably worse before they get better because we have a system of national priorities in which human needs are very low on the totem pole, very low indeed. These problems are going to grow worse because we are attempting to tackle them, as I say, with nineteenth- and eighteenth-century ideologies and values.

One of my former professors, William F. Augburn, introduced into the social science literature the concept of *cultural lag*. He perceived in our society that some things change more rapidly than others. Others lag. There are some examples, one fraught with terrific potentials, that indicate why we have some of the human needs which confront our society unresolved. As recently as 1960, there were thirty-nine states where there was a majority of urban population, but in not one of these did the urban population control the state legislature!

. . . .Why is the federal government involved . . . in urban renewal, public housing, civil rights, highways and expressways, education, mass transit? . . . The uninformed . . . say it is because the federal government has usurped states' rights. I submit that it is because these deliberately malapportioned state legislatures so callously ignore urban problems and human problems that the predominant majority of the American people (70 percent in 1960, 74 percent in 1970) turn to the federal government for the resolution of their problems.

From this point on, I think it matters little what the state governments do, despite the administration's loudly publicized Madison Avenue thing about the new federal . . . policy. It is the state governments that have made themselves the fifth wheel of the American system of government. It is not that the federal government has usurped states' rights. It is that the state legislatures have been committing suicide. This goes for the welfare front, as well as other fronts in American life. . . .

In fact, let me tell you what the new federal . . . policy means to me as set forth by this administration. It means that the state governments, which for the first seventy years of this century have demonstrated their lack of interest in urban and human problems, have demonstrated that they are much more subject to special interest pressures than is the federal government (this is not to say that the federal government is not subject to special interest pressures), and have demonstrated they do not have the personality expertise to deal with these kinds of problems.

This is the administration's way of rewarding these state governments for performance not performed for the first seventy years of this century. . . .

Let me give another example of the cultural lag. There is not a city in this nation that has either the legislative authority or the resources with which to deal with its problems (including its welfare problems) . . . not one, why? Our form of local government, municipal government, is still that which we inherited from eighteenth-century England. The English have long since gotten rid of it, but we're still stuck with it. Not only that, but we have suburban cliques (some of them are called "Save Our Suburbs") with men and women determined to chain themselves to bulldozers if necessary if anyone even talks about metropolitan planning, because that's obviously, to quote from their literature, a form of communism—metropolitan area planning. Some of us are old enough to remember when it was a form of communism when you talked about city planning. Planning has now become respectable in the United States, if you modify it with the term "city." This does not mean that many people are paying too much attention to what the planning commissions are. . . . This will be another generation's effort.

These are other examples on the ideological front of cultural lag. Let me give you some of the shibboleths from the dead past which preclude our society's dealings with any of our problems, including our human problems. Such nonsense, for example, that government is best which governs least. Each man in pursuing his own interest is guided by an invisible hand. That's in the interest of the common activity. *Caveat emptor*—Let the buyer beware. Taxes are something government takes away from people, and therefore it should be kept to a minimum. A welfare state is a pejorative, dangerous, communistic thought. Let us have rugged individualism. These are just a few of these ancient shibboleths, which we prattle as if we were still in 1790 instead of 1971 and near 1972.

Consider the first two shibboleths, that government is best which governs least and that each man in pursuing his own interest is guided by Adam Smith's invisible hand. That's in everybody's interest. Some of this nonsense, may I say, is still taught in some of our leading universities.

Back in 1790, 95 percent of the American people were on a farm or in a small town. What was there for government to do? But can anyone in his right mind visualize the United States today without a So-cial Security system, without a Pure Food and Drugs Administration, without a Public Health Service, and so on down the line? If you took care of your own family on that farm or small town in 1790, you were doing all that was necessary—not only for the economics of your family, but for the economy of the United States as well.

Caveat Emptor. In a debate with a conservative economist, he insisted that *caveat emptor* (let the buyer beware) should still regulate the markets of the United States. I'll tell you what it means to me—every woman in the United States has the right to bear one, two, maybe three deformed babies and then when she discovers thalidomide is to be blamed, she can punish the pharmaceutical house by no longer buying any more thalidomide. What utter nonsense and poop! This means that every shopper has the right to learn how to use the slide rule so that when you go to the supermarket, you discover the large-size economy package costs you more per ounce than does the small-size package. In 1790, if you exchanged a few chickens for a sack of flour, the chances are you were astute enough to determine whether or not the chickens were still alive.

Taxes are something the government takes away from people, and should be kept to a minimum. We have yet to devise in this nation, or for that matter in any nation, a mechanism as responsive to the meeting of our new, connected human needs as the market mechanism that is so elegantly responsive to meeting individual personal needs. The market is triggered by effective demand; you've got the money for something and you want it, that market's going to get it to you. But what is the equivalent when it comes to meeting collective needs—relief from air pollution and from water pollution, and the elimination of the slum? The ballot box. I challenge anyone to tell me here that that has been very responsive. The equivalent of money is demonstrations, picketing, riots, guerrilla warfare. Guerrilla warfare is just getting under way in this country. There is real reason to wonder about the bi-identity of some of our society, even though some of our politicians (few of whom are statesmen) continue to try to operate as if conditions were "normal," as usual.

THE PROBLEM OF WELFARE

Let me get more specifically to the problem of welfare. A welfare society is a nasty, socialistic, communistic concept. In my judgment one of the most interesting anachronisms I ever heard was that of the President of the United States in proposing his new welfare program, which has some good points and also some sharp punitive points to be avoided, carefully pointing out that this would not create a welfare society. It would still be a society of rugged individuals.

Let me tell you something about welfare. In our system, we assume equality of opportunity; you enter the economy; you do your work. This is the basis not only for achieving current income; it is also the basis for building up pension rights—public or private. If you fall by the wayside, there is welfare, including the categoric forms of aid. But who are on the welfare rolls disproportionately today? They are our minority groups, our poor. These are not people in the main who have fallen by the wayside. These are people who have never had the opportunity in the United States to get under way.

I want to assure those of you in public welfare, and for that matter private welfare, that you have chosen one of the most sound professions looking at the decades ahead that you could possibly choose. You are not going to be afflicted with unemployment or underemployment. You are going to have opportunities for promotions and raises indefinitely. Yours is a great career, because as long as we all live in a nation that produces millions of culturally and socially mutilated and deformed people every year, your future on the welfare front is well assured.

We are continuing. I see nothing in evidence in public policy, federal or state, that does not guarantee that in the next generation there will be as many people on the welfare rolls as there are in this generation, because there isn't a central city in the United States today that is providing the inner city children—white, black, brown, red, or otherwise—with the education, the basic skills, the salable skills, or the civic skills that will enable them to stand on their own feet in the next generation. And our welfare problem will not be resolved until we set our national priorities in such a way as to increase our investment in our own human beings.

I close, however, on a positive note. It took roughly the century from 1750 to 1850 for the physical sciences to achieve the respectability to enable physical engineers to apply physical science knowledge to physical problems. It required approximately the century from 1850 to 1950 for the biomedical sciences similarly to acquire sufficient acceptance to enable biomedical engineers—the physician and surgeon—to apply knowledge to the solution of problems of health and life. It may take from 1950 to 2050 for the social sciences to gain comparable respectability so that the social engineer is permitted to apply knowledge to the solution of social problems.

I am convinced that we have the means to deal with our problems in an effective manner to create a twentieth-century world in its social, economic, political, and technological aspects. The means to this lies in man's potential for rational behavior—in man's ability through science to acquire knowledge and in his ability through engineering to apply knowledge for the solution to his problem.

THE PROFESSIONAL SOCIAL WORKER AND THE YEAR 2000

Thomas H. Walz, Frances Hoffman

THE YEAR 2000

This reading selection addresses the subject of the future in social work. The year 1984, long the symbol of a nebulous future, has been superseded by the year 2000—a more comfortably distant time frame. Whatever year is assigned, the subject is still future issues, and with them, the issues of today. There is much truth in the oft-repeated observation, "the future is now."

The reading selection deals with the changing nature of a professional practice attempting to keep pace with a changing world. Developments in philosophical knowledge and the skill base of the profes-

---

Source: This article was specially prepared for this volume by the authors.

sion are analyzed as responses to structural and directional movements already apparent in modern society.

The key assumption in this essay is the now widely accepted concept that Western industrial societies have entered a new, postindustrial era. As Daniel Bell and others have pointed out, the profound changes in technology and its widespread application have substantively altered the nature of our society. As social work is essentially an industrial-age invention, the emergence of a postindustrial period indicates a need for extensive retooling and reshaping in the profession and practice. For a social work educator, reading this changing society and appropriately redesigning education for the profession is no simple task.

One difficulty in using a view of the future as a basis for recommending changes in professional practice is that there is no *one* view. Scenarios of the future are as common as futurists. While most futurists might agree that there are a few "probables" that will define our world in the year 2000, each exercises his or her own preferences or choices. These authors are no exception. Despite the attempt to draw most heavily upon postindustrial structural changes already evident and at work in the reshaping of North American society, our preferences are harbored.

No matter how responsibly done, forecasting is a risky business. Once before, one of us authored a similar essay ("A New Breed of Social Worker")[1] in which trends in social work practice were forecasted, and they were proven embarrassingly wrong, at least in the short run. Written at the turn of the present decade, the essay predicted the emergence of a new breed of freewheeling social workers oriented to activist social action; the author was convinced that the medical model of the profession had given way to a legal advocacy model.

While important changes did occur within the profession when confronted by the realities of the sixties, much of the social reform drive and its leadership has again receded to the margins of the profession. Traditional practice modes and orientations have been reestablished at the center of the profession; only new techniques—based on selected new knowledge—differentiate social work practice of old from that practiced today. In the schools of social work, new curriculum is largely limited to growth and behavioral control therapies. (In administration it's called *management techniques* and *accountability*.)

These modest developments in knowledge for practice are not without a direct link to societal change and need. The "self-actualizing" drive in a middle-class-dominated society is real, as is the need for a mass, corporate society to enhance its behavioral management and control over an unpredictable mass of consumers. Yet the profession's response has been traditional, conservative, and self-seeking. The social work profession has selectively addressed itself to those issues that require highly controlled investments of professional energy and that fit the usual clinical problem-solving approaches. These standard tools, even when given a fresh undercoating of new technique, are not adequate to fulfill the profession's obligatory response to the full range of new demands associated with modern society.

In other words, the emergence of a new breed of social worker, which I felt would rise out of the value conflicts of the 1960s, produced by the mid-1970s an "old breed" of social worker, not unlike its professional counterparts from the 1940s and 1950s.

The retreat from the task of social reconstruction to social treatment is not a phenomenon unique to social work. In many ways it paralleled the general posture of the society itself. Generally there has been a drift away from the concerns that occasioned the war on poverty, the civil rights movement, and the building of model cities. The issues of the poor and minorities have been replaced by the issues of the more dominant majority and its search for personal meaning and satisfaction in an impersonal society that selectively rewards its supporters with material benefits. By serving a more favored client, the profession has enhanced its status and achieved greater material rewards.

Looking ahead to the year 2000, the argument about the nature of practice must move beyond the traditional ideological debate over the merits of medical and legal models and simply face the emerging realities produced by a postindustrial society. We must choose whatever method, theory, tool, or relationship is necessary to resolve critical issues.

THE NEW ERA

For nearly four hundred years, the Western world has been moving from a rural to urban, an agrarian to industrial, orientation. This shift is nearing its completion in the last decades of the twentieth century. However, as this structural change is being completed, another somewhat more profound shift is taking place: the coming of the *postindustrial era*, to borrow Daniel Bell's favorite label for modernism.[2]

Space permits only a very brief analysis of the structural changes associated with the postindustrial society. Hopefully, enough material is presented to show how these perceptions are logically related to recommended changes in social work practice and education for that practice.

According to Bell, the threshold of postindustrialism was crossed about mid-century, when accumulated theoretical knowledge—converted to practical technology—produced such tools as the computer, laser, video, nuclear energy, and holography. The power and significance of these tools were such that the total structure of society was deeply affected: the economy, the polity, and the culture.

The postindustrial society is one of scale and interdependence. The new tools of technology have made possible a world of mass production and mass consumption. Economies of scale, based on size and functional specialization, permit maximum product at minimum cost. The achievement of these material ends requires cooperation of the entire social infrastructure; that is, human values, social institutions, and cultural lifestyles.

In Bell's analysis of postindustrial society, he identifies the presence of three catalytic variables (principles):

1. *The economizing mode* (belief in maximum production and minimum input) is the principle that governs the economy and reshapes the occupational structure;

2. *The participatory mode* (belief in egalitarianism and importance of participatory government) is the principle that explains the working of political society;

3. *The self-actualizing mode* (the search for interpersonal meaning in life through emphasis on personal growth and experience) is the principle shaping the directions of modern culture.

Social conflict and individual dysfunction within the social system can be explained in the mutual incompatability of these axial principles. Economic efficiency is often achieved only at the cost of human liberty and dignity. Participatory democracy is often realized only at the cost of time, money, and energy in attempting to reconcile group differences. (The modern bureaucracy doesn't want to expend this sort of time, energy, and money in the name of participatory democracy.) Self-fulfillment is easiest to achieve if one simply drops out of the economic-occupational structure.

Levered by these axial principles, the postindustrial world took on its own look: that of a high-energy, machine-based industrial system guided by high-speed computers requiring huge doses of knowledge input but little human energy. The model, of course, also became corporatized, and in becoming corporatized, bureaucratized. The postindustrial society is now scaled to the machine, not man, and its organizational design shows a preference for a machine metaphor: rational, mechanical, absolute.

So the postindustrial era has emerged, ominous and opportunistic; capable of mass-producing goods and longer life; adapted to cities and large corporate forms of social organization; accepting of transient values and spatial activity; experiencing interdependency both nationally and internationally; discovering the paradox of the copresence of inflation and recession; suffering from anomie and familial instability while enjoying new freedoms and unrestricted relationships.

The problems of postindustrial society may appear old, but they are new. They represent the social costs of a new socioeconomic system and will require a new social work practice if social work is to make a contribution to their resolution.[3] The total basis of practice is challenged: the values, knowledge, and appropriateness of practice skills. What follows is a look at these practice considerations, with an eye on the year 2000.

Preeminence of Scholarship

The advent of the postindustrial era, with its attendant infusion of new technology, presents the profession with an interesting dilemma. It offers a new set of tools for problem solving—for example, computer, video, cheap energy, and so on—while producing a variety of new problems and issues requiring solutions. The computer may help facilitate the payment of social security benefits, yet it threatens clients with potential abuse of confidentiality and invasion of privacy. Pharmacological research may invent new lifesaving drugs, yet it can add to the repertoire of mind-destroying drugs. The examples are many. As old problems are transferred into new ones, the very definition of social problems becomes confused. If we are unable to define and evaluate the problems appropriately, our skills could do more harm than good.

Social work will need professionals who possess both philosophical and scientific curiosity; who possess the intellectual tools necessary to rebuild the theoretical and philosophical base of the profession. Technical skills alone will be insufficient. Sometimes it seems that because of its Judeo-Christian heritage social work assumes that its value system and philosophical base have a permanence and universality that are immune from intensive questioning. As others have pointed out, however, social work is heavily tainted by the apologia of laissez-faire capitalism and frequently contributes to the ends of such a system.[4] A new social work ethic may have to be forged that allows for more responsible criticism of this postindustrial society. A new generation of social workers, if they are to grapple with new philosophical and theoretical questions, must be equipped with an improved set of intellectual tools. Knowing how to be a "good" caseworker, or even a competent social work generalist, will not be enough. The rethinking of social work theory, practice, ethics, and so forth, must be done, at least in part, by the social work professionals themselves, not contracted out to other social philosophers and theoreticians.

The scholarly tools needed include a solid background in social thought, history, political and economic theory, and philosophy, especially the tools of philosophic reasoning such as logic, epistemology, and metaphysics. The ability to identify and to ask the right questions must take priority over all other skills as social work practitioners move toward the year 2000.

With this emphasis on the preeminence of scholarship over traditional practice skills, it is possible to explore the many facets of postindustrial development in terms of their potential effects on practice and education for practice.

The New Tools

The tools of a postindustrial society are familiar to most social workers, though few practitioners are equipped to use them in their practice. The computer, with its capacity for data storage and analysis, and the video, with its capacity to record and transmit visual as well as verbal messages, are tools with which every social worker should be acquainted, if they are not at his or her command.

In a postindustrial society all persons, to some extent, require access to information. While face-to-face communication is without equal in many social situations, the computer and the video are superior in others. To be competent in only traditional forms of information-sharing and social treatment is to risk short-changing the client (or potential client) who could gain access to social work if new outreach media were employed.

The reality of a limited number of professional social workers attempting to meet the needs of 218,000,000 people ensures that only a small portion of our society could ever hope to be served. Link that same number of workers to electronic tools with greater outreach capacity and the universality of service becomes possible. With this line of reasoning, any graduate of a school of social work who has not developed a beginning command of electronic tools must be considered only partially trained.[5]

Specialist or Generalist

The need for these new tools as part of the social worker's repertoire increases the dilemma of whether students should be trained as experts in one of the existing tools—for example, therapeutic interview—or in one of the new tools, or whether they should be exposed to the entire range of possible tools.

The historic debate in social work education regarding the need for specialization is only an issue if professional education is viewed as a terminal process. By shifting to a continuing education model, social workers could manage to build skills in the entire range of tools and methodologies available and develop special expertise in those for which they proved most suited. This would, of course, include competency in the new electronic tools. We no longer have to live in a world of either/or situations. We have witnessed the horrors of those who have lived their lives as narrow specialists, as well as the horrors of those who have never advanced beyond surface knowledge of existing methods. The danger confronting the social worker of the future is that, when faced with new complexities and unbending problems, he or she will limit investments to a particular approach, believing that greater skill in one area will realize the greatest gains. At this time in social work history, if one were to err, it would decidedly be more advantageous to err on the side of being a broad-based experimentalist, a life-long student always adding new knowledge, new tools, and new skills.

Social Investor-Institution Designer

The central task of a society in transition from one era to another is that of redesigning and rebuilding the social institution base of that society. The type of social welfare organization that we have come to accept, and within which we function, is an organizational pattern largely predicated on an industrial society base. Services that once had their place in an industrial society have shown signs of running their course; for example, travelers' aid, adoptions, forms of large institutional care. The task of redesigning, reorganizing, and realigning these services requires new forms of expertise not widely found within the social work profession. There is a need for the integration of new program development, administrative policy analysis, and research skills found only in a few of today's professionals. Social welfare organization designers and builders must be prepared within the social work profession or they will, by default, be drawn out of other professions or out of a synthesis of existing professions.

Institution-building tasks require conceptual awareness of the sensitive issues implicit in the man-machine interface, especially in man-environment ecology. As a consequence, the professional worker will have to grasp a much broader domain in which a human problem and its social solution require the investments of many professions and institutions, only a small portion of which will be conventional social work. For example, dealing with the abused child and the child's family requires many actors besides the child protection worker. Citizens, police, judges, lawyers, child advocates, ministers, and school teachers are all part of the service identification–delivery domain. Rebuilding public policy and programming requires a profession with breadth of vision and confidence in interdisciplinary, multiprofessional, and interinstitutional approaches.[6]

Designing and building also require data, both clinical and epistemological. The design and conduct of research and the construction of social indicators are skills that belong in social work. Good clinical work requires persons who understand, appreciate, and are capable of producing good research. Research is a tool for evaluating clinical performance; it is an essential aspect of being a responsible professional. In this respect the computer becomes a necessary—though not exclusive—tool for data gathering. Knowing how to read a printout must become as common as knowing a case file.

As part of the process of major institutional restructuring, the full range of administrative and management skills becomes part of the social worker's repertoire. A social work professional is generally a middle-management person, responsible for working with others to produce a service requiring the collective energies of all. Such management skills cover a wide range of techniques and include components like functional job analysis, budgeting, establishing work-flow diagrams, and understanding processes of program evaluation and feedback, to mention but a few.

Humanizing the Corporate Environment

Management skills from social work's standpoint are more than the sum of administrative techniques. Like other processes, they must be fitted to an ideology and philosophy; that is, management or administration for what? This raises additional questions for the social worker in the last quarter of this century; namely, the validity of corporate organization and the danger that bureaucracy presents to the individual.[7]

The scale of social organization has increased tremendously in recent years. The efforts to rationalize patterns of production and to manage consumption present a threat to the basic needs of the individual. Schumacher's *Small is Beautiful*[8] thesis suggests the need for a more appropriate balance between the human act of production and the importance placed on the products of economic organization.[9] Social workers, with their concerns for the individual, must be wary of situations in which people are sacrificed to corporate ends, however benignly or subtly this occurs. A primary target of our professional work must be the humanization of large-scale organizations.

Humanizing organizational life requires a special knowledge base. The worker needs to understand how organizational life and administrative systems remain productive, while enhancing the individuals who make up the organization. For example, attending school should be an experience that is humanizing, growth-producing, and an end in itself. Students need not be asked to sacrifice self, even for the cause of learning. This same principle could be extended to human participation in all social organizations. School social workers, medical social workers, and even industrial social workers will find this a growing dimension of their professional work.

Humanizing organizational life requires the creation of a certain work climate or atmosphere. Building milieu through administrative interventions is a vital skill for the social work administrator. The concept of the *therapeutic milieu* should belong to all forms of social organization, not simply treatment institutions, which are too often populated by casualties from dehumanizing experiences in other institutions. At the moment, no single professional group has accepted the function of humanizing institutions as a major service area. The need is evident and the field is wide open.

Route to Social Change

Improving the human social environment goes beyond management philosophy and skill. It involves political behaviors requisite to freeing up resources and securing commitments to carry out these improvements. Political action should be a concomitant of all professions. It involves a sophisticated understanding of how questions are moved into the public arena and from the public arena into public social policy. Lobbying, presentation of expert testimony, assistance in design of public policy and the evaluation of existing programs, and critiques of existing and impending legislation all need to be part of the knowledge and skill base of the professional social worker.

It is particularly important for the clinically-oriented worker to connect with the policy area, since it is through political action that service resources and opportunities are made available. Much has been written and said about the importance of politicization of the social worker. Much still remains to be accomplished in this area.

Advocacy

Inasmuch as the social worker is one of the few professionals to make representation of the poor and powerless a major area of concern, the failure of social workers to become politically sophisticated most hurts the politically vulnerable minority poor whom they represent. The corporate business and upper-income classes are well represented in this society. We must seek to balance their power through strategies that advocate self-interest needs of other sectors.

The rise of the consumer protection movement represents a new kind of politicized effort to improve individual welfare for all people, including the poor, by making organizational systems more responsive and responsible. Consumer research, action, and service are areas that are open to many professions. Social work in the future will find it a field suitable to its concerns and many of its methods and techniques.

Role of Mass Media

Professing one's expertise to widen the possible audience is a natural professional activity. However, to profess is useless unless one reaches the target audience. To reach a wide public, to contribute to the development of public education, requires knowledge of the mass communication media and process. Each profession must develop a link to the mass media networks in order to use the new technology of these media to convey its message.[10] There is a need to merge social welfare expertise with mass media expertise to effectively reach and serve a large and disparate population.

Mass media has the potential not only for influencing public opinion in the support of new social policy positions, but also for use in basically clinical and therapeutic work. Only think for a moment of the outreach and impact of an Ann Landers column, or the popularity of a television "action line," or the significance for socialization of the young of programs like "Sesame Street" and "The Electric Company." One can readily see that the social service potential of mass communications has hardly been tapped. Social workers may soon offer correspondence counseling through a social work "Ann Landers column" or offer an information and referral action line on television. Social workers who venture into such areas, however, will require a new set of skills. Face-to-face counsel gives way to the ability to write, to diagnose written communications, and to project warmth and concern in a studio room without benefit of direct client feedback.

With the advent of new tools comes the alteration of patterns and modes of communication. Relying solely on traditional approaches to communication could render a profession obsolete.

Changing Lifestyles

Much has been said about the use of new tools of technology; little about the dangers that are increasingly inherent within its unrelenting growth. The rise of a counterculture and its new way of looking at life and mass consumption have posed questions about how much is enough in a basic material sense. The energy crisis and environmental concerns of the mid-1970s have given pause to the reconsideration of contemporary lifestyles, especially in America. One of the tasks that social workers will increasingly face (if they see it as falling within their area of professional concern) is the question of the redesign and resocialization of the population into new and less conspicuously consuming lifestyles.[11]

Insofar as there is evidence that typical middle-class living is failing to produce personal growth and satisfaction—based on such social indicators as divorce, suicide, and chemical dependencies—social work will have to argue for a new design, a truly satisfying life pattern (with plenty of variations) that achieves such spiritual considerations within the broader framework of energy conservation and environmental protection principles.

The postindustrial world mandates the rebuilding of lifeways, as well as the restructuring of institutions. Altering lifestyles is a fundamental concern for those who claim interest in the quality of human social functioning. A variety of new kinds of knowledge and skills will be required. We have traditionally intervened to influence individual ways of life. Now it is time to magnify this and think about changing cultural patterns as a more critical goal.[12] Even anthropologists have chosen to limit their concerns to understanding, describing, and analyzing life patterns; rarely to redirecting them. Escalating the goals of a profession entails increased responsibility. As with all of science, social work, if it takes on the task of influencing life patterns, must take great care that it is confident about what it professes. There should be wide variations in social functioning, but effective human ecology would argue that it takes place within a few parameters.

Synthesis in Social Work

One of the factors in a postindustrial society that affects social work development is the way in which knowledge is built. The development of knowledge through a process of reductionism—atomism—has given way to building knowledge through synthesis. Today we prefer to use a systems perspective in viewing the world. We increase what we know by experimentally putting existing things together to create new synergies. The fields with the fastest-growing knowledge bases are those that are products of such combinations, such as biochemistry. Professor John Platt has argued that the social sciences would do well to follow the experimental methods of biochemistry in this regard.[13]

Social work certainly has benefited in the past from its borrowings from the substantive areas of sociology, psychology, and anthropology and from its modeling of clinical psychology and psychiatry. It is logical to assume, with the trend toward synthesis pushing us in that direction anyway, that social work will begin importing from many other areas and professional groups. Likewise, we can expect other professions to do the same and to include social work as one of their theoretical sources.

We have found an interesting field for knowledge building in relating social work to the new field of environmental design.[14] Others have found equal success in relating social work to law, economics, mass communications, public health, and the like. More and more, curricula will be merely the intellectual bridge to other clinical and theoretical knowledge areas that have substantial relevancy to social work.

As this development is now in an incipient stage, it can be expected that the knowledge base for future social work theory will be greatly expanded. Future professional workers will have to learn more and different things from those schooled today or yesterday. The heavily interdisciplinary nature of this new knowledge will probably make workers much more cosmopolitan than their predecessors and less concerned with questions about the so-called unique role and mission of their profession. Social work will become one of many highly overlapping professions with converging interests and missions. New professions may well grow out of these syntheses; others may disappear. Social work will definitely not remain unaffected.

There is already a trend toward multiple professionalism; that is, toward persons trained in more than one professional area. Many schools of social work offer, and encourage students to pursue, joint-degree programs. A noticeable change in admissions to schools of social work is the increase in applicants who already have completed their education and practiced in another profession.[15] Two-career social workers will certainly view the world differently from those trained in more narrow, single-profession pursuits. The two-career worker may well become the more common model by the end of the century.

Deprofessionalization

Hidden among the many changes that can be credited to postindustrial forces is the changing attitude toward professionalization.[16] The growth of functional specialization and enhanced interdependencies in an urbanizing world is not without a breaking point. Rising affluence and leisure induces individuals, families, and neighborhoods to choose to contract back, or simply take over, functions that had previously been allowed to be professionalized.

A handful of social philosophers have argued the dangers of institutional approaches to social welfare.[17] Few of these have been widely read or accepted in professional social work circles. There is, however, evidence that functions that are to be given over to professionals and those that are to be held by individual consumers will be limited or changed. Social work, in many of its forms, is highly attractive and rewarding work; the underlying motivations of human service and caring exist in all persons, not just those who choose to make social work a career.

Recognizing this, the new social work profession might reduce its own service monopoly and make professional information and knowledge available for others to use as they see fit. Such a perspective could fundamentally change the direction of the field and alter the nature of professional activity. An adult education model rather than a medical model could eventuate.

Social workers have served as surrogate families for an industrial-age population stripped of its extended family affiliations. In a postindustrial age, social work could concentrate on rebuilding new primary and familial institutions to carry out these functions, without itself becoming institutionalized as the main center of caring activities. Admittedly, the rhetoric of such a perspective has long been a part of social work education. In practice, however, we have been unrequiting imperialists, sharing the company of other professional groups who have done likewise.

Global Vision

New technology in the form of mass communications and supersonic transportation has made possible multinational development. More and more, decisions made in one geographical sector affect the well-being of others. The emergence of global ecology is a reality that every profession, including social work, must face. For social work, reductionism in a global context may mean that we will once again discover poverty through increased awareness of the Third World sectors; will come to appreciate more deeply intercultural relations; and will even preempt the concept of treatment with the concept of development.[18]

Social work could conceivably take on the responsibility of drawing public attention—especially in affluent countries—to the world's tragedies, serving as the prime advocate for redistribution of the resources of the abundant nations to those less well endowed. One of the foremost tragedies of the day is the inability of people in the postindustrial world to experience the level of compassion that could lead to action for those who are starving to death on the continents of Asia and Africa. As a profession we have a long way to go before we become truly internationalized in our views and values.

The internationalization of both the social work profession and the practitioner that must come will have as by-products a greater awareness of comparative thought and a habit of cross-cultural borrowing. We have been long on exporting our ideas, but have remained limited in our imports; a sign of unhealthy professional ethnocentrism. The Third World and the Eastern countries also have much to share.

The realm of problem solving in the future will include not only the range of social institutions and occupational fields, but also the recognition of multinational variables. Social welfare, with the possible exception of the United Nations agencies, has yet to develop viable multinational social welfare models. These models will come as the domain of social welfare institutional designers is broadened along the international dimension.

All of this may appear to be somewhat overwhelming to those aspiring to social work whose field of vision has been restricted to traditional and conventional definitions of social work. There are those who would prefer to carve out a small niche of relevant professional activity and resist any pressures to broaden their base of theory and practice. They are not among the professional social workers for the year 2000 to whom this essay is addressed.

THE NEW SOCIAL WORKER

The postindustrial era will produce its own breed of social worker. The new tools, issues, and tasks of the coming age will have a decided influence on an emerging professional worker subculture. This subculture will be based on the chemistry of new professional values, functions, methods, and approaches to professional work. In this reading selection, a number of factors were identified that could influence the development of the new professional worker:

1. The probable adoption of new tools of postindustrial technology (e.g., computer and video) as standard instruments of social work practice;

2. The task of redefining human social problems and rebuilding the philosophical and theoretical bases of the profession;

3. The task of redesigning, rebuilding, and reconstructing the institutional base of social welfare policy and services;

4. The rising importance of large organizational variables in the social functioning of the individual and consequently in the locus of future social work intervention;

5. The continued need for politicization of professionals as public policy becomes a dominant variable in the viability of social welfare organization;

6. The impact of erosion of industrial lifestyles (e.g., mass production and mass consumption) and their inevitable replacement with more qualitative approaches to both;

7. The acceptance of concepts of synthesis and synergy in professional social work education and practice and the consequent contact with new theoretical sources and professional groups;

8. The meaning of deprofessionalizing trends in future assignments of human service tasks;

9. The press to extend professional work to a world community and to adopt habits of comparative thought.

Assuming that these factors will be a valid sample of some of the influences on social workers in the last quarter of this century, what will be the sum of their impact on forthcoming workers? Will they form a dominant model or style for the practitioner by the year 2000?

Currently, as was noted at the outset of this essay, there is some evidence of a return to previous professional models. The expectations expressed by a large number of students in schools of social work indicate that many prefer to limit the boundaries of professional work; that is, to direct their attention to dealing with the rising numbers of human casualties that inevitably occur under conditions of large-scale cultural revolution.

The trend toward the establishment of a highly controlled and standardized program will help to perpetuate this market view, inasmuch as the first step of professional work is essentially clinical, in the tradition of the medical model. Offsetting this trend, however, is the growth of post-master's and doctoral education with its concomitant biases toward institutional and developmental interventions. These programs are the sources for new faculty and administrators who can be expected to set the type and direction for social work education and practice.

This dual development could further bifurcate the profession, splitting it into separate entities. Should this happen, it is uncertain whether a single professional identity could umbrella both developments. If a rapprochement occurs—and this is possible—then this body of new workers, while sharing a common philosophical and theoretical base, would be even more diversified and wide-ranging than the current disparate group that now calls itself social workers.

A new style of professionalism may be forthcoming that will be open, freewheeling, and experimental and less visibly and audibly activist. The new professionals can be expected to feel at home in many new settings and surroundings, capable of communication and relationships with many different collateral groups. They will be comfortable with new tools of technology that will draw them more and more into public arenas.

Interdisciplinary trends will, in all probability, create interdisciplinary institutions that no single professional group will be able to claim as its primary setting.

The developing theoretical perspectives and knowledge will inevitably change diagnostic directions from an historic reductionism to a domain awareness. Ultimately this directional shift will level off when a world order perspective is achieved.

A new spurt of radicalism might be expected as this global perspective forces the new social worker to recognize the scale of worldwide poverty and social injustice. When this perception confronts the excessive consumption of postindustrial societies, radicalism could be converted into a major effort to alter cultural patterns in the affluent sectors of the world.

If we may be permitted a somewhat professional, egocentric prediction in concluding this essay, we might suggest that professional social work in the year 2000 could become one of the highest status professions in a postindustrial world. Given the overriding importance of world social problems, then, if the skills of social development and management were to be mastered, they would be highly sought after and recognized. The rise in status and importance of the economist as a result of the worldwide economic crisis is evidence that the solution of economic problems is now seen as central to global survival. Might not a world posteconomic crisis of a much more basic social and interactional nature be anticipated?

As many of the aforementioned developments become more visible, the social work profession will be affected and a new type of individual will be attracted to it. It will be these people who will define the profession in the year 2000.

NOTES

[1]Thomas H. Walz, "New Breed of Social Workers—Fact or Fantasy." *Public Welfare* (January 1971).

[2]Daniel Bell, *The Coming of a Post-Industrial Society: A Venture in Social Forecasting* (New York: Basic Books, 1973); and Alice Mary Hilton, ed., *The Evolving Society* (New York: Conference on the Cybercultural Revolution, 1964).

[3]One school of social work has chosen to use the concept of *social development* in lieu of social work as its organizing concept (University of Minnesota, Duluth).

[4]The social work profession was repeatedly accused, with some justification, of "welfare colonialism" by militant leaders during the 1960s.

[5]At the University of Iowa School of Social Work, graduate students are now required to be certified in the use of the computer and video.

[6]Some recent social work theorists (e.g., Hearn, Gordon) argue that social work is essentially "boundary work," assisting clients to connect better with the institutions that serve them.

[7]Thomas H. Walz, "Theory of Bureauneurosis: Implications for Social Work Practice," September 10, 1974, unpublished.

[8]E. F. Schumacher, *Small Is Beautiful* (New York: Harper & Row, 1973).

[9]The overemphasis of a therapeutic orientation toward individuals has historically limited the full politicization of social work as a profession.

[10]Schools of social work would do well to emphasize the establishment of joint degree programs between social work and mass communication departments.

[11]The Harlem Youth Project, dating back to the early days of the Youth Development Act (early 1960s) attempted to alter the total subculture of the black adolescent in Harlem, with fair success.

[12]The most important part of a school of social work's curriculum may well be its "professional concerns"—what it does, rather than what it says ought to be done.

[13]John Platt, *The Step to Man* (New York: Wiley, 1966).

[14]Thomas H. Walz, "Environmental Design: A New Source for Social Work Theory Building," *Social Work* (January 1973).

[15]The number of applicants to the University of Iowa School of Social Work with existing professional degrees has doubled since 1970.

[16]We can expect to find a rise of theoretical interest in deprofessionalization. Foremost among such theorists is Ivan Illich (*De-schooling Society, The Conviviality of Man's Tools*).

[17]One example would be Bernard de Jouvenal, ed., *Public Needs and Private Wants* (New York: Norton, 1962).

[18]A recent meeting of midwest schools of social work at Columbia, Missouri (December 5–7, 1974) focused on the relationship of the concept of development within the social work curriculum.

GENERALISTS IN HUMAN-SERVICE SYSTEMS: THEIR PROBLEMS AND PROSPECTS

Mark R. Yessian, Anthony Broskowski

Next time you are in the company of human-service professionals and find the conversation running along the same old lines, you might ask what a regional director of HHS (the Department of Health, and Human Services), an executive director of a community health and welfare planning council, a governor's human-service adviser, and a director of a neighborhood multiservice agency have in common. The question is bound to add a change of pace to the conversation. When, after an appropriate interim, you respond that they are part of a network of human-service generalists who could contribute greatly to the improved functioning of human-service programs you could, with a little luck, spark a lively discussion. It could go off in many directions, covering such areas as: (1) the current status of generalists in the human-services environment, (2) the contributions which they can make in that environment, (3) the reasons for their limited impact to date, and (4) the ways in which they could become more assertive and effective agents of change. Our aim here is to offer some insights in each of these areas and, in so doing, to provide some grist for discussions of this sort.

I. THE DIAGNOSIS

The Situation Today

Traditionally, the generalists who have played the most prominent part in the human-services field have been those working directly with people in need of service. These generalists, in their day-to-day work, have reflected a continuing concern for the overall well-being of clients and for the integrated delivery of services responsive to multiproblem client needs. In large part they have been trained social workers who have provided a broad range of personal-care services, but in their ranks there have also been many other professional and semiprofessional workers.

These clinically oriented generalists are still very much present, but in recent years they have been accompanied increasingly by another class of human-service generalists who are not directly involved with service recipients. These latter-day generalists do their work within organizational settings at all levels of government and in the private as well as the public sector. They are concerned with the internal integration of human-service organizations, with the interactions among these organizations, and, at bottom, with the responsiveness of the organizations to client needs. Some of them work as planners or evaluators, others as policy or program analysts, still others as managers. All function in a broad sense as human-service administrators.

This article is relevant to both classes of generalists, because they tend to share basic interests and to be quite dependent upon one another. Its focus, however, is on those whose jobs are oriented toward affecting the behavior of organizations. Throughout, the term *generalist* is used to refer to *organizational generalists*, unless otherwise indicated.

Personnel who work in organizational settings as generalists do not necessarily identify with the generalist label, nor do they necessarily associate much with one another or share any sense of group belongingness. They arrived at their present positions from a wide array of career backgrounds and for the most part without any specific career plans to become generalists. Yet they do appear to represent an affinity group (if not a distinct vocational breed), and they do share some basic characteristics. These include: (1) a concern with a wide range of both public and private human services covering different functional areas, different age groups, and different human problems; (2) a view of the human-services environment which tends to be systemic and to reflect an appreciation for

Source: Reprinted from *Social Service Review*, Vol. 51, No. 2, June 1977, pp. 265–87, with permission of the University of Chicago Press. © 1977 by The University of Chicago Press.

the interrelationships among human needs and among human-service programs; and (3) a perspective which focuses in large part on planning and management issues as opposed to specific techniques or technologies of service delivery.

Within their organizational environments, these generalists work in proximity to many different kinds of *human-service specialists*. By far the more widely recognized participants in the human-services arena, these specialists are also much more numerous. In contrast to the generalists they tend to: (1) focus on services covering a single major program area (e.g., health) or a single target group (e.g., the aged), (2) take a particularistic view of their enterprise and its environment, and (3) concentrate on specific techniques of a particular service. Although they, too, are concerned with organizational behavior, they are likely to concentrate their attention on only a small part of an organization's mission. For the most part

they have line responsibilities and are directly concerned with the operation of individual programs, while the generalists have staff responsibilities and are indirectly concerned with the operation of many different programs.

Table 28-1 provides an illustrative listing of the places in which these human-service specialists can be found. A thoughtful comparison of the two listings will reveal that generalists are relatively minor actors in the current service-delivery system. In any community or at any level of government or within any organization they are apt to find themselves outflanked by specialists who have a firm grip on program dollars and authority, are tightly organized within their own professional societies, possess most of the program information and technical expertise, and enjoy a greater degree of public respect and support. At federal and state levels the imbalance appears to be particularly great, as specialists within the

Table 28-1. Selected Organizational Domains of Generalists and Specialists

Generalist Domains	Specialist Domains
Office of the Secretary, U.S. Department of Health, Education, and Welfare	Public Health Service, U.S. Department of Health, Education, and Welfare
Office of the Regional Director, U.S. Department of Health, Education, and Welfare	Office of Education, U.S. Department of Health, Education, and Welfare
National League of Cities	American Medical Association
National Association of Counties	American Hospital Administrators Association
National Governors Conference	National Education Association
Federal regional councils	State public health agencies
Governors' offices	State mental health agencies
Offices of state human-service secretaries	State vocational rehabilitation agencies
Mayors' offices	Local school committees
County chief executives' offices	Local health departments
Community health and welfare councils	Community mental health centers
Neighborhood councils	Drug abuse prevention councils
Community action agencies	Child care corporations

governmental bureaucracies join forces with their counterparts in Congress and private-interest groups to develop what often amounts to a monopoly of decision-making power in their immediate spheres of interest.[1]

In itself, this imbalanced situation need not be a major cause of concern. There is no body of knowledge that suggests that generalists deserve to be in ascendance. What is disturbing is the excessive specialization which has emerged as a result of this imbalance of power.

The high costs and inefficiencies that have been incurred by excessive specialization in the human-service field have been documented in other sources and need not be reiterated here.[2] It is worth emphasizing, however, that these costs and inefficiencies have had a very pronounced human impact. From the vantage point of the person seeking service, the current, highly fragmented human-service system presents great problems. It breeds uncertainty, leaves many important services inaccessible or only remotely accessible, and results in many service gaps and discontinuities.

In this context, the client who has three or more highly interrelated problems is at a particular disadvantage. Receiving highly specialized help for only one or two of these problems, no matter how effective this help may be in its own right, may turn out to be of little overall assistance if other related problems are not addressed. The situation is analogous to repairing a car with ten malfunctioning components by giving expert attention to the distributor and carburetor difficulties, but ignoring the tires, axle, spark plugs, and other components which are in some way defective. As an operative system, the car must function as a whole, not just in a few places.

Many clinicians are quite aware of the interrelated nature of client needs and of the importance of fashioning integrative techniques and approaches at the delivery level. Some, in fact, have even been able to make some headway in this direction. But as long as integrative efforts within and among human-service organizations remain a rarity, and programs, especially at federal and state levels, continue to be developed and run within very narrow, specialized confines, these clinical efforts at integration are not likely to have much overall impact. Service providers are simply too dependent upon their organizations and programs to be able to function, in any significant way, outside their specialist sphere of influence. . . .[3]

It is our contention that organizational generalists represent a vital counterforce to excessive specialization and can be key agents in making human-service organizations more responsive to the integrative impulses of the clinical generalists. In the succeeding pages, we hope to make it clear why they have this potential and how they can take advantage of it.

The Case for the Generalists

There are some obvious questions. Why the generalists? What is it that they have to offer? What roles can they be expected to play? The answers, for the most part, rest with the basic characteristics identified earlier. Because they deal with a broader universe than individual specialists, they are in a better position to see how programs relate to one another, to spot overlaps and duplications, to identify opportunities for coordination, and at times, to determine the current relevance and effectiveness of individual programs. Less encumbered by the programmatic blinders which restrict the vision of so many specialists, they are in a better position to view the larger set of community needs and to see that programs and services are responding to these needs.

Furthermore, generalists are inclined to be much more flexible and responsive to change than are specialists. They are more likely to be able to shift perspectives and to look at the human-services environment from multiple vantage points, including those of the taxpayer, service recipient, service provider, third-party payer, legislator, program administrator, and policy planner. Specialists, as Sarason suggests below, tend to be more locked into their existing thought patterns:

In the short run specialization appears to have productive consequences in terms of new knowledge and practice, but in the long run it seems to render the individual, or field, or agency increasingly unable to assimilate and adapt to changes in surrounding social events and processes. Worse yet, the forces (individual and social) which generate specialization unwittingly increase the extent of ignorance of the larger social picture so that assimilation and adaptation are not even perceived as problems.[4]

By making the case for the generalists, we do not wish to imply that generalists should engineer power plays designed to take control from the specialists. That would be foolhardy and probably lead to a more chaotic situation than now prevails. It is imperative, however, for the generalist to search for ways of realizing the potential afforded by their systemic perspectives. How can they promote the delivery of services that are targeted toward real needs? How can they serve as cohesive elements, influencing program agencies and providers to relate more effectively and imaginatively with one another? How can they trigger reform on behalf of service recipients? These are among the vital questions with which the generalists must cope. In this process, however, we must recognize they will inevitably address issues concerning the balance of power.

There are, of course, several ways in which generalists can confront these issues and exert leadership. What methods work best will depend on the time and circumstances. Among the types of roles which generalists can play in organizational settings are the following:

1. *Broker/facilitator.* Whether on behalf of other generalists trying to tap into needed services or on behalf of specialists trying to coordinate more effectively with other specialists, generalists are in a good position to provide valuable assistance. With their comprehensive view of the human-service environment, they can identify linkage opportunities and assist generalists and specialists alike to understand and to deal effectively with the complexities of that environment. In this sense, they can serve as brokers or facilitators for getting things done.

2. *Mediator.* Generalists can play an important part in resolving disputes and conflicts which occur among providers in the human-services environment. Exercising this role successfully no doubt depends a lot on the personal skill of the individuals involved, but because they can relate more easily to the various needs of service recipients and are likely to have a broader (though not necessarily stronger) base of support, generalists are usually better equipped than individual specialists to promote negotiation and compromise.

3. *Integrator/coordinator.* Left to themselves, program specialists cannot go very far in integrating or coordinating multiple and diverse services. As soon as they reach a point where their own immediate interests appear to be threatened, they quite expectedly tend to back away. It is apparent, therefore, that if substantial progress is to be made in this direction, generalists, who are more committed to the integration and coordination of services, must provide the leadership. They can do that in many ways, ranging from outside advocacy and identification of coordination opportunities, to provision of technical assistance, to direct involvement in the development and implementation of service linkages.

4. *General manager.* Generalists can be given direct managerial responsibilities for the planning and delivery of certain human services so they can more easily and thoroughly exert an integrating influence on service operations. One of the dangers of this approach, however, is that a new and costly bureaucratic infrastructure can develop if general management is simply grafted on to the present categorical system.

5. *Educator.* Generalists can function in university or agency training programs to help educate categorical specialists on those aspects of integrated service delivery which will enhance the specialized services being provided to the citizen. Given a greater exposure to and understanding of systemic principles, professionals may become less resistant to and perhaps even supportive of the integration of certain activities.

6. *Analyst/evaluator.* By drawing heavily upon their systemic perspective and their concern for the overall impact of services on clients, generalists can play a very constructive part in the analysis and evaluation of human-service programs. They can generate information and raise vital questions on matters concerning program interrelationships or program impact which specialists are likely to overlook, and in so doing they can obtain useful feedback for subsequent planning processes. In the same context, they can serve as a significant source of information on client needs and on the type of programs necessary to meet these needs. Attkisson and Broskowski have argued that a generalist perspective is necessary for the tasks of program evaluation and planning.[5]

The Roots of the Problem

If the case for the generalists is as compelling as we believe it to be why, then, do they have so little influence at the present time? Why are they relatively minor actors in the human-services arena? Although not professing to offer definitive answers to these questions, we identify below what we regard as four basic factors responsible for the current plight of human-services generalists. We feel strongly that these factors deserve more serious inquiry than they have received thus far and emphasize that though they affect the generalists directly it is the overall impact on the well-being of our society which provides the major cause for concern.

1. *Differentiation and specialization are common human responses for coping with complex and not very well understood phenomena.*—Given a complex matter, such as the human-service needs of people, it appears easier to differentiate the separate parts and deal with them as individual components rather than trying to work with the whole or, more precisely, with the interrelationships among the components. It is this specialized approach, for example, which has led to the enormous contributions in the field of medicine during the twentieth century.

As our knowledge increases in a given field, however, differentiation and specialization in themselves emerge as less viable approaches. As we become more familiar with the bits and pieces, we find that integration and synthesis become increasingly important as ways of dealing with high rates of complexity and information overload. In fact, it could well be argued that the recent major advances in science and technology have depended on the efforts of those who were able to integrate the specialized research of many other specialist researchers.

It is sometimes argued that our current level of understanding about the complex human-services environment is insufficient to allow for bold strategies of integration and synthesis. Given the relative degree of specialization, however, we feel it is time to search out aggressively those areas in which integration may provide a reasonably better payoff. While differentiation promotes rapid responsiveness to higher specialization problems, its danger is that the pieces may not be reunited for a more powerful solution to a wider class of problems.

Probably an even more relevant concern is that we are becoming less able to afford the luxury of excessive specialization, whatever the state of our knowledge. Specialization prospers in rich and abundant environments where there are enough resources to go around to let "everybody do their own thing." In more barren environments the force of competition for limited resources puts a greater premium on consolidation and efficiency. As our country's growth rate slows and we become more conscious of the lim-its of our resources, this consideration becomes a most important one indeed.

2. *Generalists find it difficult to demonstrate the utility of their contributions.*—The benefits of integration do not tend to be immediately apparent. They are apt to take time, be rather subtle, and appear less dramatic than those achieved through specialization The necessary patience is hard to come by in a society that is enthralled by its own rapid pace and "future shock" environment.

Moreover, generalists, because they tend to focus on large-scale problems which no one person can fully comprehend or control, are likely to stimulate our fears and insecurities and to leave us uncertain about the worth of their efforts. They do not provide us with quick, ready reference points or easily identified products. For most of us the specialists are more likely to provide immediate comfort and security. They provide more easily recognized goods and services, and they seem to have better command of their own environments.

In this context, there is a particular hazard associated with any significant reliance upon the leadership of generalists. Because the contributions and standards of generalists are much harder to define than those of specialists, charlatans, particularly smooth-talking charlatans, find it much easier to penetrate their ranks. Few would deny, for instance, that it is easier for one with little or no knowledge in the given area to function as a policy analyst or program coordinator than as a mental health or vocational rehabilitation specialist. The extent of this problem is not known, but it does exist and does militate against generalists' efforts to gain greater legitimacy and respectability.

While specialists run programs and deliver services which have high external visibility and provide immediate and tangible contributions to an individual's well-being, generalists tend to work in more internal and inconspicuous capacities and to address, among other things, the ways in which specialist services can be provided more effectively. Though one can argue (convincingly, we feel) that the two functions are crucial and interdependent, the fact nevertheless remains that the services of specialists tend to be of more direct relevance to people in need of service than those of generalists. Many specialists, to extend the point, can assert, with a high degree of public credibility, that what they do can make the difference between an individual's life or death; few if any generalists can do the same. It is no wonder, then, that most generalists, be it consciously or subconsciously, are highly sensitive to criticisms from specialists. If generalists push an initiative that threatens the domain of specialists, they run the risk of a showdown, and in a showdown the specialists are the likely winners, both because they have more political power and because their services, in the final analysis, are more highly prized by the public.[6]

3. *Career rewards go to those who specialize.*—Money, prestige, and advancement come through specialization. All of us learn these facts of professional life very early in our careers, and unless we are among the few willing to sacrifice these pursuits in favor of loftier purposes we gear ourselves accordingly.

It is unfortunate that universities and governmental agencies provide particularly strong stimulants to this passion to specialize. Although some reforms are now taking place, most educational systems, especially at the graduate level, continue to focus upon specialized components of that environment and to churn out graduates who are ready and anxious to carve out careers as specialists.

Those who choose government service, whether at the federal, state, or local level, are likely to find this orientation reinforced. The career paths they see before them all seem to go in highly specialized directions, as civil service regulations and job classification practices are heavily biased toward the virtues of specialization. For those who wish to work for government in a more diversified capacity, the only real alternatives are to run for elective office or to work as personal staff for elected or politically appointed generalist officials. The more secure and numerous jobs in the career service are almost completely in the province of the specialists. . . .

II. THE CHALLENGE

What can be done to establish more appropriate roles for generalists? Are generalists inherently and inevitably minor actors in the often complex, highly differentiated organizations in which they work? Or can they become more influential in these organizations and in the human-services environment as a whole?

We feel there is no natural law or basic logic that confines generalists to a minor status. Although they may not or should not achieve the overall influence of specialists, they can assume much more constructive and significant roles. Moreover, we feel that generalists must move in this direction if significant corrective measures are to be taken in response to the ills of overspecialization.

Such a development, however, is not likely to happen by a sudden legislative or executive decree or by the sheer force of logic. It will take concerted, forceful, and long-term action by generalists themselves. They must come to view themselves as key agents of change; they must begin to press vigorously for necessary reforms in their own and other human-service organizations; and, in the process, they must start to think in terms of alliances of generalists—initially in conceptual terms but increasingly in organizational and political terms as well.

The Realities

The challenge facing generalists is a vast one, and they should address it energetically and with full confidence that it is a significant one. At the same time, however, they should not let their enthusiasm blind them to important realities. They should clearly recognize the following and, no doubt, many other such realities:

1. *Generalist-specialist tensions are an inherent part of organizational life.*—They are not unique to human-service organizations and will not be eliminated through reorganization or administrative reform. The important point is to see that an organization reflects a healthy balance between these tensions and is able to absorb them in a way that contributes to its basic mission. The concept of matrix organizations, applied in many business organizations—but hardly at all, to date, in human-service organizations—is directed to the productive interplay of these generalist-specialist tensions.[7]

2. *Resources are scarce.*—The era of large-scale growth in the human-service field is over and not likely to be replicated any time soon. It is conceivable that in time this reality will result in a greater demand for the effective integration of existing services. On the other hand, in view of the vested interests and political power of specialists, this demand could remain latent or politically insignificant for some time to come. Whatever the case, it is clear that reform efforts which call for greatly increased expenditures are not likely to get far during the years ahead.

3. *Some headway in generalist directions has been made in recent years.*—Most significant, perhaps, has been the headway made in recognizing the problems brought on by excessive specialization in the human-service field. Press accounts, congressional hearings,

and scholarly studies afford ample testimony of these problems and of the need for reforms.[8] The actual reform efforts initiated over the past decade have been less impressive, but have nevertheless opened up many opportunities for generalists.

At the national level efforts have included ... the general revenue-sharing program, the community-development and manpower special revenue-sharing programs, and the Title XX social services program. At the state and local levels they have included the establishment of umbrella human-service departments and the initiation of many formal and informal coordinative efforts which cut across program lines. And, at the university level they have included the formation at undergraduate and graduate levels of a number of multidisciplinary human-service programs.[9] Presently most generalists are more likely to look at these efforts in terms of the frustrations they have raised rather than the opportunities afforded. Although the frustrations have been very real and the gaps between promise and performance enormous, these efforts do represent a certain momentum upon which generalists should attempt to build.

An Agenda

We have outlined a seven-part agenda for reform which generalists might wish to consider. It is not a blueprint for action as much as a reference point intended to stimulate thought and constructive action. It is directed to human-service generalists in all types of organizational settings, at all levels of government, and in the private as well as public sector. In this sense it is largely inner-directed, in that it focuses on what generalists can do for themselves and among themselves.[10]

1. *Get to know one another.*—As indicated earlier, generalists do not necessarily associate with one another, recognize their commonalties, or for that matter, view themselves as generalists. Yet, organizational loyalties notwithstanding, it remains that generalists in different organizational settings are likely to have more professional interests in common with one another than with specialists in their own organizations.[11] The job of a planner in the office of the HHS regional director, for instance, is too likely to bear a much closer relationship to that of a planner in the office of a state human-service secretary or in a nonprofit human-services planning and research organization than it is to that of any program planner in any of the categorical agencies within HHS. It

makes good sense, therefore, for generalists to look beyond their own corridors and even beyond their own communities to search out and get to know one another. In so doing, they can find that there are many others who are concerned about and engaged in similar activities. They can obtain insights which will help them in performing their jobs; they can gain confidence in themselves and in the importance of their roles; and not least of all, they can begin to gain more influence within their own organizational settings and within larger political settings.

It is no easy task to forge associations or alliances (formal or informal) which are geared to the generalist perspective. For those generalists who are inclined to move in this direction, therefore, we feel that the first efforts should be small and informal ones in which interested participants attempt to carve out approaches which are likely to appeal to a larger grouping of generalists. It may very well be that the best type of appeal is one based on certain issues (e.g., Title XX planning or multidisciplinary human-service training) rather than on the generalist identity per se. We do feel, however, that the territorial scope of any such effort should not be too expansive, since identification with common turf can lend important specificity to discussions and can facilitate communication.[12]

In this context, the efforts of an informal, loosely affiliated network of generalists in New England are relevant. Known as the New England Human Services Coalition, this group meets periodically to share experiences and to discuss issues which are of major interest to those who bring a generalist perspective to the human-services environment.[13] It has grown in about two years from a core of about ten to a "membership" of about 150 individuals who come from a wide variety of organizational settings, public and private, throughout the region. On the basis of our own participation in the effort, we can say that it has elicited an enthusiastic response from most of the participants and that it has promoted greater and more effective communication among generalists in New England. Evidence along this line is provided by the fact that many of the participants have begun to communicate with one another on other than group occasions and have come to rely upon one another as resources to draw upon in dealing with their own problems in their own organizational settings.

2. *Identify commonalties with other classes of generalists and pursue closer relationships.*—Once organizational generalists begin to develop a sense of

community in their own ranks, they should begin to look for allies, especially for other classes of generalists who share many of their basic interests and who can contribute significantly to their understandings and to their political influence. There are at least four such classes of generalists to consider:

a. Clinical generalists. Clinical generalists, those who work directly with service recipients, can offer important client-level specifics which are often overlooked from more distant organizational posts. With their "bottom-up perspective" they can offer significant insights about how service delivery systems are and are not working and about how organizational changes can be made in the interests of service recipients. However, the dialogue may not always be an easy one. Clinical generalists do not tend to view the organizational generalists as generalists or as potential allies as much as cogs in the bureaucracy, too often unresponsive to the needs of their clients. Overcoming this perception could be one of the more difficult and important challenges facing the organizational generalists.

b. Elected officials. It is vital that generalists begin to develop closer alliances with representatives of general-purpose government (GPG); that is, with governors, mayors, county executives, legislators, and other elected officials who have broad governmental responsibilities. There are many good reasons for forming closer ties with these officials, but three are particularly compelling. In our form of government, these officials represent the "people" with more legitimacy and authority than is enjoyed by any other segment of our society. That does not mean that they are necessarily at the top of the ladder in terms of power or respect, but it does lend a special significance to their determinations of what is in the public interest. To the extent that generalists can draw upon such determinations in support of their efforts, their chance of succeeding, in the face of the inevitable pushing and pulling that takes place, is bound to increase.[14]

A second and more obvious reason has to do with money. It takes money to perform the roles indicated on the previous pages, and general-purpose government officials, through their control over the public purse, are in position to provide it. Yet, as many generalists have learned, this financial support is not easily obtained. It must be cultivated with care, over a long period of time, and in the midst of many competing demands. The fact that many state and local governments are being subjected to increased financial pressures because of economic and other conditions makes this job harder, but no less important.

Finally, it is important to recognize the generalized orientation which is inherent in the positions occupied by GPG officials. Their legitimacy derives from their mandate to represent the general interests of the people, not the specialized interests of certain people or groups. As agents of the people, they must respond to many different types of citizen-needs demands and oversee a wide range of specialized programs and services. As such they, too, are generalists, albeit at a broad governmental level, and are concerned about many of the same kinds of issues. It follows that if human-service generalists recognize and attempt to take advantage of this basic affiliation they can gain some important reinforcement.[15]

For many generalists such political affiliations may appear amorphous, impractical, or perhaps even repugnant. What good, many of them are apt to ask, can come from drawing closer to the politicians and from injecting more politics into the human-services environment? . . .

. . . Many of them clearly indicate that without the support and participation of GPG officials the opportunities for sustained progress in developing integrated service systems are minimal. Some of the projects show that with the commitment and leadership of such officials, particularly the chief executives, these opportunities are much enhanced.[16] It may very well be that what we need in the human-services environment is more politics, or at least more politics of the kind that involve elected officials.

In this context, generalists should address, in earnest, questions such as the following: How can they take better advantage of the generalist orientation of GPG officials? How can human-service generalists who function within the GPG orbit serve as more effective emissaries to elected officials? What lessons have been learned from previous efforts? To what extent and in what ways should they distinguish between chief executives and legislators?[17]

c. Academicians. Although academicians interested in human services tend to be as specialist-oriented as those directly involved in the provision of services, there are some whose interests are similar to those of organizational generalists and who are inclined to work closely with them. These individuals can be very helpful, not only in theoretical or conceptual terms, but also in specific terms concerning such matters as training programs, evaluation technologies, and organizational linkage mechanisms. In fact, the potential in this area, which would encompass students as well as teachers, has hardly been tapped.

d. Functional generalists. Discussion of generalists and specialists, along the lines presented in this paper, can have the unfortunate consequence of binding generalists to the importance of developing closer linkages with those who work in the organizational domains of the specialists. The dichotomy, we must emphasize, is not hard and fast. Some individuals, who would be categorized as specialists by our definition, may be receptive to closer associations with generalists. Such receptivity is especially likely to be present among specialists who, within the context of a broad program area (e.g., health) or target group (e.g., the blind, the elderly), conduct themselves in large measure as functional generalists concerned with the interaction and application of many specialist resources. These persons can make significant contributions to generalist deliberations and should not be overlooked.[18]

3. *Promote a better public understanding of the generalist perspective.*—If generalists are to become more constructive and influential participants in the human-services environment, more people who are not directly a part of that environment must come to understand the roles of generalists. The necessity of generalists' roles and the dangers of excessive specialization must be presented to the public in terms that are meaningful to their present circumstances. Generalists, we feel, can make significant contributions to their own public images primarily through better performance (albeit in the midst of major constraints) but also through the ways in which they explain themselves and their missions to the public. If, as has been the case so far, they couch such explanations around terms like "services integration," "systems analysis," "information systems," and the like, they are not likely to get far. However, if they can develop explanations which indicate in relatively simple terms how they can and hope to influence organizational behavior and the delivery of human services, they may generate more understanding and a broader base of support. The generalist-specialist distinction would seem to help in this regard.

It is our feeling that generalists have been woefully lacking in this communications task and that they would have much to gain if they recognized and addressed the issue through collective efforts. The gains, in fact, could be much greater than they would expect. For, in the process of trying to define their roles and objectives in simple terms understandable by the unindoctrinated, they could very well begin to clarify their own understandings about what they are or should be doing as human-service generalists.

4. *Search for better understanding of generalist potential and performance.*—Many people, both within and outside of the human-service field, view the generalist's job essentially as that of providing backup support to specialists. Those holding this view are not convinced that the job is of much intrinsic significance and, in fact, may feel that ascendance of generalist functions could create unnecessary and even harmful interference in the performance of specialist functions. This is a valid concern and one which generalists must confront. Edward C. Banfield, referring to the larger political environment, reflected such concerns in the following terms: "Despite the presumptions of common sense, it may be that under certain circumstances, the competition of forces which do not aim at a common interest produces outcomes which are more workable, satisfactory and effective than any that could be conceived by central decisionmakers searching for solutions in the common interest."[19] Human-service generalists are not likely to diminish such concerns immediately, but as they seek to define their roles they should recognize and understand that many of the contemporary conceptualizations and descriptions are hardly convincing enough to inspire widespread confidence.

All too often, the generalist's job is a seat-of-the-pants operation, where "success" is determined by the incumbent's skill in improvising much more than in employing any existing body of knowledge. Generalists themselves should confront this situation and do some hard thinking, in practical terms, about how they can make better use of their generalist perspectives. In the process they should ask themselves many basic questions, including the following:

a. Why is the generalist perspective important? This question is perhaps obvious, but it is usually ignored. By addressing it seriously, generalists can begin to gain a better understanding of the contexts in which they work and of the type of initiatives they should and should not undertake.

b. In what ways and under what conditions can generalists best reflect a systemic perspective? The generalist roles posed earlier in this article may provide a starting point, but they certainly do no more than that. Generalists, drawing upon their own experiences and understandings of the human-services environment, should determine for themselves what types of roles and approaches are likely to have widespread meaning for those working in generalist capacities. In this regard they should examine carefully the relevance and use of system designs. Some very thoughtful and potentially significant designs, directed toward the human-services environment, have been developed, but to date relatively little attention has been given to the ways in which these ideal designs can be adapted to the less than ideal environments in which generalists and specialists must function.[20]

c. How can generalists begin to develop standards which can be used to guide and measure their performance? Given the state of uncertainty about generalist roles, the development of performance standards may be too ambitious a task at the current time. Yet the sheer importance of it seems to leave little choice. Such standards, even if relatively crude in nature, can provide much-needed reference points for generalists and can be instrumental in gaining more public legitimacy for generalist roles. It is no small matter to recognize that standards can also help to defend generalists against charges of being charlatans or dilettantes.

5. *Promote opportunities for multidisciplinary human-services training.*—Both in universities and in public and private agencies, programs designed to train existing or potential human-service personnel are directed primarily along categorical, specialist lines. This orientation, obviously, promotes and reinforces highly specialized approaches to the planning, management, and delivery of human services.[21] As indicated earlier, there has been some movement in opening up more and better training opportunities for those inclined toward a generalist perspective. However, to date it has been slow and relatively inconsequential. For any significant level of activity to take place, it seems that generalists themselves must become the prime movers. They must recognize the crucial, long-term conditioning influence of training programs and begin to pressure forcefully and intelligently for the necessary reforms.

One line of activity in this regard is to prepare their case. They should be able to indicate, in some depth, why broad-based, multidisciplinary training programs are important and what types of skills and knowledge should be fostered through them. Such accounts, based as much as possible on the actual job demands of generalists, would provide valuable raw material for those planning or actually carrying out generalist-oriented training programs.

Finally, generalists can participate directly in efforts to initiate new training programs or to revise existing ones by designing curricula and training experiences and by serving as instructors. In this regard, programs geared to generalists should be the major concern. At the same time, however, generalists can add to specialist training programs by addressing the integration of specialist services to reflect a total system viewpoint. Through exposure to such training, specialists can gain valuable information and may become more receptive to linkage efforts involving generalists or other specialists.

6. *Cultivate organizational settings conducive to generalist perspectives.*—In order to apply their perspective, generalists must cultivate more supportive organizational settings. They must strive for the development of settings where there is more room for innovation, more receptivity to joint efforts involving specialists and generalists, and greater readiness to respond to the needs of service recipients in holistic rather than piecemeal fashion. For such movement to take place, however, generalists must develop some explicit and shared understandings about the particular elements of organizational settings which are vital to a generalist perspective and to the effective performance of generalist roles. What are these elements? To what extent and in what ways are they likely to affect generalist performance? Can more important elements be differentiated from less important ones? What are the hard political and financial realities likely to be met in trying to put them in place? By providing answers, even tentative answers, to these and other such questions, generalists can begin to develop some valuable guideposts for reform efforts in organizational settings of many different types.[22]

Many might argue that there is not enough knowledge upon which to base answers to such questions and that generalists, in any event, are not likely to reveal much agreement among themselves. This argument can be a very convincing one. Yet generalists have been coping in organizational settings for some time now, and though their "failures" are perhaps more notable than their "successes" they have learned some important lessons in the process. Unfortunately most of these lessons have not been widely shared and have not become cumulative. Inevitably, this situation has meant that the same mistakes are being made repeatedly.

In this context, the services-integration and capacity-building demonstration projects sponsored by the Federal government over the past years have provided a wealth of relevant experience. Funded with the major aim of generating increased knowledge about the development of integrated human-service systems and about the role of general-purpose governments in these systems, the projects have afforded significant opportunities for generalists. Although their overall funding level has been relatively meager,[23] they have placed generalists in important leadership positions and have enabled them to test innovative approaches and techniques in many different kinds of organizational settings. Assessments of these projects in terms of their lessons for generalists have been minimal—a situation which generalists themselves should try to correct before memories fade and relevant records and reports disappear. However, one recent report prepared for the Federal government (the former HEW) by RAND does afford a very interesting, albeit tentative conclusion. Looking closely at seventy local, comprehensive services-integration projects, not all of which were founded by HHS, RAND attempted to identify those types of linkages which were likely to foster the growth and development of an integrated service system. It found none. Such linkage mechanisms as interagency planning and budgeting, case management techniques, and information systems exhibited "a nonsignificant association with subsequent growth."[24] However, RAND did find that those integrative approaches which brought members of different agencies together fared better than those approaches which did not. The implication, RAND speculates, may be that "the key to the evolutionary growth of services-integration systems is that the links should require continuing interactions among personnel of the agencies involved."[25]

This is hardly an earth-shattering conclusion, but for generalists interested in cultivating organizational settings more conducive to integrative approaches it offers food for thought. It may mean that a vital first step to take in cultivating such settings is to foster greater interaction among generalists and specialists, even if at the outset the purposes and expected outcomes of this interaction are not sharply defined. It may mean that the gradual development of a constituency for change may be worth more emphasis than a detailed specification of the type of change being sought. Such notions may contradict the rational, orderly inclinations of many of us, but they appear to

be based on experience and quite certainly are worth further exploration.

7. *Serve as effective agents of change.*—Most of the advice we have offered heretofore is of a long-term, background nature. It concerns actions which generalists can take to maximize their strengths and to promote conditions more favorable to them. As important as they are, however, such actions in themselves will not lead to the major changes which most generalists would like to see take place. For these changes to happen generalists, individually and collectively, must be ready to enter the legislative and bureaucratic battlefields and fight intelligently and determinedly for what they perceive to be the necessary reforms.

However, it is one thing to be willing to enter these battlefields and quite another to be well prepared. The forces opposing change are in most places much stronger and more firmly entrenched. To confront them hastily and without a carefully prepared strategy is to undertake a course almost certainly destined to fail.

We do not enjoy the warfare terminology, but we use it to stress that, if generalists intend to promote major changes in the status quo,[26] they must understand that sharp conflicts are inevitable and necessary. The ways in which generalists deploy their limited resources and power will be vital in determining how well they fare. These are hard realities which must be faced and anticipated. For those generalists who are not inclined to conflict there is, as we have indicated, more than enough work to do in other arenas. For those who are so inclined and able there are great risks, but with them come the prospects of making some significant breakthroughs and contributions.

To this activist band of generalists, we offer four exhortations:

a. Be selective. At any given time and place there are likely to be numerous changes which must occur if generalists are to make significant contributions. Aside from the usual concerns for more money and authority, these are likely to involve a wide range of existing practices and requirements concerning civil service procedures, federal or state rules and regulations, and many other such factors which serve as constraints to more effective service delivery.[27] The important point here is that generalists in a particular time and place should make distinctions among these various constraints. They should identify those which are of priority concern, assess the strengths and weaknesses of the forces behind them, determine the support they could expect to obtain in opposing these forces, and, not least of all, think through the substantive grounds on which they would their case against a given constraint. Through such considerations they can put themselves in good position to select and pursue those targets for reform in which the generalist case is strong and the chance of success reasonable.

b. Promote positive alternatives. Whether a reform is focusing on a type of change that would affect many generalists in many different settings or just some generalists in a particular setting, it is important for the generalist advocates to have a clear and convincing conception of what they are for (i.e., what it is they want to do and would do, given the opportunity) as well as of what they are against. Without clear positive alternatives to replace existing procedures, advocates for change can lose credibility and become easy prey for the defenders of the status quo. Positive alternatives do not guarantee success, but they will increase one's chances, particularly if they offer specifics about how service systems would be improved and clients would be better off.

c. Use generalist allies. Generalists about to strike out at some existing constraints or about to advocate for some positive alternative should recognize that there are many potential allies and different ways in which they can help. For example, if a change is sought in a federal departmental requirement, generalists within that department could not be expected to help in the same way as could generalists in a governor's office or a private group. The latter types of generalists would probably have much more flexibility and be able to make much stronger and more open demands. As part of their homework, therefore, generalists about to go out in front on some reform issue would do well to identify their network of supporters, determine their distinctive contributions, and then, at least in some general way, try to orchestrate their actions.

d. Persevere. Most changes of any consequence are apt to take time, even under the best of conditions. Generalist architects of change, therefore, should be prepared to take a long-term view and to recognize the importance of patience and perseverance. Valuable testimony of this sort is afforded by the experience of a Connecticut group which developed a truly innovative proposal calling for the provision of integrated, community-based services to a selected population of elderly people, but which re-

quired Federal support in the form of money and waivers to myriad Medicare regulations. The story is a long one, not easily told, but the salient point here is that, although the Federal bureaucracy (the former HEW) was strongly resistant to the proposal at the outset and at many intervening points during the next two years, the proposal was eventually funded, essentially because the sponsors and the allies they cultivated refused to give up on it and continued to press HEW, vigorously and intelligently, for the necessary support. Perseverance in this case made the difference for the sponsors, and we expect could do the same for other generalists who find themselves bucking the legislative or bureaucratic tide.

A Note of Caution

The agenda set forth in the preceding pages is, we believe, a full, exciting, and important one. However, because we have presented it in terms of what generalists can and should do for themselves we feel compelled to close on a note of caution about generalists becoming too caught up in their self-interest. We do not expect generalists to be any more altruistic than any other participants in the human-service field, and we recognize that, inevitably, a good part of their energies are likely to be devoted to concerns about pay levels, working conditions, job benefits, and the like. Yet to the extent that they focus on such concerns at the expense of those dealing with the contributions they can make to the improved functioning of human-service systems, they tend to weaken their case. The strength of the generalist perspective, and of the notion of an alliance of generalists, lies in its relevance to these systems and, at bottom, to the overall well-being of service recipients, not in the inherent importance of generalists themselves. The distinction may be a fine one, but it is one that generalists would do well to keep in mind.

NOTES

The views expressed in this article are those of the authors and do not necessarily represent those of the institutions with which they are affiliated.

[1]We do not mean to suggest that this concentration of power reflects a conspiracy lacking public support or legitimacy. In fact, at least in a general sense, quite the opposite is true. Specialists in all spheres of governmental activity have for some time enjoyed far-reaching public support and have been able to derive their power largely from that support.

Herbert Kaufman, a political scientist, explains this state of affairs as a reflection of a popular long-standing quest for "neutral competence" in government; i.e., a longing to put government in the hands of experts who will make decisions on the basis of knowledge and objective standards rather than on the basis of political influences (Herbert Kaufman, "Emerging Conflicts in the Doctrines of Public Administration," *American Political Science Review* 50 [December 1956]:1057–73).

[2]The most comprehensive source for references to publications on the problems of the categorical system of service delivery is Project Share, a national clearing house for information on human-services integration (P.O. Box 2309, Rockville, Maryland 20852). Annotated bibliographies are available upon request.

[3]This interdependence is addressed in a very convincing manner in Alfred J. Kahn, "Service Delivery at the Neighborhood Level," *Social Service Review* 50 (March 1976):38–40.

[4]Seymour B. Sarason, *The Creation of Settings and Future Societies* (San Francisco: Jossey-Bass, 1972), p. 121.

[5]C.C. Attkisson and A. Broskowski, "Evaluation and the Emerging Human-Service Concept," in *Evaluation of Human-Service Programs*, eds. C.C. Attkisson, W. Hargreaves, M. Horowitz, and J. Sorensen (New York: Academic Press, 1976). For an excellent case study of the differences in evaluation and analysis when carried out under categorical as opposed to generalist auspices, see Joseph L. Falkson, "Minor Skirmish in a Monumental Struggle: HEW's Analysis of Mental Health Services," *Policy Analysis* 2 (Winter 1976):93–119.

[6]In this regard, it is significant to note that one of the most widespread criticisms of a recent reorganization of the Florida Department of Human Resources is that giving generalists more decision-making power tended to dilute the autonomy of program directors and to inhibit the department's capacity to attract top-quality specialists. This information is taken from a case analysis prepared by K.G. Heintz under the supervision of Laurence E. Lynn, Jr., for use at the John F. Kennedy School of Government, Harvard University. It is entitled "Reorganization of Florida's Human-Service Agency" and was prepared in 1975.

[7]See Fremont A. Shull, *Matrix Structure and Project Authority for Optimizing Organizational Capacity*, Business Science Monographs, no. 1 (Carbondale:

Business Research Bureau, School of Business, Southern Illinois University, May 1970); Duncan Neuhauser, "The Hospital as a Matrix Organization," *Hospital Administration* (Fall 1972):8–25; Robert W. Curtis, "From State Hospital to an Integrated Human Service System: The Management of Transition," *Health Care Management Review* 1 (1976):39–50; Donald R. Kingdon, *Matrix Organization: Managing Information Technologies* (London: Tavistock Publications, 1973; distributed in the United States by Harper & Row).

[8]See *Evaluation of Services-Integration Projects*, Human Services Bibliography Series, no. 1 (June 1976), available from Project Share, P.O. Box 2309, Rockville, Maryland 20852.

[9]Particularly notable in this regard are (1) the Community Allied Human Services Program at the College of Public and Community Services, University of Missouri, Columbia; (2) the efforts of the College for Human Services, 201 Varick St., New York, New York 10014; and (3) the Human-Services Generalist Program in the Department of Psychology at the University of Minnesota.

[10]This inner focus is not meant to suggest that a search for ways in which generalists can interact more effectively with specialists is not of great importance. Obviously, such a search is of considerable importance. However, such a search is not apt to be very successful if generalists do not have a sense of community among themselves, a sense of their own potential, and a sense of how they can best take advantage of that potential. This section is thus devoted to the quest for these basics.

[11]This is certainly true among specialists, who relate much more comfortably and easily with their counterparts in other organizations than they do with generalists in their own organizations. More often than not, it appears, they view the latter as outsiders and as threats to their professional interests rather than as members of the same team.

[12]On the other hand, if the territorial scope is too limited, say to a metropolitan area, discussions might become too detailed and might focus too heavily on personalities.

[13]The central question posed at its fall 1975 conference, for example, was: What are the major, underlying principles of services integration?

[14]Such determinations, of course, can mean different things. In one instance they can be just that and little more; i.e., a determination, official or unoffi-

cial, that a particular objective or course of action is a desirable one. In another instance they can lead to a change in the rules of the game or in the distribution of authority characterizing generalist-specialist relationships. Or, in still another instance they can lead to the provision of funds in support of certain initiatives. The important point is that in any of these instances, or others, generalists have much to gain if the determinations are supportive of their efforts.

[15]We are not naive enough to suggest that because GPG officials are in positions which call for a generalized orientation they always or even usually reflect this orientation. Obviously, many officials reflect specialized interests much more than they represent the public interest. The basic reason for this situation probably rests in the fact that the public or general interest is usually too fuzzy to be politically relevant in the midst of clear-cut and powerful specialized interests. However, at least part of the explanation, we feel, is that generalists have not been as adept as specialists in making their case in the political arena.

[16]Most of this information appears in internal departmental reports. A national evaluation of the HEW general-purpose government capacity-building projects is now underway and is very much attuned to the political dimension of the projects. It should be completed in mid-1977. An assessment of some of the earlier HEW-funded services-integration demonstration projects is less geared to political dimensions but does provide some pertinent information in this context (see Stephen D. Mittenthal, *Human-Service Development Programs in Sixteen Allied Services (SITO) Projects* [Wellesley, Mass.: Human Ecology Institute, 1975]).

[17]It is interesting to note that in the case of the Florida reorganization which elevated the status of generalists in the state's Department of Human Resources the legislative rather than the executive branch was the chief architect of the reform (see n. 6 above).

[18]There is another element here meriting the consideration of organizational generalists. Functional generalists are often appointees (or the staff of appointees) of GPG chief executives. As such, they are likely to have closer ties with GPG generalists than are the true specialists who work in the bureaus and divisions under them. Moreover, quite a few of these functional generalists are likely to have broad-based generalist backgrounds rather than specialized backgrounds in the particular functional area in which they are currently employed.

[19]Edward C. Banfield, *Political Influence: A New Theory of Urban Politics* (New York: Free Press, 1961), p. 327.

[20]See Michael Baker, ed., *The Design of Human Service Systems* (Wellesley, Mass.: Human Ecology Institute, December 1974).

[21]Frederick C. Mosher views the specialist biases of universities to be of major consequence to the public service and to be in substantial part responsible for the heavy emphasis on specialization within the public service (Frederick C. Mosher, *Democracy and the Public Service* [New York: Oxford University Press, 1968], esp. pp. 24–52 and 99–123).

[22]In this context, the mission of an organization may be a variable worth special attention. It may be that for generalists to come into their own more organizations will have to redefine their missions in ways which give more emphasis to planning, evaluation, integration, cost saving, and other concerns which are central to the generalist's agenda.

[23]Total funding between 1971 and 1975 for HEW's services-integration and capacity-building demonstration projects has been about $25 million.

[24]William A. Lucas, Karen Heald, and Mary Vogel, *The 1975 Census of Social Services Integration: A Working Note*, prepared for the Department of Health, Education, and Welfare by RAND (Santa Monica, Calif.: RAND Corporation, 1975), p. viii.

[25]Ibid., p. lx.

[26]In this context generalists would do well to understand and reflect upon the inevitable tendency of established organizations and parts of organizations not only to resist change but also to act assertively in trying to remain the same. Donald Schon refers to this characteristic as "dynamic conservatism" (Donald A. Schon, *Beyond the Stable State* [New York: Norton, 1971], esp. pp. 31–60).

[27]A major and long-standing federally induced constraint of this sort is the single state agency requirement associated with many categorical programs. This requirement, which is usually reflected in statute as well as in administrative regulation, is a device to ensure that the relevant specialist professionals at the state level retain control over the categorical program and serve as the accountable agents to counterpart federal specialists....

EXPECTATION, PERFORMANCE, AND ACCOUNTABILITY

Emanuel Tropp

The social work profession has never fully addressed the issue that Briar raised over a year ago when he stated:

> Questions about social work's effectiveness will not be stilled by rhetoric or passion. Nor will it help much to impugn the motives of those who currently demand an accounting of the costs and benefits of what social workers do. . . .
>
> What would help . . . is for the profession to increase substantially its efforts and resources devoted to evaluating and discovering more effective ways of performing its mission.[1]

This article will attempt to deal with the fundamental challenges residing within Briar's statement. It will hew closely to the issues, but will separate the concepts of accountability and effectiveness by looking at the former as a product of intent and the latter as the level of performance that derives from being accountable, with the issue of proof one more stage removed.

Much of the presentation could apply to any helping profession. In fact, the philosophical roots of the stance presented derive largely from sources outside of social work, namely, the writings of Frankl and Szasz, two psychiatrists who openly faced the shortcomings of their own profession with which social work has long had a close relation.[2]

The triad of reference points—expectation, performance, and accountability—reflects a composite area of increasing concern in almost all occupations and professions. Yet the helping professions are much more vulnerable in this area because of their intangible product. To come to grips with the three issues, one must see them in perspective, cross-referenced against three other dimensions: accountability of the social work profession to the public, accountability of the social work practitioner to users of service, and accountability of the practitioner to the agency.

ACCOUNTABILITY TO THE PUBLIC

A recent document on the future of social work education mentions the public's concern about how "money is spent in training *qualified* personnel and delivering *quality* social services" (emphasis added).[3] The public is usually identified as the people who pay for social services, but obviously persons who help provide community funds through taxes include those who use the services. Even the poorest of the poor pay taxes on practically everything purchased. A payer who is not a user has the right to know that his contributions are spent effectively. A payer who becomes a user expects and, if strong enough, demands delivery of the services promised.

Recipients of *involuntary* rehabilitation may not be in a position to claim the consumer's role, but an informed public is asking increasingly whether involuntary rehabilitation is effective, simply because it appears self-defeating and does not produce the desired results. Deprivation of liberty may deter crime, but rehabilitation can only make sense as an agreed-on endeavor—unless one believes in totalitarian mind control.[4]

On the other hand, those who voluntarily seek social services or who at least respond voluntarily to an outreach from those services have found ways to let providers know what they think of services. If they receive the help needed, they usually show by what they do or say that an effective "piece of business" was carried out. When they do not receive help they need, the users, rather than complain, tend to find easier ways to let providers know—for example, by dropping out.

It used to be simple for social workers to explain within the professional family that a dropout was "resistant" or "apathetic," but it is now much harder for the profession to accept this interpretation. The tendency has been to absolve the provider from any charge of ineffectiveness and to blame the user for his own inadequacy (which, ironically, was why he first sought help). Too many questions have been raised for too long a time to permit such self-serving explanations to be the rule. They are far more likely to be valid merely as exceptions.

Social workers need only view themselves in their roles of taxpayers or consumers to get an idea of the performance and accountability expected. Like others, they pay taxes for some services they use and for some they do not use. In either case, they have a valid claim on the services and frequently create quite a disturbance about them. A social worker, say, who has no children of school age is alarmed to learn about the low level of performance of local public schools. As a taxpayer, he has a right to be heard, even if he does not directly need the service. Why then is the taxpayer stereotyped as someone "on the other side"?

If a store sells a faulty product to a social worker so that he does not get his money's worth, is he not angry? Is it wrong to object when goods are misrepresented or overpriced? Of course it is possible that "social work as a way of life" may have so enveloped a practitioner's existence that he dare not judge an inefficient salesperson or clerk too harshly.

PURSUIT OF EXCELLENCE

Although the devaluation of excellence is widespread today, it is especially pronounced in the helping professions. As Szasz noted, role evaluations in psychiatry have become reversed: failure is elevated to a state of grace deserving compassion, while success is suspected of pretension and is lowered in status so that other people will not feel inferior.[5]

Dorothy Thompson once said it was becoming ever harder to find good repairmen for household equipment, and she added that watching a worker execute a job with genuine skill and pride was a "delicious" experience. In effect, such a proud worker was doing what a leading spokesman for the counterculture advocates when he urges that one "make his work a performance" as though for an audience.[6] From experiences with those attracted to teach in his "free schools," even so radical an educational critic as Kozol has noted ruefully:

It is time for us to face head-on this problem of our own inherent fear of strength and effectiveness. We must be prepared to strive with all our hearts to be strong teachers, efficacious adults, unintimidated leaders.[7]

Kozol expressed his dismay at "those who look upon

effectiveness itself as bearing the copyright of evil men."[8]

Just as the social worker as citizen has the right to demand the most effective use of his tax dollar, all people as citizens have the right to demand effectiveness in social services and in social workers. To act with the *intention* of delivering the services effectively and humanely is to fulfill accountability to the public.

The standard of accountability includes various functions that may be expected of a profession:

To provide services to the public, as claimed, within the scope of the particular professional knowledge and skill;
To deliver these services to those who contract for their use;
To educate individuals for social work practice and to certify that these individuals, when they have obtained a degree or have met other requirements, are qualified to practice their profession responsibly. Thus the public will know whom the profession deems capable of delivering the services promised.

The standard of accountability needs to spell out what a qualified person *knows* of a disciplined professional nature, what he can *do* professionally with his knowledge, and how well he can *explain* what he knows and what he does. When his knowledge and skill are put to use, it is assumed they are translated into competent practice.

To be accountable is to be liable or legally bound to account for the terms of a contracted transaction. To be accountable means to keep an agreement to deliver promised services. Thus accountability involves "accounts payable" and "accounts receivable" that are mutually agreed to. Accountability to the public provides the ground on which accountability to the agency necessarily rests, since the agency is the publicly supported vehicle for service delivery. Accountability to the agency provides the ground on which the accountability to the user must then rest, because the public sponsors the agency for the benefit of those using services. Accountability to the user is the ultimate goal of both accountability to the public and to the agency.

EFFECTIVENESS

The step from accountability to proved effectiveness is a tremendous jump. In discussing the age of accountability, it should be sufficient to demonstrate that the social work profession is acting accountably—and that alone is a large order today. To prove effectiveness in discharging responsibilities is a larger order. First, effectiveness can be related only to the tasks contracted for. When the profession agrees, for example, to be party to a contract calling for performance of police functions, it is merely guaranteeing the dismal results evident in any study of these services, since they are not fruitful or appropriate tasks for social workers. But the social work profession should be able to agree on the areas to which it can contribute significantly through amelioration, prevention, or fulfillment. For these areas, social workers need to find more refined measuring instruments to trace the attitudinal, cognitive, and behavioral movements that occur.

Even with more refined instruments, criteria for effectiveness would have to consider such factors as Ripple's "motivation, capacity, and opportunity" and Reid's "target problems."[9] Furthermore, attainments should be evaluated in relation to the extent of success within a given population and the degree of success with given users of service. By way of comparison, an inept lawyer might achieve a fine record of success by accepting the simplest and most-likely-to-be-won cases, while a highly competent lawyer who accepted only the most difficult cases might have a much lower rate of success. Which lawyer, then, would be considered more effective?

The triad of expectation-performance-accountability is on one level; the triad of effectiveness-guarantee-proof on another. A worker may be accountable by intent, but his performance may not be competent enough to live up to what is expected of him. Further, a worker may be highly accountable and highly competent, but not effective in given situations because of external limitations. Finally, a worker may perform effectively, but there may be no available measuring instruments to prove that effectiveness.

All that can be asked for in effectiveness in any human-service profession is that a person perform well enough to meet reasonable expectations, with the best available knowledge and skill, under given circumstances. This does not imply that effectiveness is guaranteed; the proof varies with each profession according to what is to be accomplished. In the medical profession, for example, respiratory ailments such as colds, virus infections, and influenza are common and frequent. Yet, since these are recognized to be be-

yond the ability of present medical knowledge, physicians who cannot cure them are not labeled ineffective. It might be said that the same kind of situation exists for social work in regard to the common problems of people on welfare or those convicted of crimes. In both professions, when specific cures to problems are lacking, there are still ways to help people cope more effectively.

Like other human-service professions, social work can be held accountable for a reasonable degree of effective performance in delivering claimed services. Everything starts from the expectation of service that user and provider agreed to. When social work has made unrealizable claims, it has not been able to match expectation with performance. However, once having defined a claim and shown it to be within acceptable bounds of realization, social work has created an expectation that it must fulfill by performance.

How does the public determine expected performance for industries producing physically tangible items for public consumption? For instance, a customer who purchases from a reliable company a pair of shoes that fall apart within a week can reasonably expect a replacement or a refund. This is a kind of guarantee of basic satisfaction.

GUARANTEED PERFORMANCE

In the many human services, guaranteed performance is rarely expected, except within restricted ground rules, simply because outcomes for people are not as tractable or predictable as for materials. In law, for instance, the public generally expects an attorney to do the best he can to represent the interests of his client. This does not guarantee that he will win the case, since many variables exist, such as vulnerability and available evidence on either side. Therefore the attorney's accountability and effectiveness are measured by how well he represents his client, win or lose. A refund for alleged ineffective service would not be dreamed of.

One does not expect refunds or replacements from human service professions because no guarantees can conceivably be given for the favorable outcome of such actions as a surgical operation or a lawsuit. Sometimes, however, there may be suits for malpractice—for example, in cases of gross negligence. This principle is further compounded in social work by the fact that in a voluntary service the user makes the final decision about how to lead his life and carries out that decision (or does not, as the case may be). There is truly no legal guarantee on the part of the social work practitioner when the service is voluntary and choices rest with the user.

Another view of the guarantee can be seen by comparing social work and the practice of medicine. Social work has allowed itself to be saddled with implicit guarantees of a sort in relation to criminal recidivism, repeated pregnancies, and other subjects that tend to be studied for effectiveness. The practice of medicine has achieved broad public acceptance without making comparable claims. It is sufficient for the public that a physician give a person the best available professional treatment. Certain types of illness respond to treatment with a high rate of success; others do not respond, or else they recur, sometimes repeatedly.

The case of a boy who crushed his leg in an accident may offer a useful analogy. A physician may be able to avoid amputation, but may not be able to prevent a permanent limp. Many social workers have been working with "crushed lives," and persons with severe traumatic experiences are far less likely to respond favorably to treatment than those with multiple bone fractures. The only guarantees that a realistic social worker can give against such formidable odds is that he can help a person having chronic and multiple life-fractures cope with the limitations with realism, dignity, clarity, and hope—and that perhaps there may be the possibility of correcting conditions. Social workers deal not only with such unpromising situations, but with many temporary crisis situations as well. If a social worker can help a significant number of people cope more successfully with such conditions, then that social worker has been both accountable and effective.

It is the broad contract-guarantee covering services of this kind that the social work profession should be offering to the public. Once the issues are defined more clearly and realistically, then the demands that those restated claims be honored become an unquestioned obligation for the profession, namely, the obligation to be accountable for performance at a professional level of effectiveness.

ACCOUNTABILITY TO CONSUMER

It is today generally realized that many who enter the human-service professions do so to get some kind of help for themselves in the process. This is a recognition of the magnetic power of becoming a helper and an acceptance of the reality that people who have suffered deeply are more likely to be drawn into a profession that helps others who suffer. They are also likely to be persons who can empathize with those in need or those seeking greater fulfillment.

Yet motivation to help others is usually identified with a polar opposite to the triad under consideration, namely, need, compassion, and help. Thus the general life-view of the social worker has been oriented more closely to nurturing than to the expectation-performance-accountability triad. The thought of converting an apparently humane set of values into what looks like its hard-nosed opposite presents an alarming prospect to the social worker. If this conversion was intended, it would be cause for alarm. Yet social work and other helping professions have lived through many pendulum swings. The one that lasted longest was the swing from the demands of the work ethic to an ethic calling for sympathetic understanding of why people could not reasonably be expected to live up to earlier demands.

This swing process may be historically necessary, but it inflicts a heavy price until a higher level of integration is reached. Those who moved from an exaggerated posture of "demands without compassion" to "compassion without demands" find that the current ethic suffers from a defect similar to the one it replaced. Life becomes insufferable without compassion, and it becomes unworkable without demands. It is time the two were brought together in a livable way to form a basis for a professional orientation.

Just as expectation without help does not require a helping profession, help without expectation tends to "cripple self-respect and initiative" rather than activate those forces.[10] Szasz used the following quotation from Popper to introduce the final chapter of his book, *The Myth of Mental Illness:*

The strain of civilization . . . is created by the efforts which life in an open and partially abstract society continually demands from us—by the endeavor to be rational, to forego at least some of our emotional social needs, to look after ourselves, and to accept responsibilities. We must, I believe, bear this strain, as the price to be paid for every increase in our knowledge, in reasonableness, in cooperation and in mutual help, and consequently in our chances of survival . . . It is the price we have to pay for being human.[11]

Frankl added another perspective when he stated:

Man should not ask what he may expect from life but should rather understand that life expects something from him. . . . Life is putting its problems to him, and it is up to him to face these problems by shouldering his responsibility, thus answering for his life.[12]

If, like Szasz, one sees life as a series of games or social transactions that have rules, roles, and expectations, then there is an objective ground against which one can deal with subjective reactions.[13] Those who deal with the subjective alone tend to focus primarily on attitudes and feelings. They make the serious error of overlooking not only knowledge and judgment but also the real tasks to which emotions are attached. If they continue to fix their expectations solely on feelings, other elements are blocked. Then they never arrive at the end product that both users of services and the society want. That is, they do not find a way of taking cognitive and emotional steps toward better performance, including the crucial element of accountability for performance—all of which leads to greater effectiveness and satisfaction for self and others.

Social work and psychiatry have lived through a long period that might be called the "time of the id," and have more recently turned to the "time of the ego." Yet they have carefully avoided entering the third part of Freud's world, the superego. When the id rode high, the concept of responsibility vanished because man was seen as trapped by his instincts. Now with the ego having its turn, there seems to be a sense of shame associated with using this concept.

Truly, then, the superego is yet to be liberated. Since people remain at the levels of the id and the ego, it has not been possible to see or deal with the complete person who has achieved the self-respect and liberation that expectations of performance and accountability can produce. Social workers are among those who have failed to deal completely with those they serve. In doing so, they have applied the same overprotective standards to themselves as professionals that they have applied to their clients—almost as if in recompense for not expecting too much from others.

EXPECTATIONS

The expectation-performance-accountability complex now parallels the lines developed between the profession and the public. Thus a two-way set of expec-tations is operating—expectations both for the user and for the practitioner.

What does the user expect of the practitioner? There are as many different answers to this question as there are different services and different applicants for those services. In the following example, the user is a voluntary applicant at a mental health center. She is a married woman concerned about her deteriorating relationship with her adolescent daughter. Alienation has become so severe that she fears her daughter will run away from home, and this fear is creating a deep sense of panic in her.

What would be a reasonable expectation on the part of the mother? If she perceives the situation accurately, she is likely to expect that the skills of the center's staff will help her find out what happened between her and her daughter, help them deal more successfully with each other, and prevent a rupture in family relations.

If a social worker assigned to the case performed his job effectively, it might be assumed that he would enable the mother to cope with the situation in a satisfying manner. In this sense, then, his performance would be accountable in intent and effective for the purpose, and the applicant's expectations would be met. If his efforts were not successful, this might be because of his own ineffectiveness, the mother's unwillingness to face realities, or other variables. If the worker's inability to perform hinders success, then his work needs to be called to the attention of a skilled person within the agency who has supervisory responsibility and is in the role of quality-control agent. If the supervisor cannot help this worker overcome his limitations, then the agency is not performing effectively. However, if the worker meets reasonable expectations and the mother is unwilling to carry out her part of the agreement, then despite the lack of a "satisfied customer," the worker can rightfully claim to have acted accountably to the client.

The major implication of this example emerges clearly: accountability does not guarantee fulfilling the expectations of the user. However, it cannot be so easily assumed that practice is effective, because the guidelines to effective practice have not been clearly established. A recent review of many studies of social work effectiveness revealed a recurrent theme: social agencies do not deliver what is expected of them.[14] A question frequently raised about these studies is whether expectations were unrealistic—that is, whether extremely unpromising missions were to be accomplished. It is increasingly evident that more so-phisticated instruments are needed to evaluate what social work service can accomplish. These can con-tribute substantially to human renewal, even though the "missions impossible" are not accomplished.[15]

A major difficulty in developing more refined measuring instruments lies in the professional dilem-mas presented when expectation-performance-accountability demands are applied to the user of ser-vice. The central reason that social workers have not been able to apply these demands fully may lie in their blocked view of dealing with the people they serve.

HEART AND HEAD

This leads full circle from what the user expects of the provider to what the provider expects of the user. And here is probably the most crucial obstruc-tion which has prevented the intention of accounta-bility from becoming actual, effective performance by practitioner and user.

Social work practice has been living far too long with far too great a proportion of heart to head. Does this statement reinforce the common public image of the social worker as a "bleeding heart"? Hardly. So-cial workers who live long on a diet of ultrasen-sitivity to human needs tend to become frustrated at not being able to satisfy all needs. Their frustration easily leads to anger at those unamenable to their efforts or to subtle manipulation of clients who may accede to their wishes without realizing it. If exces-sive stress of compassion can so easily lead to irrita-tion or manipulation, then of what value is that kind of compassion? Is it surprising that the public sees so-cial workers as softhearted but many users consider them hardhearted?

An excessive stress of either heart or head, to the neglect of the other, creates hazards. Even more damaging than ultrasensitivity to needs is the avoid-ance of potential strength and responsibility. As Frankl quotes Goethe:

If we treat people as they are, they will become worse. If we treat them as if they were what they ought to be, we help them to become what they are capable of becoming.[16]

The underlying life-view of social workers today too often contradicts Goethe's dictum. They are too likely to protect weakness. By feeling sorry for the client and creating increased self-pity, they may bring about immobilization. This protectionist stance re-flects fear of asking others to be responsible for their own behavior.

Szasz describes the "game of helpfulness" as one that perpetuates the "game of helplessness" in which "sick" people are so entitled to help that they lose their power to demand.[17] According to the rules of this game, he says, the sick are rewarded and the able are somehow made to feel ignoble. These "rules of irresponsibility and childish dependency" have cre-ated a situation in which the helper "becomes the captive of the help-seeker"—a way of life ultimately dysfunctional for both.[18]

Robert Kennedy used to say that some people looked at what was and asked why, while others looked at what could be and asked why not. When a social worker asks a client why—but fails to follow through with why not—what is he doing to a person he aims to serve? How does a worker relate to or communicate with a client? How do they do business with each other? The terms "relating" and "commu-nicating" imply a gingerly treading on ice, as though the client or the relationship mught crack at any moment.

What does a client think when a social worker fails to ask him to look at the demands of reality? He may think at first that the worker is understanding and supportive. However, this feeling may soon evaporate into "I guess I really can't do much," be-cause the worker does not deal directly with expecta-tions or with alternatives and consequences of action or inaction. Nor is the worker confronting the client with the challenge that it is truly up to him to take his life in his hands, decide, and act.

It is a strong tonic for the client's spirit when someone who is responsible and professionally knowledgeable treats him as though he can and is ex-pected to rise to the occasion. The client says to him-self, "The social worker sees the strengths in me, has faith in me." Relationships that remain at the empa-thy-support-ventilation level dehumanize the client because the worker is failing to show expectations for coping. And all people expect and are able to cope in some way, whatever their restrictions and limitations may be. Emphasizing strengths brings out strengths, while emphasizing limitations reinforces weaknesses. Besides being an invaluable tonic, expectation is es-sential in showing respect for any human being's ca-pacities, whatever the conditions.

The realities of life, when approached openly and freely, demand responsibility and performance.

Recognizing that a person is responsible is actually to liberate him. A person regarded as responsible can truly feel free to influence his future. Each person determines for himself how to perform and how to be accountable, but that sense of freedom is a source of real strength.

A clear and firm blend of compassion for realistic limitations and of expectations for realistic performance is the balance much needed today in practice. As the social worker moves from relating and communicating toward the firmer ground of transacting business with people, it is much easier to conceive of transactions expressed freely, openly, and responsibly. As he moves away from ultrasensitivity and cautiously maneuvered discussion, he can still find ways to transact business with empathy as well as with relaxed, direct, and challenging "straight-talk." Such an approach is needed with those served; it is also needed in transactions among social workers, which have strongly tended to overemphasize the game of ultrasensitivity.

It is in the practice of social work—in the transactions between user and provider—that the core of the problem exists. It is in practice that the social work profession must first jump the expectation-performance-accountability hurdles. And this must be done before these same barriers can be overcome through changed approaches to the public or to the agency.

ACCOUNTABILITY TO AGENCIES

Much has been written about what is wrong with social agencies and what social workers should do to change them. Whatever changes may be deemed necessary, there are obligations that agencies have to the public supporting them and that practitioners have to the agencies employing them. These obligations are unavoidable if the profession is to face its own problem of accountability to the public.

A social work practitioner may be accountable to an agency—and through it to a community—without being considered effective in some instances, because an agency looks at intent while the community looks at results. On the other hand, a practitioner may be effective in a fashion without being accountable. This is the clear road of certain client-advocacy approaches in which accountability is not essential to the agency. Thus, one may be effective either by being against the agency or by subtly subverting agency policies. Obviously, the questions in this case are: Effective-

ness for whom and in doing what? With what direction of accountability?

Until all evils are corrected, which is never, one must still be accountable to an agency as the authorized instrument of the community. If a practitioner's effectiveness in obtaining certain concrete results flows from his commonsense ability to fight or get around obstacles rather than from special professional competence, then he is effective despite professional identity. This would not be an example of professional accountability or effectiveness, because anyone with the same common sense might have accomplished the same results, perhaps even better.

Kadushin shows how social workers' ways of doing business with each other in an agency tend to subvert the effectiveness of the operation.[19] Administrators and supervisors are seen, from whatever perspective, as being quality-control agents or guarantors of service delivery. However, social workers have always been plagued by the tendency to live out the supervisor-worker operation as though it were the same as the worker-client system.

As identified by Kadushin, the names of the games that social workers are playing with willing supervisors tell the story with relentless impact: "Two against the Agency," "Be Nice to Me Because I Am Nice to You," and "Protect the Sick and Infirm." These are, of course, the same games played by workers and clients. The supervisor is induced to play, says Kadushin, because he identifies with the worker's concerns, resents bureaucratic demands just as the worker does, and "is hesitant to assert his authority in demanding firmly that the requirements be met." The supervisor also finds it gratifying to be considered helpful, and he "needs the supervisee as much as the supervisee needs the supervisor" as his "principal source of gratification." The supervisor "is induced to play because the game appeals to the social worker in him."

In this statement, Kadushin has really said all that needs to be said about what is wrong with internal staff lines of accountability in the profession. If these faults represent the weaknesses in the ways that social workers do business with those they serve, they represent these same weaknesses to a much higher degree in staff relationships. It is debilitating enough to treat clients with overprotective attitudes. It is close to farce to deal with supposedly self-sufficient workers in the same way, as though they were in the agency to obtain some "service." And of course this holds for graduate students, that is, workers-in-training who are experiencing a pattern-forming internship that tends to perpetuate traditions.

EDUCATION AND ACCOUNTABILITY

How do accountability and related issues affect the education and certification of those who tomorrow will become social work practitioners? People have every right to expect the social work profession—as well as the legal and medical professions—to exercise internal controls in approving training schools and requirements for degrees and for certification. People can expect those who have received a degree in social work to be qualified, since they have acquired specific knowledge and skills so that they can provide accountable professional service to the community. To meet the expectations there must be a clear upgrading of present standards, especially at the graduate level. This issue opens up painful problems for the social work profession because of existing currents: the widening range of acceptable content of graduate school curricula and the major emphasis on the baccalaureate degree, with a tendency to reduce and perhaps eventually eliminate the master's program and a hope that the terminal degree will thus become a doctorate—a hope completely unreal for the practice level.

Seeing the social worker at the bachelor's level as the "generalist" and the worker at the master's level as the "specialist," Boehm presents considerations that are particularly serious in this age of accountability.[20] If it is true that the public is demanding quality in social services and if it is also true that the current trend may lead to the elimination of the master's program, then the profession will be left essentially with lower-quality generalists! Is that being responsive to the real needs of the social work profession at this time in history? Can generalists of lower quality effectively deliver services in an accountable way? Thus, besides having to face an inheritance of a professional style that has prevented effective performance, social work has to deal with its own self-made "inevitabilities," which may lead to the lowering of standards even further. There is much to be done if the social work profession is to take its rightful position in the human services and exercise its potential influence to the maximum degree.

NOTES

[1]Scott Briar, "The Age of Accountability," Editorial Page, *Social Work*, 18 (January 1973), p. 2.

[2]*See* Viktor Frankl, *The Doctor and the Soul* (New York: Alfred A. Knopf, 1962); and Thomas S. Szasz, *The Myth of Mental Illness* (New York: Dell Publishing Co., 1961).

[3]Michael J. Austin and Robert O. Turner, Foreword, *Curriculum Building for the Continuum in Social Work Education* (Tallahassee: State University System of Florida, 1972), p. 9.

[4]*See* James Q. Wilson, "If Every Criminal Knew He Would Be Punished and Caught," *New York Times Magazine* (January 28, 1973), p. 9.

[5]Szasz, op. cit., pp. 195–196.

[6]Charles A. Reich, *The Greening of America* (New York: Random House, 1970), p. 372.

[7]Jonathan Kozol, "Free Schools: A Time for Candor," *Saturday Review* (March 4, 1972), p. 54.

[8]Ibid.

[9]*See* Lilian Ripple, *Motivation, Capacity, and Opportunity* (Chicago: School of Social Service Administration, Social Service Monographs, 1964); and William J. Reid, "Target Problems, Time Limits, Task Structure," *Journal of Education for Social Work*, 8 (Spring 1972), pp. 58–68.

[10]For an illuminating perspective on the effects of the concerted application of the work ethic, *see* Ruth Sidel, "Social Services in China," *Social Work*, 17 (November 1972), pp. 5–13.

[11]Karl R. Popper, *The Open Society and Its Enemies* (Princeton, N.J.: Princeton University Press, 1950), p. 172; and Szasz, op. cit., p. 294.

[12]Frankl, op. cit., p. xiv.

[13]Szasz, op. cit., pp. 167–182.

[14]Edward J. Mullen, James R. Dumpson, and Associates, *Evaluation of Social Intervention* (San Francisco: Jossey-Bass, 1972).

[15]*See* Carol Meyer, "Practice on a Microsystem Level," in ibid., pp. 180–181.

[16]Frankl, op. cit., p. 9.

[17]Szasz, op. cit., pp. 187–188.

[18]Ibid., pp. 197, 264.

[19]Alfred Kadushin, "Games People Play in Supervision," *Social Work*, 13 (July 1968), pp. 23–32.

[20]*See* Werner Boehm, "Continuum in Education for Social Work," in Mullen, Dumpson, and Associates, op. cit., pp. 222–223, 230–232.

APPENDIX A

THE NASW CODE OF ETHICS

PREAMBLE

This code is intended to serve as a guide to the everyday conduct of members of the social work profession and as a basis for the adjudication of issues in ethics when the conduct of social workers is alleged to deviate from the standards expressed or implied in this code. It represents standards of ethical behavior for social workers in professional relationships with those served, with colleagues, with employers, with other individuals and professions, and with the community and society as a whole. It also embodies standards of ethical behavior governing individual conduct to the extent that such conduct is associated with an individual's status and identity as a social worker.

This code is based on the fundamental values of the social work profession that include the worth, dignity, and uniqueness of all persons as well as their rights and opportunities. It is also based on the nature of social work, which fosters conditions that promote these values.

In subscribing to and abiding by this code, the social worker is expected to view ethical responsibility in as inclusive a context as each situation demands and within which ethical judgment is required. The social worker is expected to take into consideration all the principles in this code that have a bearing upon any situation in which ethical judgment is to be exercised and professional intervention or conduct is planned. The course of action that the social worker chooses is expected to be consistent with the spirit as well as the letter of this code.

In itself, this code does not represent a set of rules that will prescribe all the behaviors of social workers in all the complexities of professional life. Rather, it offers general principles to guide conduct, and the judicious appraisal of conduct, in situations that have ethical implications. It provides the basis for making judgments about ethical actions before and after they occur. Frequently, the particular situation determines the ethical principles that apply and the manner of their application. In such cases, not only the particular ethical principles are taken into immediate consideration, but also the entire code and its spirit. Specific applications of ethical principles must be judged within the context in which they are being considered. Ethical behavior in a given situation must satisfy not only the judgment of the individual social worker, but also the judgment of an unbiased jury of professional peers.

This code should not be used as an instrument to deprive any social worker of the opportunity or freedom to practice with complete professional integrity; nor should any disciplinary action be taken on the basis of this code without maximum provision for safeguarding the rights of the social worker affected.

The ethical behavior of social workers results not from edict, but from a personal commitment of the individual. This code is offered to affirm the will and zeal of all social workers to be ethical and to act ethically in all that they do as social workers.

The following codified ethical principles should guide social workers in the various roles and relationships and at the various levels of responsibility in which they function professionally. These principles also serve as a basis for the adjudication by the National Association of Social Workers of issues in ethics.

In subscribing to this code, social workers are required to cooperate in its implementation and abide by any disciplinary rulings based on it. They should also take adequate measures to discourage, prevent, expose, and correct the unethical conduct of colleagues. Finally, social workers should be equally ready to defend and assist colleagues unjustly charged with unethical conduct.

Source: *NASW News*, Vol. 25, No. 1 (January 1980), pp. 24, 25. Reprinted with permission of the National Association of Social Workers.

I. **The Social Worker's Conduct and Comportment as a Social Worker**

    A.   Propriety—The social worker should maintain high standards of personal conduct in the capacity or identity as social worker.

        1.   The private conduct of the social worker is a personal matter to the same degree as is any other person's, except when such conduct compromises the fulfillment of professional responsibilities.

        2.   The social worker should not participate in, condone, or be associated with dishonesty, fraud, deceit, or misrepresentation.

        3.   The social worker should distinguish clearly between statements and actions made as a private individual and as a representative of the social work profession or an organization or group.

    B.   Competence and Professional Development—The social worker should strive to become and remain proficient in professional practice and the performance of professional functions.

        1.   The social worker should accept responsibility or employment only on the basis of existing competence or the intention to acquire the necessary competence.

        2.   The social worker should not misrepresent professional qualifications, education, experience, or affiliations.

    C.   Service—The social worker should regard as primary the service obligation of the social work profession.

        1.   The social worker should retain ultimate responsibility for the quality and extent of the service that that individual assumes, assigns, or performs.

        2.   The social worker should act to prevent practices that are inhumane or discriminatory against any person or group of persons.

    D.   Integrity—The social worker should act in accordance with the highest standards of professional integrity and impartiality.

        1.   The social worker should be alert to and resist the influences and pressures that interfere with the exercise of professional discretion and impartial judgment required for the performance of professional functions.

        2.   The social worker should not exploit professional relationships for personal gain.

    E.   Scholarship and Research—The social worker engaged in study and research should be guided by the conventions of scholarly inquiry.

        1.   The social worker engaged in research should consider carefully its possible consequences for human beings.

        2.   The social worker engaged in research should ascertain that the consent of participants in the research is voluntary and informed, without any implied deprivation or penalty for refusal to participate, and with due regard for participants' privacy and dignity.

        3.   The social worker engaged in research should protect paticipants from unwarranted physical or mental discomfort, distress, harm, danger, or deprivation.

        4.   The social worker who engages in the evaluation of services or cases should discuss them only for professional purposes and only with persons directly and professionally concerned with them.

        5.   Information obtained about participants in research should be treated as confidential.

6. The social worker should take credit only for work actually done in connection with scholarly and research endeavors and credit contributions made by others.

II. The Social Worker's Ethical Responsibility to Clients

F. Primacy of Clients' Interests—The social worker's primary responsibility is to clients.

1. The social worker should serve clients with devotion, loyalty, determination, and the maximum application of professional skill and competence.
2. The social worker should not exploit relationships with clients for personal advantage or solicit the clients of one's agency for private practice.
3. The social worker should not practice, condone, facilitate or collaborate with any form of discrimination on the basis of race, color, sex, sexual orientation, age, religion, national origin, marital status, political belief, mental or physical handicap, or any other preference or personal characteristic, condition, or status.
4. The social worker should avoid relationships or commitments that conflict with the interests of clients.
5. The social worker should under no circumstances engage in sexual activities with clients.
6. The social worker should provide clients with accurate and complete information regarding the extent and nature of the services available to them.
7. The social worker should apprise clients of their risks, rights, opportunities, and obligations associated with social service to them.
8. The social worker should seek advice and counsel of colleagues and supervisors whenever such consultation is in the best interest of clients.
9. The social worker should terminate service to clients, and professional relationships with them, when such service and relationships are no longer required or no longer serve the clients' needs or interests.
10. The social worker should withdraw services precipitously only under unusual circumstances, giving careful consideration to all factors in the situation and taking care to minimize possible adverse effects.
11. The social worker who anticipates the termination or interruption of service to clients should notify clients promptly and seek the transfer, referral, or continuation of service in relation to the clients' needs and preferences.

G. Rights and Prerogatives of Clients—The social worker should make every effort to foster maximum self-determination on the part of clients.

1. When the social worker must act on behalf of a client who has been adjudged legally incompetent, the social worker should safeguard the interests and rights of that client.
2. When another individual has been legally authorized to act in behalf of a client, the social worker should deal with that person always with the client's best interest in mind.
3. The social worker should not engage in any action that violates or diminishes the civil or legal rights of clients.

H. Confidentiality and Privacy—The social worker should respect the privacy of clients and hold in confidence all information obtained in the course of professional service.

1. The social worker should share with others confidences revealed by clients, without their consent, only for compelling professional reasons.
2. The social worker should inform clients fully about the limits of confidentiality in a given situation, the purposes for which information is obtained, and how it may be used.
3. The social worker should afford clients reasonable access to any official social work records concerning them.
4. When providing clients with access to records, the social worker should take due care to protect the confidences of others contained in those records.
5. The social worker should obtain informed consent of clients before taping, recording, or permitting third party observation of their activities.

I. Fees—When setting fees, the social worker should ensure that they are fair, reasonable, considerate, and commensurate with the service performed and with due regard for the clients' ability to pay.

1. The social worker should not divide a fee or accept or give anything of value for receiving or making a referral.

III. The Social Worker's Ethical Responsibility to Colleagues

J. Respect, Fairness, and Courtesy—The social worker should treat colleagues with respect, courtesy, fairness, and good faith.

1. The social worker should cooperate with colleagues to promote professional interests and concerns.
2. The social worker should respect confidences shared by colleagues in the course of their professional relationships and transactions.
3. The social worker should create and maintain conditions of practice that facilitate ethical and competent professional performance by colleagues.
4. The social worker should treat with respect, and represent accurately and fairly, the qualifications, views, and findings of colleagues and use appropriate channels to express judgments on these matters.
5. The social worker who replaces or is replaced by a colleague in professional practice should act with consideration for the interest, character, and reputation of that colleague.
6. The social worker should not exploit a dispute between a colleague and employers to obtain a position or otherwise advance the social worker's interest.
7. The social worker should seek arbitration or mediation when conflicts with colleagues require resolution for compelling professional reasons.
8. The social worker should extend to colleagues of other professions the same respect and cooperation that is extended to social work colleagues.
9. The social worker who serves as an employer, supervisor, or mentor to colleagues should make orderly and explicit arrangements regarding the conditions of their continuing professional relationship.
10. The social worker who has the responsibility for employing and evaluating the performance of other staff members should fulfill such responsibility in a fair, considerate, and equitable manner, on the basis of clearly enunciated criteria.
11. The social worker who has the responsibility for evaluating the performance of employees, supervisees, or students should share evaluations with them.

K. Dealing with Colleagues' Clients—The social worker has the responsibility to relate to the clients of colleagues with full professional consideration.

1. The social worker should not solicit the clients of colleagues.
2. The social worker should not assume professional responsibility for the clients of another agency or a colleague without appropriate communication with that agency or colleague.
3. The social worker who serves the clients of colleagues during a temporary absence or emergency should serve those clients with the same consideration as that afforded any client.

IV. The Social Worker's Ethical Responsibility to Employers and Employing Organizations

L. Commitment to Employing Organization—The social worker should adhere to commitments made to the employing organization.

1. The social worker should work to improve the employing agency's policies and procedures and the efficiency and effectiveness of its services.
2. The social worker should not accept employment or arrange student field placements in an organization which is currently under public sanction by NASW for violating personnel standards or imposing limitations on or penalties for professional actions on behalf of clients.
3. The social worker should act to prevent and eliminate discrimination in the employing organization's work assignments and in its employment policies and practices.
4. The social worker should use with scrupulous regard, and only for the purpose for which they are intended, the resources of the employing organization.

V. The Social Worker's Ethical Responsibility to the Social Work Profession

M. Maintaining the Integrity of the Profession—The social worker should uphold and advance the values, ethics, knowledge, and mission of the profession.

1. The social worker should protect and enhance the dignity and integrity of the profession and should be responsible and vigorous in discussion and criticism of the profession.
2. The social worker should take action through appropriate channels against unethical conduct by any other member of the profession.
3. The social worker should act to prevent the unauthorized and unqualified practice of social work.
4. The social worker should make no misrepresentation in advertising as to qualifications, competence, service, or results to be achieved.

N. Community Service—The social worker should assist the profession in making social services available to the general public.

1. The social worker should contribute time and professional expertise to activities that promote respect for the utility, the integrity, and the competence of the social work profession.
2. The social worker should support the formulation, development, enactment, and implementation of social policies of concern to the profession.

O. Development of Knowledge—The social worker should take responsibility for identifying, developing, and fully utilizing knowledge for professional practice.

1. The social worker should base practice upon recognized knowledge relevant to social work.

2. The social worker should critically examine, and keep current with, emerging knowledge relevant to social work.

3. The social worker should contribute to the knowledge base of social work and share research knowledge and practice wisdom with colleagues.

VI. The Social Worker's Ethical Responsibility to Society

P. Promoting the General Welfare—The social worker should promote the general welfare of society.

1. The social worker should act to prevent and eliminate discrimination against any person or group on the basis of race, color, sex, sexual orientation, age, religion, national origin, marital status, political belief, mental or physical handicap, or any other preference or personal characteristic, condition, or status.

2. The social worker should act to ensure that all persons have access to the resources, services, and opportunities which they require.

3. The social worker should act to expand choice and opportunity for all persons, with special regard for disadvantaged or oppressed groups and persons.

4. The social worker should promote conditions that encourage respect for the diversity of cultures which constitute American society.

5. The social worker should provide appropriate professional services in public emergencies.

6. The social worker should advocate changes in policy and legislation to improve social conditions and to promote social justice.

7. The social worker should encourage informed participation by the public in shaping social policies and institutions.

APPENDIX B

A SCHEDULE FOR COMMUNITY ANALYSIS

It is perhaps a truism to note that every social worker works in "a community." Unfortunately, the traditional methods-centered orientation of most social workers—casework, group work, community organization—often led to a belief that understanding communities was a job only for the "community organizers." Thus services were frequently provided in a way that tended to isolate both clients and services from the context of their larger communities. The fallacies in this type of thinking—especially for the social work generalist—should be obvious. All social workers must be able to understand the communities in which they work; that is, the resources, norms, values, and the people who live there. Understanding the community in general can facilitate not only case-by-case services, but also the worker's assessment of and intervention in a problem or situation whose cause stems not from the individual client but from some deficiency in the community-at-large.

This appendix consists of a community schedule developed by Gottschalk and provides specific questions that social workers can think about—if not di-

Source: From Simon S. Gottschalk, *Communities and Alternatives* (Cambridge, Mass.: Schenkman Publishing Co., 1975). Reprinted by permission.

rectly ask—in the process of analyzing the community in which they work. This is done on the grounds that services provided without recognition and consideration of the various factors that can and do make up these communities will, at best, touch only the "tip of the iceberg." The purpose of this schedule, then, is to provide a practical method for social workers to use in order to gain an understanding of their own and their clients' communities and thereby increase the breadth and the relevance of their services.

I. History

    A. Who took the first step toward the creation of the community?

    B. What has been the subsequent role of these initiators and their heirs?

    C. What are the most significant milestones in the development of the community?

    D. What changes have taken place in the formal structure of the community over the years?

        1. Statement of purpose or purposes

        2. Legal status and political structure

        3. Boundaries and location

        4. Economic base

        5. Membership: nature and size

Note: Each of the following items is to be examined historically, i.e., what are the facts today, what changes have taken place over time, what were the facts at the time of the creation of the community?

II. Community Level Specific Goals

    A. Is there an explicit or implicit statement of goals? What is it and what is its origin?

    B. Does the goal of the community include a product which may serve as an input into another system? Is the product measurable? Is it amenable to contract?

    C. Are there specific, identifiable steps which lead to the attainment of the goals of the community? Is there a specific process or technology? Give examples.

    D. Are there specific, identifiable negative steps which lead away from the goals? Give examples.

    E. How do individual members or families contribute to the attainment of the goals of the community?

    F. Are organizations external to the community essential to the community in the attainment of its goals? Which ones, and how?

III. Initiation of Members and Role Allocation

    A. Is there a formal process of initiating new members into the community? Who administers and who controls this process?

    B. How are roles allocated to new members? By whom?

    C. Is there a method whereby roles are rotated among members? Who controls this process? Who would be authorized to make changes in the system?

    D. By whom are the membership boundaries of the community defined, i.e., who is considered a member, what kind of person may become a member, how large should the total number of members be?

    E. Is there disagreement among groups of members, or between members on the one hand and leaders on the other, concerning the principles of membership or the allocation of roles? What is the nature of this disagreement?

IV. Leadership

A. Are there identified or identifiable community leaders? How do the leaders demonstrate their leadership?

B. How are leaders chosen from among the members (residents) of the community? Is there a formal selection process or are leaders identified informally?

C. Is there a second group of leaders, i.e., officials or staff, appointed by individuals or organizations external to the community?

D. To whom is the staff primarily responsible? Who has the authority to dismiss them? To whom is the staff primarily responsive?

E. Is there a formal leadership hierarchy with specified levels of authority?

　　1. Among the resident leaders?
　　2. Among the staff?

F. What appear to be the major sources of high social status among the residents?

G. Does high social status coincide with leadership status?

H. Are there processes for the prevention of centralization of leadership, power, and authority? Is there a policy:

　　1. Of collective decision making?
　　2. Of distributing authority among many individuals or subgroups?

V. Central Decision Making

A. Is there a central decision-making structure in the community?

B. Does this central decision-making structure regularly make decisions affecting the total community:

　　1. Does it allocate space within the community?
　　2. Does it rule on the acceptance of new members?
　　3. Does it negotiate contracts in behalf of the community?

C. Do officials or resident leaders predominate in the central decision-making structure?

　　1. Is there is single structure in which both types of leaders participate?
　　2. Are there two separate structures? If so, what is the authority and the domain of each?

D. If there is no central decision-making structure which allocates space, accepts new members, and makes contracts in behalf of the community, how are such decisions made?

　　1. By an organization external to the community?
　　2. By a variety of decentralized decision-making systems within the community?
　　3. By all members of the community together?
　　4. Central decision making is avoided; there are no important central decisions purposefully made by any individual or group.

VI. Community Control of Deviant Behavior

A. Is there a central mechanism in the community which has the authority to exercise social control?

　　1. Under what circumstances does it use coercive power?
　　2. Under what circumstances does it use utilitarian power?
　　3. Under what circumstances does it use normative power?

B. In the absence of, or in addition to the central social control mechanism, how is deviant behavior controlled? What kinds of power are utilized?

1. By the residents among each other
   a. When is normative power (social control) used exclusively?
   b. When is utilitarian power used?
   c. When is coercive power used?
2. By an external system

C. Under what circumstances are individuals or families forced out of the community and by whom?

VII. Community and Its Subsystems (i.e., Families and Individuals)

A. What are the major subsystems of the community? Are they families, individuals, and/or other kinds of groupings?

B. What is the nature of the legal and economic ties between the community qua community and its subsystems?

C. Are there ideological commitments between the community and its members? What is their significance?

D. Do individuals view themselves as having important social or moral obligations to the community and its leaders, i.e., they "cannot let them down"?

E. Is the idea of community largely coincidental to the individual concerns of the members?

F. How are differences between families and the community adjudicated? By whom?

VIII. External Systems

A. What are the major external systems to which the community is linked, specifically:

1. Economic systems (production, consumption, distribution)
2. Political systems (social control)
3. Educational systems and communications (socialization)
4. Voluntary associations (social participation)
5. Systems of social welfare (mutual support)

B. What are the principal inputs of each of the external systems into the community?

C. Does the community have outputs which contribute to one or more of the external systems? What are they? How essential are they to the external system?

D. To what extent do individual members, families, or groups of members create an output which serves the goals of one or more of the external systems?

1. Are these outputs made directly to the external system?
2. Are these outputs made via the community?

IX. Community, Its Members, and Their Linkage to External Systems

A. Which links between the community and the external systems are specifically defined and limited as to function?

B. Are there specific agreements concerning the outputs of one system serving as inputs into the other system?

1. The community into external systems
2. External systems into the community

C. Does the community attempt to maximize its autonomy of external systems? Which systems? How?

D. Are there direct linkages between external systems and individuals in the community? Are these relationships contractual in nature?

E. Are most of the linkages between individuals and external systems via the community qua community?

F. Are most of the linkages between individuals and external systems via subsystems of external systems which are located within the community?

G. Are most of the linkages between individuals and external systems of an undefined, undeclared, laissez-faire nature?

X. Control of External Systems over the Community and Its Members

A. Are the behavioral norms of members dictated primarily by the external environment or by the community itself?

B. Which norms are enforced by utilitarian power, (i.e., primarily by economic means) which derives from outside the community?

C. Which norms are enforced by coercive power which derives from outside the community?

D. To what degree is the community dependent upon external systems for its survival? Which ones? To what degree are these systems benign or threatening?

XI. Why Individuals and Families Enter the Community

A. Have the members joined voluntarily?

B. Can residents leave whenever they want?

    1. Temporarily, on what conditions?
    2. Permanently, on what conditions?

C. How do the reasons for the residents having joined the community relate to the goals of the community?

D. How do the reasons for the residents having joined the community relate to the goals of any of the external systems?

XII. Linkage of Individuals and Families (Horizontally) to Each Other

A. Are there multiple formal links, regulations, or rituals which bind the residents to each other?

B. Are there explicit ideological links among the residents?

C. Are most of the links between residents informal, voluntary, supported by friendship and mutual concern for each other (but *not* by mutual concern for a common goal)?

D. Are links between individuals and among families casual, accidental, and of secondary importance in the lives of the residents?

E. Do families exist within the community in the same sense that they exist in the larger society?

    1. What is the role and status of women within the family?
    2. What is the role and status of children within the family?
    3. What is the role of the head of household?

F. Are there important subsystems within the community which have an important influence upon its organization which have not been mentioned above? What are they?

ABOUT THE EDITORS

DANIEL S. SANDERS

Daniel S. Sanders received his B.A. in social science from the University of Ceylon; diploma in social welfare, University of Wales; M.S.W. and Ph.D. in social work, University of Minnesota. Dr. Sanders was a British Council Scholar, 1957–58; World Council of Churches Ecumenical Fellow, 1965–66, and Institute of International Education Development Fellow, 1966–67.

He has had substantial experience in social work education and practice in Sri Lanka (Ceylon), the United Kingdom, and the United States. He has published extensively in the areas of social policy, social work education, social work practice, and international cross-cultural social work, in professional journals in the United States, United Kingdom, India, and Sri Lanka. He is also the author of *The Impact of Reform Movements on Social Policy Change: The Case of Social Insurance* (R.E. Burdick Publishers).

Dr. Sanders is currently Dean, Professor, and Director of International Programs at the School of Social Work, University of Hawaii.

OSCAR KURREN

Oscar Kurren received his B.A. and M.S.W. degrees from the University of Pittsburg and his Ph.D. in social welfare from Brandeis University. Dr. Kurren's professional interests include social policy, social planning, administration, and community organization. He has held a variety of leadership positions in social work education and practice in the United States, including Executive Director, Hamerville Rehabilitation Center, 1954–58; Consultant on Rehabilitation Facilities, National Society for Crippled Children and Adults, Chicago, 1958, 1963; and Institute Director, National Institute on Public Health and Rehabilitation, 1963–65. From 1965–69 Dr. Kurren was Professor, School of Social Work, Portland State University, and Director, Continuing Education for Social Work, Oregon State System of Higher Education. He has published several articles and monographs in the areas of social policy, mental health, and social work education.

Dr. Kurren is currently Professor at the School of Social Work, University of Hawaii.

JOEL FISCHER

Joel Fischer received his B.A. and M.S.W. degrees from the University of Illinois and his Ph.D. in social welfare from the University of California, Berkeley. Dr. Fischer's major professional interests are in the areas of effectiveness research, the development of an eclectic and empirically based approach to clinical practice, and human sexuality. He is the author of several books and over 100 articles and papers. One of his recent books, written with Harvey Gochros, is *Treat Yourself to a Better Sex Life*, a self-help guide to sexual enhancement (published in January 1980 by Prentice-Hall). His most recent book is *Evaluating Practice: A Guide for the Accountable Professional*, co-authored by Martin Bloom (published by Prentice-Hall).

Dr. Fisher, who has been a visiting professor at the University of Wisconsin and Washington University in St. Louis, is currently Professor of Social Work at the University of Hawaii.